Scholastic Success With

1st GRADE

WORKBOOK

SCHOLASTIC

Teaching Resources

NEW YORK • TORONTO • LONDON • AUCKLAND • SYDNEY
MEXICO CITY • NEW DELHI • HONG KONG • BUENOS AIRES

Acknowledgments

Maps workbook copyright © 2002 by Linda Ward Beech

Cover art by Tom Ungrey and Reggie Holladay
Cover design by Anna Christian
Interior illustrations by Jon Buller, Reggie Holladay, Anne Kennedy,
Kathy Marlin, Bob Masheris, Sherry Neidigh, and Carol Tiernon
Interior design by Quack & Company

ISBN 0-439-56969-9

11 12 13 14 15 08 14 13 12 11

Table of Contents

TRADITIONAL MANUSCRIPT

GRAMMAR

WRITING

MAPS

ADDITION & SUBTRACTION

MATH

"Nothing succeeds like success."

Alexandre Dumas the Elder, 1854

Dear Parent,

Congratulations on choosing this excellent educational resource for your child. Scholastic has long been a leader in educational publishing—creating quality educational materials for use in school and at home for nearly a century.

As a partner in your child's academic success, you'll want to get the most out of the learning experience offered in this book. To help your child learn at home, try following these helpful hints:

- Provide a comfortable place to work.
- Have frequent work sessions, but keep them short.
- Praise your child's successes and encourage his or her efforts. Offer positive help when a child makes a mistake.
- Display your child's work and share his or her progress with family and friends.

In this workbook you'll find hundreds of practice pages that keep kids challenged and excited as they strengthen their skills across the classroom curriculum.

The workbook is divided into eight sections: Reading Comprehension; Reading Tests; Traditional Manuscript; Grammar; Writing; Maps; Addition & Subtraction; and Math. You and your child should feel free to move through the pages in any way you wish.

The table of contents lists the activities and the skills practiced. And a complete answer key in the back will help you gauge your child's progress.

Take the lead and help your child succeed with the *Scholastic Success With: 1st Grade Workbook!*

The activities in this workbook reinforce age-appropriate skills and will help your child meet the following standards established as goals by leading educators.

Mathematics

- ★ Uses a variety of strategies when problem-solving
- ★ Understands and applies number concepts
- ★ Uses basic and advanced procedures while performing computation
- ★ Understands and applies concepts of measurement
- ★ Understands and applies concepts of geometry

Writing

- ★ Understands and uses the writing process
- ★ Uses grammatical and mechanical conventions in written compositions

Reading

- ★ Understands and uses the general skills and strategies of the reading process
- ★ Can read and understand a variety of literary texts
- ★ Can understand and interpret a variety of informational texts

Geography

- ★ Understands the characteristics and uses of maps and globes
- ★ Knows the location of places, geographic features, and patterns of the environment

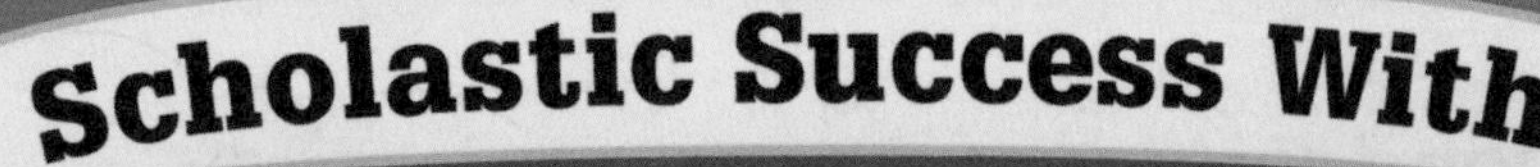

READING COMPREHENSION

Name ______________________________

Tim Can Read

Tim is a good reader. He uses clues to help him read. First, he looks at the picture. That helps him know what the story is about. Next, he reads the title of the story. Now he knows a little more. As he reads the story, the words make pictures in his mind.

Color in the book beside the correct answer.

1. Who is Tim?

 a good reader  a math whiz

2. What does Tim do first?

 reads the story  looks at the picture

3. What else helps Tim know what the story will be about?

 the title  the page number

4. As he reads, what makes pictures in Tim's mind?

 the letters  the words

Now you can try reading the stories in this book the way that Tim does. If you do, you will be a good reader, too! Write the name of your favorite book here.

Trucks

The **main idea** *tells what the whole story is about.*

Trucks do important work. Dump trucks carry away sand and rocks. Cement trucks have a barrel that turns round and round. They deliver cement to workers who are making sidewalks. Fire trucks carry water hoses and firefighters. Gasoline is delivered in large tank trucks. Flatbed trucks carry wood to the people who are building houses.

Find the sentence in the story that tells the main idea. Write it in the circle below. Then draw a line from the main idea to all the trucks that were described in the story.

Write the sentence that tells the main idea on another sheet of paper. Draw a picture that tells about the sentence.

Circus Clowns

The **main idea** *tells what the whole story is about.*

Today I went to the circus. My favorite part of the circus was the clowns. Clowns can do funny tricks. A clown named Pinky turned flips on the back of a horse. Fancy Pants juggled balls while he was singing a funny song. Happy Hal made balloons into animal shapes. Then twelve clowns squeezed into a tiny car and rode away.

Color in the ball that tells the main idea.

Clowns drive tiny cars.

Balloons can be shaped like animals.

Pinky rides a horse.

Clowns can do funny tricks.

Fancy Pants sang a song.

Name ______________________________ 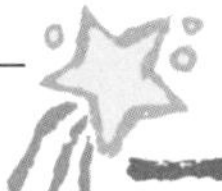

George W. Bush

George W. Bush grew up in Texas. When he finished college, he worked in the oil business. Later on, he became the governor of Texas, then the 43rd president of the United States. His wife's name is Laura. They have twin daughters named Jenna and Barbara. The Bush family owns a ranch in Texas. They have two dogs named Barney and Spotty.

The Bush family also has a cat. To find out the name of their cat, write the answers in the blanks. Then copy the letters that are in the shapes into the empty shapes below.

1. Mr. Bush grew up in ___ ___ ___ ___ ___.
2. He worked in the ___ ___ ___ business.
3. He became the 43rd ___ ___ ___ ___ ___ ___ ___ ___ ___ of the United States.
4. Laura Bush is Mr. Bush's ___ ___ ___ ___.

5. His daughter's names are Barbara and ___ ___ ___ ___ ___.

His cat's name is ___ ___ ___ ___ ___.

If you were president of the United States, what new law would you make? Write it in a complete sentence, including three details.

Mr. Lee's Store

Story events that can really happen are **real***. Story events that are make-believe are* **fantasy***.*

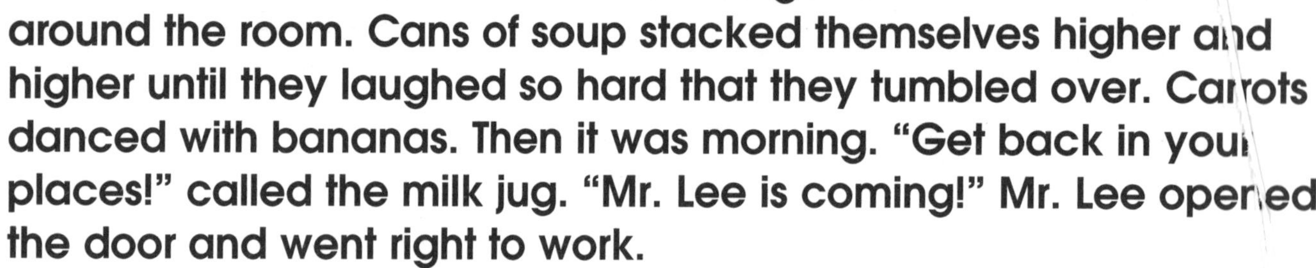

At night, Mr. Lee locked the store and went home. That's when the fun began! The ketchup bottles stood in rows like bowling pins. Then the watermelon rolled down the aisle and knocked them down. The chicken wings flew around the room. Cans of soup stacked themselves higher and higher until they laughed so hard that they tumbled over. Carrots danced with bananas. Then it was morning. "Get back in your places!" called the milk jug. "Mr. Lee is coming!" Mr. Lee opened the door and went right to work.

Circle the cans that are make-believe.

Draw a picture of the story on another piece of paper.

Name ______________________________

Cool Clouds

Have you ever looked up in the sky and seen a cloud that is shaped like an animal or a person? Big, white, puffy clouds float along like soft marshmallows. In cartoons, people can sit on clouds and bounce on them. But clouds are really just tiny drops of water floating in the air. You can understand what being in a cloud is like when it is foggy. Fog is a cloud on the ground!

Read each sentence below. If the sentence could really happen, color the cloud blue. If the sentence is make-believe, color it orange.

Clouds float in the sky.

A cartoon dog sleeps on a cloud.

Clouds are made of tiny drops of water.

Animal shapes in clouds are made by the Cloud Fairy.

Clouds are big blobs of whipped cream.

Clouds are made of marshmallows.

Fog is a cloud on the ground.

Birds can hop around on clouds.

Draw a picture to show a real cloud. Then draw a make-believe cloud.

Name ______________________________

Fun at the Farm

Story events that can really happen are **real***. Story events that are make-believe are* **fantasy***.*

Read each sentence below. If it could be real, circle the picture. If it is make-believe, put an X on the picture.

Dairy cows give milk.

The farmer planted pizza and hamburgers.

The pig said,"Let's go to the dance tonight!"

The mouse ate the dinner table.

The hay was stacked in the barn.

The chickens laid golden eggs.

The green tractor ran out of gas.

The newborn calf walked with wobbly legs.

The goat and the sheep got married by the big tree.

Two crickets sang "Mary Had a Little Lamb."

Horses sat on the couch and watched TV.

Rain made the roads muddy.

Four little ducks swam in the pond.

The farmer's wife baked a pumpkin pie.

On another sheet of paper, write one make-believe sentence about the farmer's house and one real sentence about it.

Ready for School

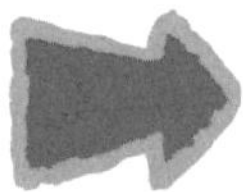

Sequencing *means putting the events in a story in the order they happened.*

Tara could hardly wait for school to start. Mom drove her to the store to buy school supplies. They bought pencils, crayons, scissors, and glue. When Tara got home, she wrote her name on all of her supplies. She put them in a paper sack. The next day, Tara went to school, but the principal told her and the other children to go back home. A water leak had flooded the building. Oh no! Tara would have to wait another whole week!

Number the pictures in the order that they happened in the story.

Color the supplies that Tara bought.

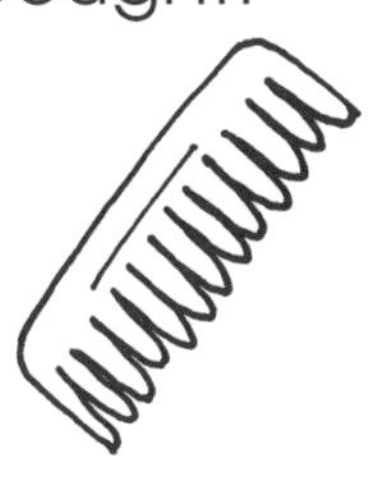

Swimming Lessons

Sequencing *means putting the events in a story in the order they happened.*

Last summer I learned how to swim. First, the teacher told me to hold my breath. Then I learned to put my head under water. I practiced kicking my feet. While I held on to a float, I paddled around the pool. Next, I floated to my teacher with my arms straight out. Finally, I swam using both my arms and my legs. I did it! Swimming is fun! This summer, I want to learn to dive off the diving board.

Number the pictures in the order that they happened in the story.

Unscramble the letters to tell what the person in the story wants to do next.

EALNR **OT** **IVDE**

___ ___ ___ ___ ___   ___ ___   ___ ___ ___ ___

What would you like to learn to do? Draw four pictures on the back of your paper to show how to do it.

Shapes in the Sky

Be sure to read directions carefully.

Follow the directions.

1. **Outline each star with a blue crayon. Then color each one red.**
2. **Color one moon yellow. Color the other one orange.**
3. **Draw a face on every sun.**
4. **Write the number of stars inside the star.**
5. **Write the number of moons inside the moon.**
6. **Write the number of suns inside the sun.**

7. **Add the three numbers you wrote together to find the total number of shapes.**

_____ + _____ + _____ = _____

8. **Which two shapes belong in the night sky?**

__________ and __________

Draw a picture of the sun with nine planets around it. Write EARTH on our planet.

My Monster

Be sure to read directions carefully. Look for key words like circle, underline, *and* color.

I saw a scary monster who lived in a cave. He had shaggy fur and a long, striped tail. He had ugly, black teeth. His three horns were shaped like arrows. His nose was crooked. One of his feet was bigger than the other three. "Wake up! Time for breakfast," Mom said. Oh, good! It was only a dream.

Follow the directions.

1. **What did the monster's tail look like? Circle it.**

2. **What did the monster's teeth look like? Draw a box around them.**

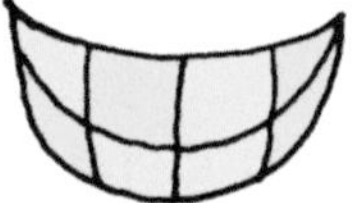   

3. **What did the monster's horns look like? Color them green.**

 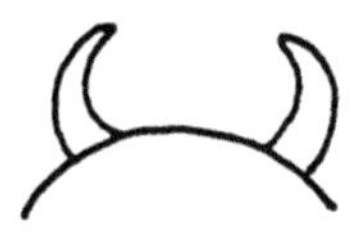  

4. **What did the monster's nose look like? Underline it.**

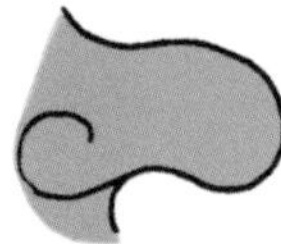 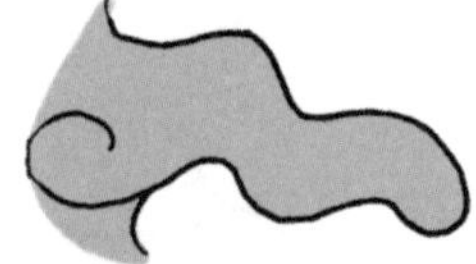  

5. **What did the monster's feet look like? Color them red.**

  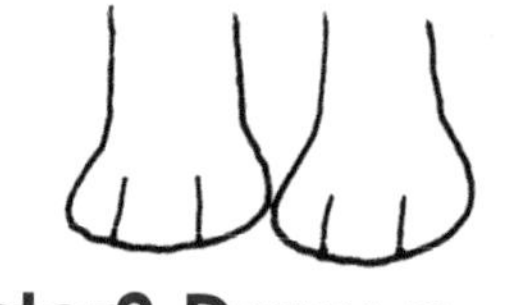

6. **Which one of these is the correct picture of the monster? Draw a cave around him.**

Fun at the Beach

Jack and Joni went to the beach today. Mom spread a blanket on the sand, and they had a picnic. It got very hot, so Jack and Joni jumped into the cold water. They climbed onto a big yellow raft. The waves made the raft go up and down. Later, they played in the sand and built sandcastles. Jack and Joni picked up pretty shells. Joni found a starfish. What a fun day!

1. Color the pictures below that are from the story. Put an X on the ones that don't belong.

2. In the third sentence, find two words that are opposites of each other and circle them with a red crayon.
3. In the fifth sentence, find two more words that are opposites of each other and circle them with a blue crayon.
4. Draw a box around the compound word that tells what Joni found.
5. What color was the raft? Show your answer by coloring the picture at the top of the page.

Write three sentences that tell how to get ready to play your favorite sport.

My New Rug

When you use your own thoughts to answer the question, "How could that have happened?", you are **drawing conclusions**.

I bought a fancy rug today. It was made of brightly-colored yarn. I placed it on the floor in front of the TV and sat on it. All of a sudden, it lifted me up in the air! The rug and I flew around the house. Then out the door we went. High above the trees, we soared like an eagle. Finally, it took me home, and we landed in my backyard.

How could that have happened? To find out, use your crayons to trace over each line. Use a different color on each line. Write the letter from that line in the box at the bottom of the rug.

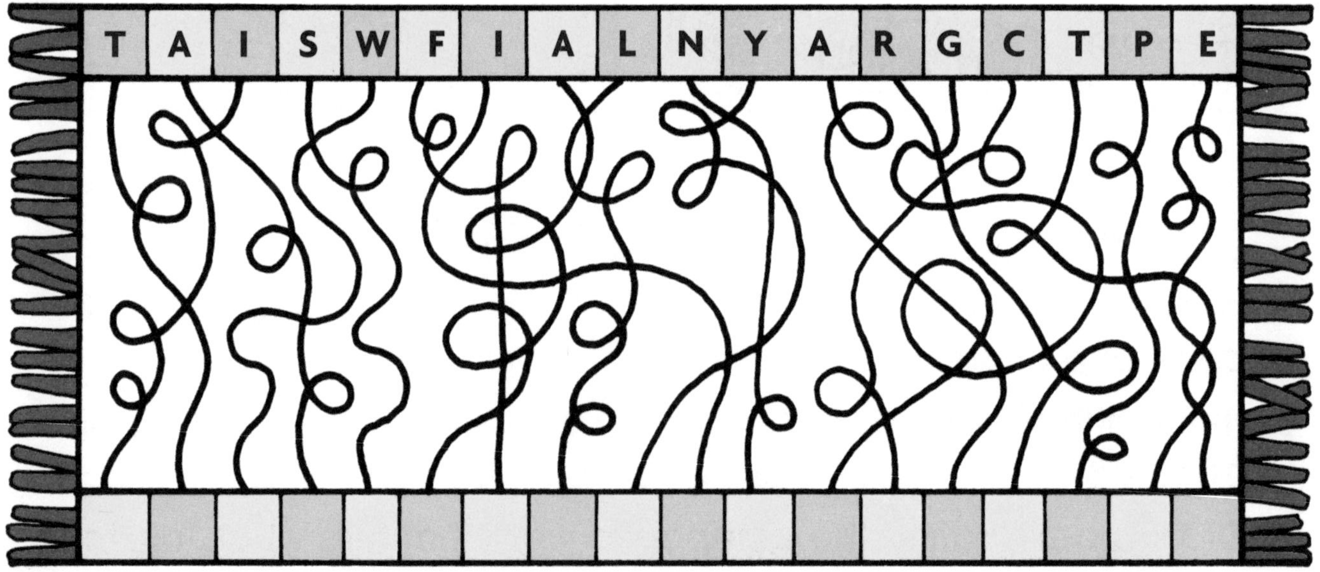

Could this story really happen? Draw a rug around your answer.

Yes **No**

You left your ball on the steps. Your mother came down the steps carrying the laundry basket. Draw a picture of what you think happened.

Polly Want a Cracker?

Have you ever heard a parrot talk? Parrots are able to copy sounds that they hear. You can train a parrot to repeat words, songs, and whistles. But a parrot cannot say words that it has never heard. People can use words to make new sentences, but a parrot cannot.

Read each sentence. If it is true, color the parrot under True. If it is false, color the parrot under False.

1. You could teach a parrot to sing "Happy Birthday."
2. You could ask a parrot any question, and it could give the answer.
3. A parrot could make up a fairy tale.
4. If a parrot heard your mom say, "Brush your teeth," every night, he could learn to say it, too.
5. It is possible for a parrot to repeat words in Spanish.

Write what would happen if a parrot heard you say, "No, I can't" too often.

You Be the Artist

Picturing a story can help the reader understand it better.

An artist drew the pictures that are in this book. Now it is your turn to be the artist! Read each sentence very carefully. Draw exactly what you read about in the sentence.

1. **The green and yellow striped snake wiggled past the ants.**

2. **Wildflowers grew along the banks of the winding river.**

3. **On her sixth birthday, Shannon had a pink birthday cake shaped like a butterfly.**

Now write your own sentence and illustrate it.

Name ____

A Stormy Day

Big, black clouds appeared in the sky. Lightning struck the tallest tree. The scared cow cried, "Moo!" It rained hard. Soon there was a mud puddle by the barn door. Hay blew out of the barn window.

Read the story above. Then go back and read each sentence again. Add to the picture everything that the sentences describe.

Who Am I?

Use details from the story to make decisions about the characters.

Circle the picture that answers the riddle.

1. **I have feathers. I also have wings, but I don't fly. I love to swim in icy water. Who am I?**

2. **I am 3 weeks old. I drink milk. I cry when my diaper is wet. Who am I?**

3. **I live in the ocean. I swim around slowly, looking for something to eat. I have six more arms than you have. Who am I?**

4. **I am an insect. If you touch me, I might bite you! I make tunnels under the ground. I love to come to your picnic! Who am I?**

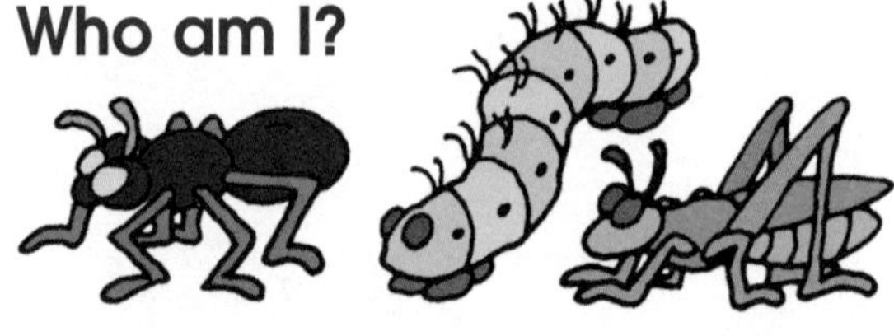

5. **I am a female. I like to watch movies and listen to music. My grandchildren love my oatmeal cookies. Who am I?**

6. **I am a large mammal. I live in the woods. I have fur. I stand up and growl when I am angry. Who am I?**

7. **I wear a uniform. My job is to help people. I ride on a big red truck. Who am I?**

Write your own riddle and let the class guess the answer.

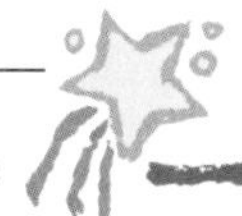

What's Going On?

Use story details to help you make decisions about the story.

James was the first boy in Miss Lane's class to find red spots on his face and arms. He scratched until his mom came to take him home. A week later, Amy and Jana got the spots. The next Monday, six more children were absent. Finally, everyone got well and came back to school. But, this time Miss Lane was absent. Guess what was wrong with her!

Color red spots on the correct answers.

1. What do you think was wrong with the children?

broken arms

2. How do you know the spots were itchy?

James scratched them.

Amy said, "These spots itch!"

3. How many children in all got sick?

4. Why do you think Miss Lane was absent? Write your answer.

Draw a picture of what Miss Lane might look like with chickenpox!

Make a Cartoon

Read the sentence below each picture. In the bubbles, write what each character could be saying.

Mr. Giraffe asked Mr. Zebra why he had stripes. Mr. Zebra didn't know.

Mr. Giraffe said that he should ask Mrs. Owl. Mr. Zebra agreed.

Mr. Zebra asked Mrs. Owl why he had stripes. Mrs. Owl laughed.

Mrs. Owl told Mr. Zebra that the Magic Fairy painted him that way!

If Mr. Giraffe asked Mrs. Owl why he had such a long neck, what do you think she would say?

Clean Your Room

 *Grouping like things together makes it easier to remember what you read.*

Mom says, "Let's go out for ice cream! Clean your room, and then we will go." Your room is a mess. You need to put the blocks in the basket. The crayons must go in their box. The books must go on the shelf, and the marbles go in the jar. You can do it. Just think about that hot fudge sundae!

Draw a line from each item on the floor to the place it belongs. Color what you could use in school red. Color what are toys blue.

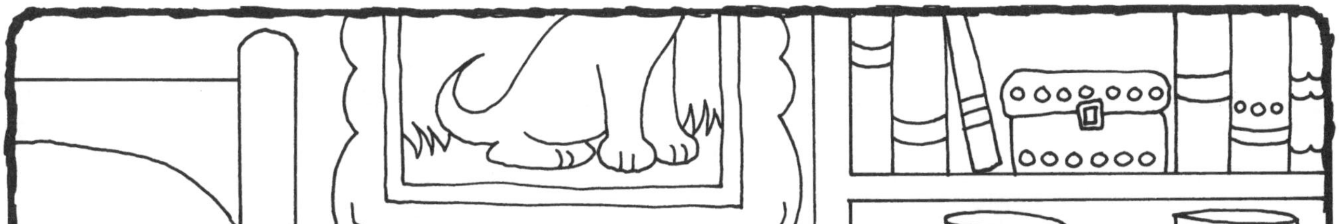

Circle the food that does not belong in an ice cream store.

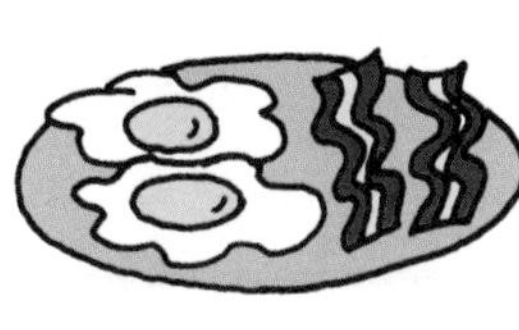

Fold a sheet of paper in half. Write "hot" on one side and "cold" on the other side. Draw four foods on each side of the paper that go with the heading.

Going to the Mall

Look for similarities when grouping items.

Read the words in the Word Box. Write each word in the place where you would find these things at the mall.

Word Box

tickets	sandals	high heels	beans	big screen	
tulip bulbs	peppers	fertilizer	popcorn	gardening gloves	
sneakers	burritos	boots	pots	candy	tacos

Sandie's Shoe Store

____
____
____
____

On another sheet of paper, draw the following items in a toy store or a clothing store: jump rope, blue jeans, basketball, doll, sweatshirt, stocking cap, wooden train, pajamas.

Name ______________________________

My Favorites

This page is all about you! Read the categories and write your own answers.

My Favorite TV Shows	My Favorite Foods	My Favorite Sports
________	________	________
________	________	________
________	________	________

Draw two of your favorite people here and write their names.

Favorite Color

____

Favorite Holiday

____

Favorite Song

____

Favorite Movie

____

Favorite School Subject

____

Favorite Thing to Do After School

____

Favorite Thing to Do With My Family

____

Trade pages with friends and read what they wrote. You might get to know them a little better!

Ouch!

Use story details to make a guess of what will happen next.

Mia and Rosa were playing hospital. Mia was the patient, and Rosa was the doctor. Rosa pretended to take Mia's temperature. "You have a fever," she said. "You will have to lie down." Mia climbed onto the top bunk bed. "You need to sleep," Dr. Rosa said. Mia rolled over too far and fell off the top bunk. "O-o-o-h, my arm!" yelled Mia. Her mother came to look. It was broken!

What do you think happened next? Write your answer here.

____

To find out if your answer is correct, finish the sentence below by coloring only the spaces that have a dot in them.

Mia had to go to

If Mia hadn't fallen off the bed, how do you think this story would have ended? Draw your answer.

What Will Sam Do?

One day, Sam was riding his bike to the baseball game. He had to be on time. He was the pitcher. Just ahead, Sam saw a little boy who had fallen off his bike. His knee was bleeding, and he was crying. Sam asked him if he was okay, but the boy couldn't speak English. Sam knew the boy needed help getting home. If he stopped to help, he might be late for the game. Sam thought about it. He knew he had to do the right thing.

What do you think Sam did next? There are two paths through the maze. Draw a line down the path that shows what you think Sam did next.

What sentence from the story gives you a hint about what Sam decided to do? Write that sentence below.

____

The maze shows two ways the story could end. Draw a different ending to the story and tell about your picture.

Riddle Fun

Compare *means to look for things that are the same.*
Contrast *means to look for things that are different.*

To solve the riddles in each box, read the clues in the horse. Then write the letters in the blanks with the matching numbers.

What kind of food does a racehorse like to eat?

___ ___ ___ ___   ___ ___ ___ ___
11 5 10 3   11 9 9 2

1. What letter is in LOG, but not in DOG?
2. What letter is in DIME, but not in TIME?
3. What letter is in BITE, but not in BIKE?
4. What letter is in WEST, but not in REST?
5. What letter is in FAN, but not in FUN?
6. What letter is in BOX, but not in FOX?
7. What letter is in CAR, but not in CAN?
8. What letter is in ME, but not in MY?
9. What letter is in SOCK, but not in SACK?
10. What letter is in SEE, but not in BEE?
11. What letter is in FULL, but not in PULL?

What does a rose sleep in at night?

___ ___ ___ ___ ___ ___   ___ ___ ___
11 1 9 4 8 7   6 8 2

Twins

Holly and Polly are twins. They are in the first grade. They look just alike, but they are very different. Holly likes to play softball and soccer. She likes to wear her hair braided when she goes out to play. She wears sporty clothes. Recess is her favorite part of school. Polly likes to read books and paint pictures. Every day she wears a ribbon in her hair to match her dress. Her favorite thing about school is going to the library. She wants to be a teacher some day.

Look at the pictures of Holly and Polly. Their faces look alike. Circle the things in both pictures that are different from each other.

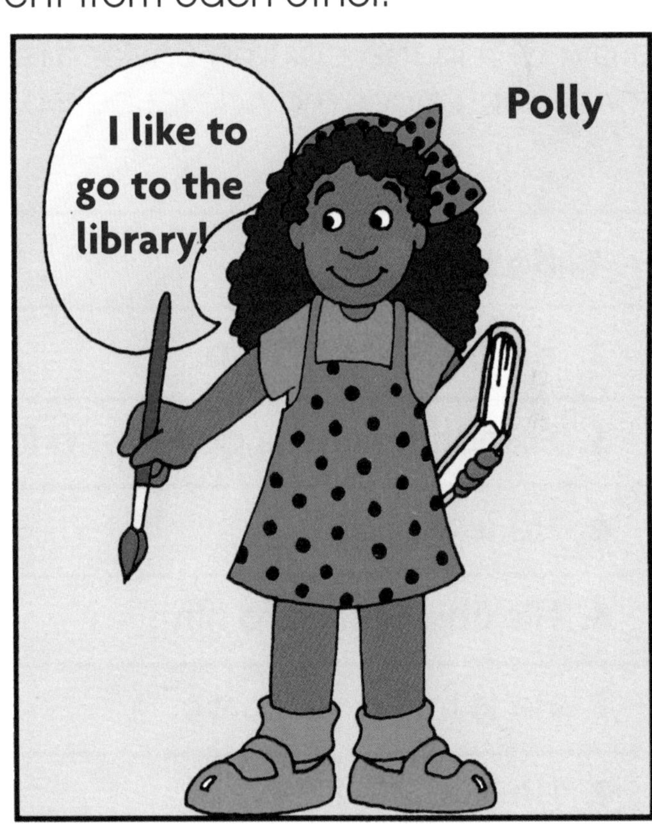

Draw two lines under the words that tell what Holly and Polly do that is the same.

They play sports. They love to paint. They are in the first grade.

Write rhyming names for twins that are boys. What is alike about them? What is different?

Soldier Dads

Juan's dad and Ann's dad are soldiers. Juan's dad is a captain in the Navy. He sails on the ocean in a large ship. Ann's dad is a pilot in the Air Force. He flies a jet. Juan and Ann miss their dads when they are gone for a long time. They write them letters and send them pictures. It is a happy day when their dads come home!

Draw a ☺ in the column under the correct dad. Some sentences may describe both dads.

	Juan's dad	Ann's dad	Both dads
1. He is a captain.			
2. He works on a ship.			
3. Sometimes he is gone for a long time.			
4. He is a pilot.			
5. His child writes to him.			
6. He is in the Air Force.			
7. He is in the Navy.			
8. It is a happy time when he comes home.			
9. He flies a jet.			
10. He is a soldier.			

Dinosaur Clues

How do we know that dinosaurs were real? It is because their bones have been found in rocks. Sometimes scientists have found dinosaur footprints where mud later turned to stone. These kinds of rocks are called fossils. Fossils give us clues about how big the dinosaurs were. Some were small and some were very large. Scientists say a diplodocus was as big as three school buses!

1. Color the picture that shows scientists working.

2. Color the picture of a fossil.

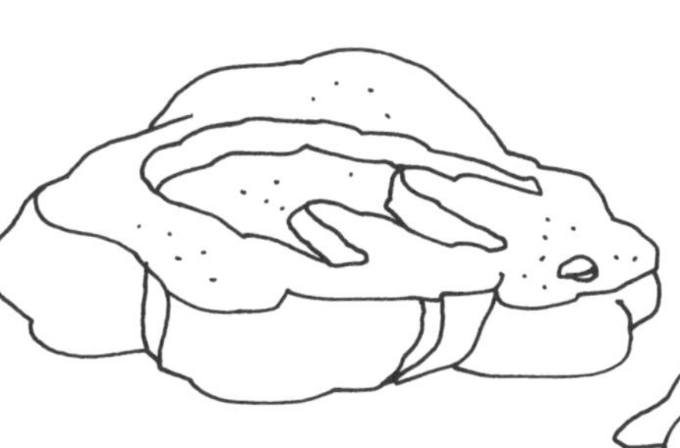

3. Color the picture of a diplodocus.

Find and write the names of three more dinosaurs.

Name ______________________________

Amazing Animal Facts

Read each sentence. Then color the picture that tells the meaning of the underlined word.

1. Sea lions sleep in the water with one flipper up in the air.

2. Even though whale sharks are the biggest fish in the world, they are harmless to people.

3. Horses use their tails to swat pesky flies.

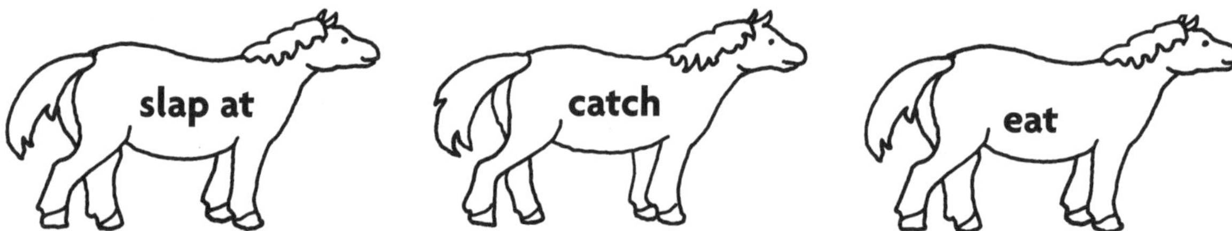

4. Snakes shed their old skins and grow new ones.

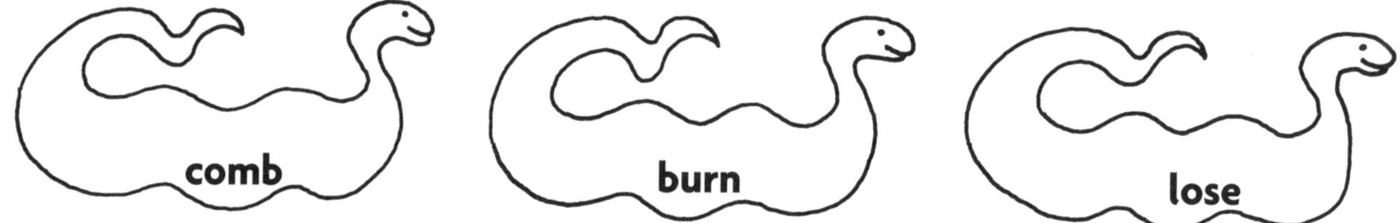

5. Squirrels bury acorns and nuts to eat when winter comes.

Write an interesting fact about two other animals.

Name ______________________________

A Tiny Town

Have you ever seen a prairie dog town? That's where prairie dogs live, but there are no buildings or houses. They live underground. They dig deep into the dirt making burrows. Along the burrows, here and there, are chambers for sleeping or storing food. One chamber is lined with grass for the babies. Sometimes prairie dogs have unwanted guests in their town, like rattlesnakes!

Use the code below to learn what some of the words in the story mean. Copy the matching letters in the blanks.

1. town ___ ___ ___ ___ ___ ___ ___ ___ ___ ___

2. prairie dogs ___ ___ ___ ___ ___ ___

___ ___ ___ ___ ___ ___ ___ ___ ___ ___ ___ ___

3. burrows ___ ___ ___ ___ ___ ___ ___

4. chambers ___ ___ ___ ___ ___

5. unwanted guests ___ ___ ___ ___ ___

Oops!

In a story, there is usually a reason something happens. This is the **cause**. *What happens as a result is the* **effect**.

1 2 3
4 5 6
7 8 9
0

Sandy went on a vacation in the mountains with her parents and little brother Austin. They were staying in a small cabin without any electricity or running water. It was fun to have lanterns at night and to bathe in the cold mountain stream. The biggest problem for Sandy was she missed her best friend, Kendra. Sandy found her dad's cell phone and called Kendra. They talked for nearly an hour! When Sandy's dad went to call his office, the cell phone was dead. He was NOT a happy camper!

Draw a line to match the first part of each sentence to the second part that makes it true.

1. **Sandy used lanterns at night because**
2. **Sandy and Austin bathed in a stream because**
3. **Sandy felt better about missing Kendra because**
4. **Sandy's dad could not call his office because**

she talked to her on the cell phone.
the cabin had no running water.
the cabin had no electricity.
the cell phone was dead.

Write about something you did that caused a huge "effect."

Wanda Wiggleworm

In a story, there is usually a reason something happens. This is the **cause**. *What happens as a result is the* **effect**.

Wanda Wiggleworm was tired of living alone in the flowerpot, so she decided to live it up. Last night, Wanda went to the Ugly Bug Ball. She looked her best, all slick and slimy. Carl Caterpillar asked her to dance. They twisted and wiggled around and around to the music. All of a sudden, they got tangled up. They tried to get free, but instead, they tied themselves in a knot! What would they do? They decided to get married, and they lived happily ever after.

Unscramble each sentence about the story.
Write the new sentence on the line.

tangled	worms	when	got	danced.	they	The	up

____

____

in	knot	They	married.	a	they	were	so	got	tied

____

____

Tim fell asleep on his raft while playing in the lake. Draw a picture of what you think the effect was on Tim.

School Rules

It is important to follow the rules at school. Read each rule below. Find the picture that shows what would happen if students DID NOT follow that rule. Write the letter of the picture in the correct box.

1. You must walk, not run, in the halls. ☐
2. Do not chew gum at school. ☐
3. Come to school on time. ☐
4. When the fire alarm rings, follow the leader outside. ☐
5. Listen when the teacher is talking. ☐
6. Keep your desk clean. ☐

Write a school rule that you must obey. Draw a picture of what might happen if you do not.

Name ______________________________ 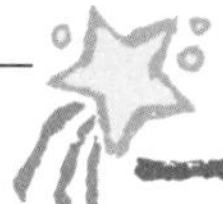 Analyzing characters

Mixed-Up Margie

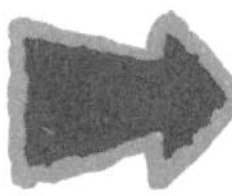

A character is a person or animal in a story. To help readers understand a character better, a story often gives details about the character.

Once upon a time there was a mixed-up queen named Margie. She got things mixed up. She wore her crown on her arm. She wore a shoe on her head. She painted every fingernail a different color. Then she painted her nose red! She used a fork to hold her hair in place. She wore a purple belt around her knees. The king didn't mind. He always wore his clothes backward!

Use the story and your crayons to help you follow these instructions:

1. **Draw Margie's crown.**
2. **Draw her shoe.**
3. **Paint her fingernails and nose.**
4. **Draw what goes in her hair.**
5. **Draw her belt.**

Circle the correct answer:

6. **What makes you think Margie is mixed up?**

   the way she dresses

   the way she talks

7. **What makes you think the king is mixed up, too?**

   He talks backward.

   He wears his clothes backward.

Pretend tomorrow is Mixed-Up Day. Describe what you will wear as a mixed-up character.

Name ______________________________

Miss Ticklefoot

I love Miss Ticklefoot. She is my first-grade teacher.

To find out more about her, read each sentence below. Write a word in each blank that tells how she feels. The Word Box will help you.

Word Box

sad	scared	silly	worried	happy	surprised

1. Miss Ticklefoot smiles when we know the answers.

   ____

2. She is concerned when one of us is sick.

   ____

3. She makes funny faces at us during recess.

   ____

4. She cried when our fish died.

   ____

5. She jumps when the fire alarm rings.

   ____

6. Her mouth dropped open when we gave her a present!

   ____

Different Friends

When Ty was four years old, he had two make-believe friends named Mr. Go-Go and Mr. Sasso. They lived in Ty's closet. When there was no one else around, Ty talked to Mr. Go-Go while he played with his toys. Mr. Go-Go was a good friend. He helped put Ty's toys away. Mr. Sasso was not a good friend. Some days he forgot to make Ty's bed or brush Ty's teeth. One day he even talked back to Ty's mother. Another day Dad said, "Oh my! Who wrote on the wall?" Ty knew who did it . . . Mr. Sasso!

Read the phrase inside each crayon. If it describes Mr. Go-Go, color it green. If it describes Mr. Sasso, color it red. If it describes both, color it yellow.

1. helpful
2. probably sassy
3. forgets to do chores
4. friends that live in the closet
5. could get Ty in trouble
6. make-believe characters
7. does the right thing

Draw Mr. Go-Go.

Draw Mr. Sasso.

Write something you think Mr. Sasso and Mr. Go-Go might do.

Poetry

A poem paints a picture with words. It often uses rhyming words.

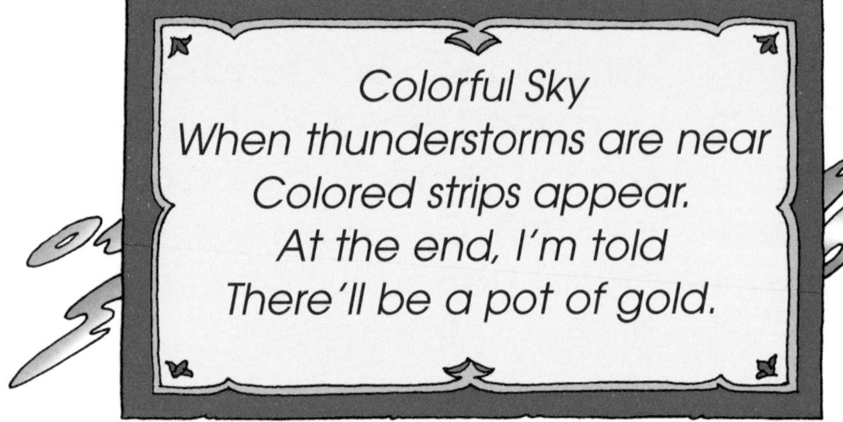

Colorful Sky
When thunderstorms are near
Colored strips appear.
At the end, I'm told
There'll be a pot of gold.

Draw what it is.

1. **Draw a red line under the word that rhymes with <u>near</u>.**
2. **Draw a green line under the word that rhymes with <u>told</u>.**

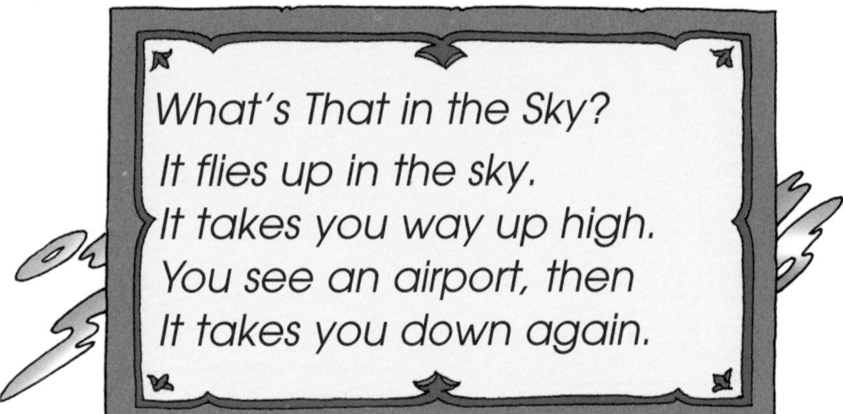

What's That in the Sky?
It flies up in the sky.
It takes you way up high.
You see an airport, then
It takes you down again.

Draw what it is.

3. **Draw a blue circle around the word that rhymes with <u>sky</u>.**
4. **Draw a brown circle around the word that rhymes with <u>then</u>.**
5. **Finish this two-line poem:**

I wish that I could see

A giant bumble______.

Draw what it is.

Now see if you can make up your own two-line poem using these rhyming words at the end of each line: GO and SNOW.

A Fable

A fable is a story that teaches a lesson. This fable was written many, many years ago.

The Dog and His Shadow

A dog carried a piece of meat in his mouth. He crossed over a river on a low bridge. He looked down into the water and saw his reflection. It looked like another dog with a piece of meat larger than his. The dog snapped at the other dog's meat. When he did, his own meat dropped into the water. Now the dog didn't have any meat at all.

Draw a box around the lesson that the story teaches:

1. **Two dogs are better than one.**
2. **Don't be greedy. Be happy with what you have.**

Color only the pictures of things that you read about in the story:

Write a complete sentence telling what the dog should have done.

Library Books

A library has many different kinds of books.

It is fun to check books out of the library. Have you ever read *Rainbow Fish* by Marcus Pfister? It is a story about a very special fish. His scales were blue, green, and purple. He also had some shiny, silver scales. The other fish wanted him to share his shiny scales with them, but he said no. No one would be his friend. Later, he decided to give each fish one of his shiny scales. It was better to lose some of his beauty and have friends than to keep them to himself.

Connect the dots. You will see something from the book.

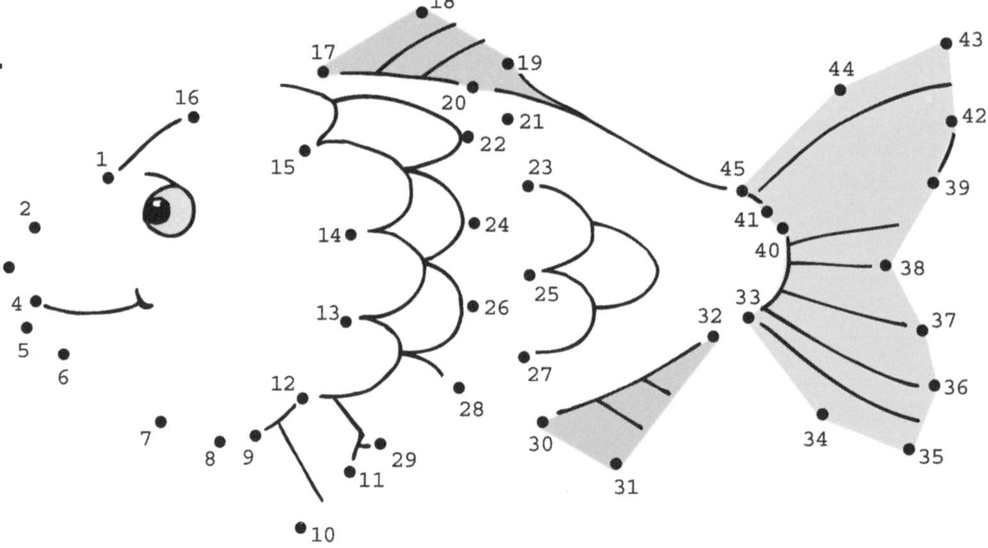

1. Draw a blue circle around the word that tells what this book is about:

running **lying** **sharing** **eating**

2. Copy the name of the author here.

____

If you grew up to be an author, what would you write about? Make a pretty book cover that includes the title of your book.

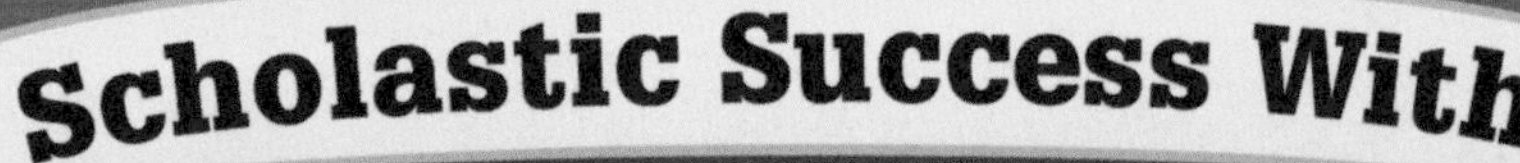

TESTS: READING

Name ______________________________ 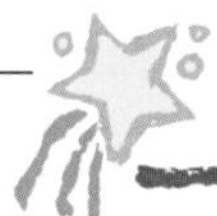

E. Grammar, Usage, and Mechanics

Read each sentence. Fill in the bubble next to the word or words that best complete each sentence.

Sample

________ walk to school.

- O we
- O look
- O We

1. My kitten likes to ____________

- O jump.
- O jump?
- O Jump

2. I went to see ____________ for a checkup.

- O dr. Jones
- O Dr. Jones
- O dr. jones

3. May ________ play with you?

- O i
- O It
- O I

4. My family went to ____________ on a trip.

- O New York
- O NEW YORK
- O new york

5. The girl ____________ the bus.

- O ride
- O rides
- O rided

F. Story Comprehension

Read the story. Then answer each question.
Fill in the bubble next to the best answer.

Jane Goodall

MICHAEL NEUGEBAUER/COURTESY OF NORTH-SOUTH BOOKS

Jane Goodall is a famous scientist. She learned about wild chimpanzees in Africa.

Jane learned that baby chimpanzees ride on their mothers' backs until they are 3 years old. She learned that chimpanzees hold hands like people do. She also learned that chimpanzees use sticks to catch insects. Jane learned all about chimpanzees by watching them closely.

1. What is a good title for this story?
- O Scientists
- O Jane Goodall
- O Baby Chimpanzees

2. Where did Jane Goodall learn about chimpanzees?
- O Africa
- O South America
- O Asia

3. Baby chimpanzees ride on their mothers' backs until what age?
- O 5 years old
- O 6 months old
- O 3 years old

4. Write a sentence telling something that Jane Goodall learned about chimpanzees.

____

____

E. Grammar, Usage, and Mechanics

Read each sentence. Fill in the bubble next to the word or words that best complete each sentence.

Sample

The cat ______ its food.

- O eat
- O eats
- O Eats

1. _____ teacher is nice.

- O My
- O my
- O me

2. Grandma ______ in a house.

- O live
- O Lives
- O lives

3. Careful! The fire _____ hot.

- O are
- O is
- O Is

4. _____ you like ice cream?

- O does
- O Does
- O Do

5. I _____ a loose tooth.

- O have
- O Have
- O has

6. _____ eat some cake.

- O They
- O Him
- O Her

F. Story Comprehension

Read the story. Then answer each question.
Fill in the bubble next to the best answer.

Baby penguins come from eggs. When a penguin is ready to be born, it starts to peck the shell. The shell is thick. It can take three days to get out! When the penguin is born, it has soft fluff all over. Its eyes are shut. It peeps to be fed! The mother and father take turns feeding and caring for their chick.

1. What is a good title for this story?
- O Baby Penguins
- O Penguins
- O Eggs

2. How long can it take for a baby penguin to peck out of its shell?
- O one day
- O two days
- O three days

3. Who takes care of a baby penguin?
- O the mother
- O the father
- O the mother and father

4. Write a sentence that tells something about baby penguins.

____

____

Scholastic Success With

TRADITIONAL MANUSCRIPT

Trace and write.

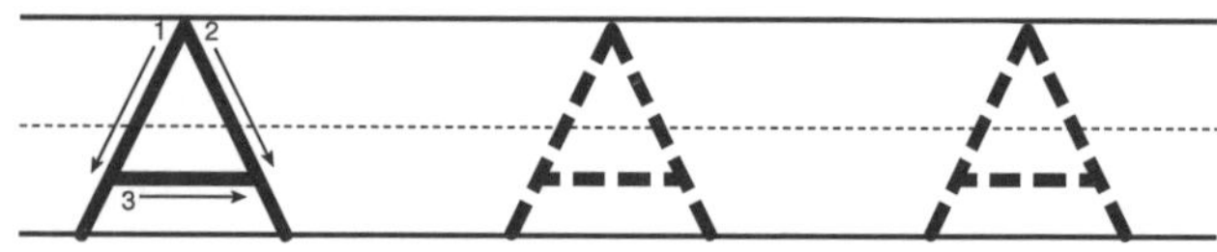

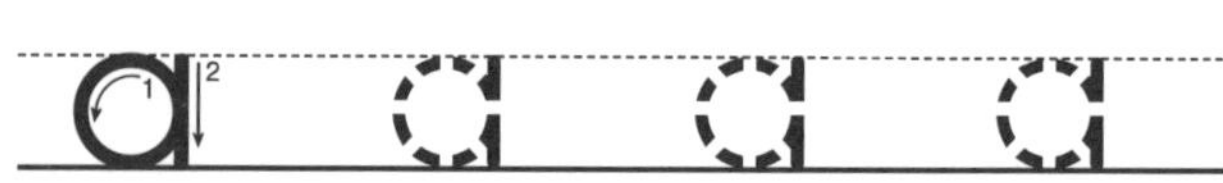

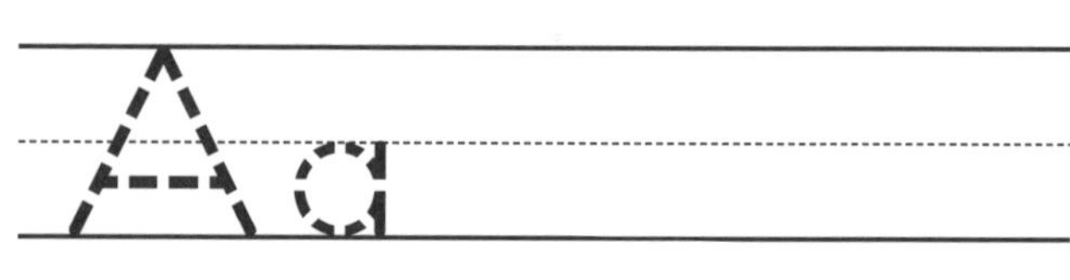

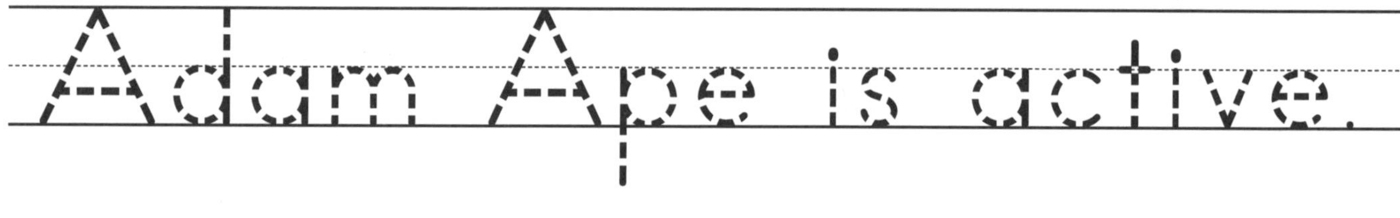

Annie asked Alice.

B b

Trace and write.

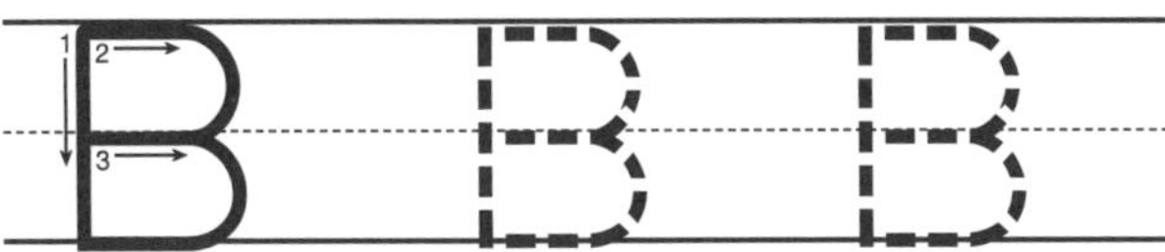

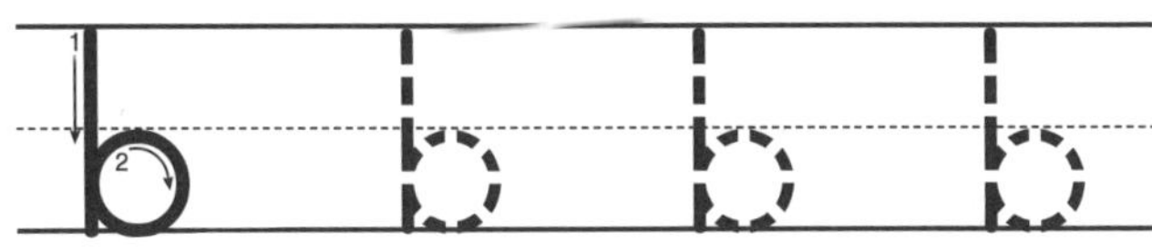

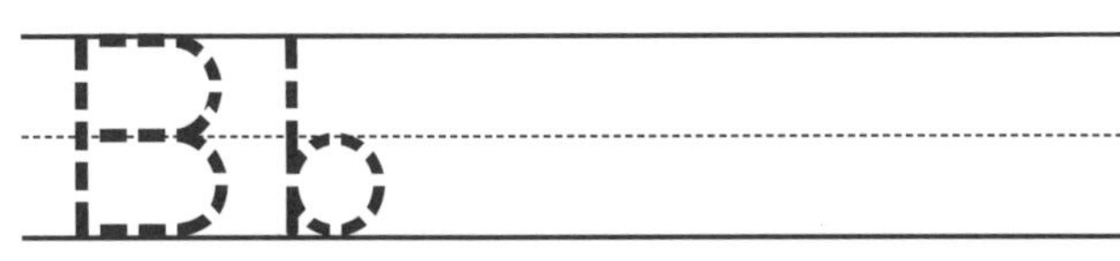

Betsy bee buzzes.

Bobby buys balloons.

Name ______________________________ Cc

Cc

Trace and write.

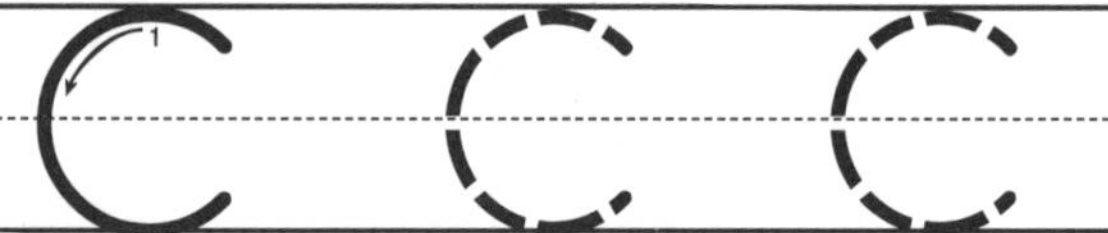

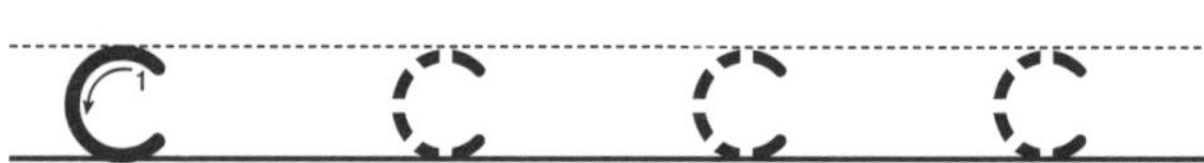

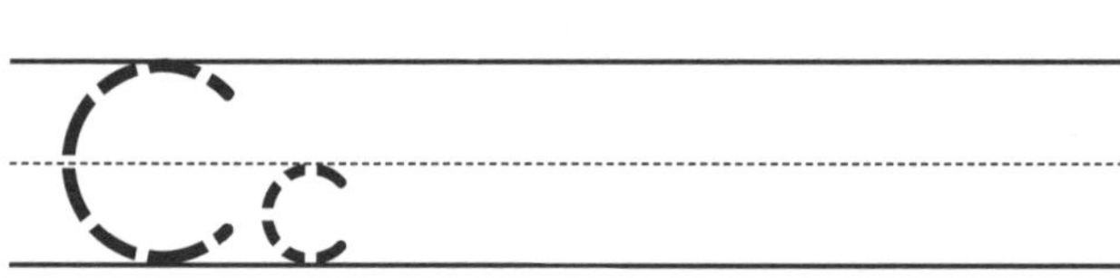

Cows crave color.

Callie carries cats.

Name ________________________________  Dd

D d

Trace and write.

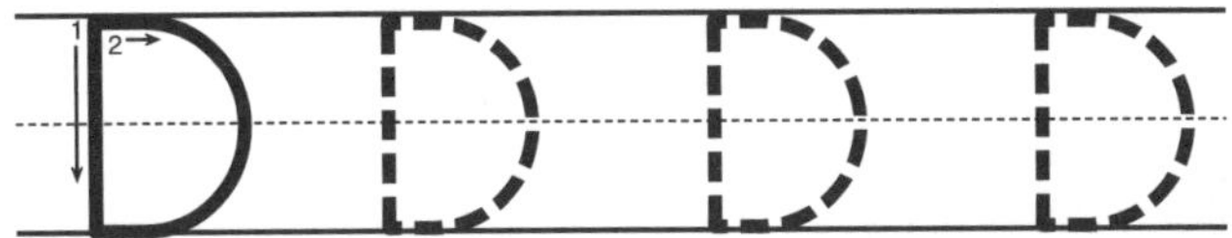

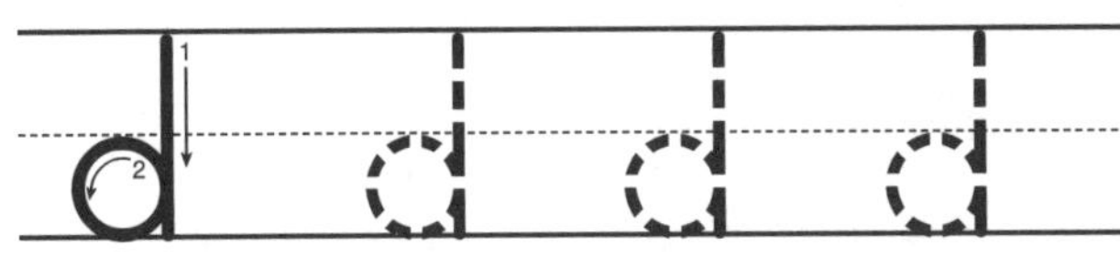

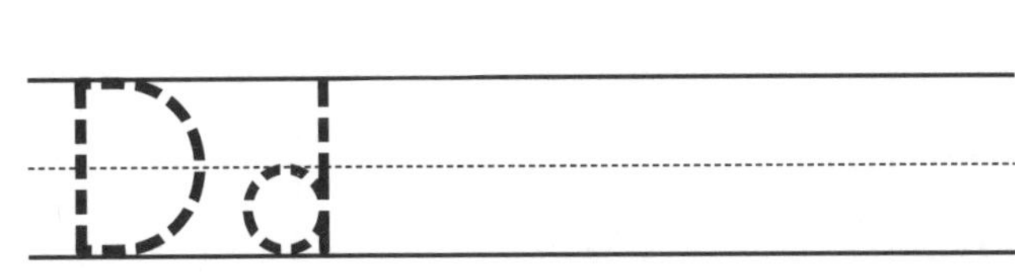

Dandy Duck dances.

Dragons draw dogs.

Name ______________________________

Ee

Trace and write.

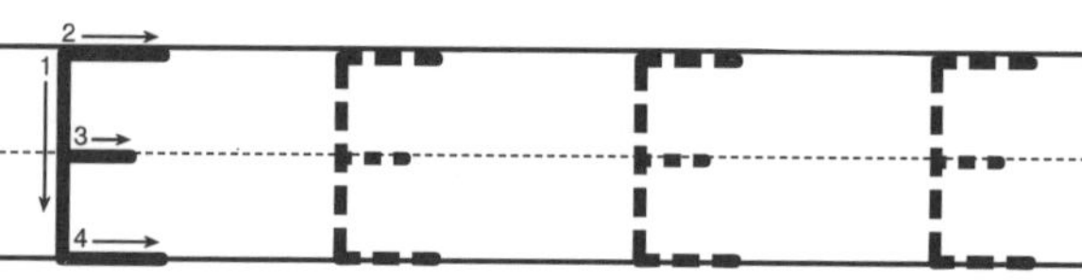

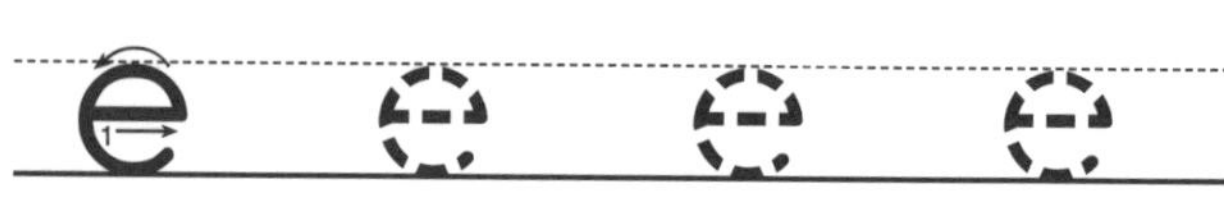

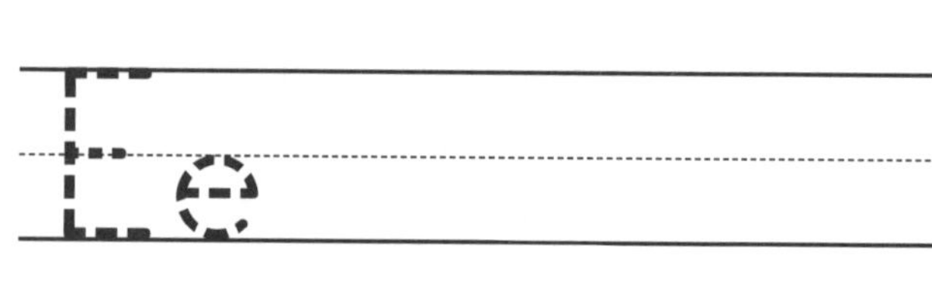

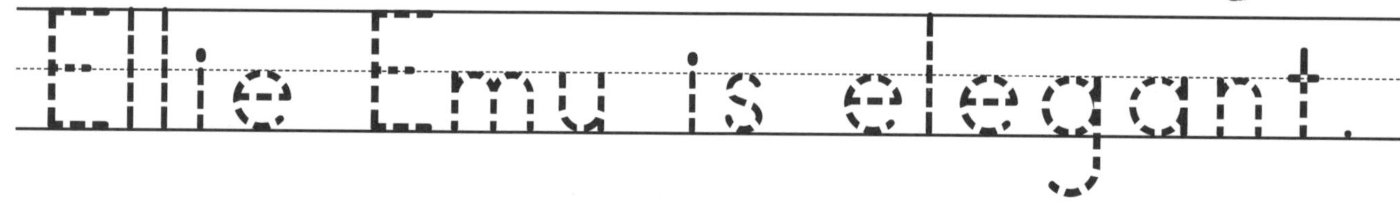
Ellie Emu is elegant.

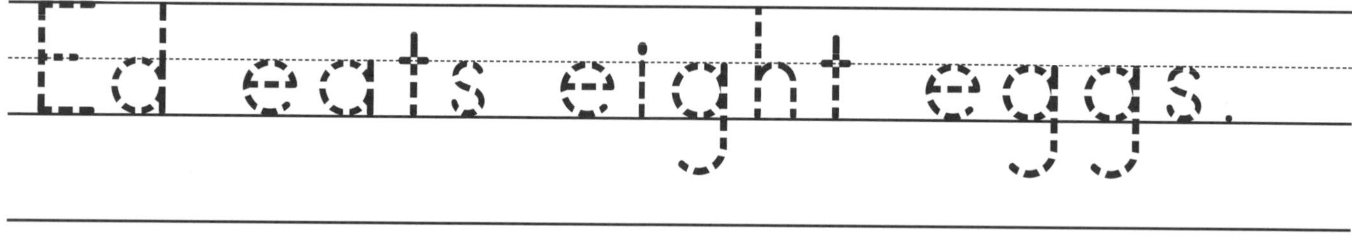
Ed eats eight eggs.

Name ______________________________ 

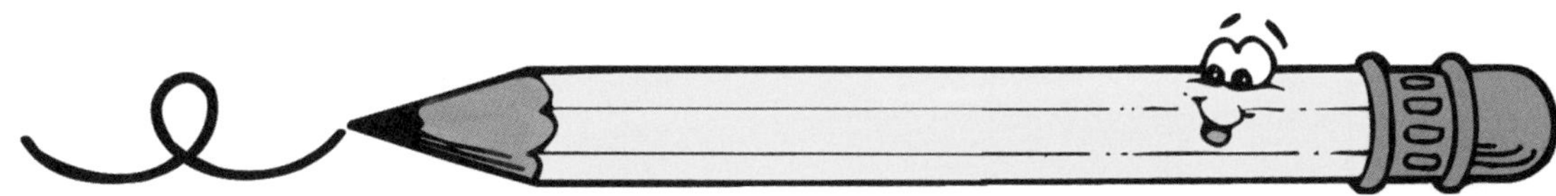

Trace and write.

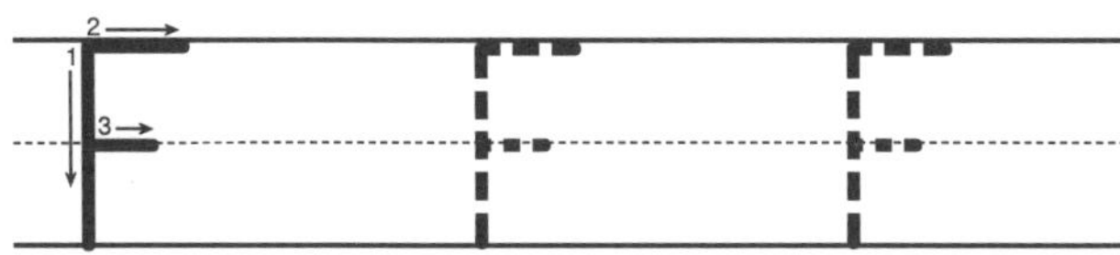

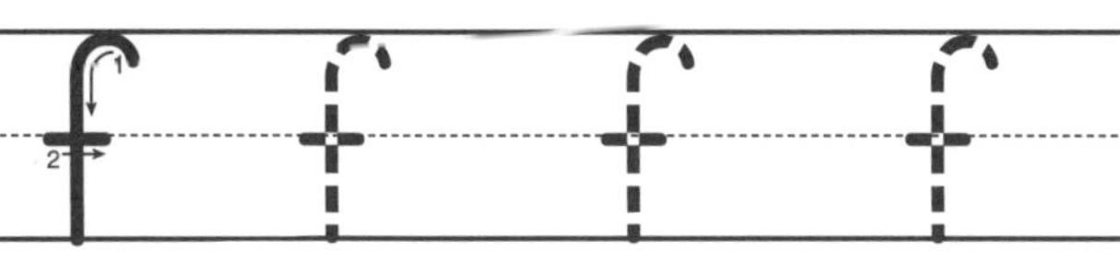

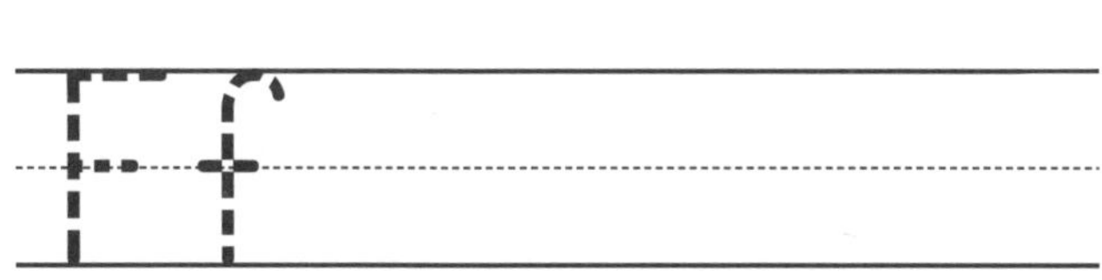

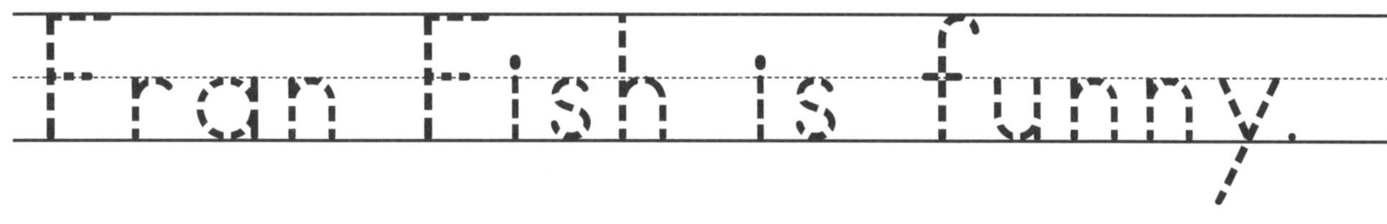

Footballs fly fast.

Name ______________________________

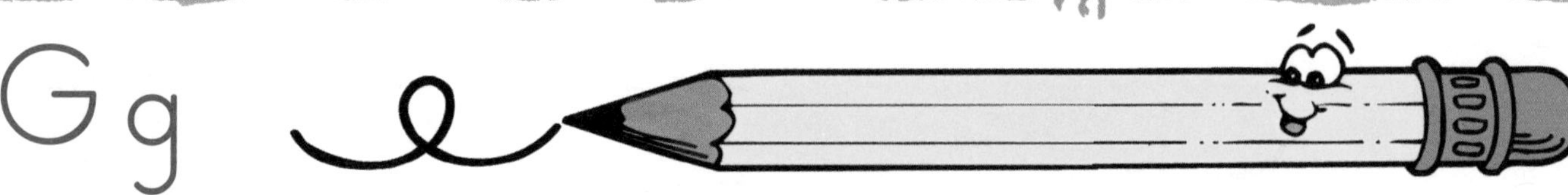

Trace and write.

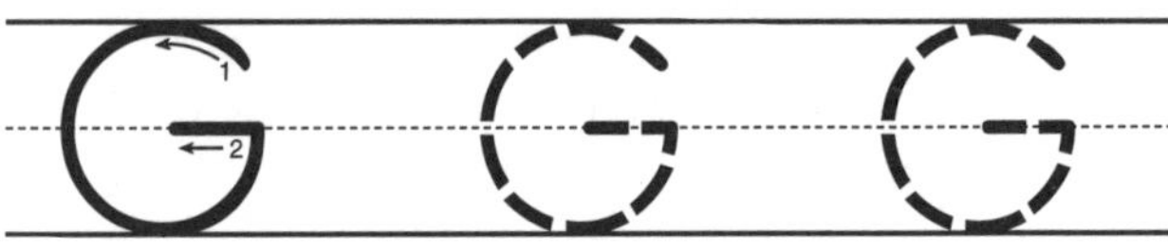

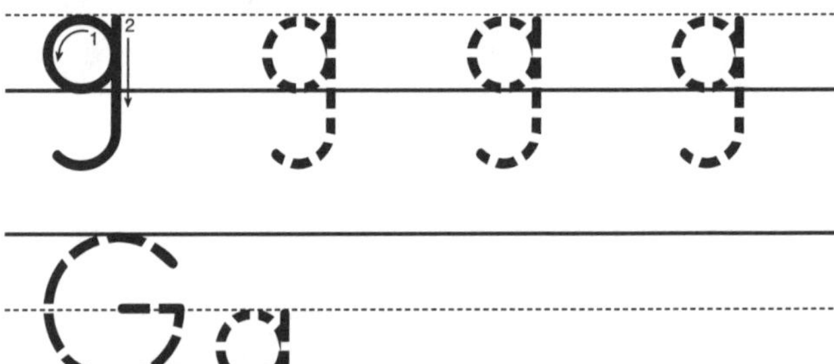

Gg

Gus Goose giggles.

Greta grows greens.

Name ________________________________

Hh

Trace and write.

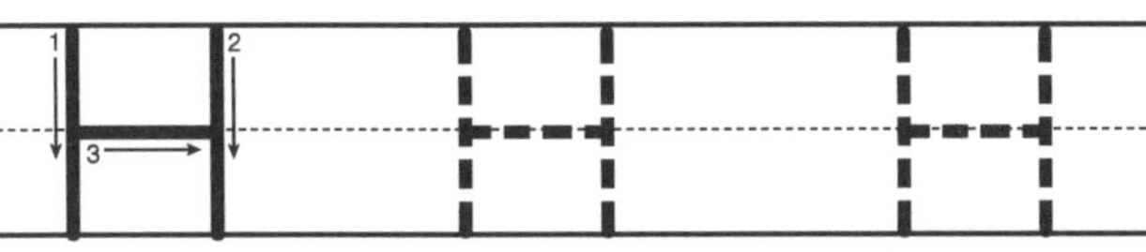

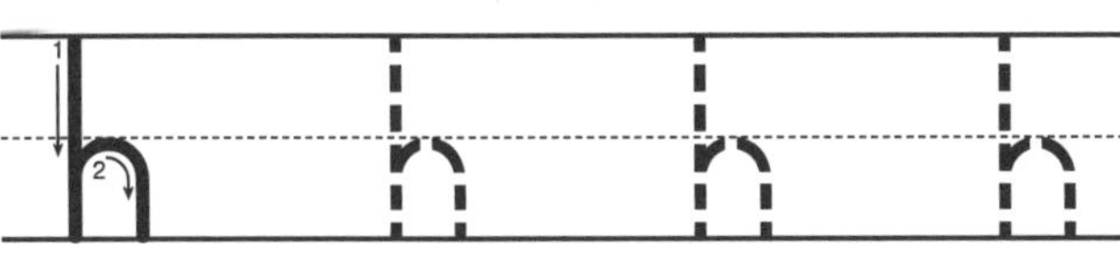

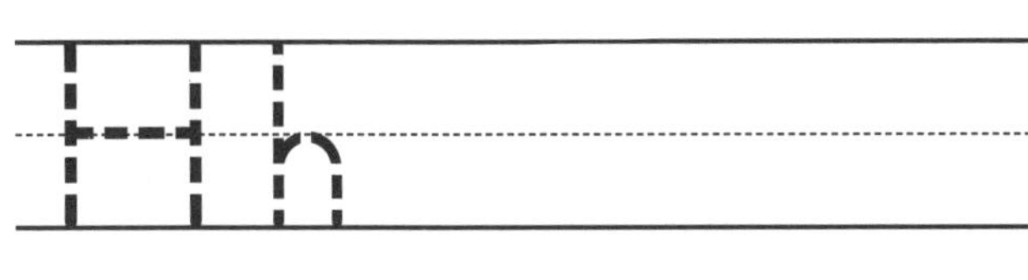

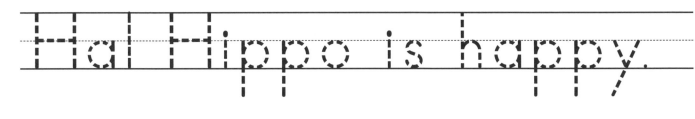

Hal Hippo is happy.

Hannah hangs hats.

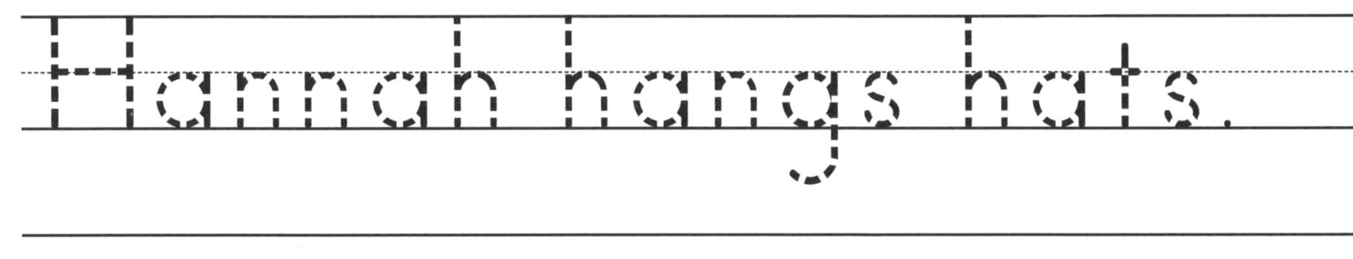

Name ____

Trace and write.

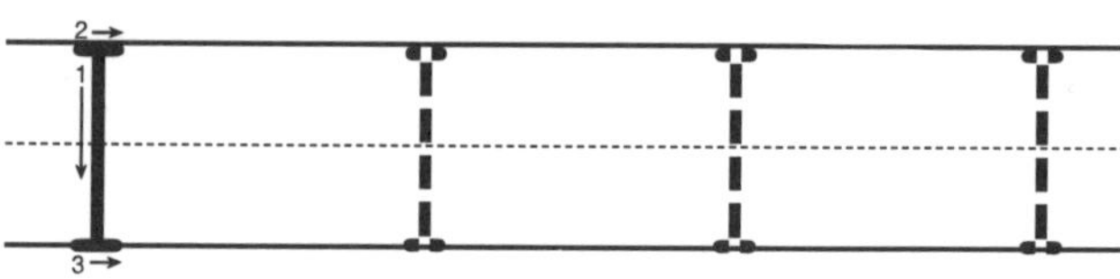

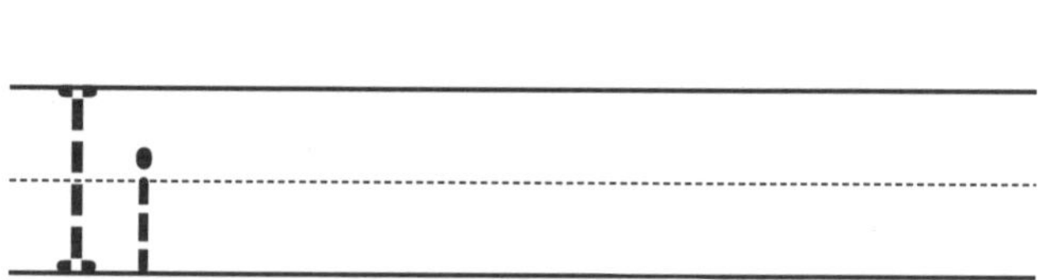

Irina Iguana is itchy.

Invite Irving inside.

Name ______________________________

Trace and write.

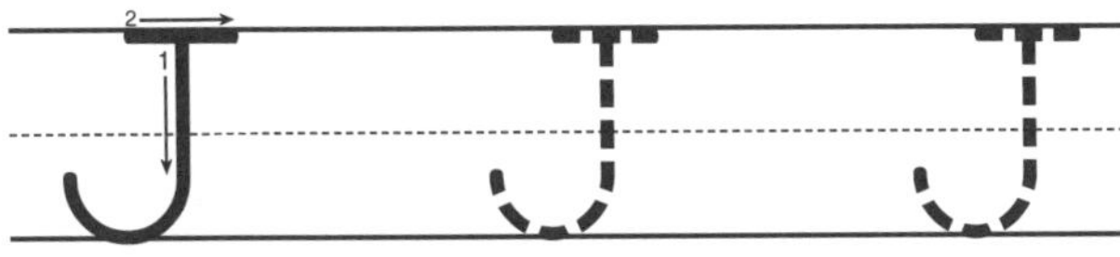

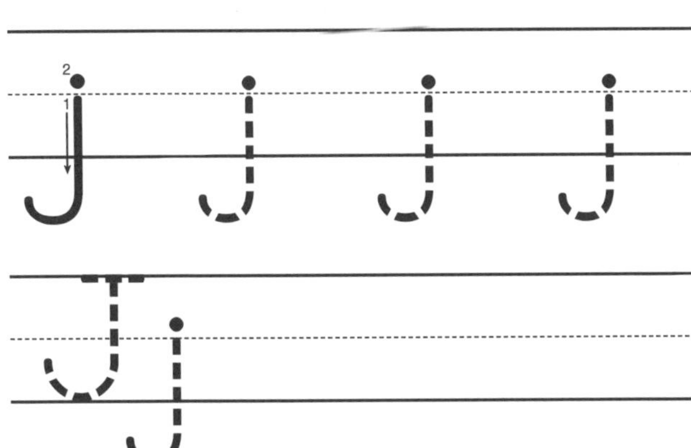

Jim Jellyfish is jazzy.

Jill juggles jelly jars.

Name ______________________________

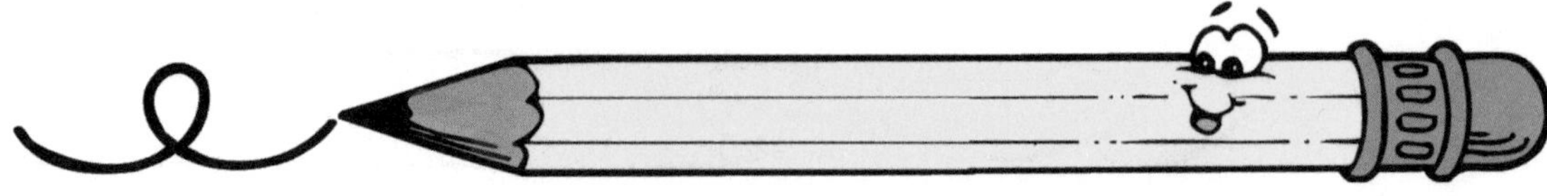

Trace and write.

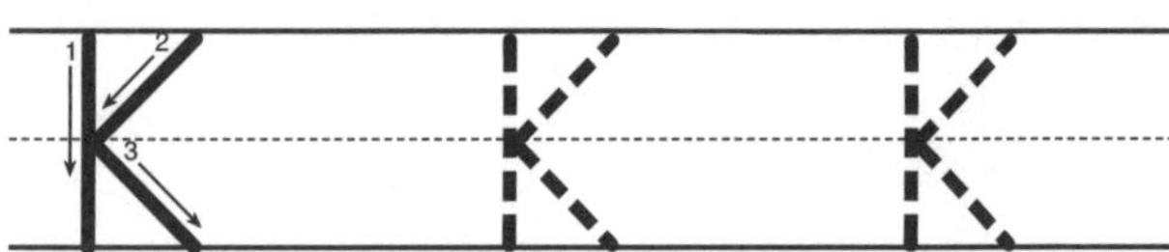

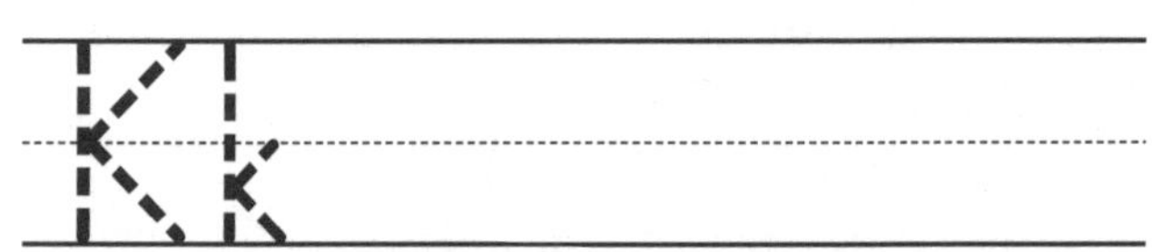

Kyle Kangaroo kicks.

Katie keeps kittens.

Name ____________________

Ll

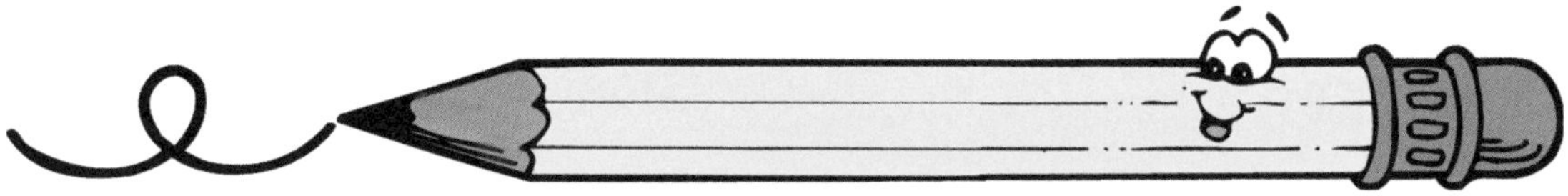

Trace and write.

L L L L

l l l l l

L l

Lyle Lion looks lost.

Lindy loves lollipops.

Name ______________________  **Mm**

Mm

Trace and write.

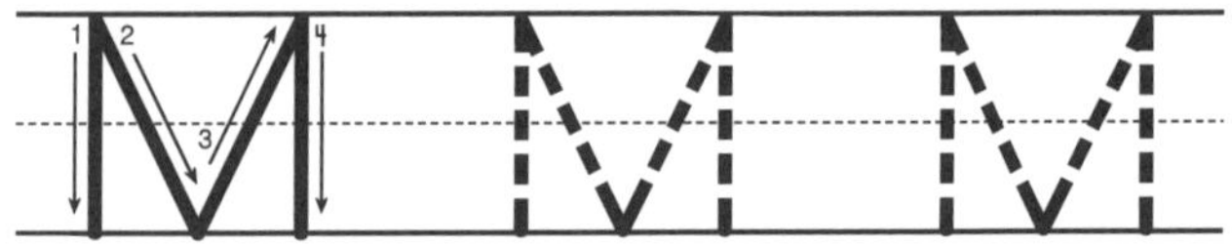

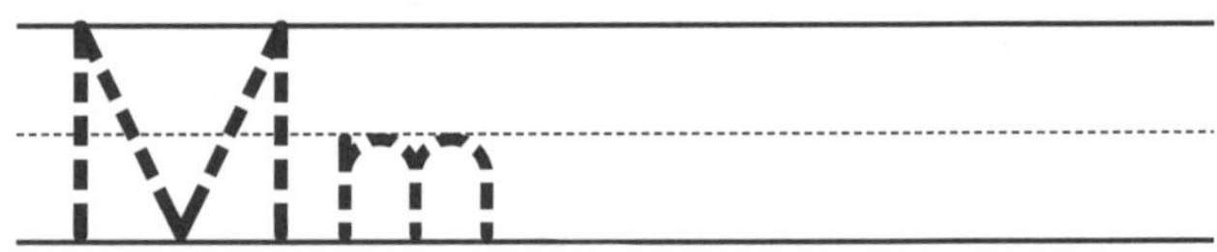

Mike Mouse is messy.

Mom met Madeline.

Name ______________________________

Nn

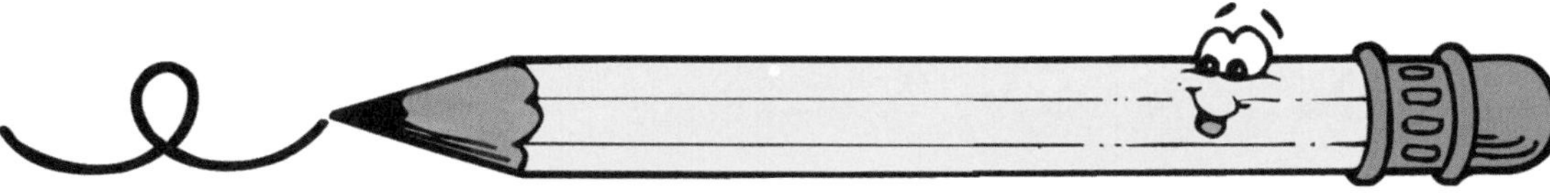

Nn

Trace and write.

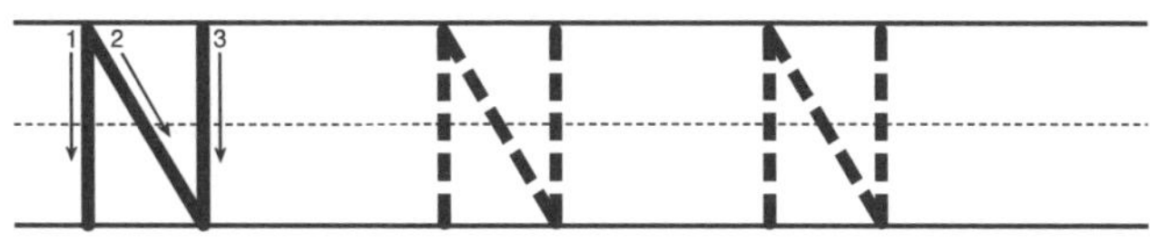

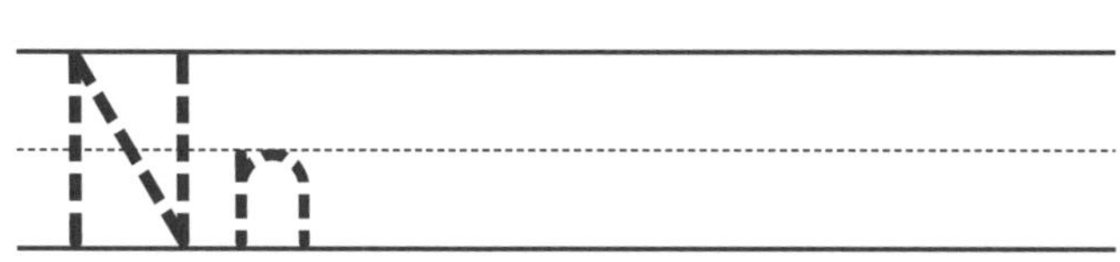

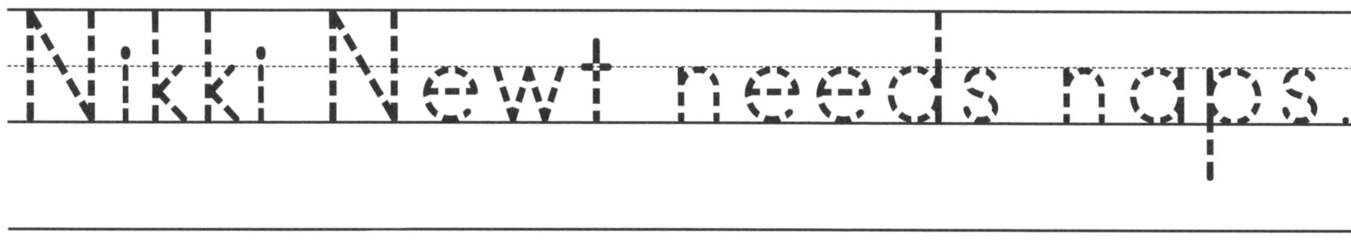

Nurse Ned nibbles.

Name ________________________________ Oo

Trace and write.

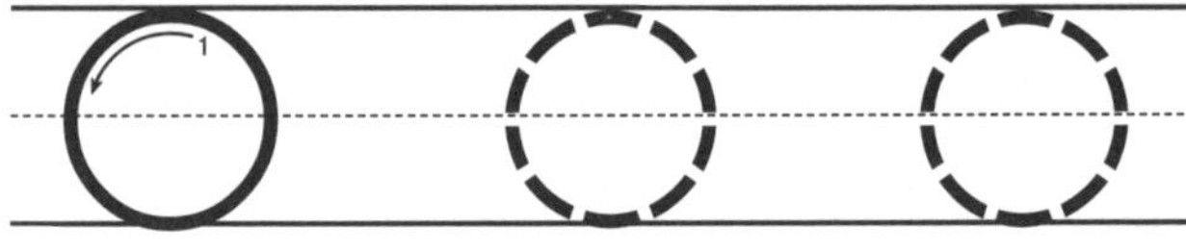

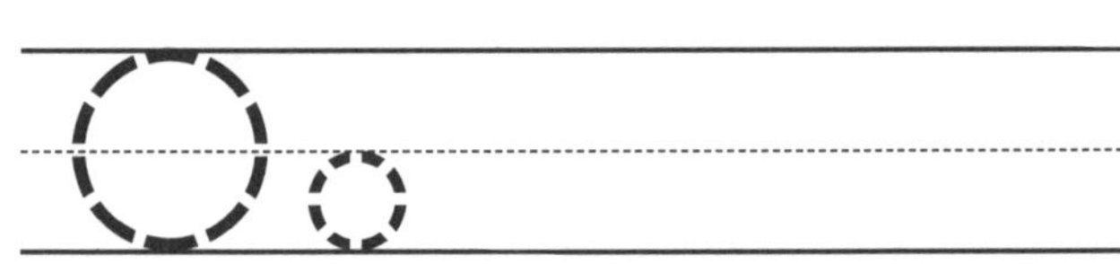

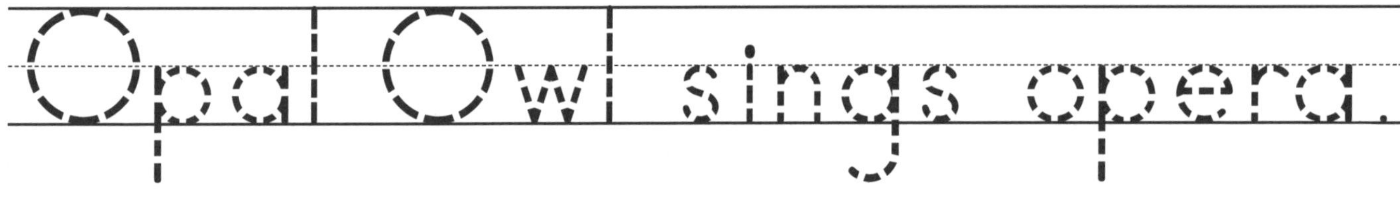

Opal Owl sings opera.

Otis orders oranges.

Scholastic Professional Books

Name ______________________________

Trace and write.

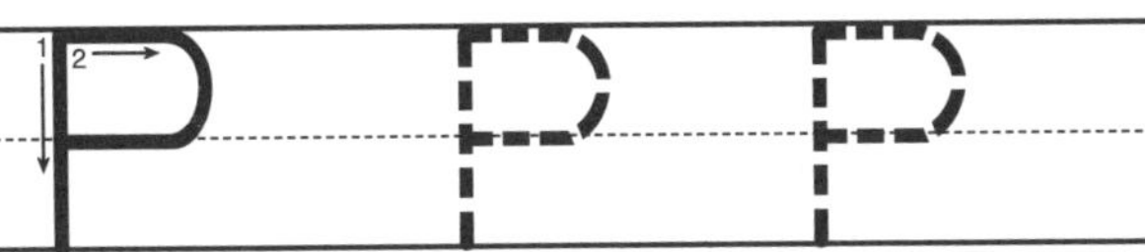

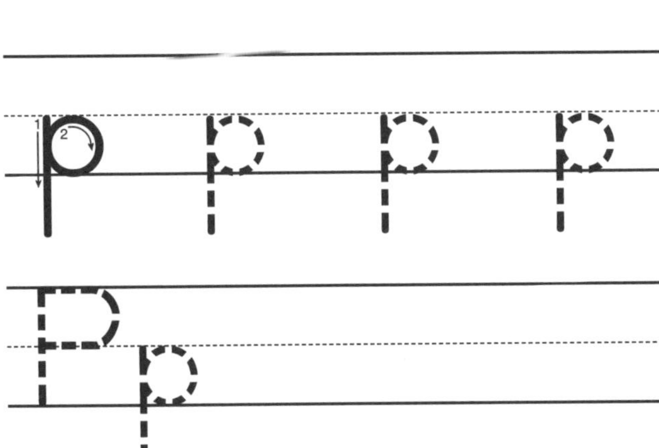

Pam Pig paid a penny.

Peter Pig says please.

Name ______________________________

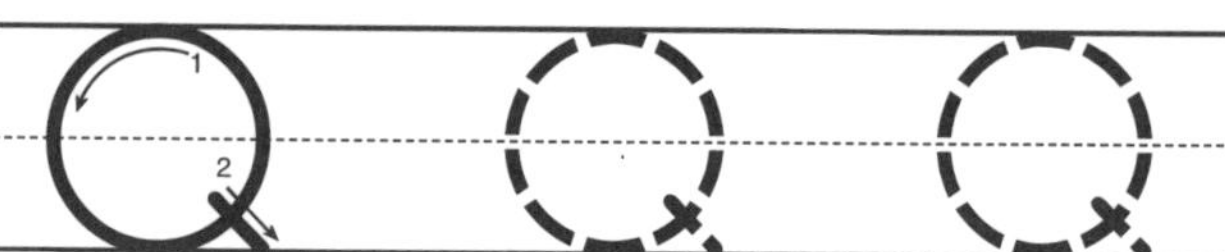

Trace and write.

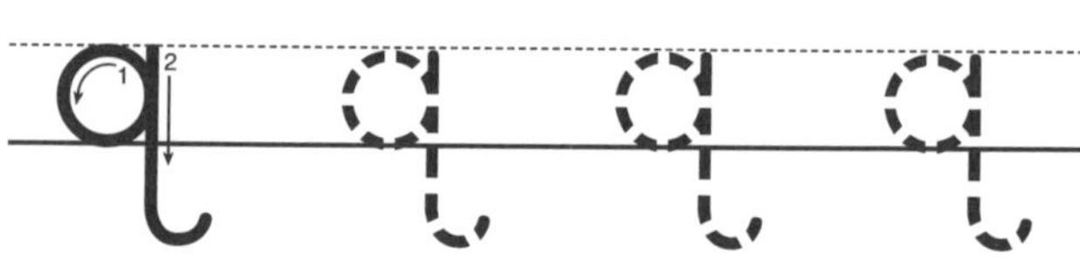

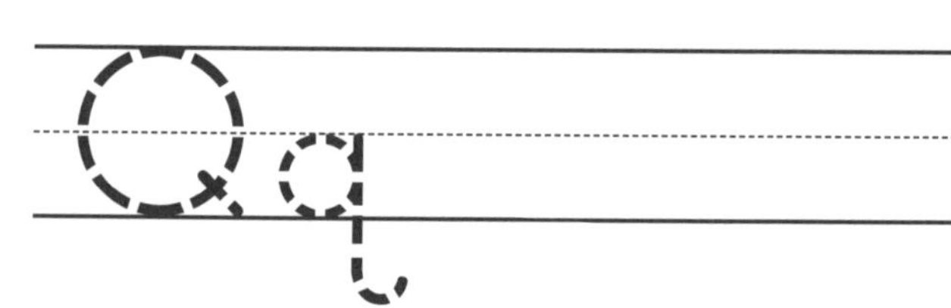

Quinn Quail is quiet.

Quebec is quite nice.

Name ______________________________

Rr

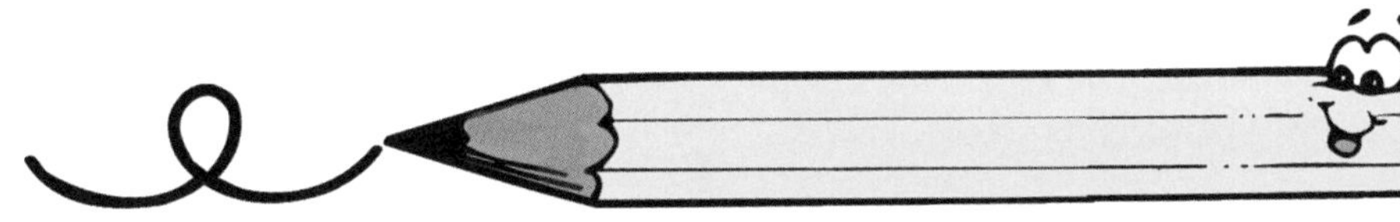

Trace and write.

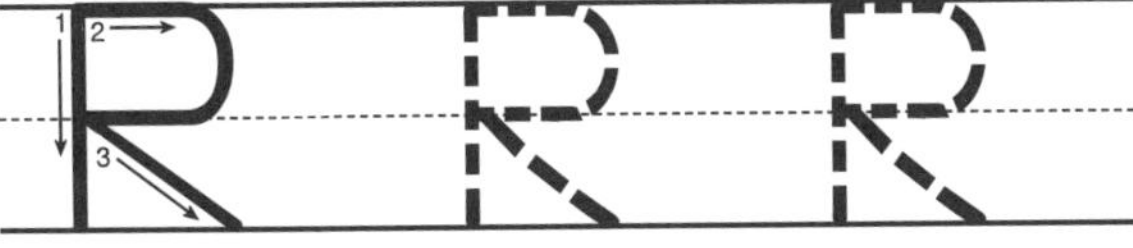

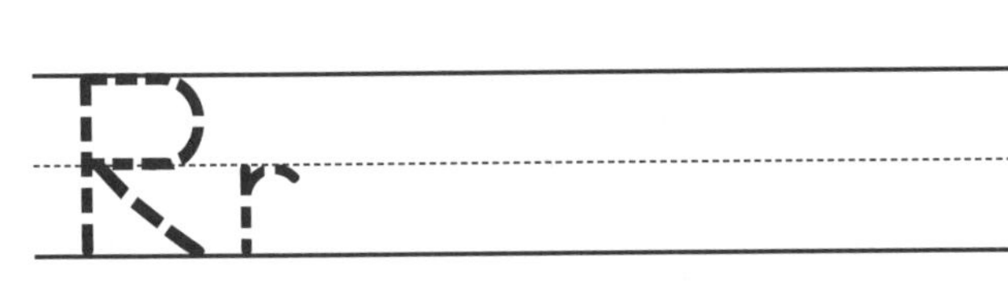

Randy Rabbit races.

Robin reads rapidly.

Name ______________________________

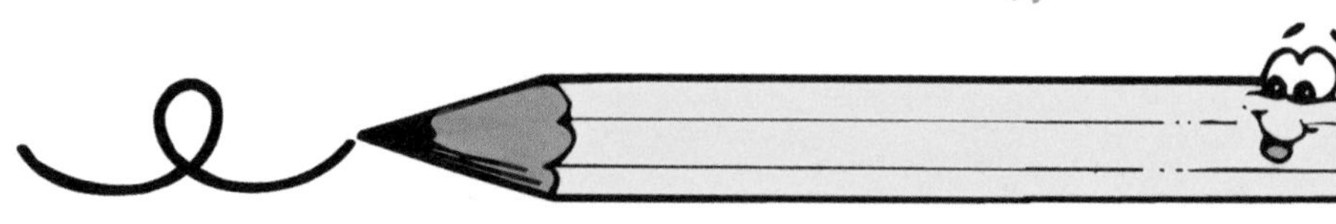

Trace and write.

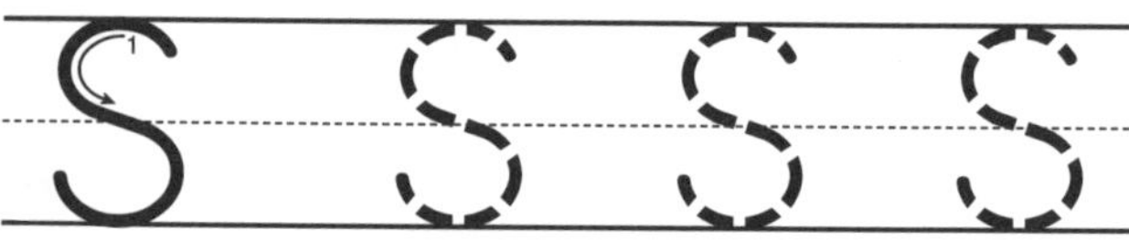

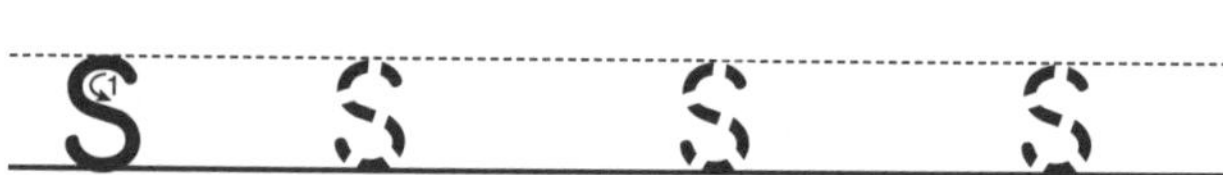

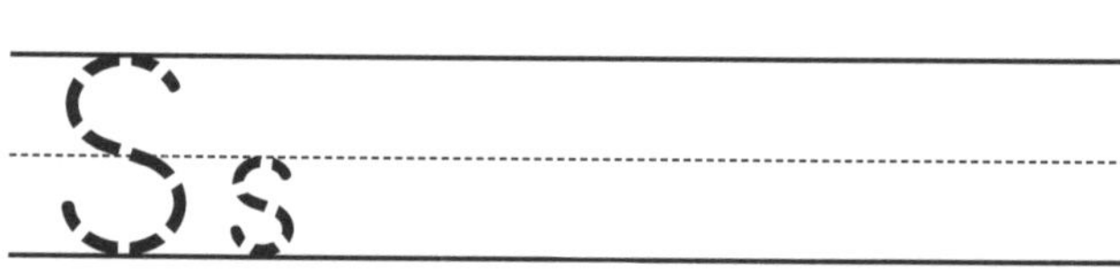

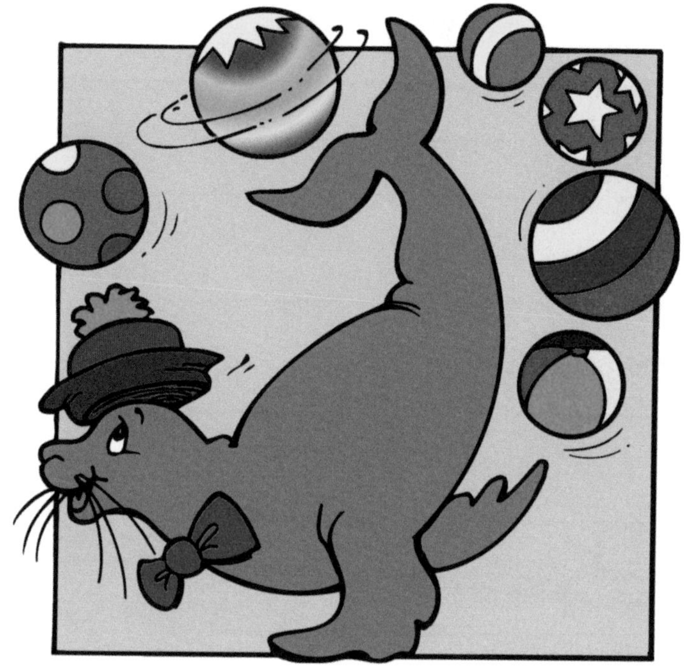

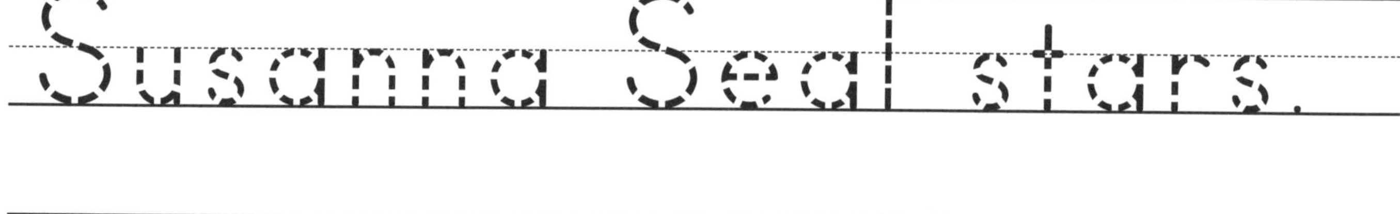
Susanna Seal stars.

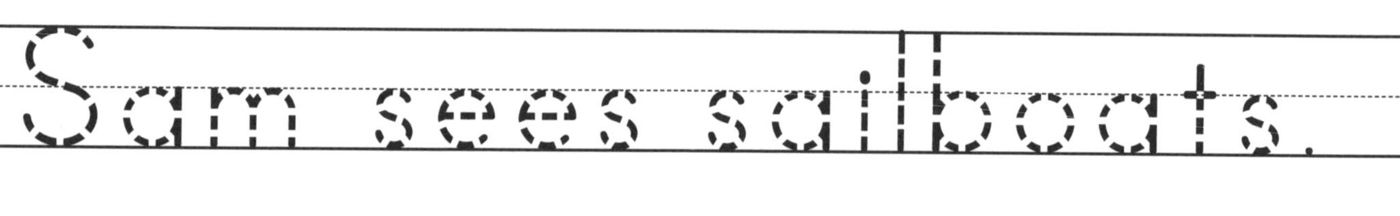
Sam sees sailboats.

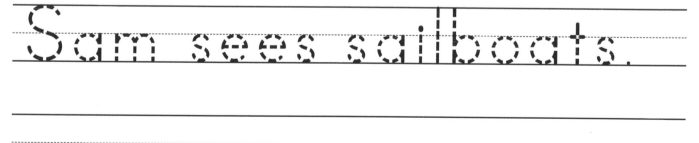

Name ____________________

Tt

Trace and write.

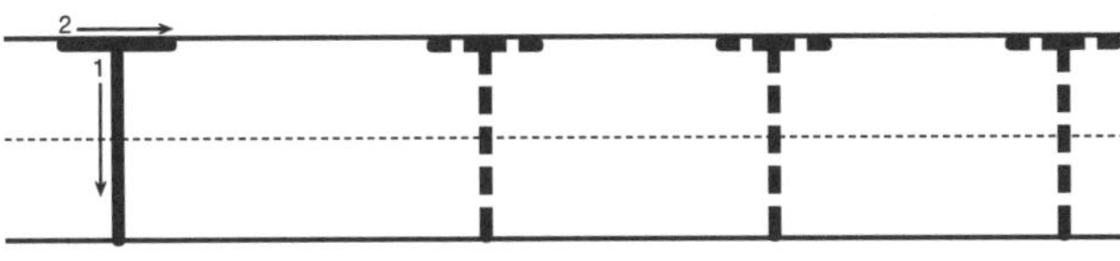

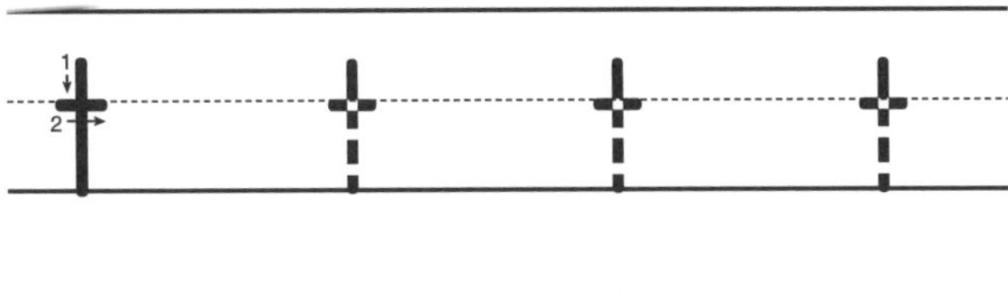

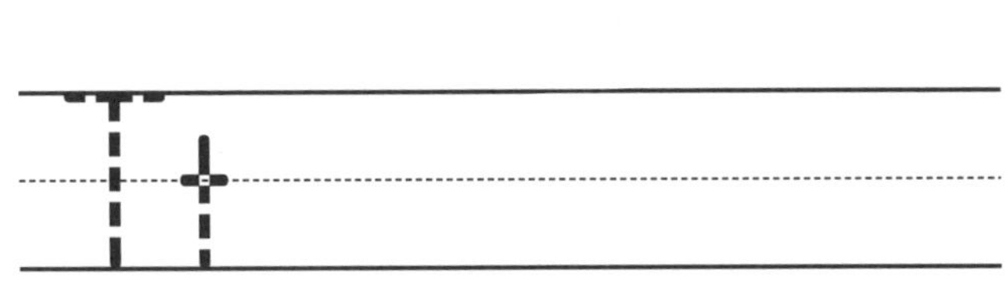

Tristan Toad is toothy.

Tigers taste terrible.

Name ______________________________

U u

Trace and write.

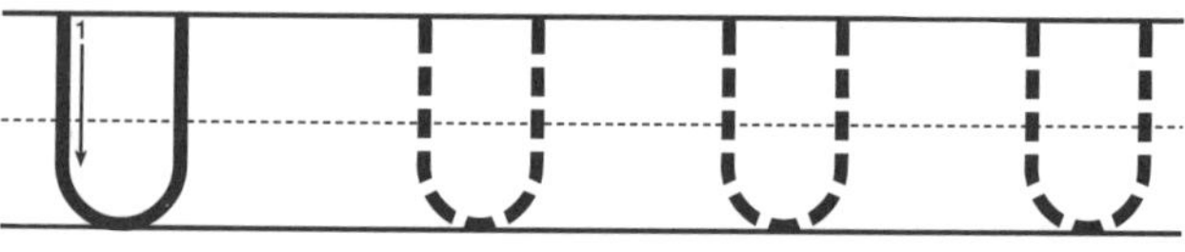

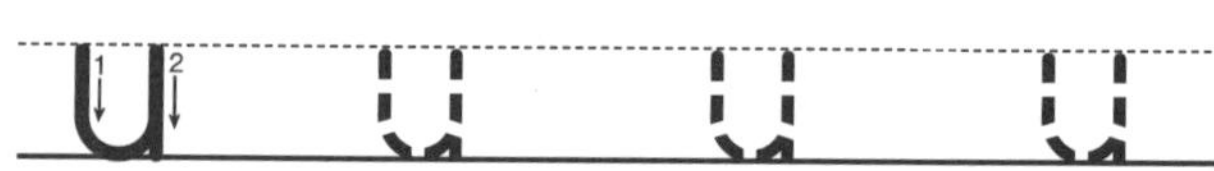

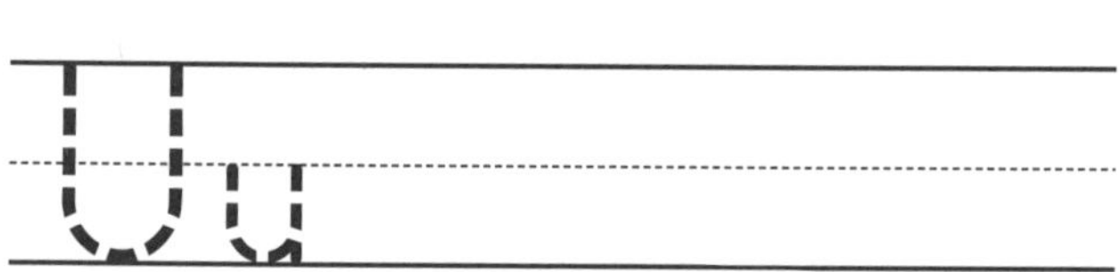

Ula uses an umbrella.

Uncle Uno umpires.

Name ____________________  Vv

Trace and write.

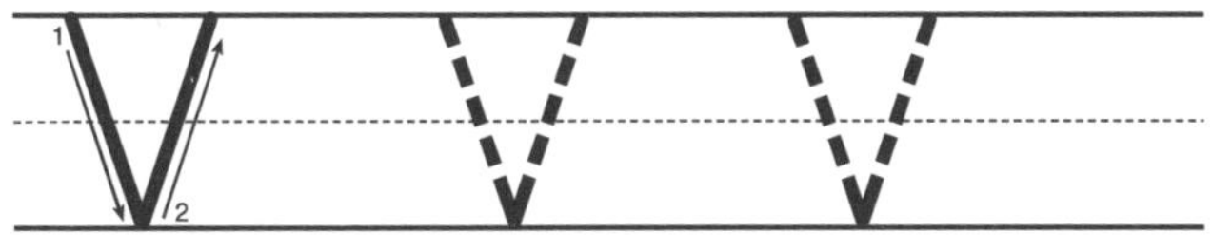
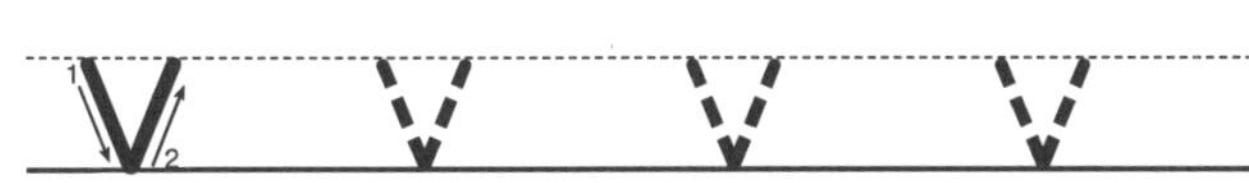
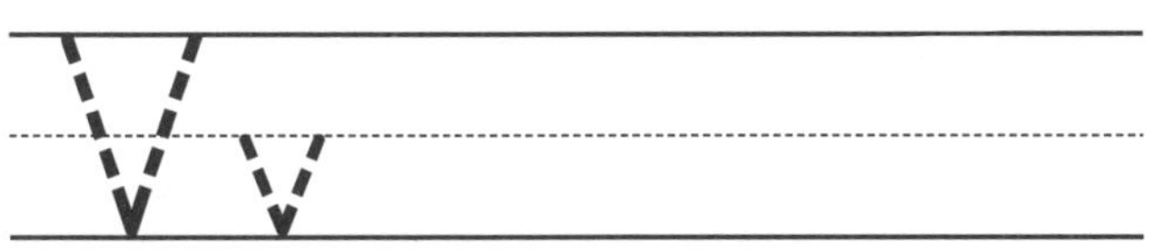

Vic Vulture is vain.

Vegetables vary.

Name ____________________

Ww

Trace and write.

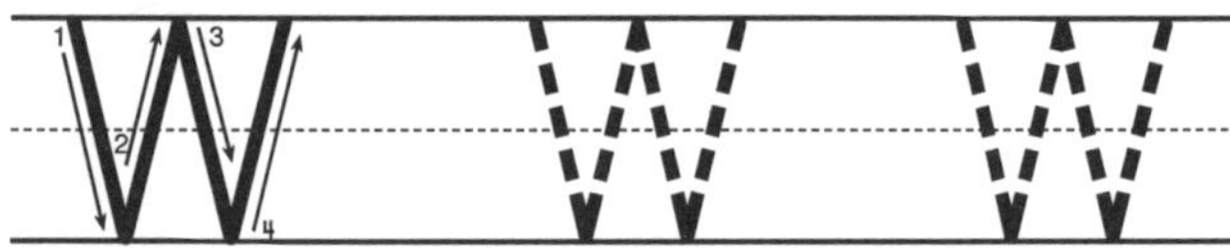

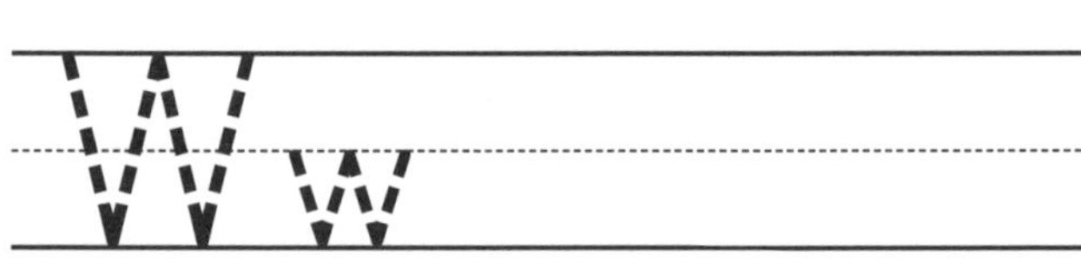

Will Worm is wealthy.

Wilma wipes windows.

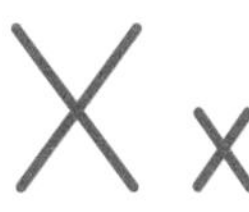
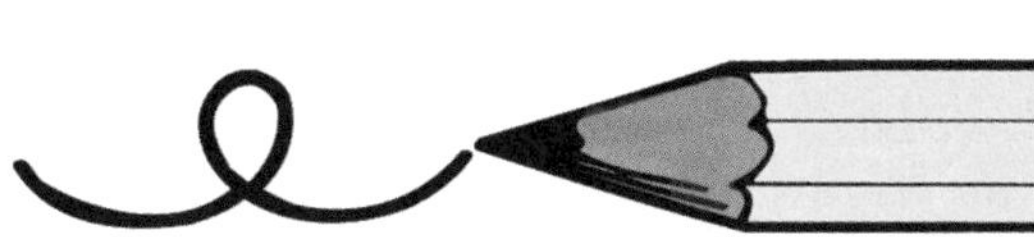
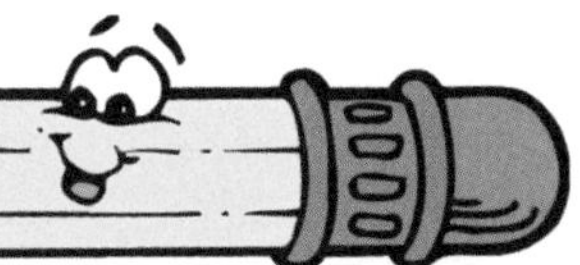

Trace and write.

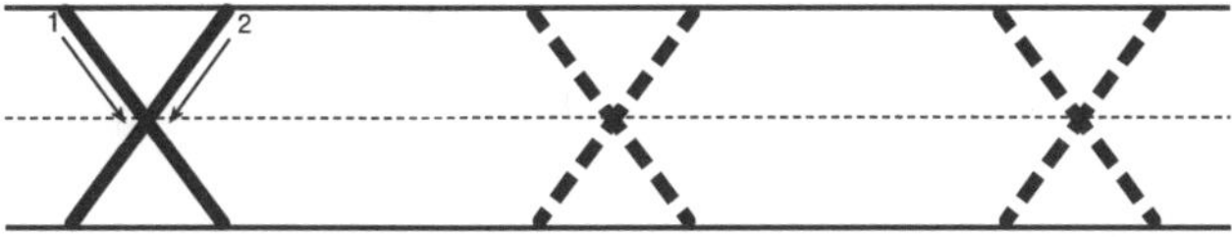
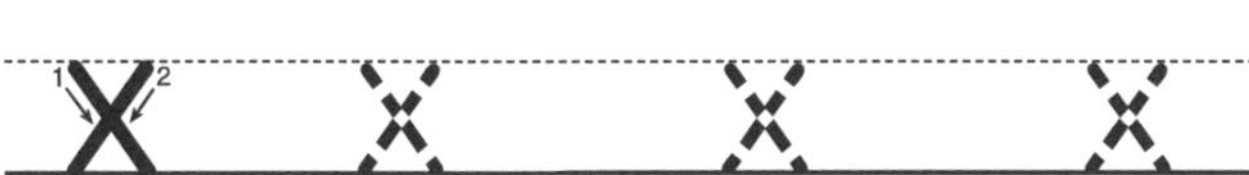
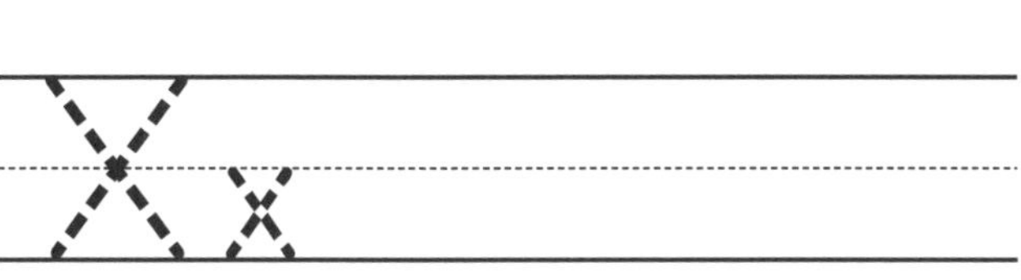
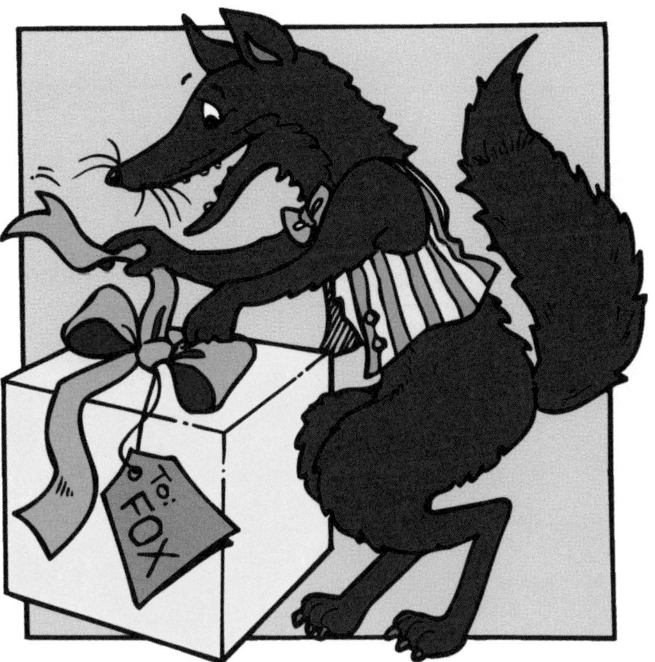
To:
FOX

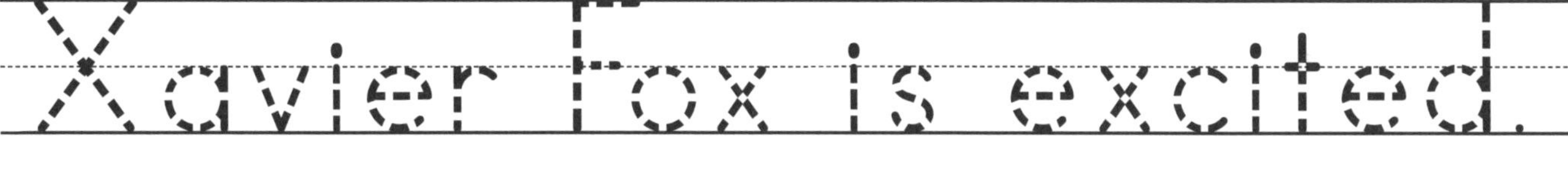
Xavier Fox is excited.

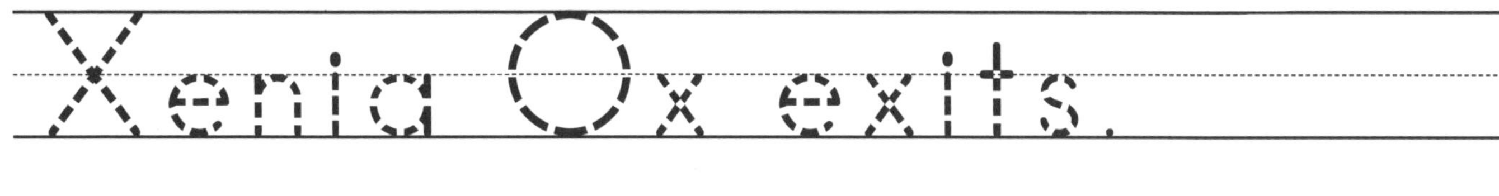
Xenia Ox exits.

Name ______________________ 

Trace and write.

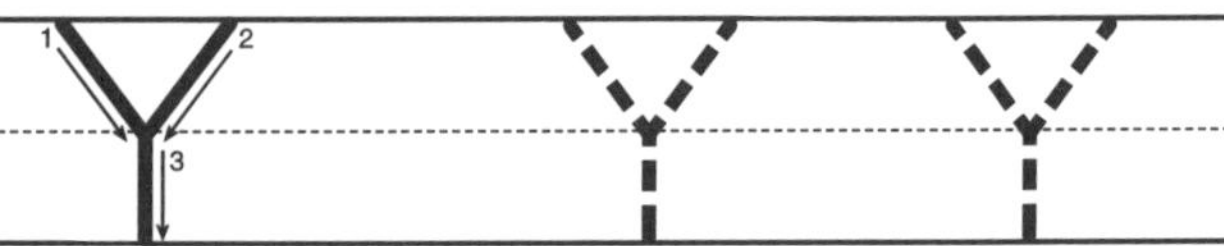

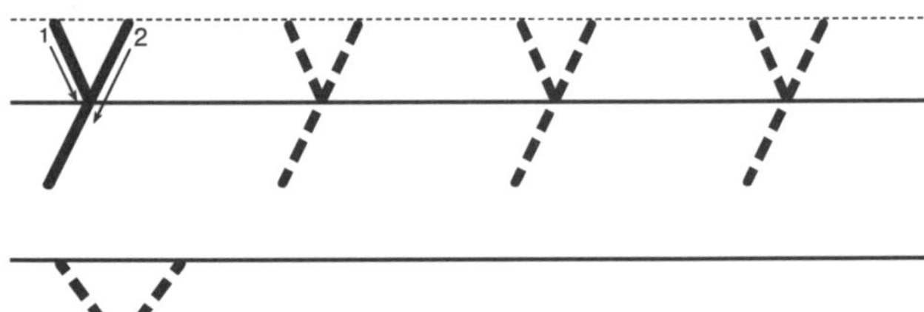

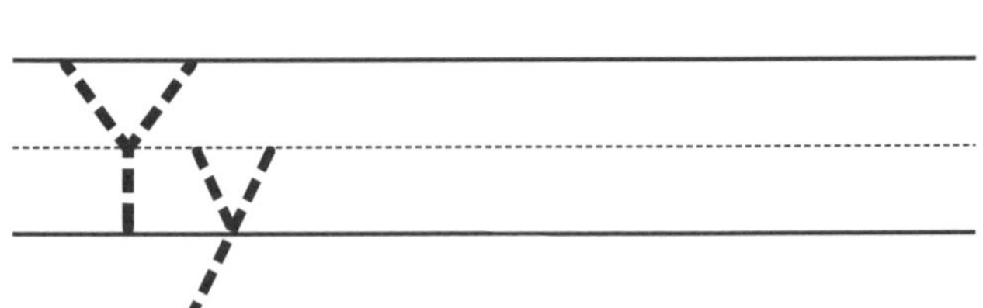

Yvonne Yak yawns.

Young yaks yodel.

Name ______________________________________  Zz

Z z

Trace and write.

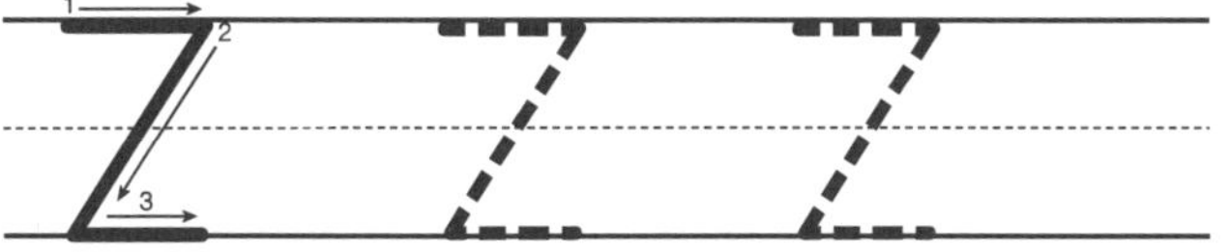

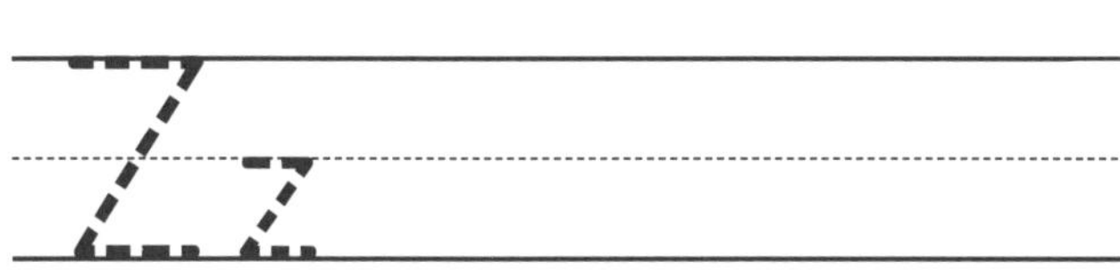

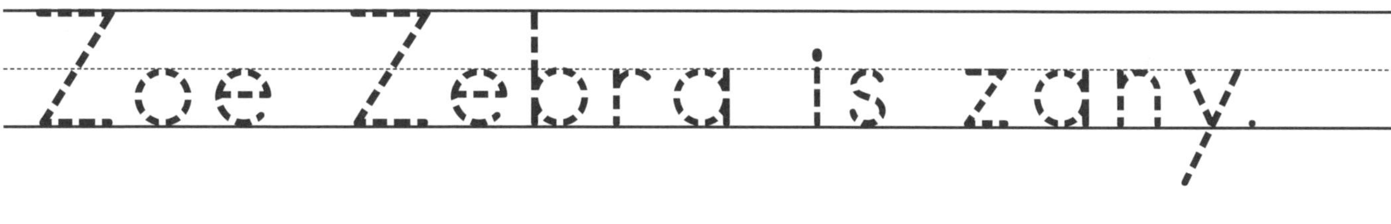

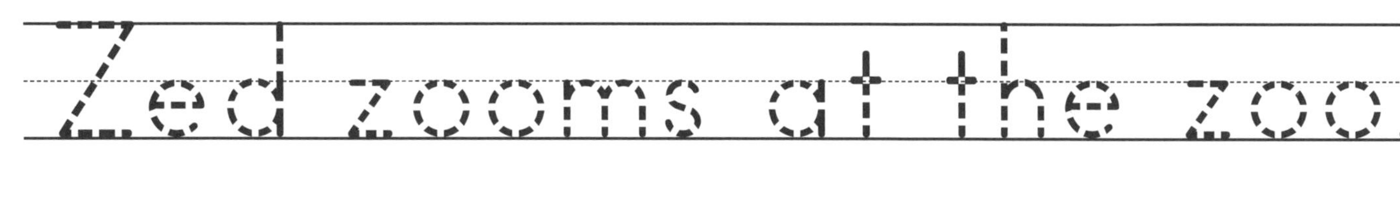

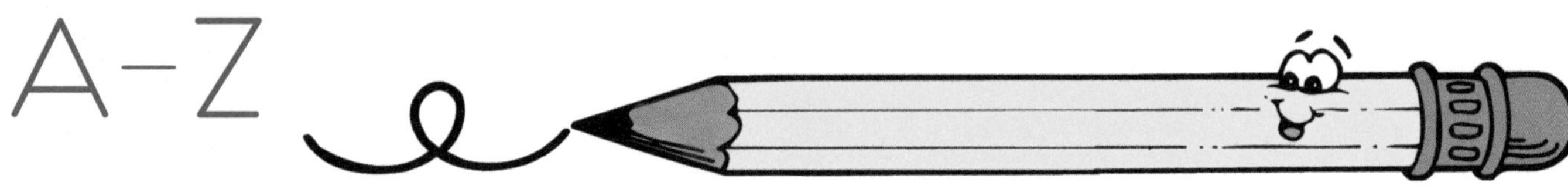

Trace and write.

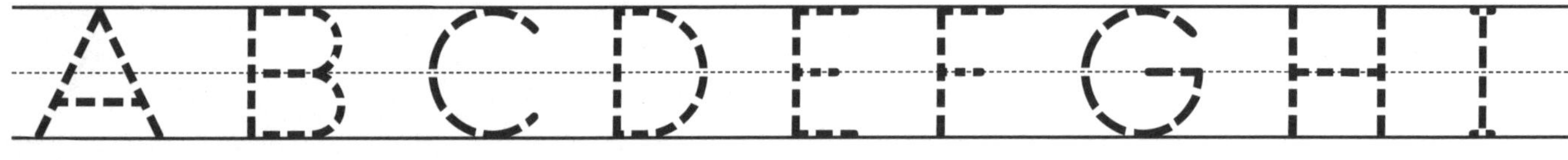

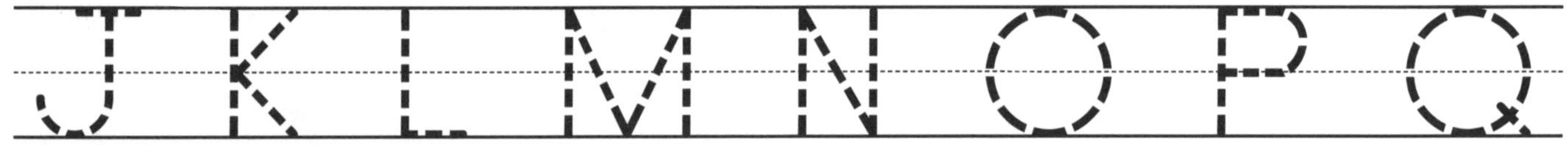

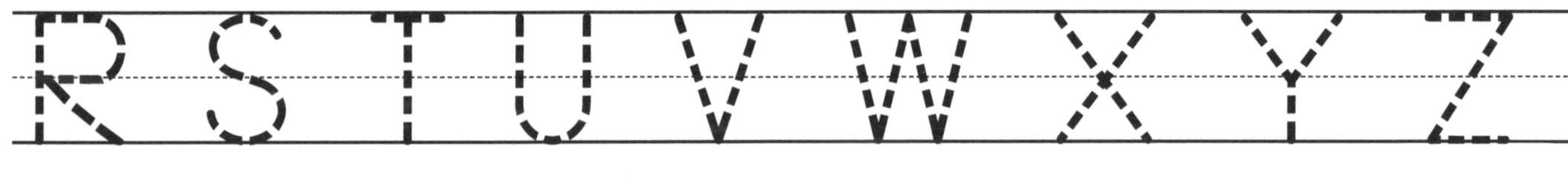

Name ______________________________

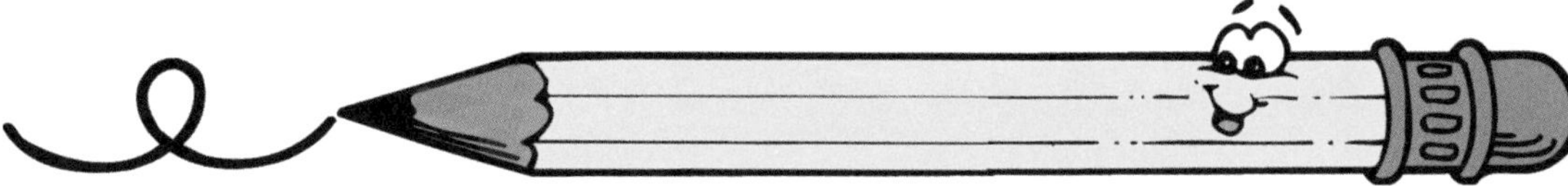

a–z

Trace and write.

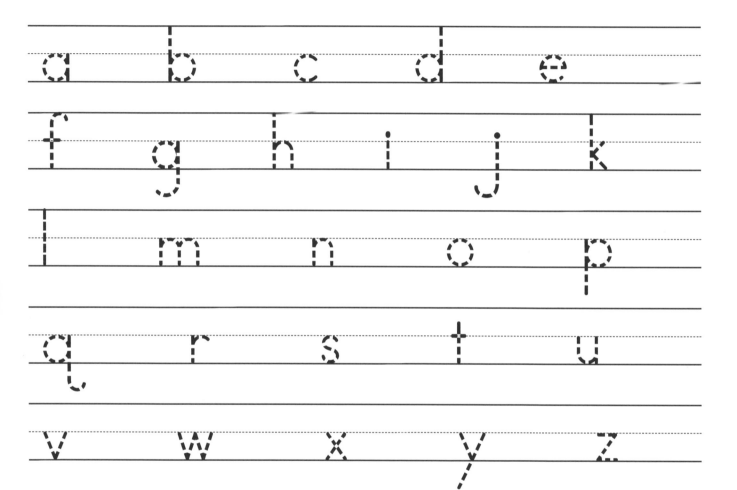

a b c d e

f g h i j k

l m n o p

q r s t u

v w x y z

1–5

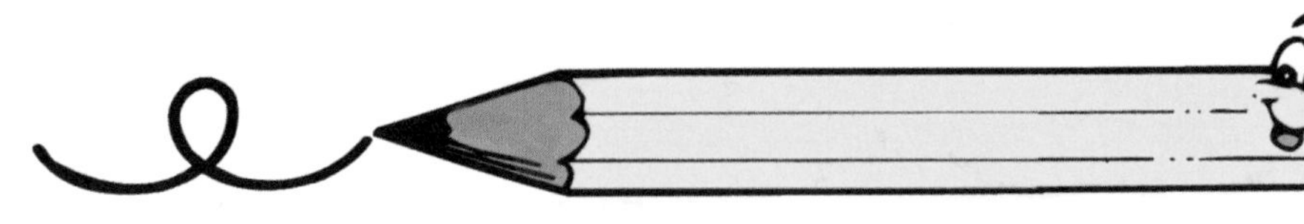

Trace and write.

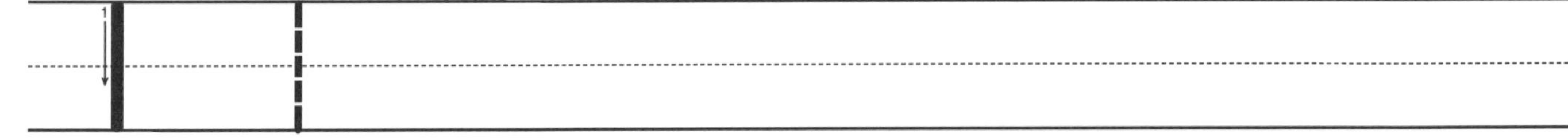

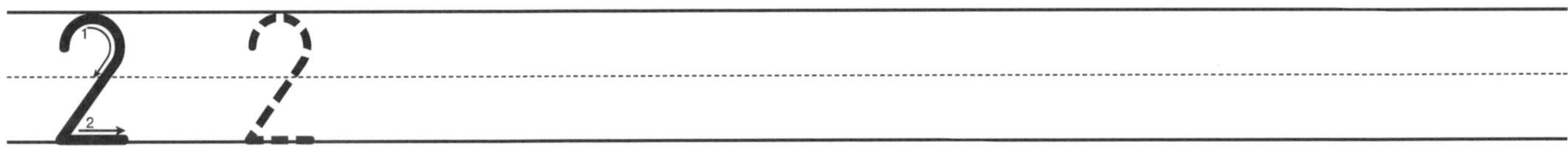

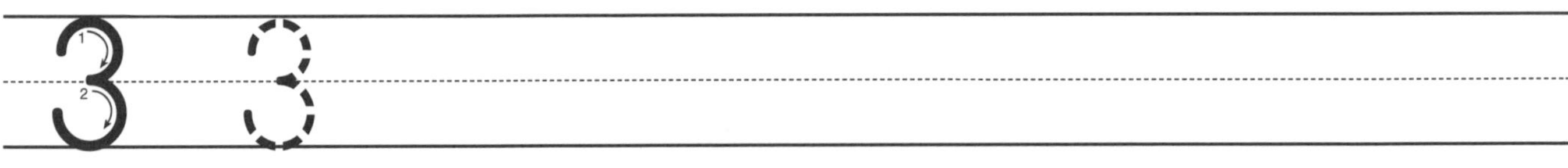

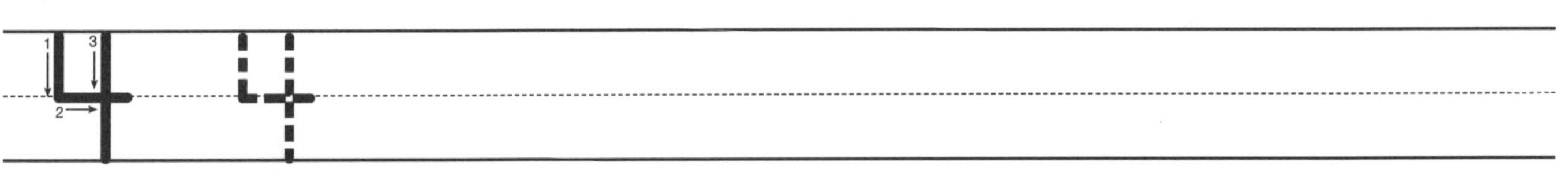

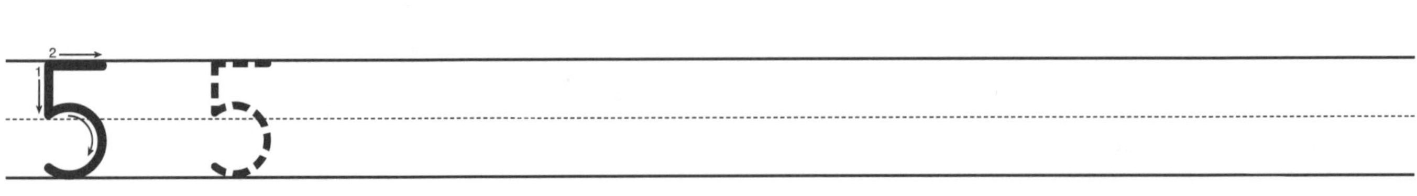

Name ____________________ 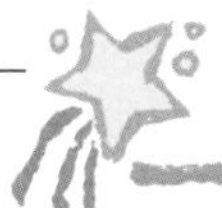

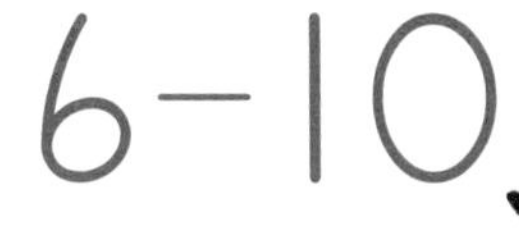

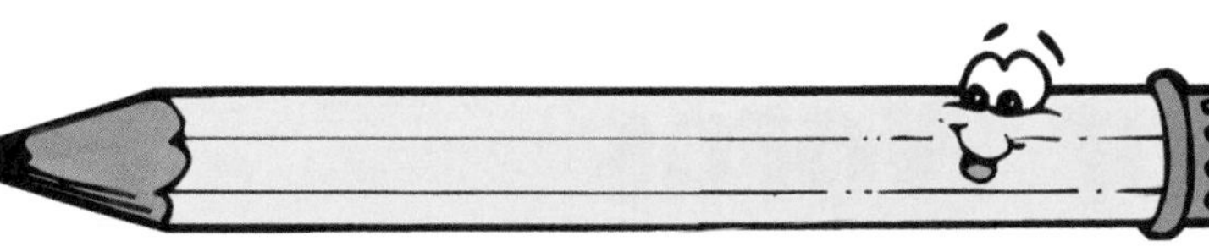

Trace and write.

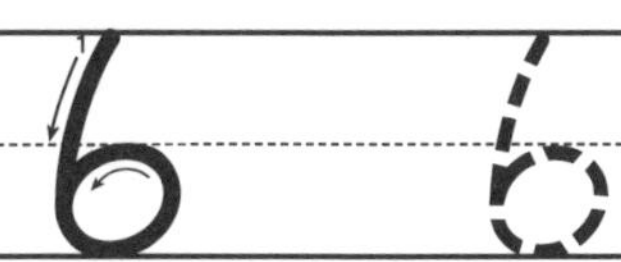

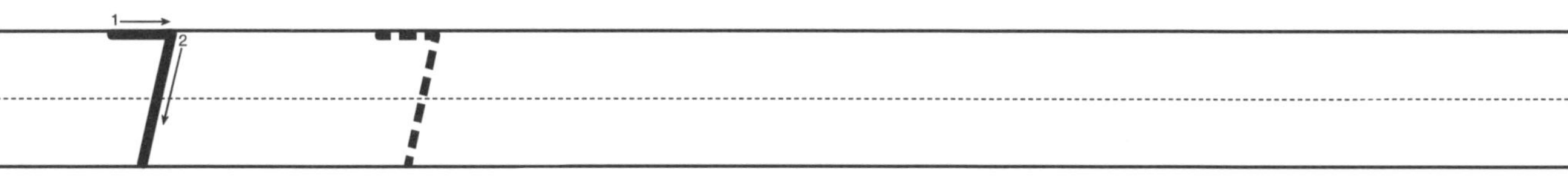

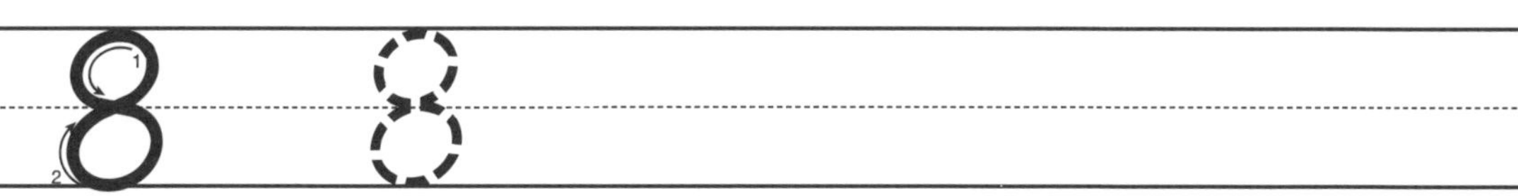

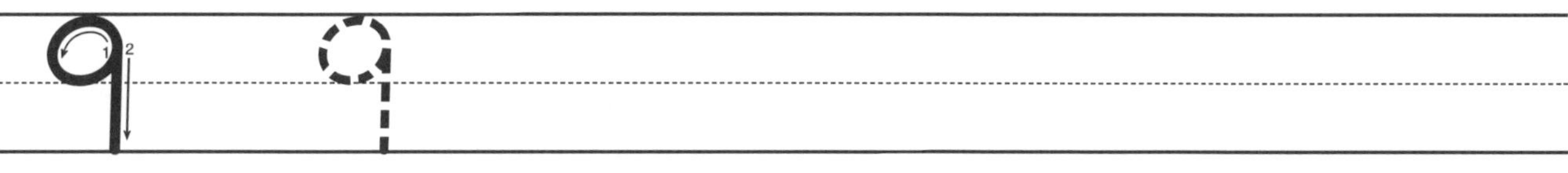

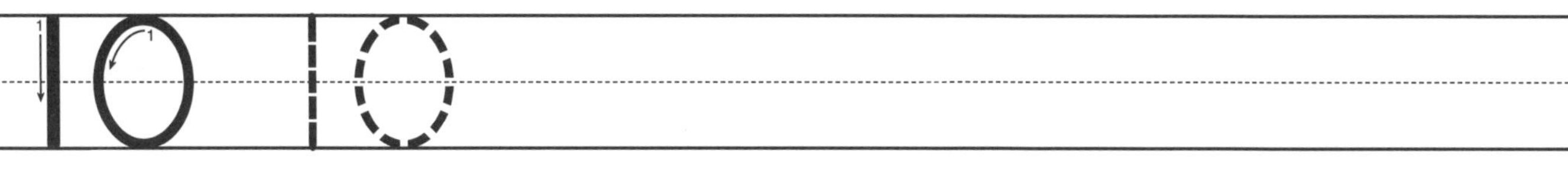

Color Words

Trace and write.

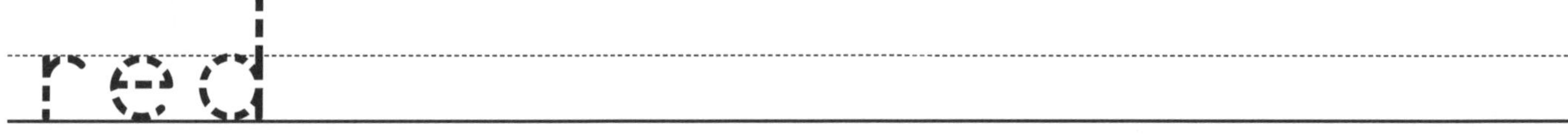

green

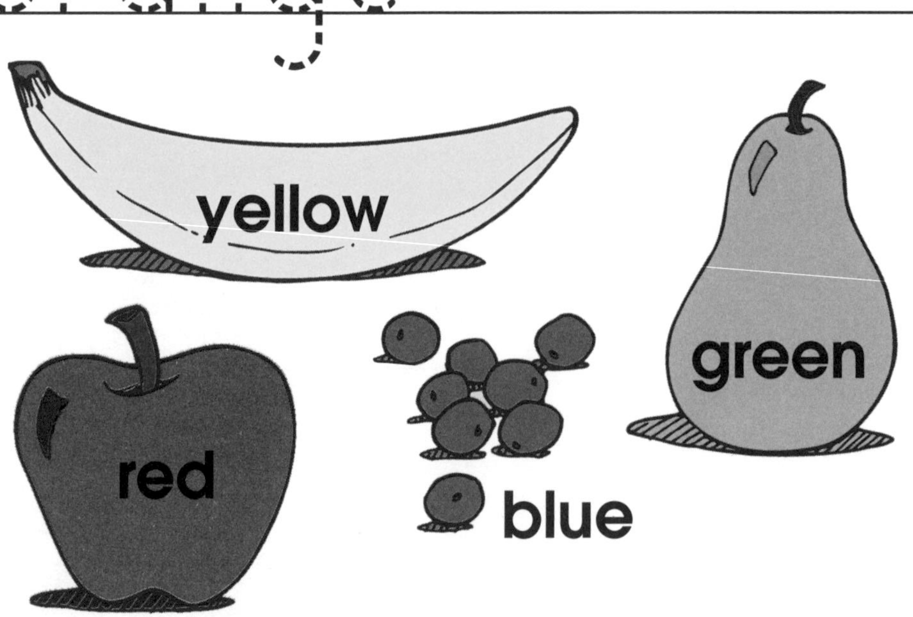

More Color Words

Trace and write.

brown

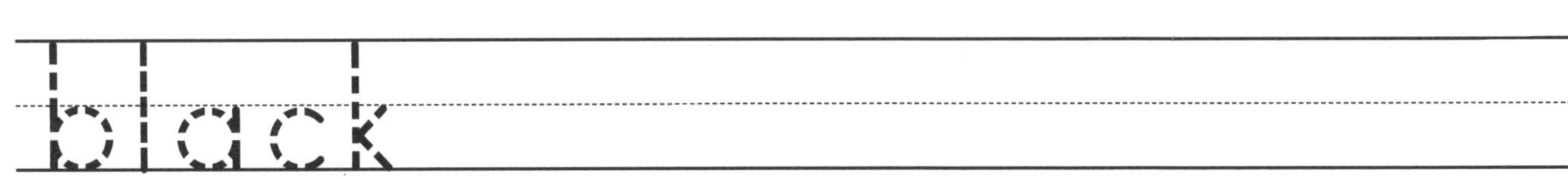

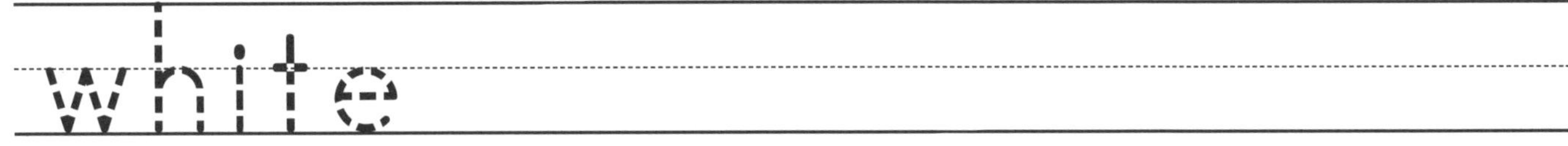

pink

Name ______________________________

Number Words

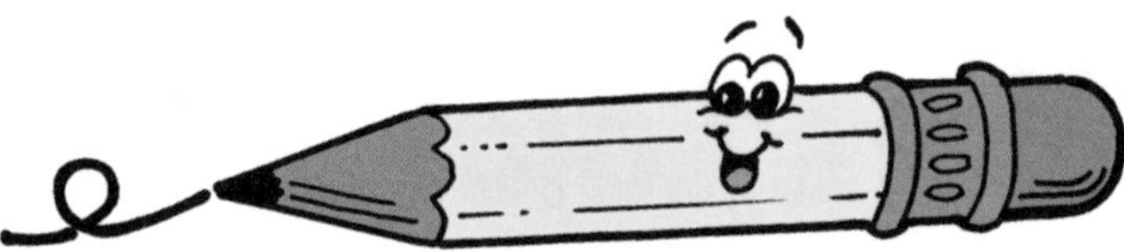

Trace and write.

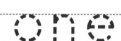

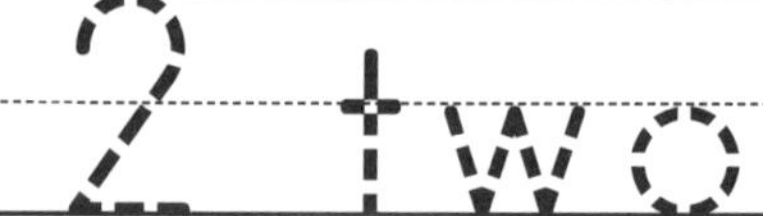

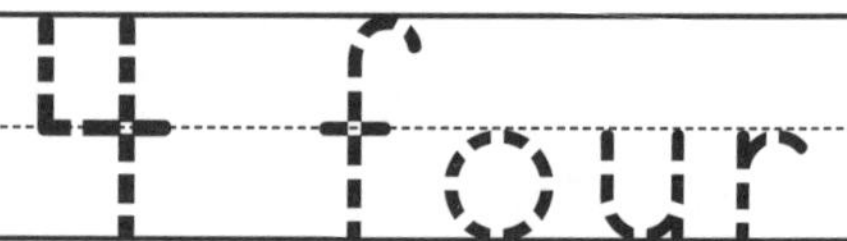

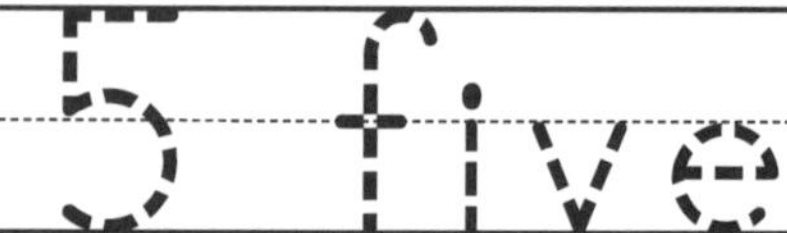

More Number Words

Trace and write.

6 six

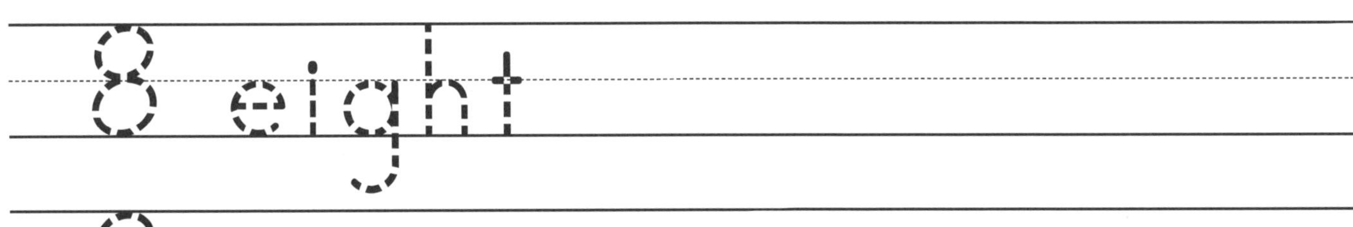

9 nine

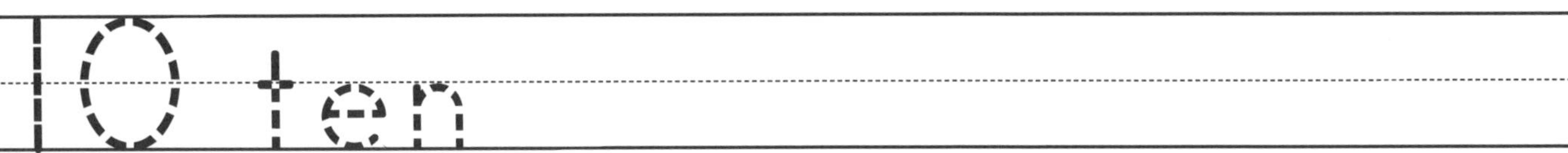

Shapes

Trace and write.

oval

heart

circle

square

triangle

diamond

rectangle

Days of the Week

Trace and write.

Sunday

Monday

Tuesday

Wednesday

Thursday

Friday

Saturday

Months

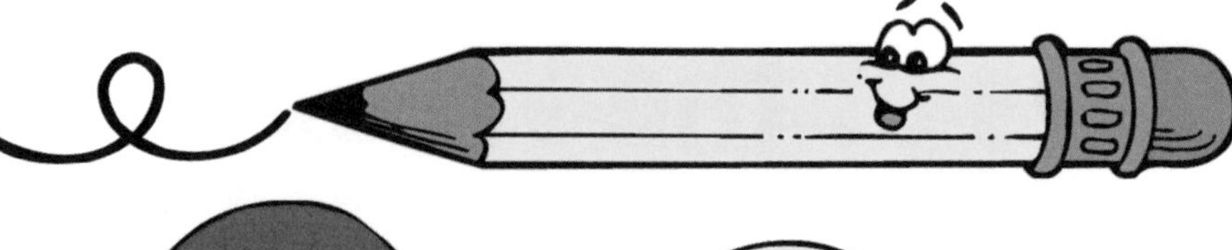

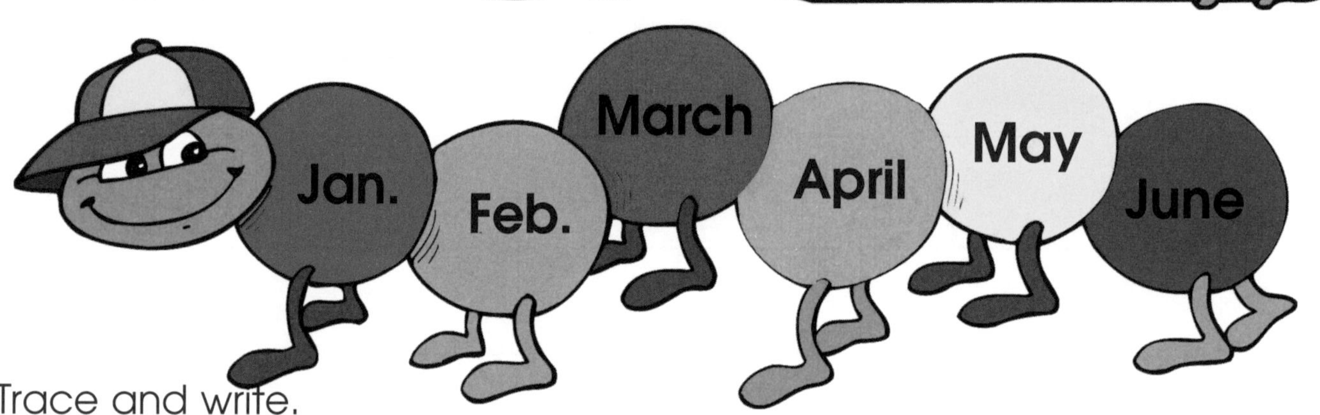

Trace and write.

January

February

March

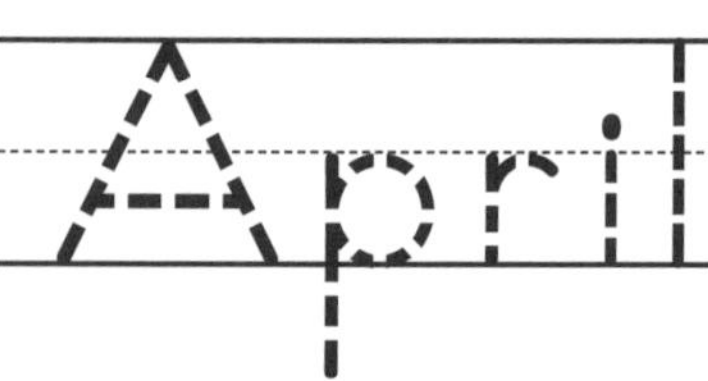

April

May

June

Months

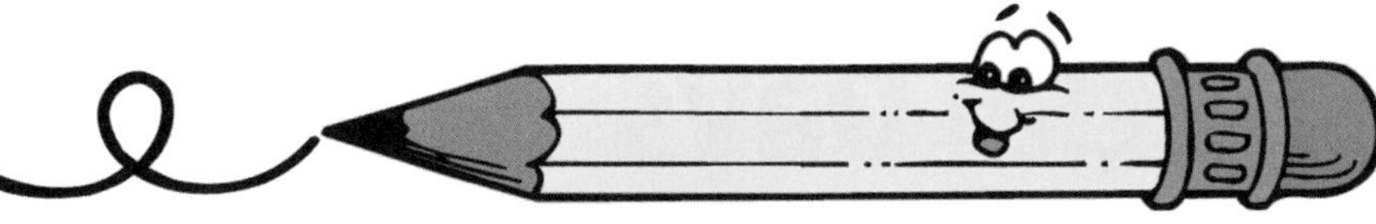

Trace and write.

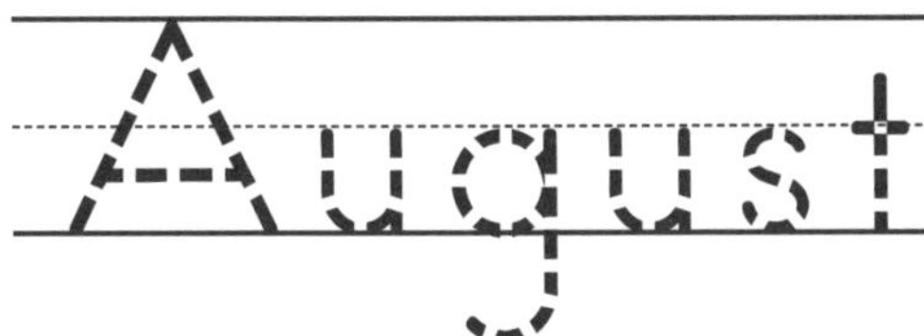

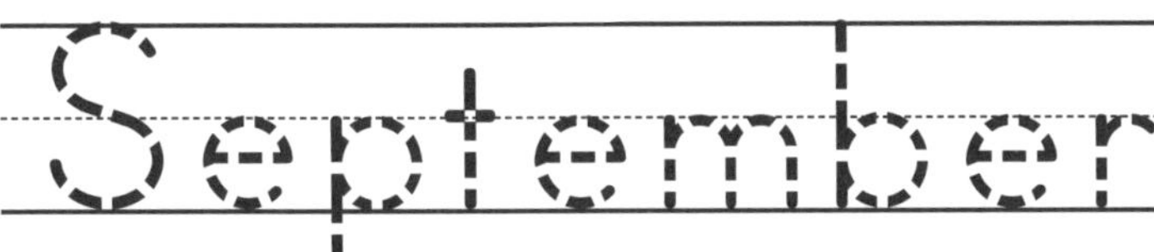

September

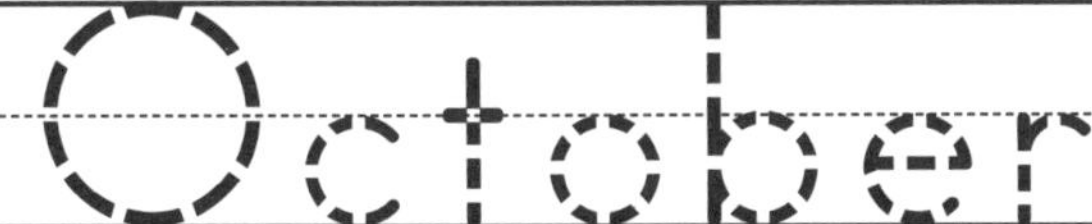

Name ______________________________

Special Days

Write each special day.

New Year's Day

Valentine's Day

Presidents' Day

St. Patrick's Day

Mother's Day

Father's Day

Fourth of July

Name ______________________ 

Special Days

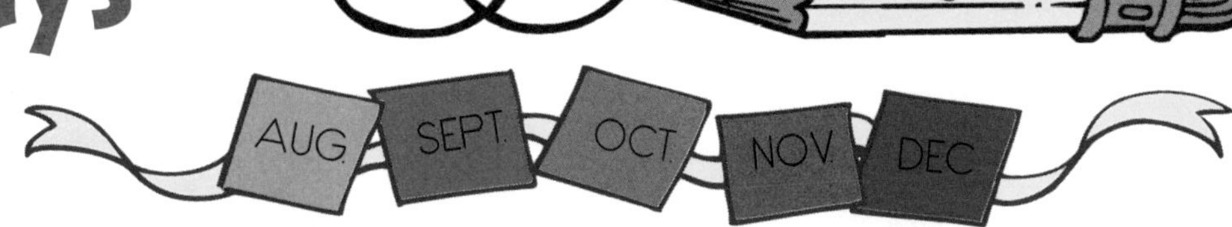

Write each special day.

Labor Day

Halloween

Veterans Day

Thanksgiving

Hannukah

Christmas

Kwanzaa

Name ___________________________

Animals From A to Z

Write the animal names on the lines below.

alligator
bear
cougar
duck

elk
frog
giraffe
horse

iguana
jaguar
kangaroo
leopard

moose
newt
ostrich

Name ______________________________

Animals From A to Z

Write the animal names on the lines below.

parrot
quail
raccoon
squirrel
tiger
urchin
vulture
whale
X-ray fish
yak
zebra

Name ______________________

The Continents

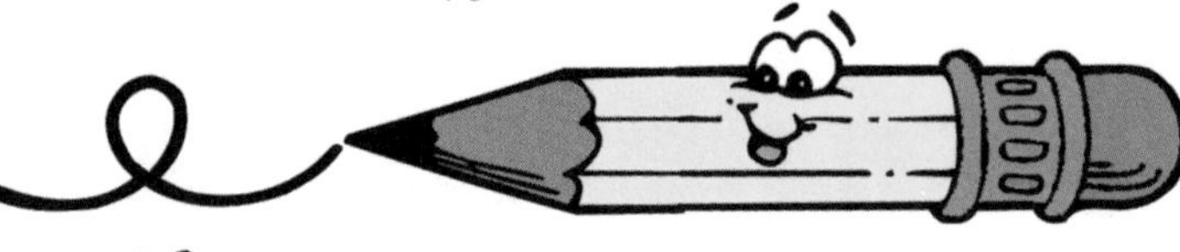

Write the names of the continents.

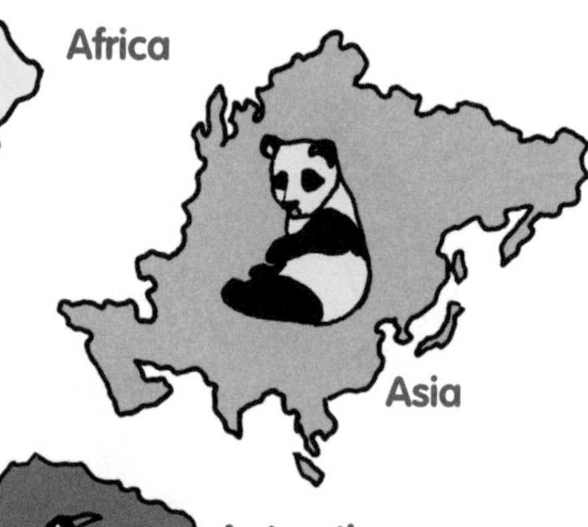

Africa

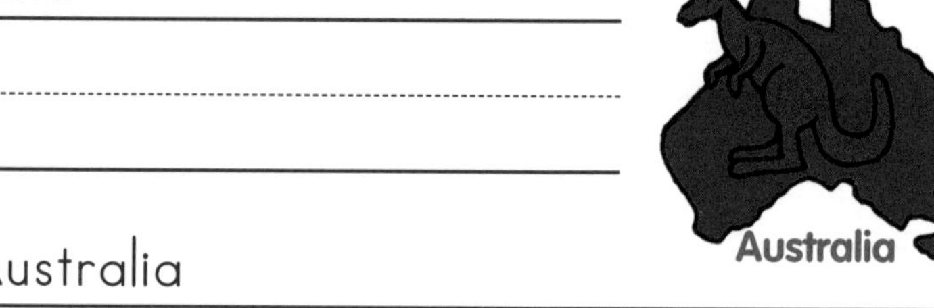

Asia

Australia

Antarctica

Europe

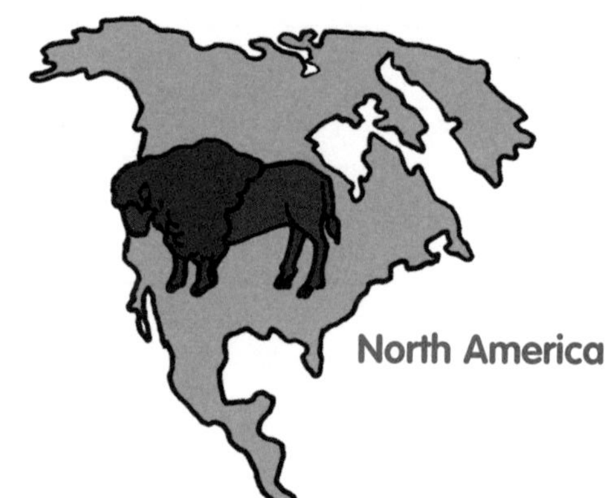

North America

South America

South America

The Planets

Write the names of the planets.

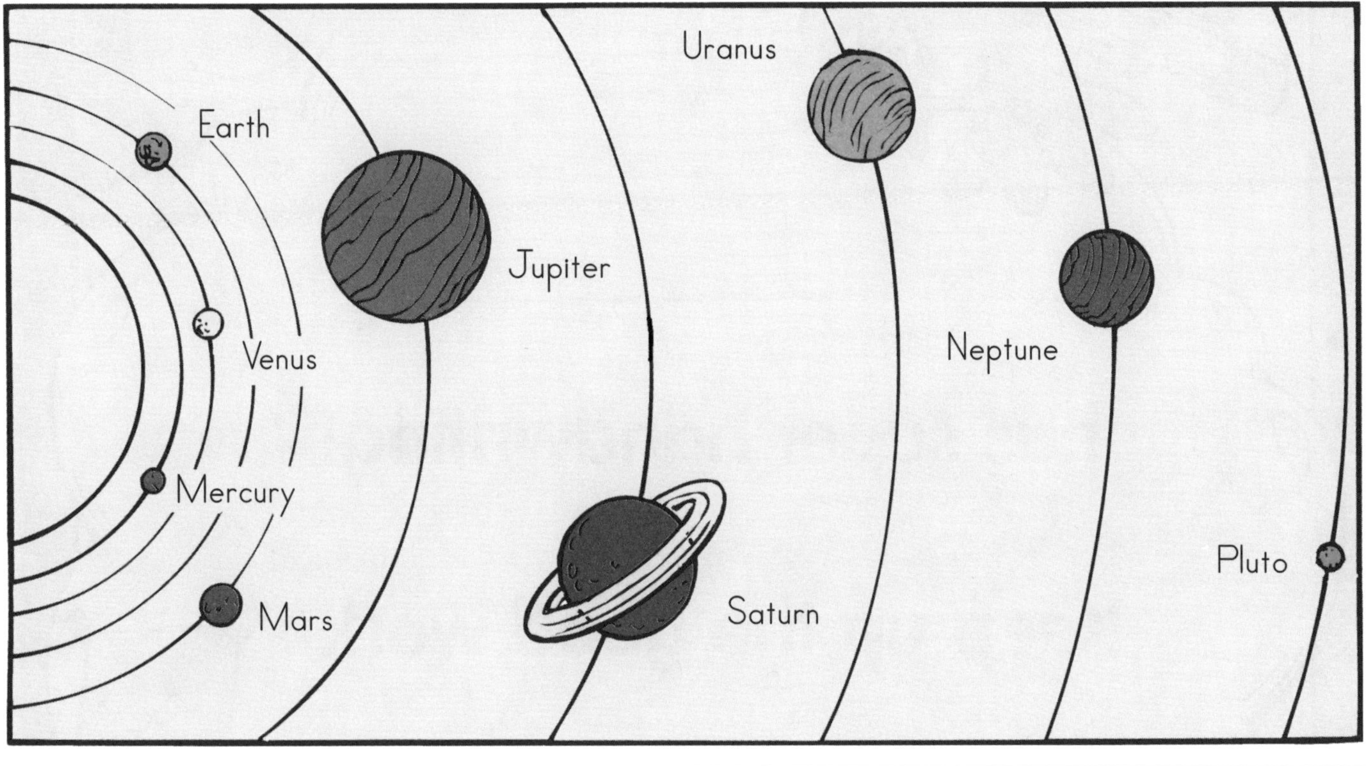

has super handwriting!
Keep up the good work!
signed
date

Name ______________________________ 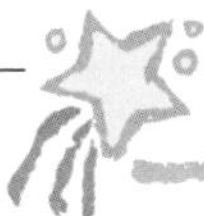

Capitalizing First Word

A sentence always begins with a capital letter.

Copy each sentence correctly on the line.

1. the cat sat.

2. the dog sat.

3. i see the cat.

4. i can see.

Capitalizing First Word

Read each sentence. Then fill in the circle next to the word with the capital letter that begins the sentence.

1. **The cat is in the van.**
   - ◯ cat
   - ◯ The

2. **My dog can run.**
   - ◯ My
   - ◯ dog

3. **Jan can hop.**
   - ◯ Jan
   - ◯ hop

4. **I like ham.**
   - ◯ ham
   - ◯ I

5. **Ants like jam.**
   - ◯ jam
   - ◯ Ants

Name ______________________________ 

Periods

A telling sentence ends with a period.

Circle the period at the end of each sentence.

1. **I see Jan.**
2. **I go with Jan.**
3. **We see Dan.**
4. **I go with Dan and Jan.**

Draw a line under the last word in each sentence.
Add a period to each sentence.

5. **We go to school**
6. **We like school**

Periods

A telling sentence ends with a period.

Write a period where it belongs in each sentence. Read the sentences to a friend.

1. **Dan is in the cab**
2. **The cat is in the cab**
3. **Mom is in the cab**
4. **We see Dan and Mom**

Read the words. Write each word at the end of the correct sentence.

van.	red.

5. **We can go in the** ______________

6. **The van is** ______________

Name ______________________________ 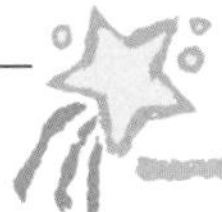

Periods

Read each group of words. Fill in the circle next to the correct sentence.

1

- ◯ The cat is on the mat.
- ◯ the cat is on the mat
- ◯ the cat on the mat

2

- ◯ the rat is on the mop
- ◯ the rat is on the mop
- ◯ The rat is on the mop.

3

- ◯ The rat sees the cat
- ◯ The rat sees the cat.
- ◯ the rat sees the cat

4

- ◯ The rat can hop.
- ◯ The rat can hop
- ◯ the rat can hop

5

- ◯ the cat and rat sit
- ◯ The cat and rat sit
- ◯ The cat and rat sit.

Name ______________________________ 

Capitalizing I

Always write the word I with a capital letter.

Circle the word I in each sentence.

1. I like to hop.
2. Pam and I like to hop.
3. I can hop to Mom.
4. Mom and I can hop.

Draw what you like. Use the word I to write about it.

5. ______________________________

Name ______________________________  **Practice**

Capitalizing I

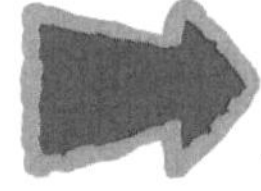

Always write the word I with a capital letter.

Read the sentences. Write I on the line.

1. ______ will ride.

2. ______ will swim.

3. Mom and ______ will sing.

4. Then ______ will read.

What will you do next? Write it on the line.

5. I will ______________________________

Name ________________________________

Capitalizing I

Read each group of words. Fill in the circle next to the correct sentence.

1

- ◯ i sit on a mat.
- ◯ I sit on a mat.
- ◯ i sit on a mat

2

- ◯ Pam and I like cats.
- ◯ Pam and i like cats.
- ◯ pam and i like cats

3

- ◯ I see the van.
- ◯ i see the van.
- ◯ i see the van

4

- ◯ i like jam.
- ◯ i like jam
- ◯ I like jam.

5

- ◯ i like to nap.
- ◯ I like to nap.
- ◯ i like to nap

Name ______________________________

Simple Sentences

Read each group of words. Fill in the circle next to the complete sentence.

1

- ○ on a mat
- ○ The cat sits on a mat.
- ○ The cat

2

- ○ Pam and Dan like jam.
- ○ Pam and Dan
- ○ like jam

3

- ○ I see Mom.
- ○ I see
- ○ Mom

4

- ○ my hat
- ○ I like
- ○ I like my hat.

5

- ○ Ben.
- ○ Ben can hop.
- ○ hop

Name ____________________ 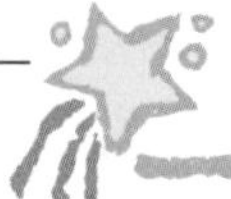 **Practice**

Word Order

Words in a sentence must be in an order that makes sense.

Read each group of words. Draw a line under the word that should go first in each sentence.

1. **dots. I like**
2. **Pam dots. likes**
3. **like We hats.**
4. **hats with dots. We like**

Now write each group of words in the right order.

1. ____________________
2. ____________________
3. ____________________
4. ____________________

Question Sentences

Question sentences ask something.

Read each sentence. Circle each question mark.

1. **Who hid the hat?**
2. **Is it on the cat?**
3. **Can you see the hat?**
4. **Is it on the man?**

Write two questions. Draw a line under each capital letter at the beginning of each question. Circle the question marks.

5. ___________________________________

6. ___________________________________

Question Sentences

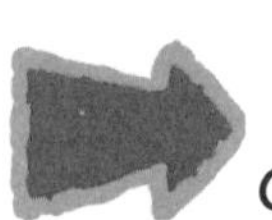

Question sentences ask something.

Draw a line under each sentence that asks a question.
Circle the question mark.

1. **Who hid the cat?**
2. **Can the cat see the rat?**
3. **The cat is in the van.**
4. **Can the van go?**

Read the sentences. Circle each sentence that asks something.

5. **Can we sit in the van?**

   We can sit in the van.

6. **Dan can nap in the van.**

   Can Dan nap in the van?

Question Sentences

Read the sentences. Fill in the circle next to the sentence that asks a question.

1

◯ Who hid my hat?

◯ My hat is with him.

◯ My hat is big.

◯ The hat has spots.

◯ The hat has dots.

◯ Did the hat have dots?

3

◯ Jan likes my hat.

◯ Did Jan like my hat?

◯ Jan did like my hat.

◯ Can you see the hat?

◯ You can see the hat.

◯ She can see the hat.

◯ Dan can get a hat.

◯ Dan likes hats.

◯ Dan has the hat?

Name ______________________________  **Practice**

Naming Words

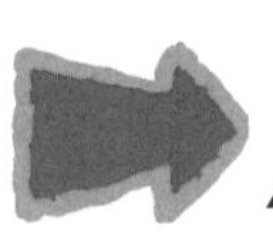

A naming word names a person, place, or thing.

Read each sentence. Draw a line under the word or words that name the person, place, or thing in each sentence.

1. **The pig is big.**
2. **The pan is hot.**
3. **Pam hid.**
4. **Can you run up the hill?**

Draw a line from each sentence to the picture that shows the naming word in that sentence.

5. **The sun is hot.**
6. **Sam ran and ran.**
7. **Is the cat fat?**

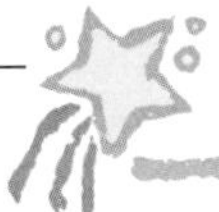

Naming Words

A naming word names a person, place, or thing.

Circle the naming words in the sentences.

1. **Al can go in a van.**
2. **The cat sat on a mat.**
3. **Pat ran up the hill.**
4. **Dan and Jan will mop.**

Draw a picture of a person, place, or thing. Write a sentence about your picture. Circle the naming word.

Naming Words

Read each sentence. Fill in the circle next to the naming word.

1. **I see a big cat.**

   (a) see (b) big (c) cat

2. **The rat ran fast.**

   (a) ran (b) rat (c) fast

3. **Can you see the map?**

   (a) Can (b) map (c) see

4. **The van is tan.**

   (a) van (b) is (c) tan

5. **The fan is not on!**

   (a) not (b) on (c) fan

Name ______________________________ 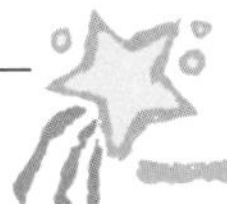 Practice

Capitalizing Special Names

The names of people, places, and pets are special. They begin with capital letters.

Draw a line under the special name in each sentence. Then circle the first letter or letters in that name.

1 **They go to Hill Park.**

2 **Pam sees the ham.**

3 **Don sees the cat.**

4 **They like Frog Lake.**

Write a special name of a person, place, or pet you know.

5 ______________________________

Name ________________________________  **Practice**

Capitalizing Special Names

The names of people, places, and pets are special. They begin with capital letters.

Circle each special name. Draw a line under each capital letter in each name.

1. **I am Pam.**
2. **I sit on Ant Hill.**
3. **Ron likes the lake.**
4. **He likes Bat Lake.**

Read the special names in the box.
Write a special name for each picture.

Spot	Hill Street

5. ________________________________

6. ________________________________

Capitalizing Special Names

Read each sentence. Fill in the circle next to the special name.

1. **Can Don go to the picnic?**
   - ⬭ picnic
   - ⬭ Don
   - ⬭ Can

2. **The picnic will be on Pig Hill.**
   - ⬭ Pig Hill
   - ⬭ picnic
   - ⬭ The

3. **The hill is on Jam Street.**
   - ⬭ hill
   - ⬭ The
   - ⬭ Jam Street

4. **Jan will go to the picnic.**
   - ⬭ go
   - ⬭ picnic
   - ⬭ Jan

5. **She will go in Ham Lake.**
   - ⬭ She
   - ⬭ Ham Lake
   - ⬭ will

Action Words

An action word tells what happens.

Read each sentence. Circle the word that tells what happens.

1. **The hen sits.**
2. **The cat ran.**
3. **Pam hid.**
4. **The dog naps.**

Read the words. Use the words to finish the sentences.

5. **I will ______________ up the hill.**

6. **I ______________ a big pig.**

Name ______________________________ 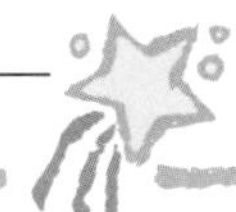

Action Words

An action word tells what happens.

Look at each picture. Read the words. Write the action word.

  **I can see.** ______________________________

  **The cat sits.** ______________________________

3  **Mom mops.** ______________________________

4  **We run fast.** ______________________________

5  **It hops a lot.** ______________________________

Action Words

Read each sentence.
Fill in the circle next to the action word.

1. **I sit on a hill.**

   (a) I (b) sit (c) hill

2. **The rat ran fast.**

   (a) ran (b) rat (c) fast

3. **We mop a lot.**

   (a) We (b) lot (c) mop

4. **The dog digs up sand.**

   (a) dog (b) sand (c) digs

5. **Pam hops up and down.**

   (a) hops (b) up (c) Pam

Describing Words

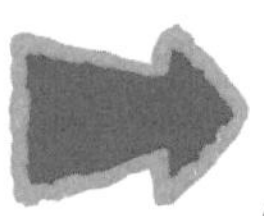

A describing word tells more about a person, place, or thing.

Read each sentence. Circle the word that tells about the cat.

1. **I see a big cat.**
2. **The fast cat ran.**
3. **My cat is bad.**
4. **The fat cat naps.**

Look at each cat. Circle the word that tells about it.

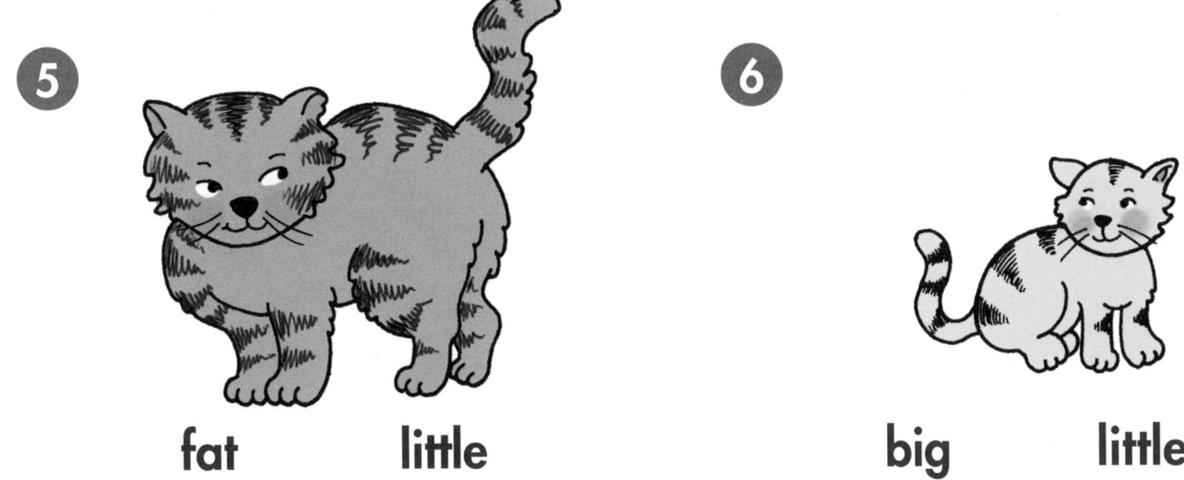

5. **fat** **little**

6. **big** **little**

Name ____________________ 

Describing Words

A describing word tells more about a person, place, or thing.

Look at each picture. Circle the words that tell about it.

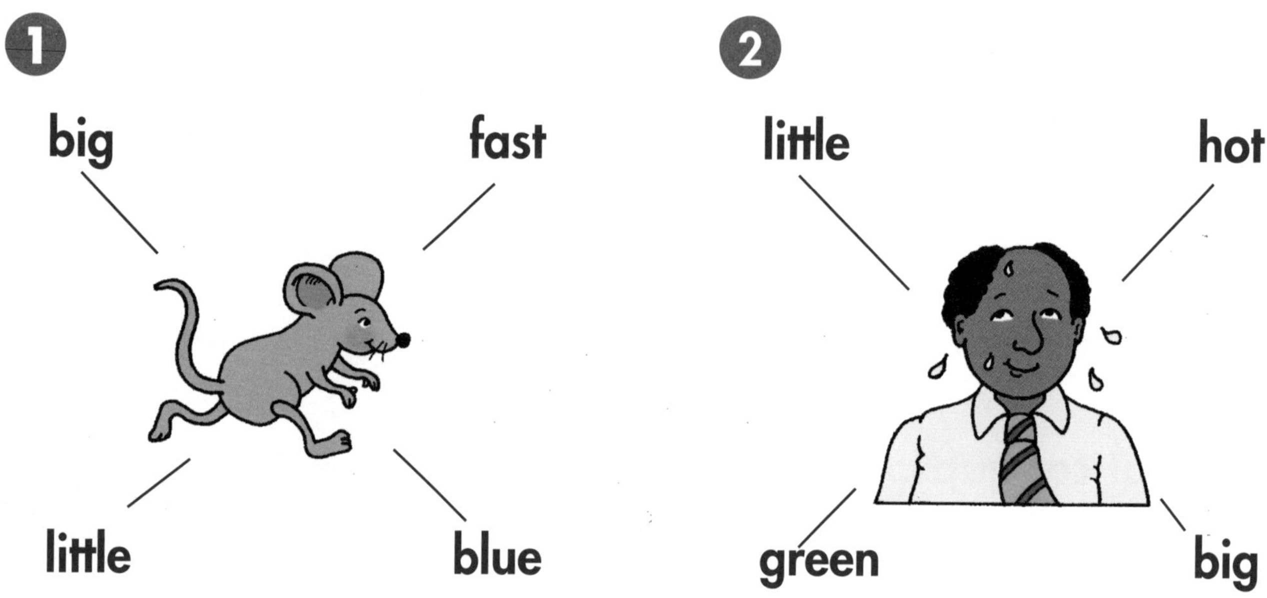

Draw a line between each sentence and the picture that shows what it describes.

3 **It is fat.**

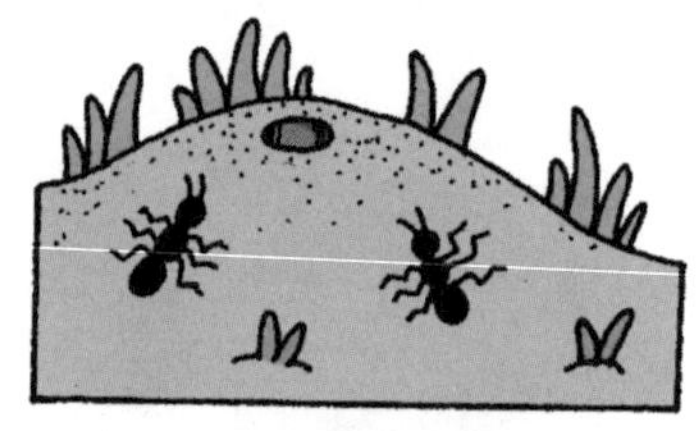

4 **They are little.**

Name ________________________________ 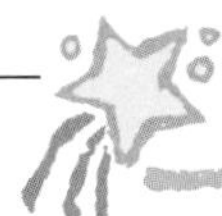

Describing Words

Read each sentence. Fill in the circle next to the describing word.

1 The silly cat can play.

- ◯ silly
- ◯ cat
- ◯ play

2 The bad rat will run.

- ◯ bad
- ◯ run
- ◯ rat

3 The black dog naps.

- ◯ dog
- ◯ black
- ◯ naps

4 The cow is big.

- ◯ cow
- ◯ is
- ◯ big

5 A green frog can hop.

- ◯ frog
- ◯ green
- ◯ hop

Telling Sentences

A telling sentence tells something.

Circle the capital letter at the beginning of each telling sentence. Then circle the period at the end of each telling sentence.

1. **I see the basket.**
2. **The cat is in the basket.**
3. **Hats can go in it.**
4. **The sock can go in it.**

Draw a line under each telling sentence.

5. **I can fill the basket.**
6. **Can you get the mop?**
7. **We can clean.**

Telling Sentences

A telling sentence tells something.

Draw a line to match each sentence with the picture that shows what the sentence tells.

1. **She has a mop.**

2. **The dog is on top.**

3. **Dan gets the hats.**

4. **Ron can clean spots.**

Read the sentences. Circle the capital letter and period in the telling sentence.

5. **Put it in the pot.**

6. **Is it in the pan?**

Telling Sentences

Read the sentences. Fill in the circle next to each sentence that tells something.

1

- ⬭ **Can you get the basket?**
- ⬭ **You can get it.**
- ⬭ **Can you fill it?**

2

- ⬭ **The basket is big.**
- ⬭ **Is the basket big?**
- ⬭ **Why is it big?**

3

- ⬭ **What can go in it?**
- ⬭ **Will the hat go in?**
- ⬭ **The hat is in the basket.**

4

- ⬭ **A cat can not go in it.**
- ⬭ **Can a cat go in?**
- ⬭ **Will a cat go in it?**

5

- ⬭ **Can we fill it?**
- ⬭ **We can fill the basket.**
- ⬭ **Will you fill it?**

Name ____________________ 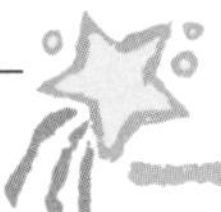

Exclamation Sentences

Exclamatory sentences show strong feelings such as excitement, surprise, or fear. They end with exclamation marks. (!)

Read each sentence. Circle each exclamation mark. Draw a line under the capital letter at the beginning of each sentence.

1. **Help! The rat is on top!**
2. **Get the cat!**
3. **This cat is bad!**
4. **Uh-oh! The cat is wet!**

Read each set of sentences. Draw a line under the sentence or sentences that show strong feeling.

5. **Oh my! Get the dog!**

   Let's get the dog.

6. **The dog runs.**

   Oh! The dog runs!

Name ______________________________  **Practice**

Exclamation Sentences

Choose the sentence in each pair that shows strong feeling. Write it on the line. Put an exclamation mark at the end.

> Exclamatory sentences show strong feeling, such as excitement, surprise, or fear. They end with an exclamation mark. (!)

1. **Run to the show** **We will go to the show**

____

2. **I'm late for it** **Oh my, I'm very late**

____

3. **What a great show** **I liked the show**

____

4. **The floor is wet** **Watch out, the floor is wet**

____

5. **We had fun** **Wow, we had lots of fun**

____

Name ______________________________ 

Exclamation Sentences

Read each group of sentences. Fill in the circle next to the sentence or sentences that show strong feeling.

1

- ⬭ The cow is on the hill.
- ⬭ The cow likes grass.
- ⬭ Yes! The cow can kick!

2

- ⬭ That cat is bad!
- ⬭ That cat naps.
- ⬭ Is the cat on the mat?

3

- ⬭ The rat will run.
- ⬭ That rat runs fast!
- ⬭ The rat can hop.

4

- ⬭ Oh no! A frog is in my house!
- ⬭ A frog hops.
- ⬭ The frog is green.

5

- ⬭ The pot can get hot.
- ⬭ The pot is hot!
- ⬭ Fill the pot with mud.

Name ______________________________  **Practice**

Singular/Plural Nouns

Many nouns, or naming words, add -s to show more than one.

Read each sentence. Draw a line under each naming word that means more than one.

1. **I see hats and a cap.**
2. **It sits on eggs.**
3. **The girls swim.**
4. **Pam can pet cats.**

Read each sentence. Write the naming word that means more than one.

5. **The mugs are hot.** ______________________

6. **Mud is on my hands.** ______________________

Name ________________________________ 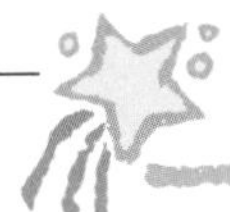

Singular/Plural Nouns

 *Many nouns, or naming words, add -s to show more than one.*

Read the sets of sentences. Draw a line under the sentence that has a naming word that names more than one.

1 **Jan has her mittens.**

Jan has her mitten.

2 **She will run up a hill.**

She will run up hills.

3 **Jan runs with her dogs.**

Jan runs with her dog.

4 **The dogs can jump.**

The dog can jump.

Look at each picture. Read each word. Write the plural naming word that matches the picture.

5  **cat** ________________

6  **sock** ________________

Name ______________________________ **Assessment**

Singular/Plural Nouns

Read each sentence. Fill in the circle next to the naming word that means more than one.

1 **Jim gets mud on his hands.**

- ◯ gets
- ◯ hands
- ◯ mud

2 **Pam can fill the pots with mud.**

- ◯ pots
- ◯ mud
- ◯ fill

3 **The dogs dig fast.**

- ◯ dig
- ◯ fast
- ◯ dogs

4 **The ants are on the plant.**

- ◯ ants
- ◯ plant
- ◯ are

5 **The frogs hop.**

- ◯ The
- ◯ frogs
- ◯ hop

Name ______________________ 

Action Words

 *An action word tells what happens.*

Read each sentence. Circle the word that tells what happens.

1. **The hen sits.**
2. **Mom sees the hen.**
3. **The dog digs.**
4. **The cat naps.**

Read the words. Use the words to finish the sentences.

sees	**run**

5. **She** ______________ **eggs.**

6. **It can** ______________ **fast.**

Name ________________________  **Practice**

Action Words

An action word tells what happens.

Look at the pictures. Read the action words in the box.
Write the correct action word on the line.

talk
play
dance
run

1 **Sue and Al** 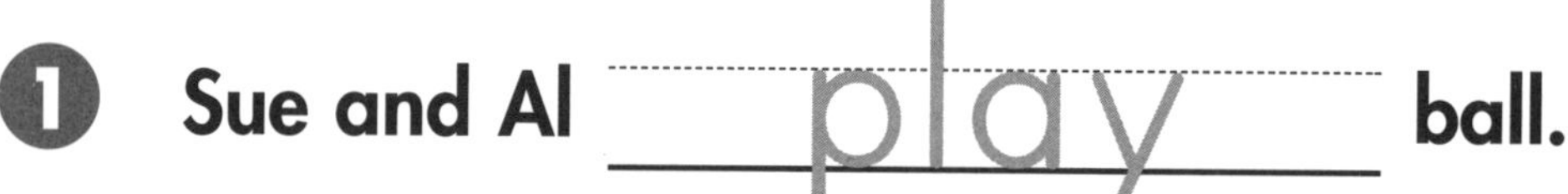 **ball.**

2 **The bears** ________________ .

3 **Rabbit and Pig** ________________ .

4 **Tami and Lee** ________________ **fast.**

To the Teacher: Read the words in the box with children. Help children understand that they tell what the characters in the pictures are doing.

Name ____________________ 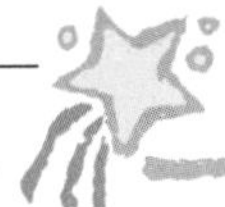

Action Words

Read each sentence. Fill in the circle next to the action word.

1. **The hen sits.**
   - ○ hen
   - ○ sits
   - ○ The

2. **The cat naps in the van.**
   - ○ naps
   - ○ cat
   - ○ van

3. **The green frog hops.**
   - ○ frog
   - ○ green
   - ○ hops

4. **The dog digs.**
   - ○ digs
   - ○ dog
   - ○ The

5. **The big pig ran.**
   - ○ big
   - ○ pig
   - ○ ran

Naming Words

A naming word names a person, place, or thing.

Read each sentence. Draw a line under the naming word.

1. **We play at school.**
2. **The ball is fast.**
3. **The girl kicks.**
4. **The friends run.**

Look at each box. Circle the naming word that belongs in that box.

Person	Place	Thing
girl	ball	Pam
school	Bill	man
ball	school	ball

Name ____________________  Practice

Naming Words

 *A naming word names a person, place, or thing.*

Read each sentence. Circle each naming word. Draw a line to match the sentence to the picture of the naming word.

1. **Run and kick in the park.**

2. **Kick with a foot.**

3. **Kick the ball.**

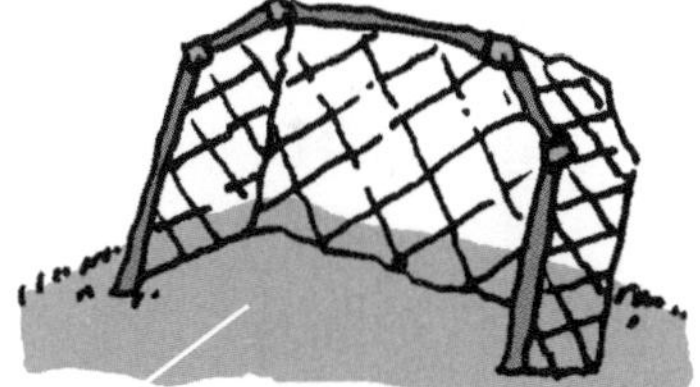

4. **The girl will run to get it.**

5. **Kick it to the net.**

Name ____________________

Naming Words

Read each sentence. Fill in the circle next to the word that names a person, place, or thing.

1. **Let's play in the park.**
   - ○ play
   - ○ Let's
   - ○ park

2. **The girl can run and kick.**
   - ○ girl
   - ○ run
   - ○ kick

3. **Kick the ball.**
   - ○ ball
   - ○ the
   - ○ kick

4. **The friend can jump.**
   - ○ can
   - ○ jump
   - ○ friend

5. **Jump to the net.**
   - ○ get
   - ○ net
   - ○ jump

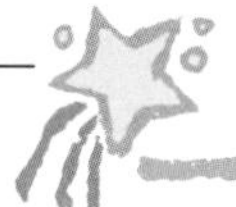

Word Order

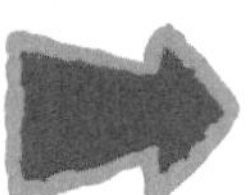

Words in a sentence must be in an order that makes sense.

Read each group of words. Circle the words that are in an order that makes sense. Draw a line under each capital letter.

1 **The king is sad.**

sad. king is The

2 **bake Let's cake. him a**

Let's bake him a cake.

3 **the king Tell to come.**

Tell the king to come.

4 **Let's eat the cake.**

eat Let's the cake.

Read the words. Write them in order.

king The eats .

____

Name ______________________________  **Practice**

Word Order

Words in a sentence must be in an order that makes sense.

These words are mixed up. Put them in order.
Then write each sentence.

1. **snow. bear likes This**

____

2. **water cold. The is**

____

3. **fast. The runs bear**

____

4. **play. bears Two**

____

Name ______________________________________ 

Capitalizing Titles

Important words in a title are capitalized.

Read the titles. Circle all the words that should be capitalized.

1. **look at the stars!**
2. **the moon shines at night**
3. **we see planets**
4. **many moons shine**
5. **night and day**

Read each set of titles. Draw a line under the correct title.

6. **The Sun in the Sky**

   the sun in the sky

7. **See the stars!**

   See the Stars!

Name ______________________________ 

Capitalizing Titles

Read the titles. Fill in the circle next to the title with the correct words capitalized.

1

- ◯ **Where Is the Sun?**
- ◯ **Where is the sun?**
- ◯ **Where Is The Sun?**

2

- ◯ **many cats to see**
- ◯ **Many cats To See**
- ◯ **Many Cats to See**

3

- ◯ **Day and Night**
- ◯ **day And night**
- ◯ **Day And Night**

4

- ◯ **how many pigs?**
- ◯ **How Many Pigs?**
- ◯ **How many pigs?**

5

- ◯ **the Big Bad wolf**
- ◯ **the big, bad wolf**
- ◯ **The Big, Bad Wolf**

Naming Words

A naming word names a person, place, or thing.

Read each sentence. Draw a line under the word or words that name the person, place, or thing in each sentence.

1. **The pot is big.**
2. **The pan is big.**
3. **See the top?**
4. **Jim can mop.**

Draw a line from each sentence to the picture that shows the naming word in that sentence.

5. **The pot is hot.**

6. **See the pan?**

7. **Jim is fast.**

Naming Words

A naming word names a person, place, or thing.

Circle the naming words in the sentences.

1. **Jan can go in a van.**
2. **The van can go fast.**
3. **The van is on a hill.**
4. **Dan sees Jan.**

Draw a picture of a person, place, or thing.
Write a sentence about your picture.
Circle the naming word.

5. ______________________

Name ______________________________

Naming Words

Read each sentence. Fill in the circle next to the naming word.

1 See the hot pans?

- ◯ hot
- ◯ See
- ◯ pans

2 See Jim mop fast.

- ◯ fast
- ◯ Jim
- ◯ See

3 The cat naps.

- ◯ cat
- ◯ The
- ◯ naps

4 The rat hid.

- ◯ The
- ◯ rat
- ◯ hid

5 Can the cat see?

- ◯ see
- ◯ cat
- ◯ Can

Name ___________________________ 

Linking Verbs

Is, are, was, and *were* are linking verbs. *Is* tells about one. *Are* tells about more than one. *Was* tells about one in the past. *Were* tells about more than one in the past.

Read each sentence. Draw a line under the linking verb is, are, was, or were.

1. **The hen is digging.**
2. **The chicks were helping.**
3. **The pig was having fun.**
4. **The cat and duck are playing.**

Read each sentence. Circle now or in the past to show when it happens or happened.

5. **The hen is planting.** now in the past
6. **The cat was not helping.** now in the past
7. **The chicks are with the hen.** now in the past

Name ______________________ 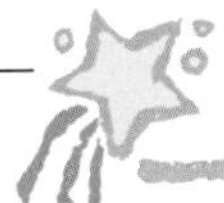

Linking Verbs

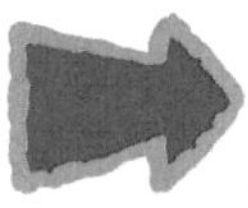

Is, are, was, and *were* are linking verbs. *Is* tells about one. *Are* tells about more than one. *Was* tells about one in the past. *Were* tells about more than one in the past.

Circle the linking verb. Write now or past to tell when the action happens or happened.

1. The chicks are eating. ______________
2. The duck is swimming. ______________
3. The cat was napping. ______________
4. The pig is digging. ______________
5. They were playing. ______________

Name ________________________________ **Assessment**

Linking Verbs

Fill in the circle next to the linking verb that completes each sentence.

1 **The hen ___ sitting.**

- ◯ **was**
- ◯ **are**
- ◯ **were**

2 **They ___ playing.**

- ◯ **were**
- ◯ **is**
- ◯ **was**

3 **The pigs ___ digging.**

- ◯ **was**
- ◯ **is**
- ◯ **are**

4 **The duck ___ swimming.**

- ◯ **were**
- ◯ **is**
- ◯ **are**

5 **The chicks ___ napping.**

- ◯ **was**
- ◯ **is**
- ◯ **are**

Name ______________________________  **Practice**

Capitalizing Names and First Words

The first word in a sentence starts with a capital letter. Sometimes words that name a person, place, or thing begin with a capital letter.

Read the sentences. Circle the words that are capitalized.

1. **The goats Gruff have a problem.**
2. **They do not like the Troll.**
3. **His name is Nosey.**
4. **He is big and bad.**

Draw a line to match each sentence to why the underlined word is capitalized.

5. **Dan and <u>Pam</u> like the play.**	**First word in a sentence.**
6. **<u>They</u> will read it Jim.**	**Names a person, place, to or thing.**

Name ______________________________

Capitalizing Names

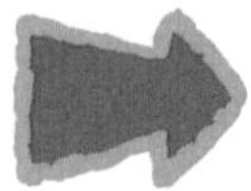

Sometimes the names of people, places, and things are special. They begin with a capital letter.

Circle the special names in the picture. Write each one correctly on a line.

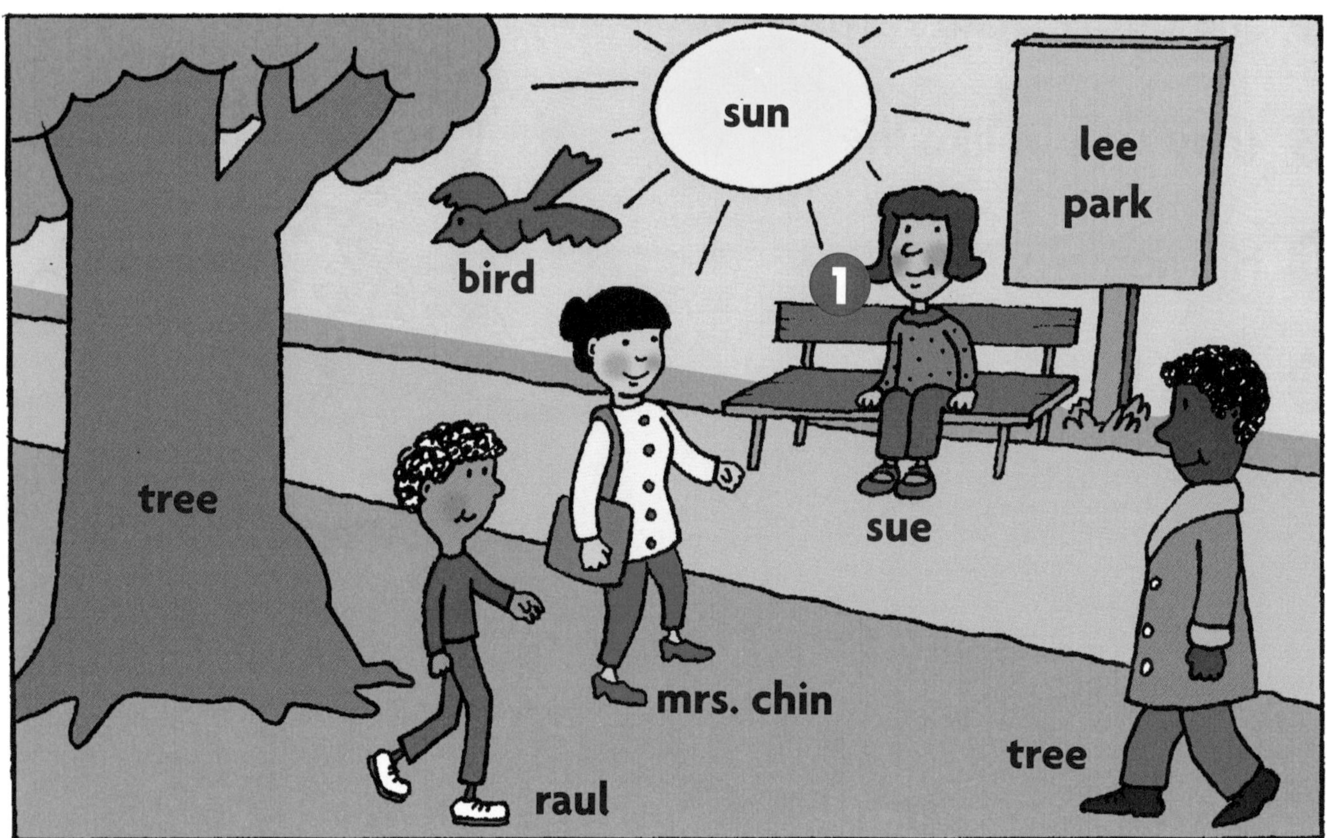

1 ______________________________ 2 ______________________________

3 ______________________________ 4 ______________________________

Name ________________________________ 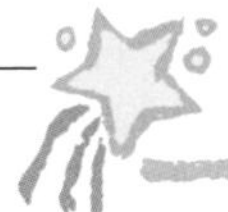

Capitalizing Names and First Words

Read each sentence. Fill in the circle next to the word that needs a capital letter.

1 i like the goats Gruff.

- ◯ Goats
- ◯ The
- ◯ I

2 I read the story with ron.

- ◯ Read
- ◯ Story
- ◯ Ron

3 Little gruff had a problem.

- ◯ Had
- ◯ Gruff
- ◯ Problem

4 troll was on the bridge.

- ◯ A
- ◯ Bridge
- ◯ Troll

5 His name was nosey.

- ◯ Name
- ◯ Nosey
- ◯ His

Scholastic Success With

WRITING

Name ______________________________________

That's Amazing!

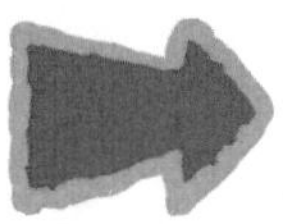

A sentence begins with a **capital letter**.

Help the mouse through the maze by coloring each box with a word that begins with a capital letter.

The	For	That	with	know	but
here	on	When	Have	next	we
as	after	good	Make	there	see
Go	Look	Are	Could	is	why
This	who	said	in	come	them
Has	Name	Before	Her	Where	The

Read the back of a cereal box. How many capital letters did you find? Write the number next to the cheese.

Squeak!

Circle the words that show the correct way to begin each sentence.

1\. 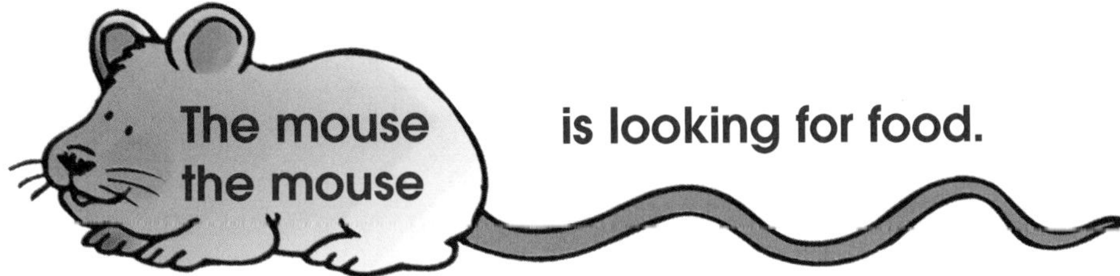
The mouse
the mouse
is looking for food.

2\. 
he finds
He finds
a cracker on the floor.

3\. 
he Eats
He eats
the cracker.

4\. 
Then he
then He
takes a nap.

5\. 
oh No,
Oh no,
He hears a cat!

6\. 
the Mouse
The mouse
runs home fast!

Name ________________________________

Counting Sheep

Write the beginning words correctly to make a sentence.

1. 

________________________ books before bed.

2. 

________________________ hug good night.

3. 

________________________ is soft and cozy.

4. 

________________________ sleeps with me.

5. 

________________________ has turned dark.

6. 

________________________ close.

On another piece of paper, copy a sentence from your favorite bedtime book. Circle the capital letter at the beginning.

Sweet Dreams!

Write each beginning word correctly to make a sentence.

1. 

___________________ runs in her sleep.

2. 

___________________ be dreaming.

3. 

___________________ is chasing a cat.

4. 

___________________ even barks.

5. 

___________________ it is funny.

On another piece of paper, write a sentence about a dream you remember. Circle the capital letter at the beginning.

Name ______________________________

The Night Sky

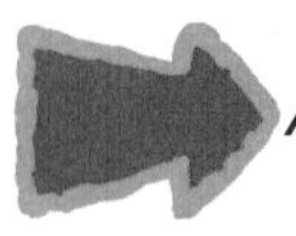

A **telling sentence** *ends with a* **period.**

period ⟶ .

Add a period to each sentence.

1. Many things shine in the sky at night____

2. The moon looks the brightest____

3. It is closest to Earth____

4. The stars look like tiny dots____

5. They are very far away____

6. The sun is a star____

7. Planets look like colored stars____

8. Their light does not twinkle____

9. Shooting stars look like stars that are falling____

10. There are many things to see in the night sky____

Name ______________________

Twinkle, Twinkle Little Star

Rewrite each sentence using periods.

1. Tonight I saw a star

2. I saw the star twinkle

3. It looked like a candle

4. It was very bright

5. I made a wish

6. I hope it comes true

Look for the brightest star in the sky. Make a wish. On another piece of paper, write a sentence about your wish.

Name ______________________________

Hop to It!

A **telling sentence** *begins with a* **capital letter** *and ends with a* **period**.

Rewrite each sentence correctly.

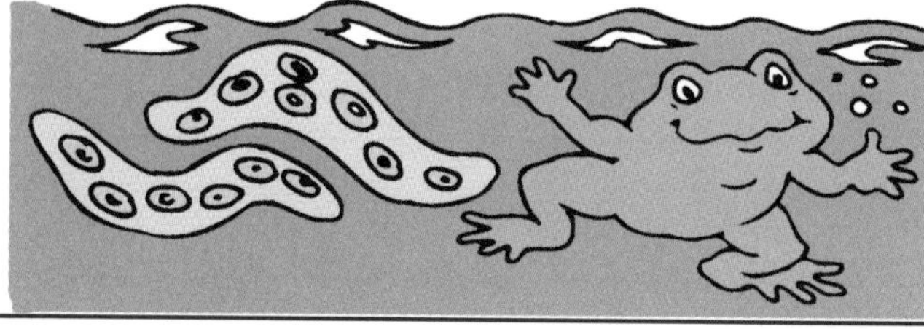

1. frogs and toads lay eggs

____

2. the eggs are in the water

____

3. tadpoles hatch from the eggs

____

4. the tadpoles grow legs

____

5. the tadpoles lose their tails

____

Name ______________________

Hop to It Some More!

Rewrite each sentence correctly.

1. tadpoles become frogs or toads

2. frogs live near water

3. toads live under bushes

4. frogs have wet skin

5. toads have bumpy skin

On another piece of paper, write three sentences about a time that you saw a frog or toad. Make sure you use capital letters and periods correctly.

Patriotic Sentences

A **sentence** *tells a complete idea. It should always make sense.*

Color the flag to show:

RED = sentence WHITE = not a sentence

★ ★ ★ ★ ★ ★ (flag stars)	This is a flag.
	The flag
	The flag has stars.
	The stars
	The stars are white.
	The stripes
	The stripes are red.

And white
The stripes are white.
Blue part
The flag has a blue part.
There are
There are 50 stars.

Color the star part of the flag with a blue crayon. Then on another piece of paper, write a complete sentence about your colorful flag.

Name ____________________

High-Flying Sentences

Color each flag that tells a complete thought. Leave the other flags blank.

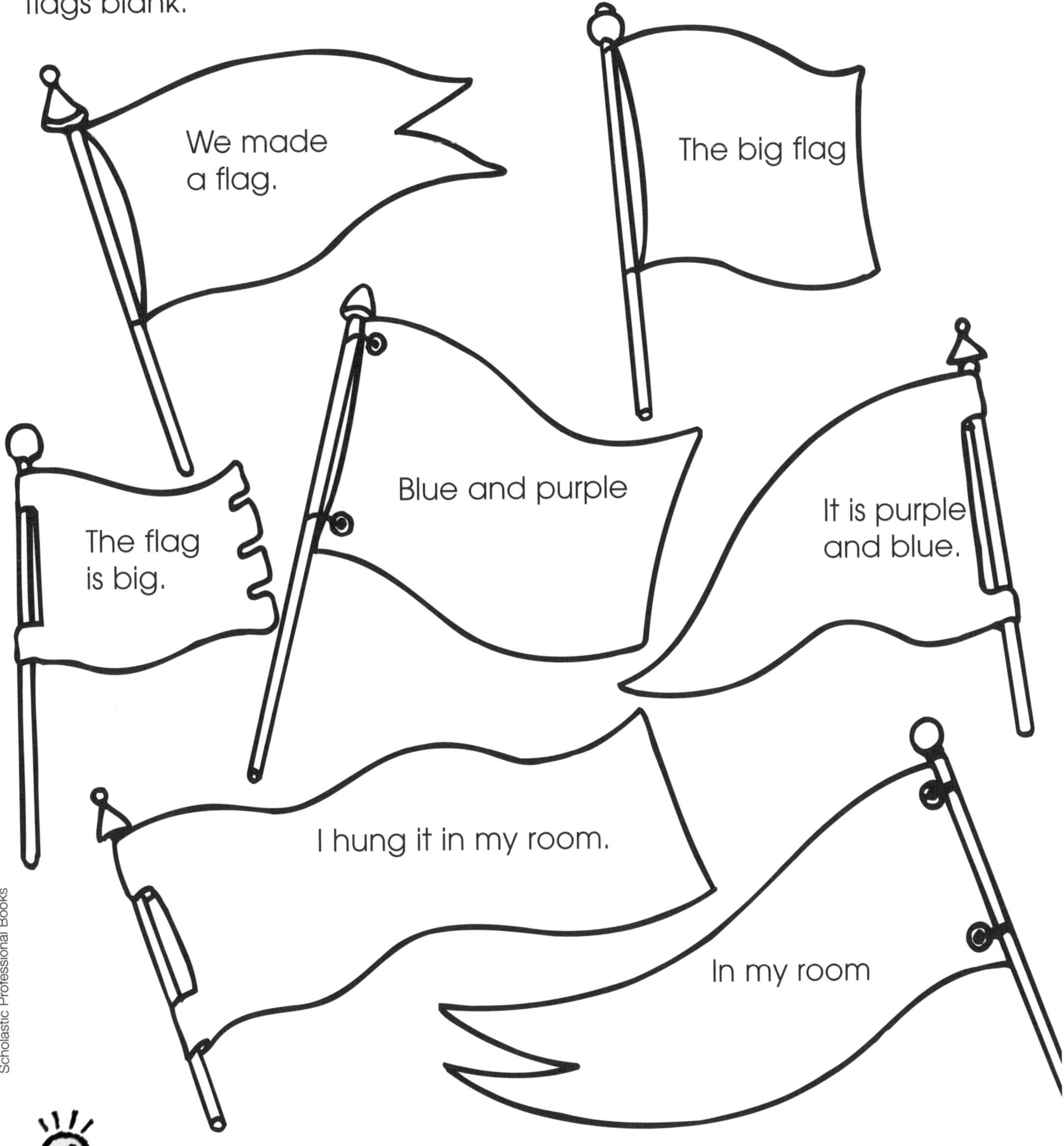
We made a flag.
The big flag
The flag is big.
Blue and purple
It is purple and blue.
I hung it in my room.
In my room

On another piece of paper, turn this into a sentence: The biggest flag.

Name ______________________________ 

At the Seashore

Unscramble the words to make a sentence. Write the new sentence below each picture. Finish each picture to match the sentence.

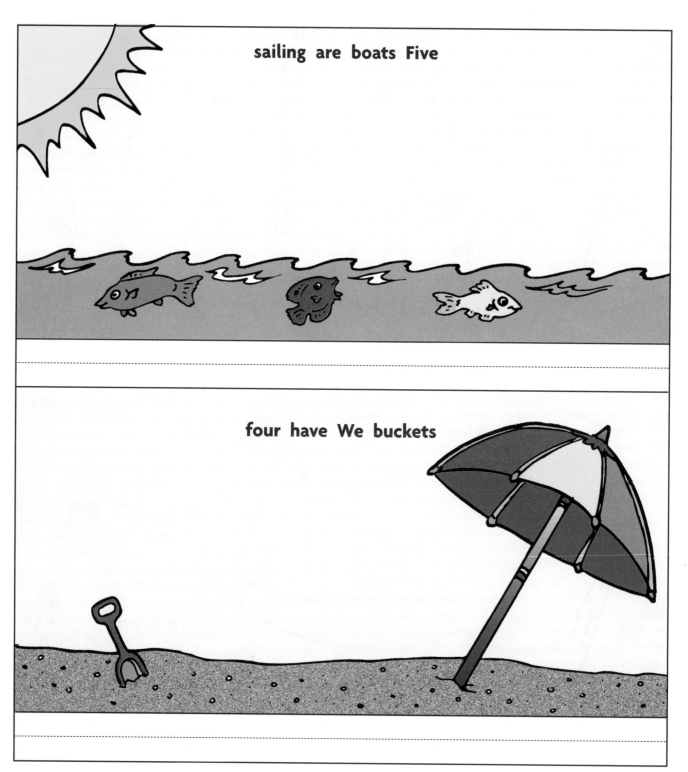

sailing are boats Five

____

four have We buckets

____

Name ______________________________

In the Rain Forest

Unscramble the words to make a sentence. Write the new sentence. Do not forget to put a period at the end.

A hiding jaguar is

blue Some butterflies are

water in jump the Frogs

snakes trees Green hang from

very tall grow The trees

Scramble a sentence for someone at home. Be sure the first word begins with a capital.

Snakes Alive!

*A sentence has a **naming part**. It tells who or what the sentence is about.*

Color the snake that tells the naming part in each sentence below.

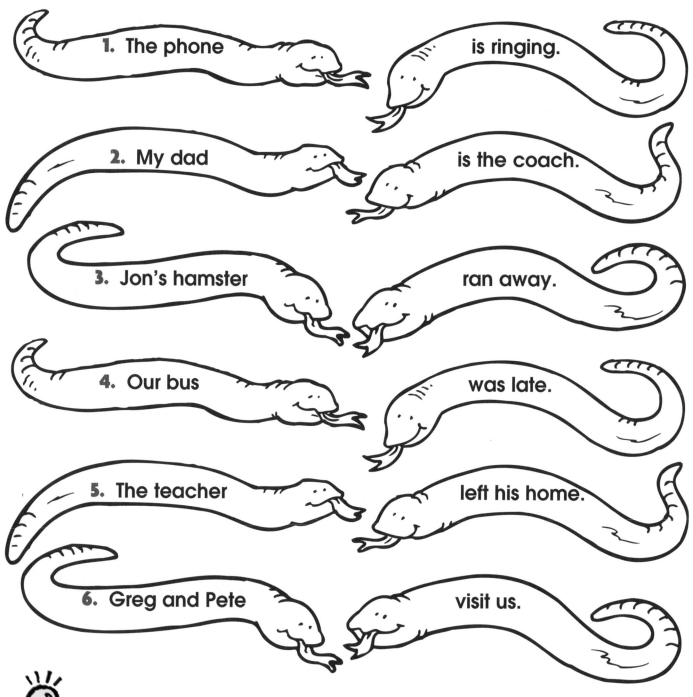

1. The phone — is ringing.

2. My dad — is the coach.

3. Jon's hamster — ran away.

4. Our bus — was late.

5. The teacher — left his home.

6. Greg and Pete — visit us.

On another piece of paper, write one of the sentences using a different naming part.

Name ______________________________________

Slithering Sentences

Circle the naming part in each sentence below.
Then color the picture to match.

1. The blue snake is playing with a friend.
2. The yellow snake is climbing a tree.
3. The green snake hides under rocks.
4. The brown snake is swimming.
5. The red snake is hanging on a tree.
6. The purple snake sleeps in trees.
7. The black snake rests on a rock.
8. The orange snake is near an egg.

Look around you. On another piece of paper, write three people or things that could be the naming part of a sentence.

Name ______________________

Who Is That?

The naming part of a sentence can be a person.

Use the pictures to find naming parts to make each sentence complete.

1. ______________________ **fell on the ice.**

2. ______________________ **won the race.**

3. ______________________ **went inside the dark cave.**

4. ______________________ **climbed the hill.**

5. ______________________ **swam across the pool.**

Name ______________________________

Where Is That?

The naming part of a sentence can be a place or a thing.

Use naming parts to complete each sentence that tells about the map.

1. ______________________________ is near the swings.

2. ______________________________ is far from the cave.

3. ______________________________ is a good place to fish.

4. ______________________________ has bats inside.

5. ______________________________ is along Tree Lane.

Find the naming part of three sentences in your favorite book.

Name ______________________________ 

Family Photos

 *The naming part of a sentence can be a person, a place, or a thing.*

Use your own naming parts to write a complete sentence about each picture.

Name ______________________

More Family Photos

Use your own naming parts to write a complete sentence about each picture.

Look at your family pictures. On another piece of paper, write a sentence telling about two of them.

Name ________________________________

No Bones About It!

A sentence has an ***action part****. It tells what is happening.*

Color the bone that tells the action part in each sentence below.

1. The dog | chases the cat.

2. The dog | hides the bone.

3. The dog | plays with a ball.

4. The dog | jumps in the air.

5. The dog | eats a bone.

6. The dog | sleeps on a rug.

On another piece of paper, rewrite your favorite sentence.

Mighty Good Sentences

Choose the ending that tells what each dog is doing. Remember to use periods.

is eating.
is sleeping.
is jumping.
is barking.

1. The white dog ______________________

2. The gray dog ______________________

3. The spotted dog ______________________

4. The striped dog ______________________

On another piece of paper, draw another dog and write a sentence about it.

Name ____________________

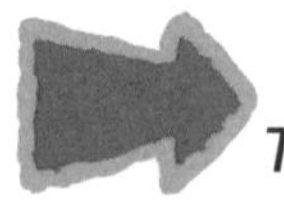

A Busy Classroom

The action part of a sentence is called the **verb**.

Complete each sentence with an action verb to tell what is happening in the picture. Remember to use periods.

1. Mr. Downs ____________________

2. The fish ____________________

3. James ____________________

4. Cara ____________________

On another piece of paper, write a sentence about your teacher. Circle the action word.

Name ___________________________

Pencil It In

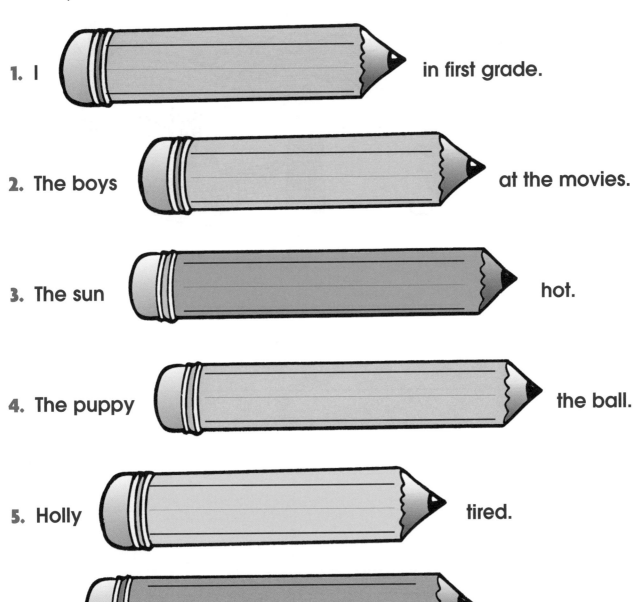

Sometimes the verb does not show action. It still tells what is happening.

For example: I **know** *the answer.*

I **am** *hungry.*

Word Bank

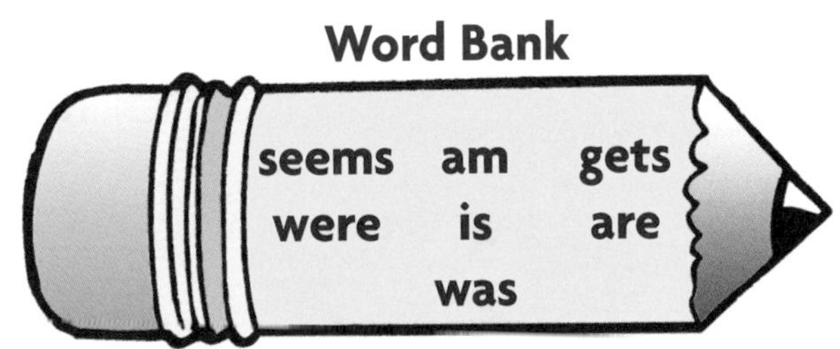

Choose a verb from the Word Bank to complete each sentence.

1. I ____________ in first grade.

2. The boys ____________ at the movies.

3. The sun ____________ hot.

4. The puppy ____________ the ball.

5. Holly ____________ tired.

6. We ____________ at the park.

Topsy-Turvy!

A sentence has a verb that tells what is happening.

Write five silly sentences that tell what is happening in the pictures.

1. ______________________

2. ______________________

3. ______________________

4. ______________________

5. ______________________

Name ______________________

What Is Going On?

Look around you. Write four sentences that tell what is happening.

1. ______________________

2. ______________________

3. ______________________

4. ______________________

Find five action words in your favorite book. Write them on another piece of paper.

Name ______________________________

The Caboose

A sentence is more interesting when it tells ***where*** *the action is happening.*

In each caboose, draw a picture to show where each sentence takes place.

1.

The plane flew into the clouds.

2.

The princess played in the castle.

3.

The boys fished in the lake.

Name ____________________

Chugging Along

Write an ending for each sentence that tells where the action takes place.

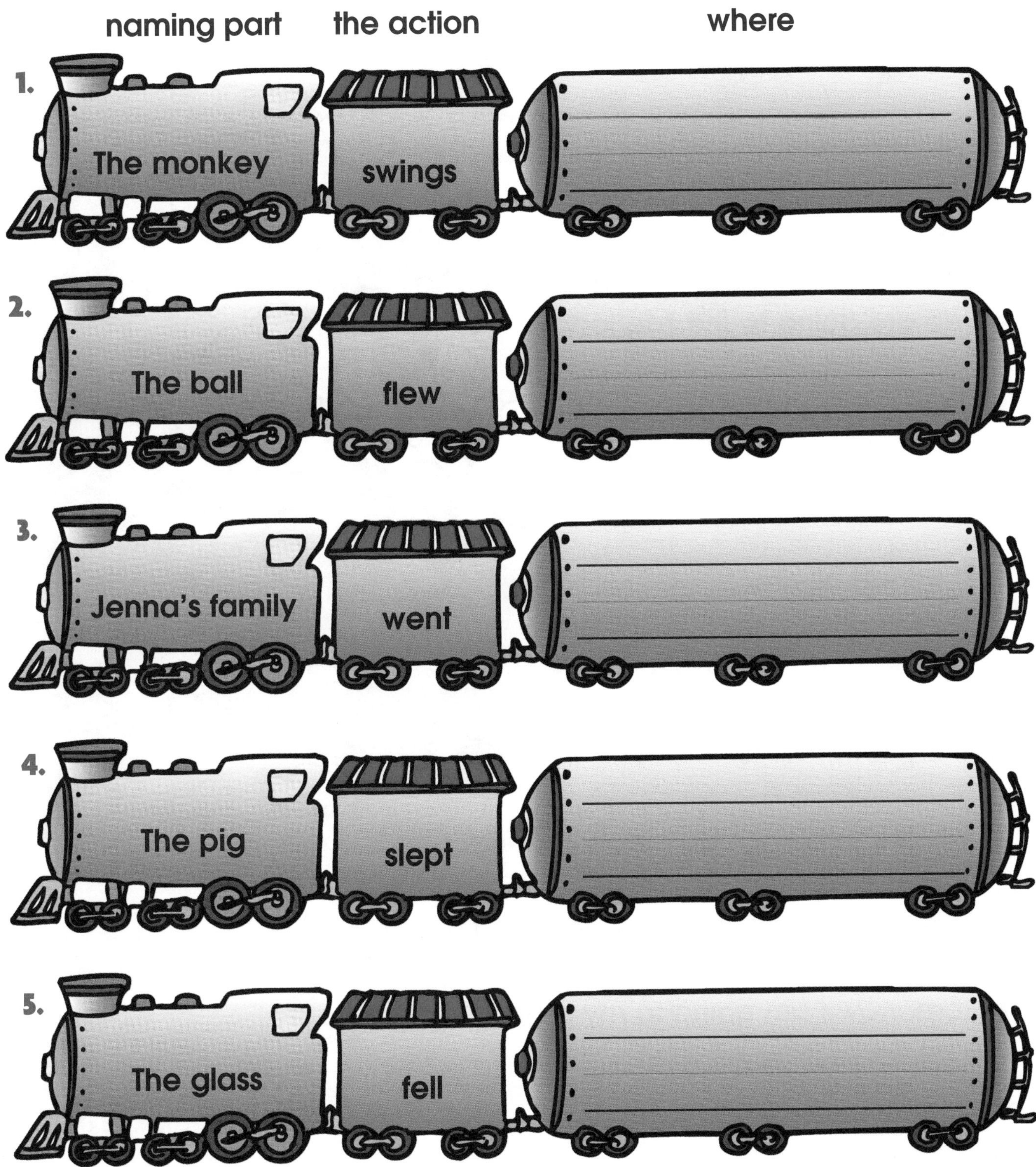

Name ________________________________ Identifying sentence parts

When Was That?

A sentence may also tell ***when*** *the action takes place.*

Circle the part that tells when in each sentence.

1. George Washington lived long ago.
2. The mail carrier was late yesterday.
3. The bear slept in winter.
4. We are going to the zoo today.
5. The leaves change in the fall.
6. I lost my tooth last night.
7. It rained all day.
8. The party starts at noon.
9. We got home yesterday.
10. We ate turkey on Thanksgiving Day.
11. The kitten was playing this morning.
12. Tomorrow I am going to my grandmother's house.

On another piece of paper, make a time line of your life. Use it to write two sentences that tell when.

Name ____________________

My Busy Day

Part of a sentence may tell ***when*** *the action happened.*

Write the beginning part of each sentence to tell about your day. Draw a picture to match each sentence.

____________________ ____________________	this morning.
____________________ ____________________	this afternoon.
____________________ ____________________	tonight.

On another piece of paper, write four sentences and draw four pictures to tell about your best day ever.

Silly Sentences

A sentence may have three parts: a naming part, an action, and a part that tells where or when.

Complete each missing part to make silly sentences.

	the naming part	the action	where or when
1.	The monkey		on his head.
2.	My dad	is hopping	
3.		flipped	in the forest.
4.	The ball	bounced	
5.	My shoes		at the pool.
6.	The snake	twisted	
7.	The bubbles	filled	

On another piece of paper, write a new sentence by scrambling three parts listed above. For example, use the naming part from #1, the action part from #2, and where or when from #3. Draw a picture of your sentence.

Sweet Sentences

Use choices from each part to make three "sweet" sentences.

naming part	action	where or when
I	ate doughnuts	at the bakery
She	ate candy	at the party
He	chewed gum	at the circus

On another piece of paper, name the three parts of this sentence: The doughnut shop closed at noon.

Home Sweet Home

Write three sentences about the picture. For example: The dog is sleeping outside.

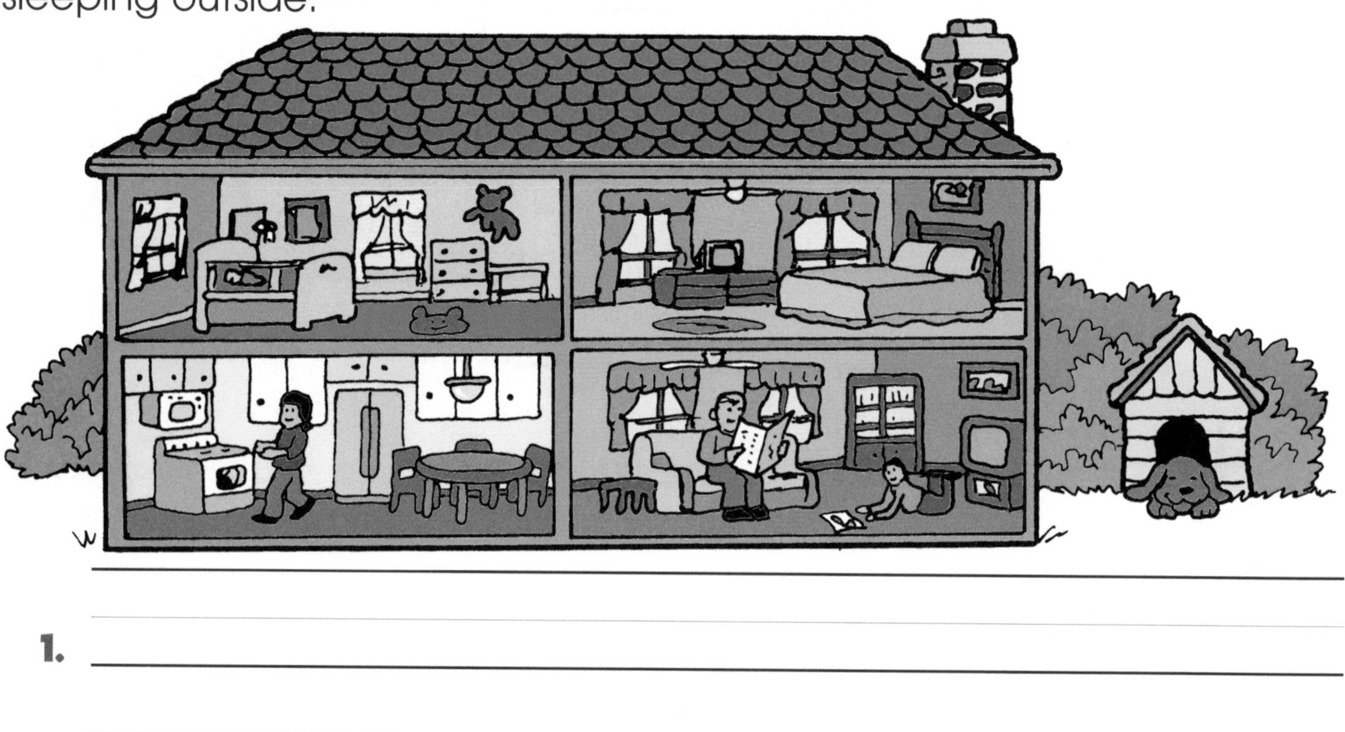

1. ______________________________

2. ______________________________

3. ______________________________

Name ______________________________

The Construction Crew

Write three sentences about the picture. Include three parts in each sentence.

1. ______________________________

2. ______________________________

3. ______________________________

Name ______________________ 

Mystery Boxes

Describing words help you imagine how something looks, feels, smells, sounds, or tastes.

Read the describing words to guess the mystery object. Use the Word Bank to help you.

Word Bank

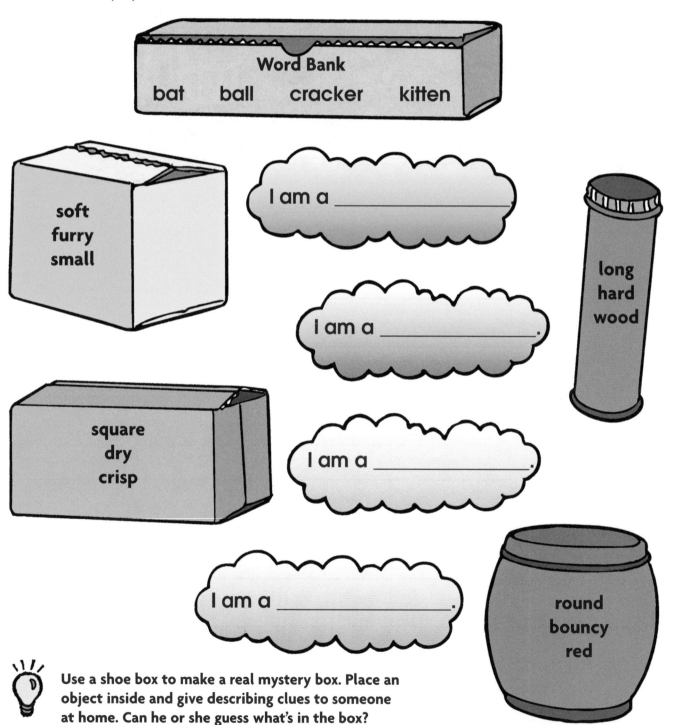

bat ball cracker kitten

soft
furry
small

I am a ______________.

long
hard
wood

I am a ______________.

square
dry
crisp

I am a ______________.

round
bouncy
red

I am a ______________.

Use a shoe box to make a real mystery box. Place an object inside and give describing clues to someone at home. Can he or she guess what's in the box?

Name ______________________________ 

Sensational Words

Choose words from the Word Bank to describe each picture.

It tastes ______________.

It looks ______________.

It feels ______________.

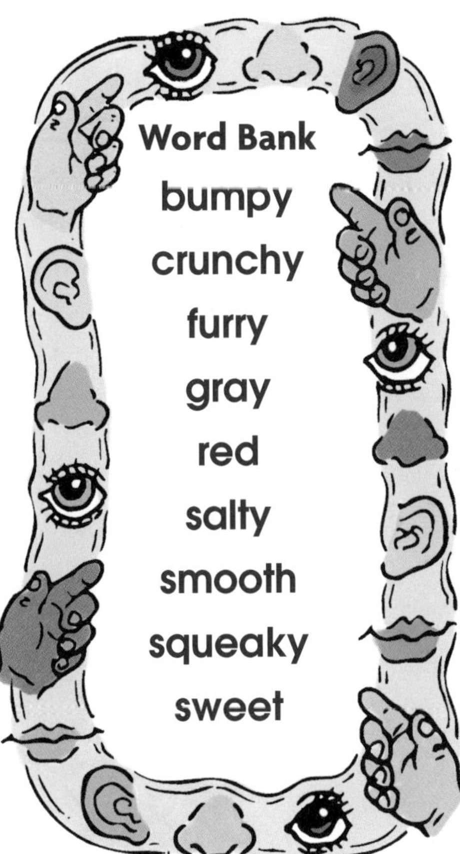

Word Bank

bumpy
crunchy
furry
gray
red
salty
smooth
squeaky
sweet

It feels ______________.

It tastes ______________.

It sounds ______________.

It looks ______________.

It sounds ______________.

It feels ______________.

Find two objects outside. On another piece of paper, write two adjectives to describe each object.

Name ____

Pretty Packages

The describing words in a sentence help the reader paint a picture in his or her mind.

Write three words to describe each gift. Then color them to match.

________________ (color)

________________ (color)

________________ (pattern)

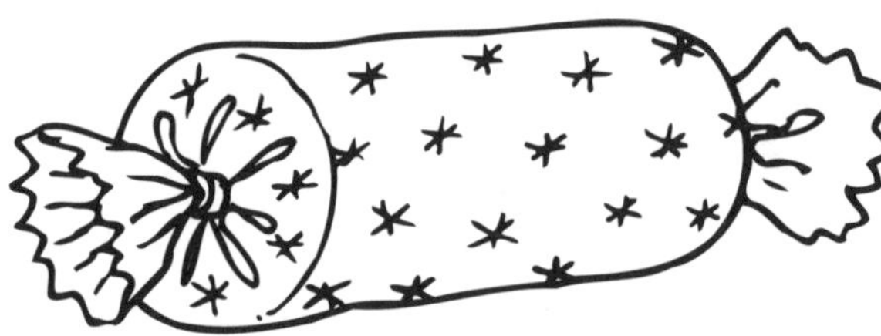

________________ (color)

________________ (color)

________________ (pattern)

________________ (color)

________________ (color)

________________ (pattern)

________________ (color)

________________ (color)

________________ (pattern)

Describe a "mystery object" to a friend. Can he or she guess what you are describing?

Name ___________________________  Completing describing sentences

What's Inside?

Use the describing words from page 244 to write a sentence about each package. For example: I found a swimsuit in the **yellow square** box.

1. I found ______________________ **in the** ______________________ **package.**

2. I found ______________________ **in the** ______________________ **package.**

3. I found ______________________ **in the** ______________________ **package.**

4. I found ______________________ **in the** ______________________ **package.**

A Walk in the Park

Describing words make a sentence more interesting.

Write describing words to finish each sentence.

1. A ______________ duck is swimming in the ______________ pond.

2. A ______________ man is walking his ______________ dog.

3. A ______________ girl is flying a ______________ kite.

4. A ______________ woman is sitting on a ______________ .

On another piece of paper, draw a picture of your favorite animal at the zoo. Then write two words to describe this animal.

Name ____

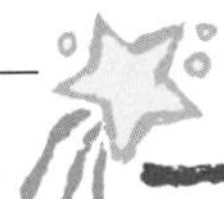

Around Town

Write a sentence for each picture. Use the describing word in the sentence.

large

beautiful

crowded

noisy

On another piece of paper, write five words that describe your street.

Name ______________________________ 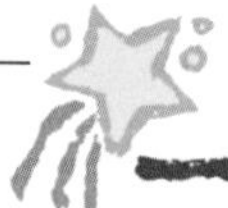

Keep It in Order

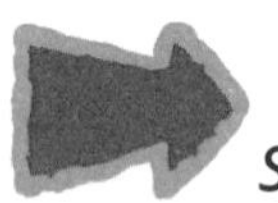

Sentences can be written in order to tell a story.

Finish each story by writing sentences about the last pictures.

1. First, the spider crawls up.

Next, ______________________________

Last, ______________________________

2. First, there is a tadpole.

Next, ______________________________

Last, ______________________________

Name ______________________________

What's Next?

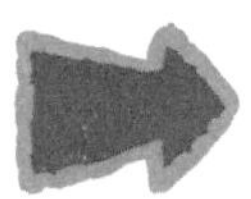

Sentences can be written in order to give directions.

Finish each set of directions by writing sentences about the last pictures.

1. First, mix all the ingredients.

Next, ______________________________

Last, ______________________________

2. First, put your dog in the tub.

Next, ______________________________

Last, ______________________________

Which Title Fits?

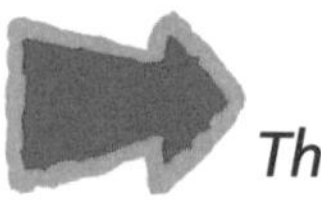

The name of a story is called the ***title****. It matches with the story. Most of the words in a title begin with capital letters.*

Match each title with its story. Write the title above the picture.

A Big Beak	**The Big Win**
My Space Friend	**A Knight's Tale**

____

(title)

____

(title)

____

(title)

____

(title)

A Terrific Title

Fill in the missing words to make your own story. Then write a title that fits with your story. Draw a picture about your story in the box.

____

(title)

One ______________________________ day,

______________________________ took his pet

______________________________ for a walk. First,

they went to the ______________________________.

Then they walked to ______________________________'s

house. Last, they went home to ____________________

______________________________. It was a

______________________________ day!

Name ______________________________

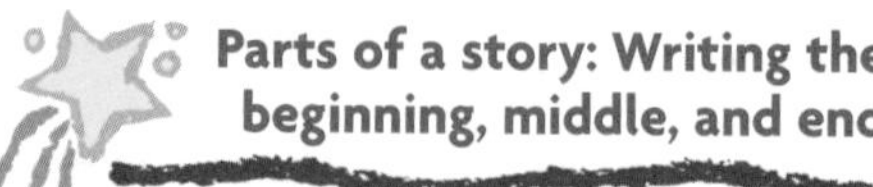

Story Strips

A story has a beginning, middle, and end.

Write a sentence to tell about each part of the story. Remember to give the story a title.

Beginning

____
(title)

____

Middle

____

End

____

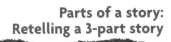

Name ______________________

More Story Strips

A story has a beginning, middle, and end.

Think of a story you know well. Write about the beginning, middle, and end parts. Draw pictures to match. Be sure to give your story a title.

____
(title)

Beginning

Middle

End

Fold a piece of paper two times to make a storybook. Write a story and draw pictures to match. Do not forget to write a title for your story.

Scholastic Success With

MAPS

Name ______________________________

Places in Pictures

Pretend you are on
cloud in the sky.
You look down.
You take a photo.
Here it is!

Circle **YES** if you see the thing in the photo.
Circle **NO** if you do not.

1. house YES NO
2. street YES NO
3. tree YES NO
4. pond YES NO
5. What else do you see? ______________________________

Name ____________________

You can show a place on a map.
A map is a drawing of a place from above.
This map shows the same place that the photo does.

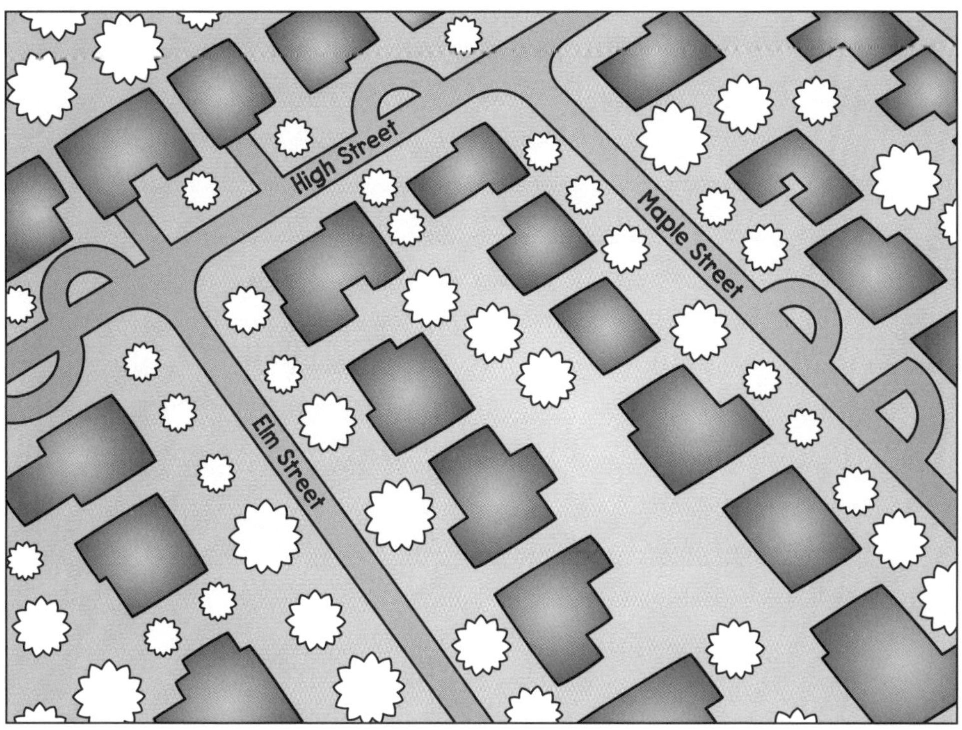

6. Find a street on the photo.
   Then find the same street on the map.
   Write the name of the street. ____________________

7. The trees on the map are not colored.
   Color them green.

8. Find a swimming pool in the photo.
   Draw it in the same place on the map.

Making a Map

This picture shows a toy store.

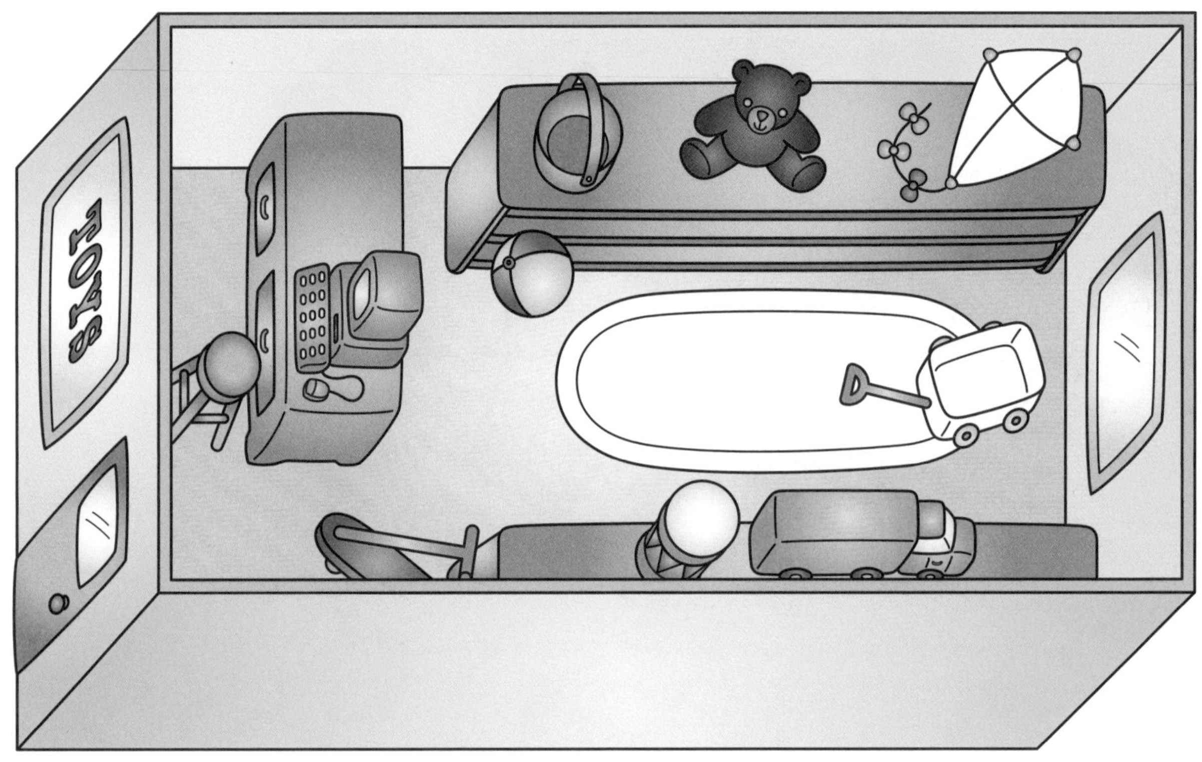

1. Color the kite yellow.

2. Color the rug green.

3. Color the wagon red.

4. What is next to the drum? ______________________

5. Can you buy a teddy bear here? ______________________

This map shows the same toy store.
You can help draw the map.

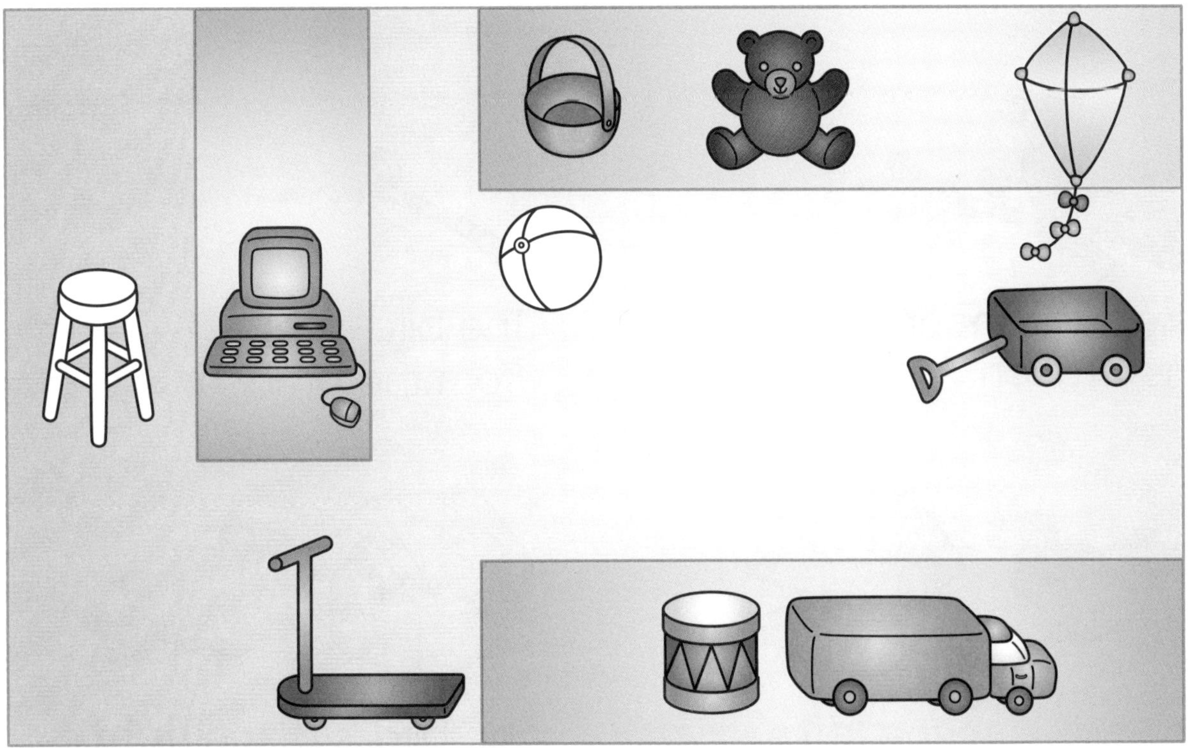

6. Find the ball in the picture.
   Make it the same color on the map.

7. Find the stool in the picture.
   Make it the same color on the map.

8. Find the rug in the picture.
   Draw it on the map in the same place.

Map Words

Many map words tell where things are.

The bird is **near** the branch.

The bird is **far** from the branch.

The bird is to the **left** of the bird house.

The bird is to the **right** of the bird house.

The bird is **above** the bath.

The bird is **below** the bath.

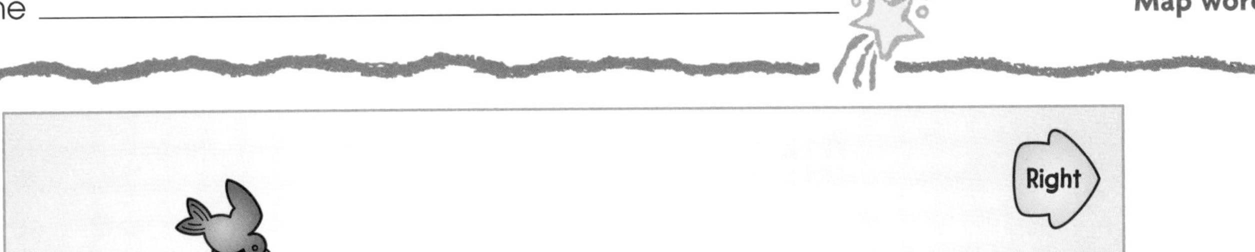

Name ______________________________

Write a word to complete each sentence.

near **far** **left** **right** **above**

1. The bird is ______________ from the bird house.

2. The girl is ______________ the bird house.

3. The bird is ______________ the grass.

4. The bird house is to the ______________ of the girl.

5. The path is to the ______________ of the girl.

Big and Small Spaces

Maps can show big spaces or small spaces.

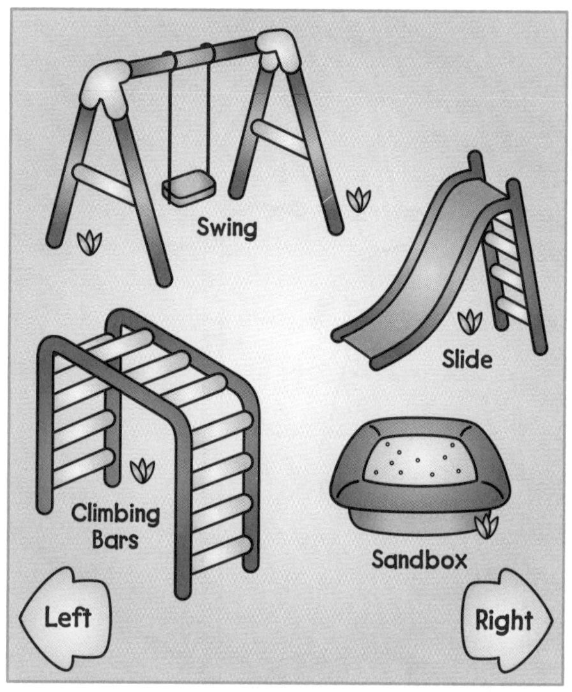

Map 1: This map shows a school playground.

Map 2: This map shows all of the school grounds.

Circle **YES** if the sentence is true.
Circle **NO** if the sentence is not true.

1. **The school is bigger than the trees.** YES NO
2. **The playground is bigger than the parking lot.** YES NO
3. **The school is to the right of the playground.** YES NO
4. **The trees are to the right of the playground.** YES NO

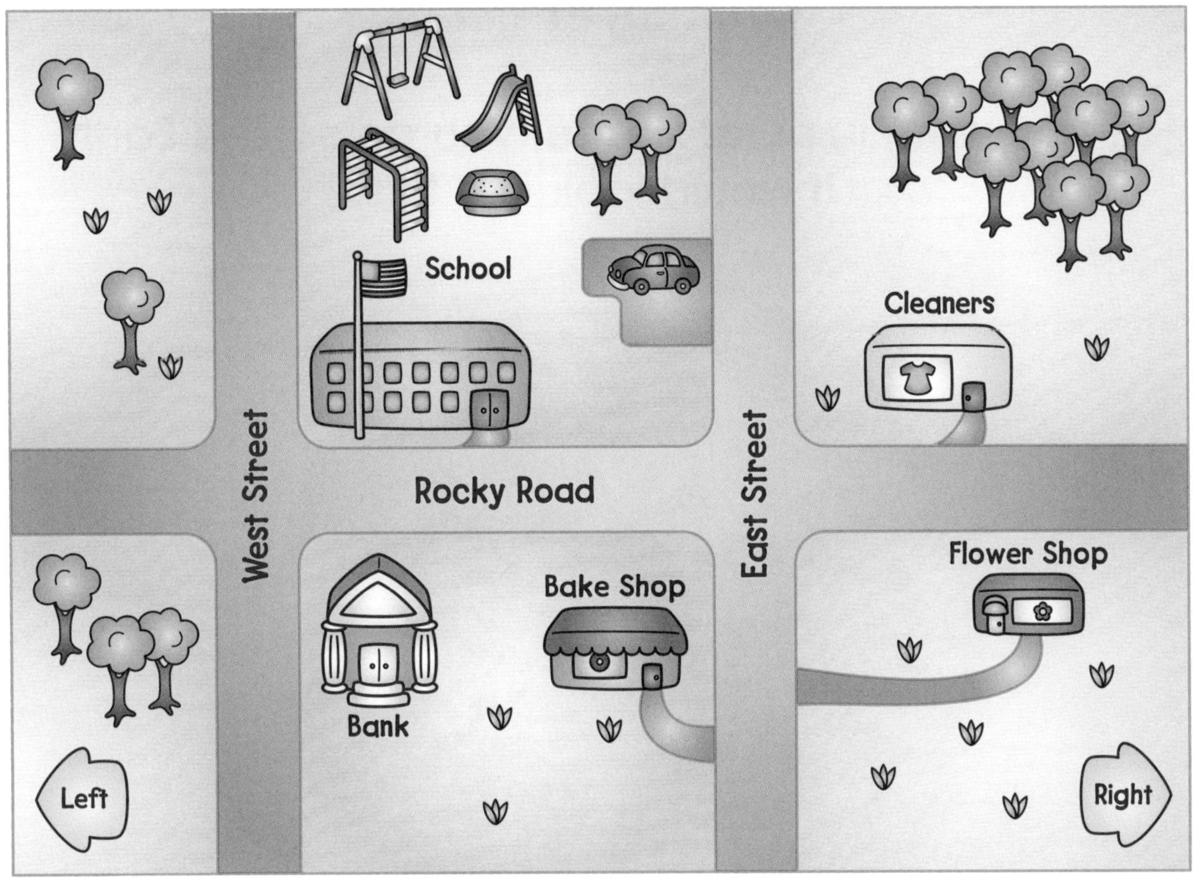

Map 3: This map shows three streets. Can you find the school?

5. **What is the biggest building on this map?** ______________________

6. **What is the smallest building on this map?** ______________________

7. **Look at all three maps. Which map shows the biggest space?** ____________

8. **Which map shows the smallest space?** ____________

Looking at Earth

If you were in outer space, you could see Earth. It would look like this.

1. **What shape is Earth?** ______________________

2. **Who lives on Earth?** ______________________

3. **Draw something that is the same shape as Earth.**

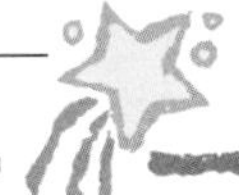

A Globe

A globe is a model of Earth.
It is the same shape as Earth.

1. What colors do you see on the globe?

____

2. What color stands for water?

____

3. Is a globe smaller or bigger than Earth?

____

Directions

**Earth has four main directions.
They are north, south, east, and west.**

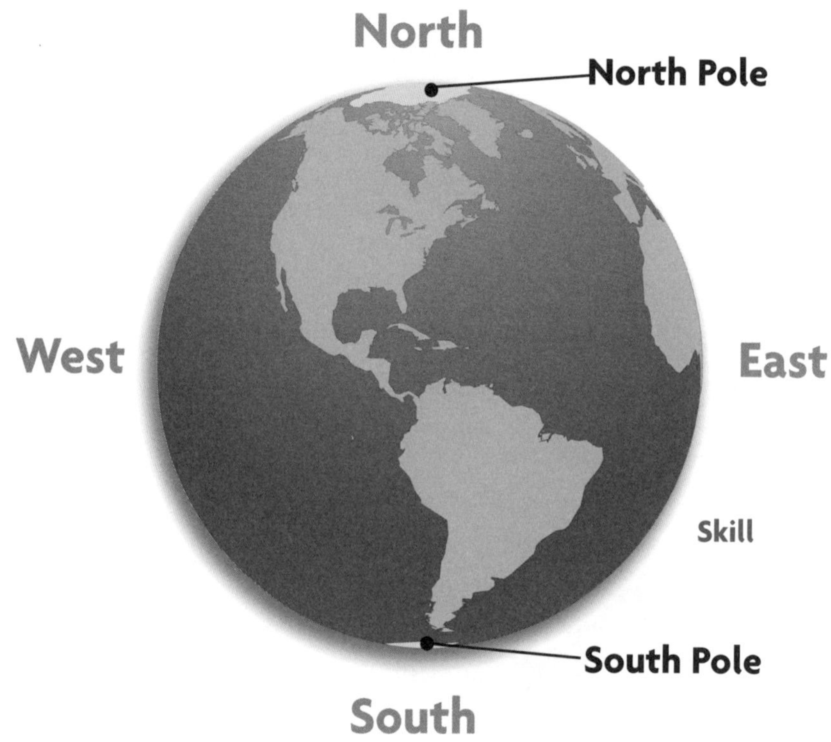

North is the direction toward the North Pole.
South is the direction toward the South Pole.

Can you find east and west on the picture, too?

1. What direction is the opposite of north? ____________

2. What direction is the opposite of west? ____________

Name ______________________

Directions help you find places on a map.
This map shows a camp.
Point to the four directions.

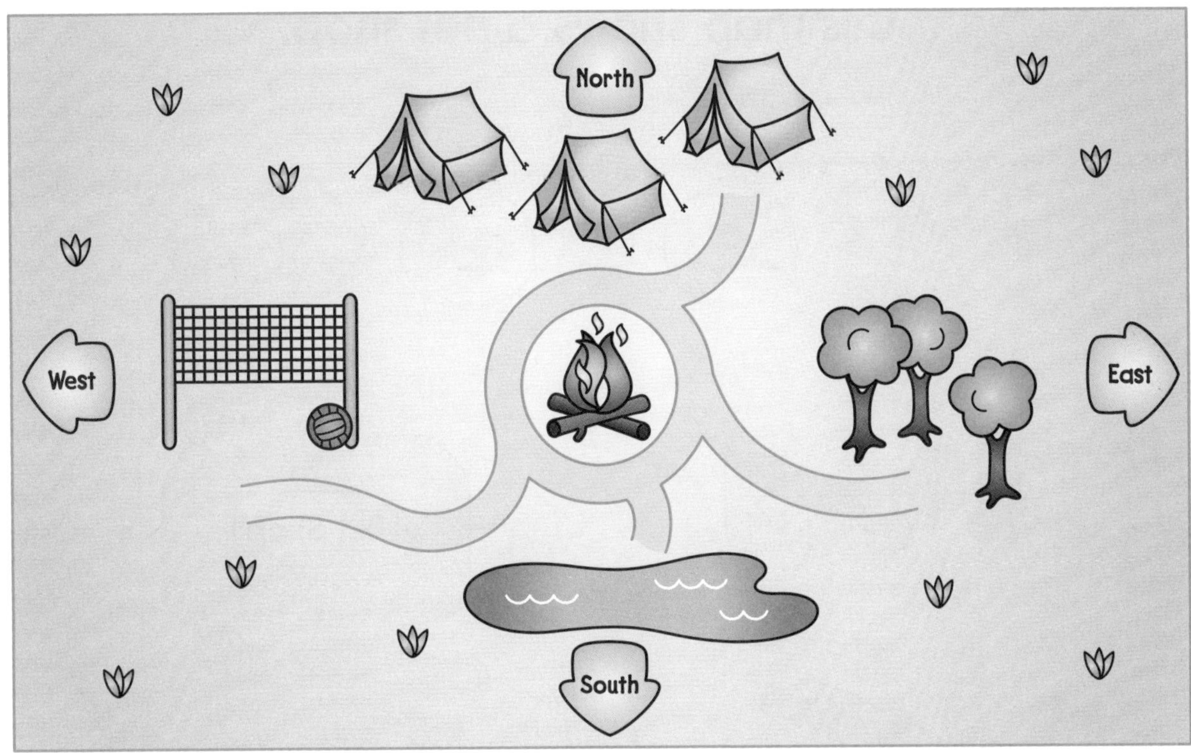

Where is each thing?
Write a direction word to describe it.

1.  ______________________

2.  ______________________

3. 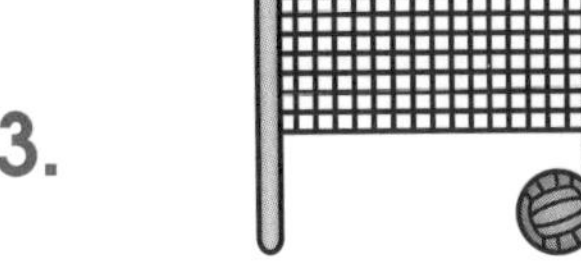 ______________________

4. 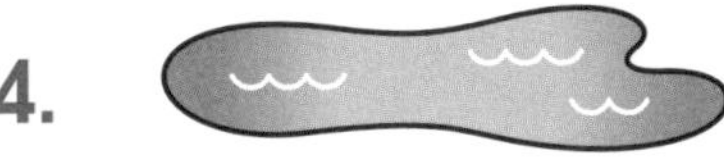 ______________________

Using Directions

**Directions tell you which way to go.
This map shows a pet shop.**

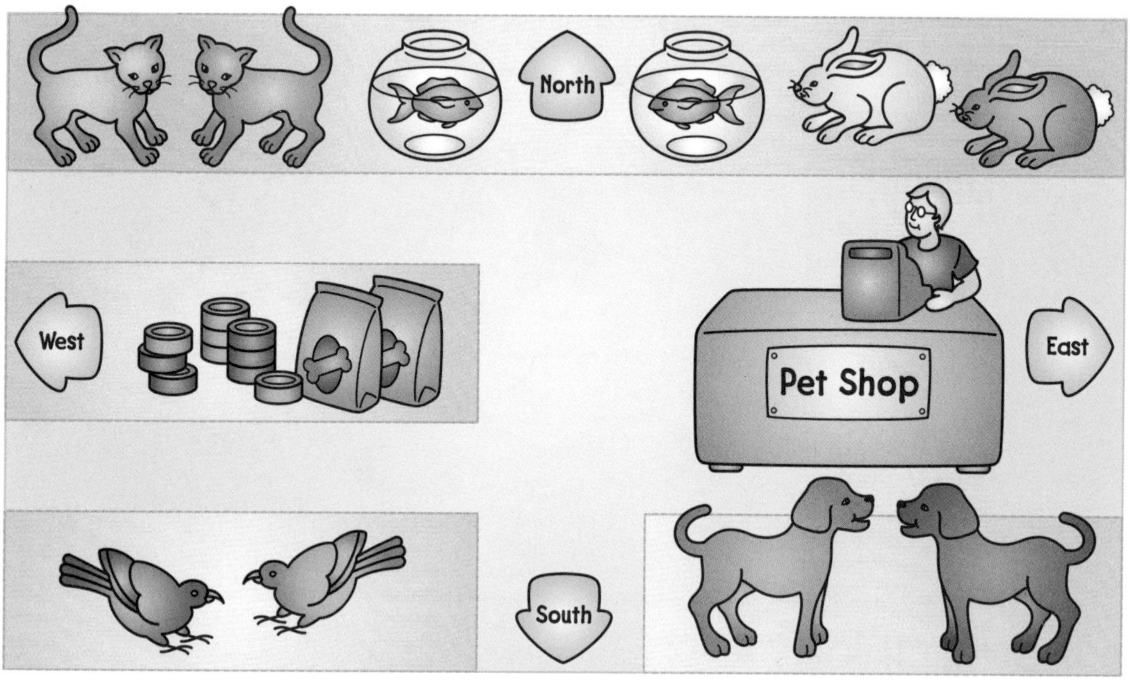

Write the direction word that tells how to get there.

1. from  to 

2. from  to 

3. from  to 

4. from 

to 

Name ___________________________ 

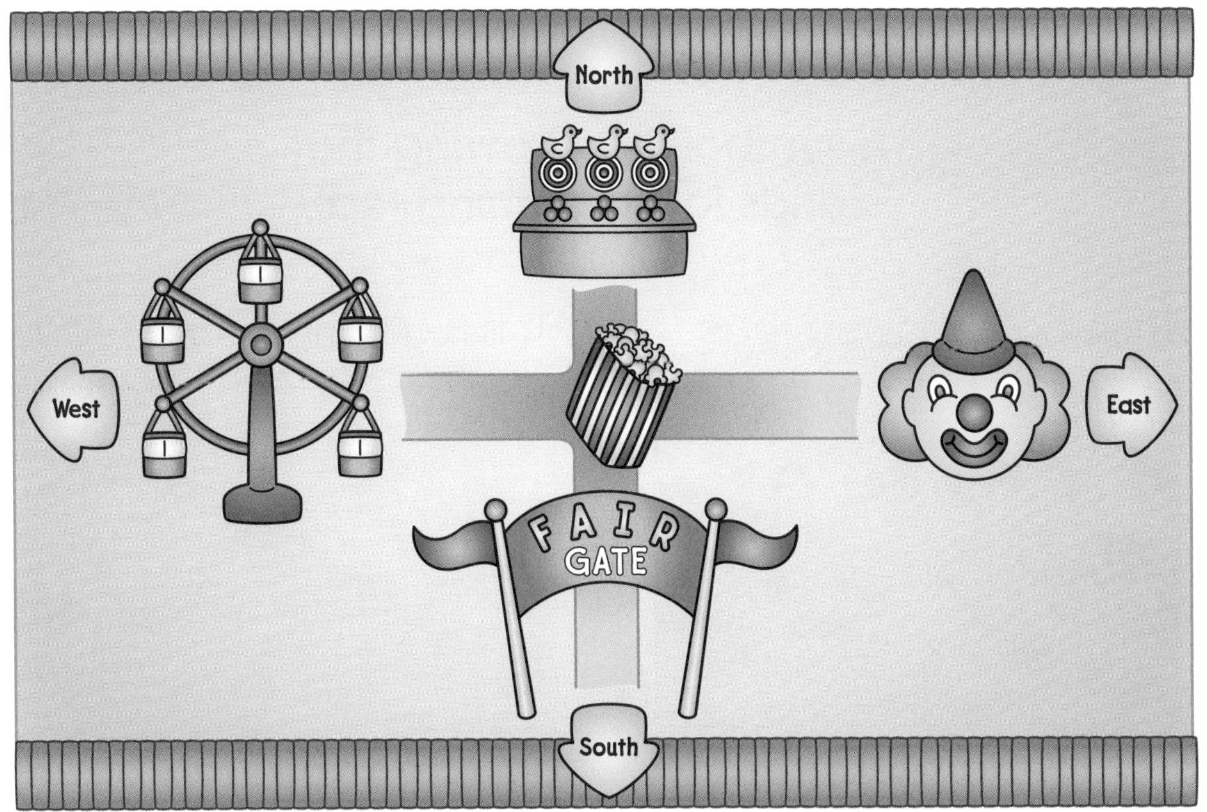

Come to the fair! You can have fun.

Draw a line to show where you go.

1. **Start at the gate. Go north to the . Mmmm!**

2. **Now go west. Stop and ride on the .**

3. **Walk to the east. Get your face painted like a .**

4. **From here, go west and then north. Stop and play at the .**

5. **In which direction is the gate from the ?**

Symbols

A symbol is a drawing that stands for something real.

The photo shows a road.

This is a symbol for a road.

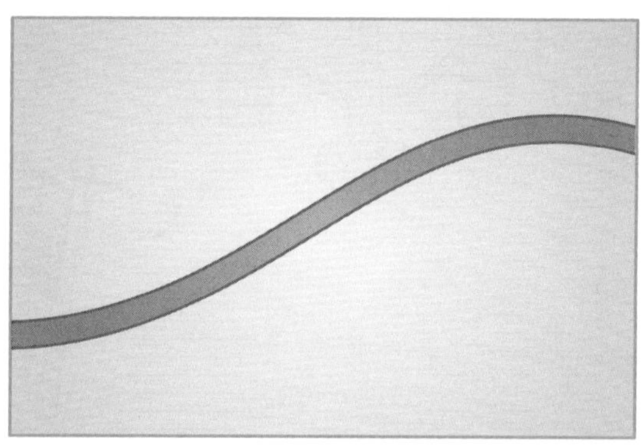

Draw a line to match each photo to the correct symbol.

1.

2.

3.

4.

a.

b.

c.

d.

Name ______________________________________

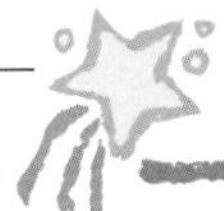

Here are some more symbols.

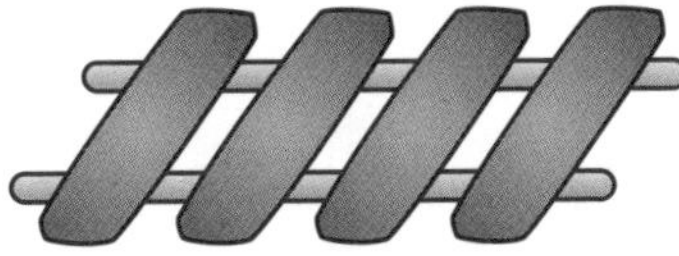

Draw the correct symbol next to each photo.

1.

3.

2.

4.

Name ____________________  Key

Symbols on Maps

Most maps have symbols.
A map key tells what each symbol stands for.

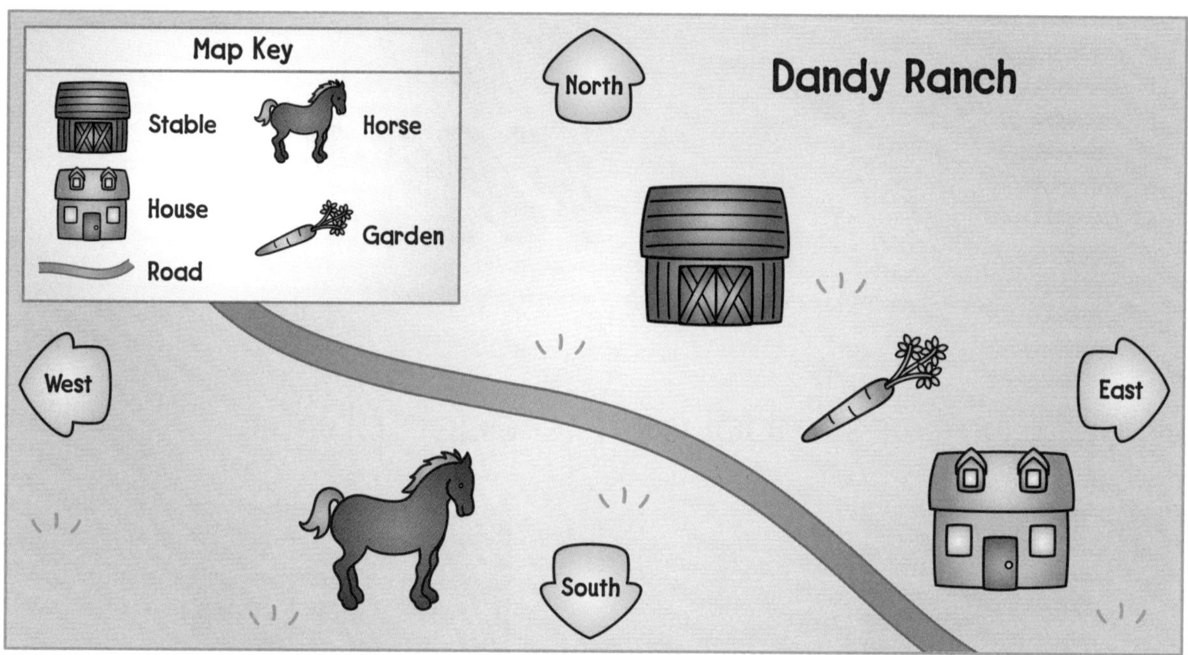

Use the map key.
Write what each symbol stands for.

1. 

3. 

2.

4. 

Name ______________________________ Key

The ranch has one new animal.

Circle the new animal on the map.
Use the map key to answer the questions.

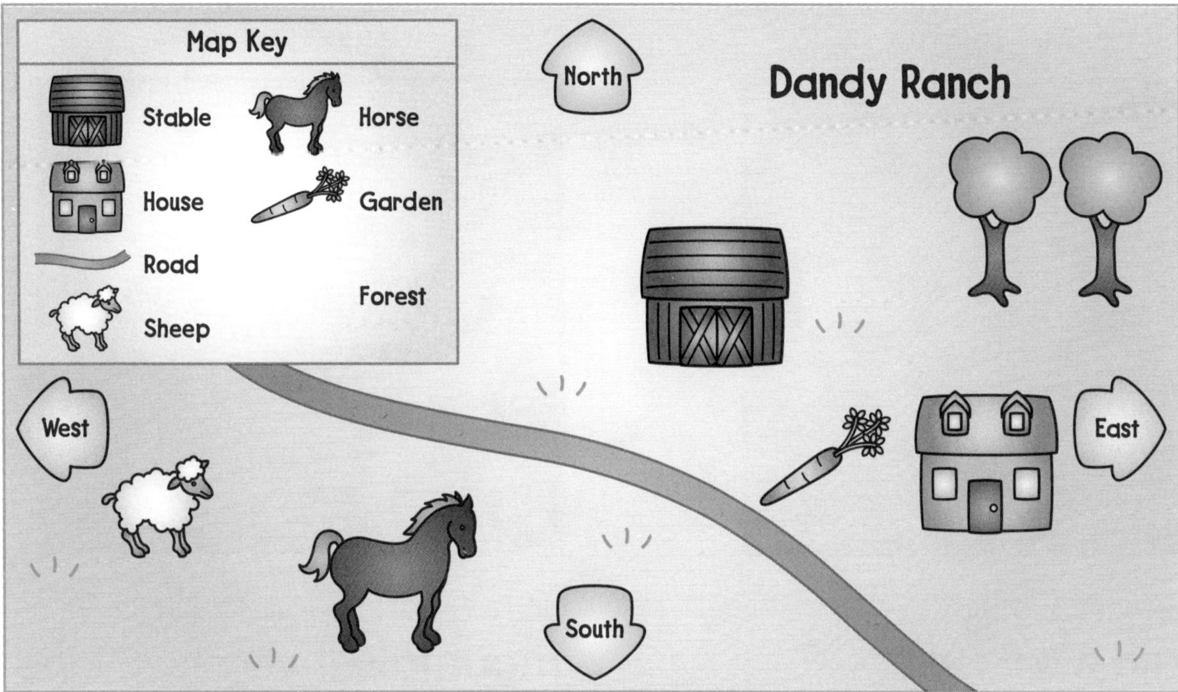

1. **Is the horse north or south of the road?** ______________

2. **What does [sheep] mean?** ______________

3. **Is the garden east or west of the house?** ______________

4. **Find the forest on the map.**
   Add a tree symbol to the map key.

Land and Water

Earth has different kinds of land.

Some land is flat.
A **plain** is flat land.

Some land is very high. A **mountain** is very high land.

Some land is higher than a plain but not as high as a mountain. This land is called a **hill**.

1. What is the highest kind of land?

____

2. What is the flattest land?

____

3. Which is higher, a hill or a plain?

____

Name ____________________

Earth has lots of water.

Some water runs across the land. This water is called a **river.**

Some water has land all around it. This water is called a **lake**.

These symbols stand for different kinds of land and water. Write a word to tell what each symbol stands for.

4. 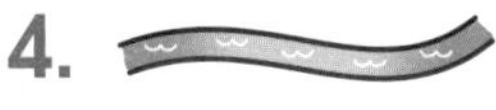 ____________________

6. ____________________

5.  ____________________

7. ____________________

A Land and Water Map

This picture shows different kinds of land and water.

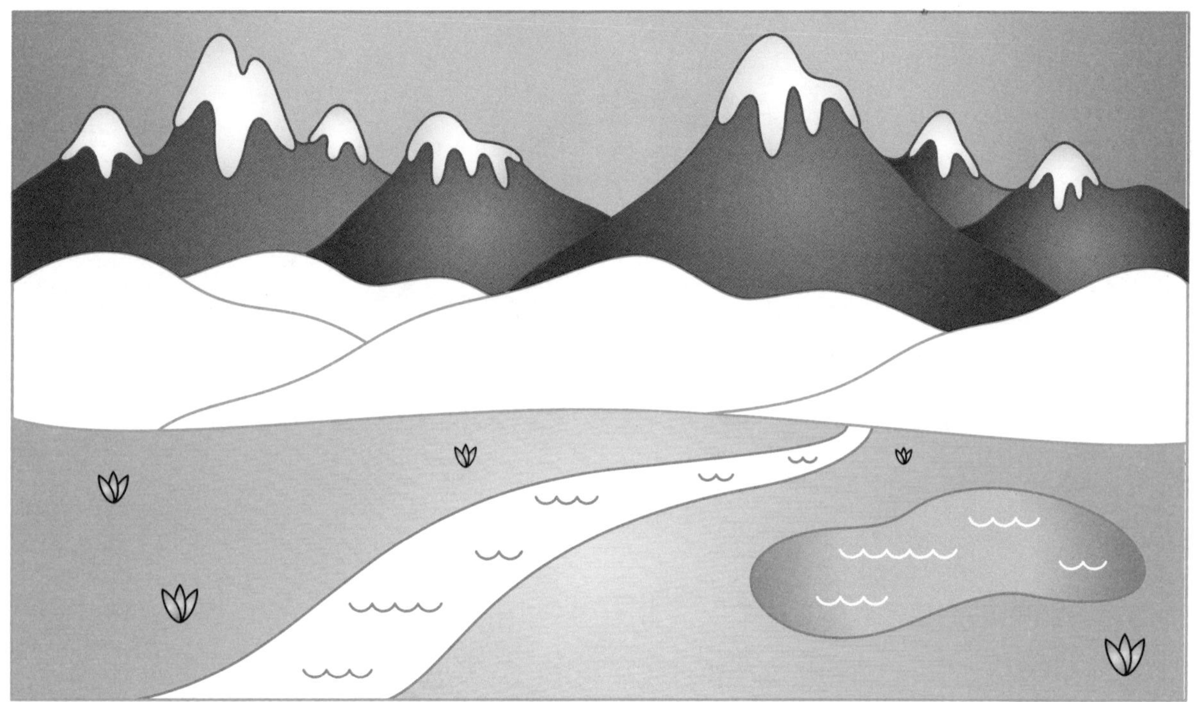

1. Find the river. Color it blue.
2. Find a body of water with land all around it. Write "lake" on it.
3. Find the hills. Color them light green.
4. Find the flat land. Write "plain" on it.

Name ______________________

This map shows land and water, too.

1. What does [plain symbol] mean? ______________________

2. Is the lake to the east or west of the river? ______________________

3. Are the mountains to the east or west of the hills? ______________________

4. Write a place where you can do each thing.

climb ______________________ run ______________________

swim ______________________ fish ______________________

A Park Map

This map shows a big park.
A park can have different kinds of land and water.

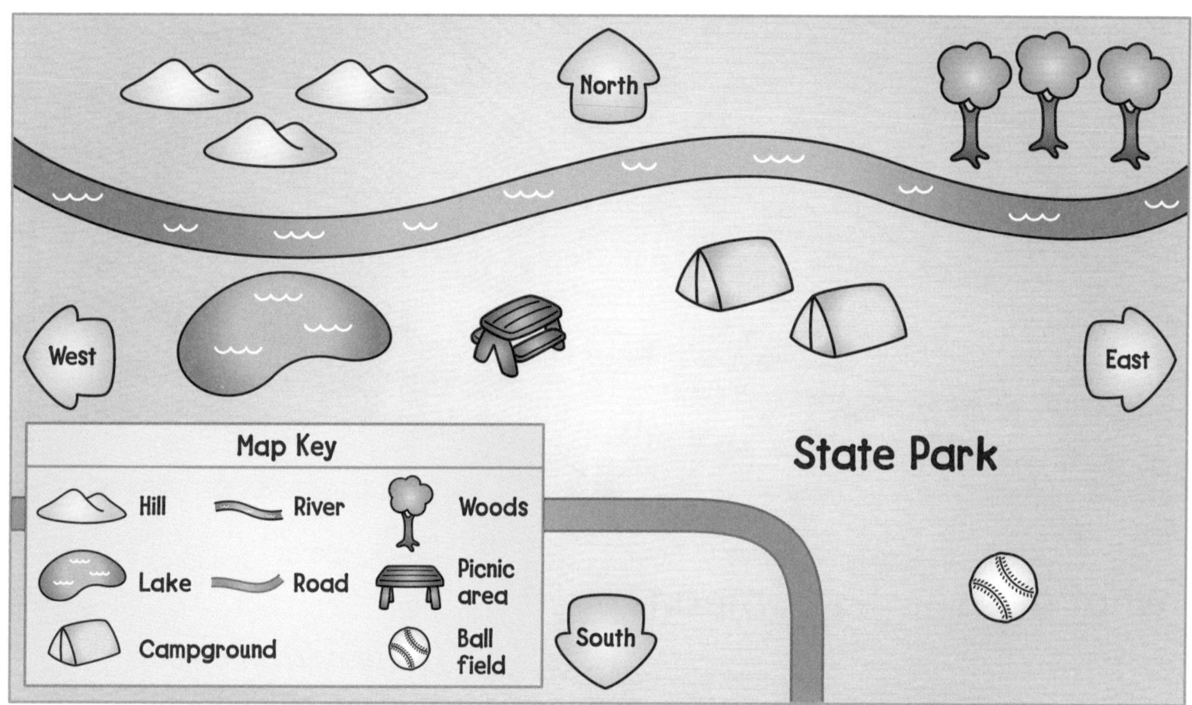

1. What does this symbol [hill symbol] mean? ____________

2. Where can you sleep in this park? ____________

3. What symbol shows where you can have a picnic? ____________

4. Where can you ride a raft in this park? ____________

5. Is the road to the east or west of the ball field? ____________

Name ______________________________

This map shows a city park.

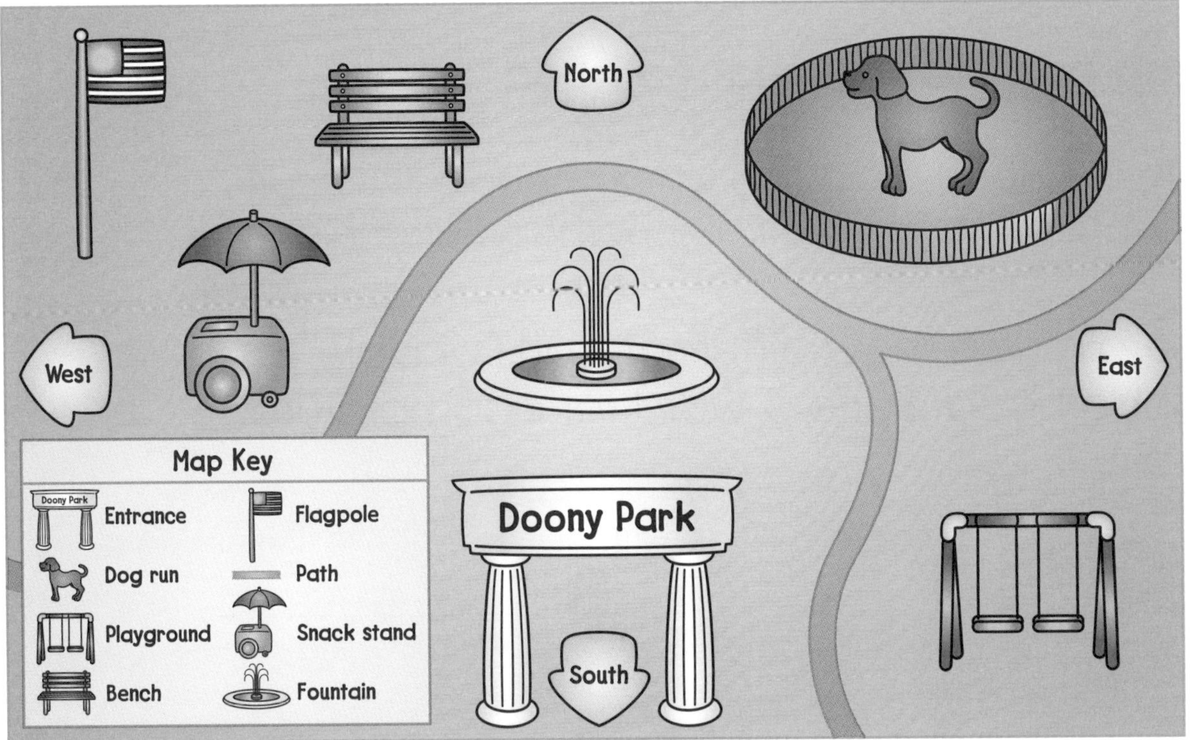

1. What is the name of this park? ______________

2. Where can you get something to eat? ______________

3. What is north of the entrance? ______________

4. Where can your dog play in this park? ______________

5. Where can you ride a swing? ______________

6. In which direction would you walk from the  to the  ______________

A Neighborhood Map

A map can show a neighborhood.

A neighborhood is a place where people live, work, and play. The people who live in a neighborhood are neighbors.

These pictures show different parts of Dale's neighborhood. Write a word for each picture.

1.  ____________

2.  ____________

3. 

____

4.  ____________

5. Draw a picture of something in your neighborhood.

This map shows the neighborhood where Dale lives.

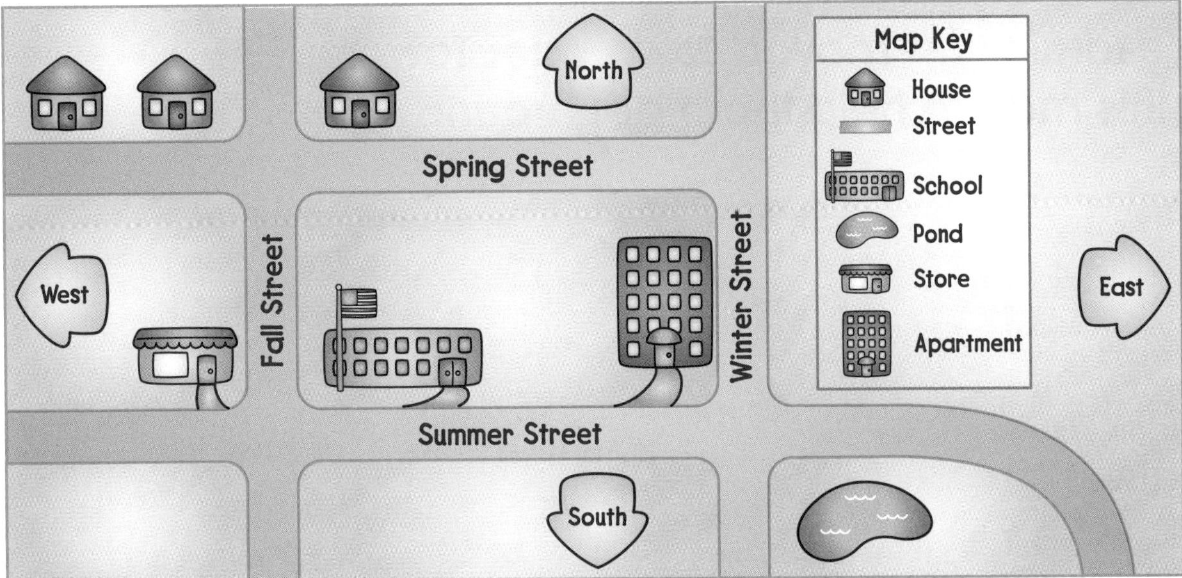

1. What does the symbol

stand for? ______________________

2. Find the symbol for house.
On what street are the houses? ______________________

3. Dale lives in an apartment.
On what street does Dale live? ______________________

4. Dale is going to the store
with her father. In which direction
is the store from her home? ______________________

Name ______________________

Going Places

Hari's family just moved to Wonder Town. Use this map to help them get around.

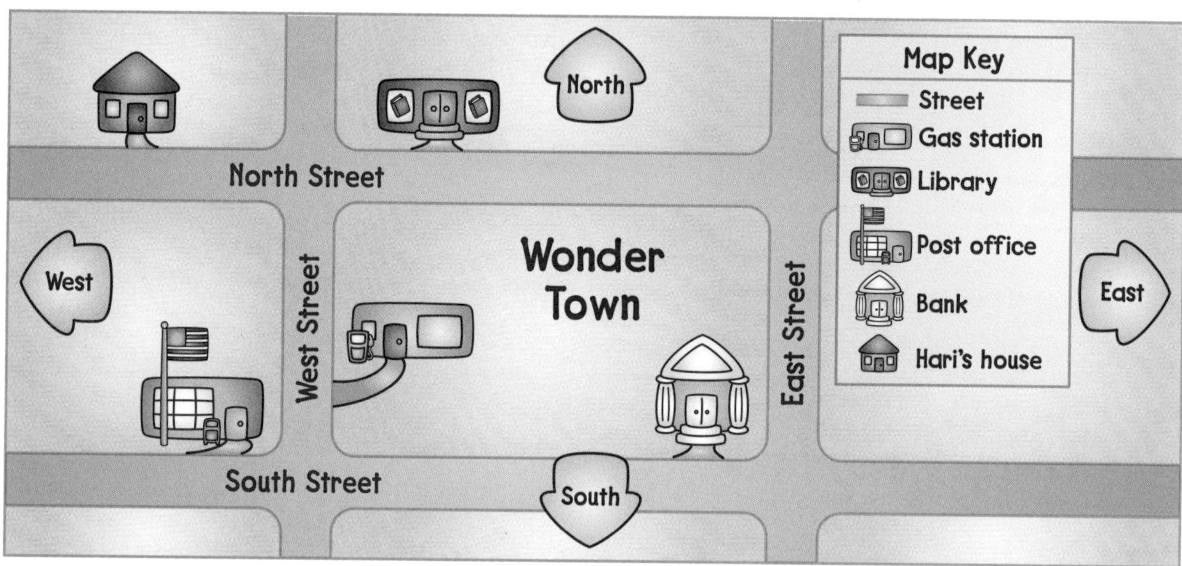

Tell Hari's family the street for each place.

1. **Hari's mother is going to the bank. It is on ______________________.**
2. **Hari's father is going to the gas station. It is on ______________________.**
3. **Hari's big brother is going to the library. It is on ______________________.**
4. **Hari's grandma is going to the post office. It is on ______________________.**

Name ____________________

Hari goes to school the same way each day. He follows a route. A route is a way to go from one place to another.

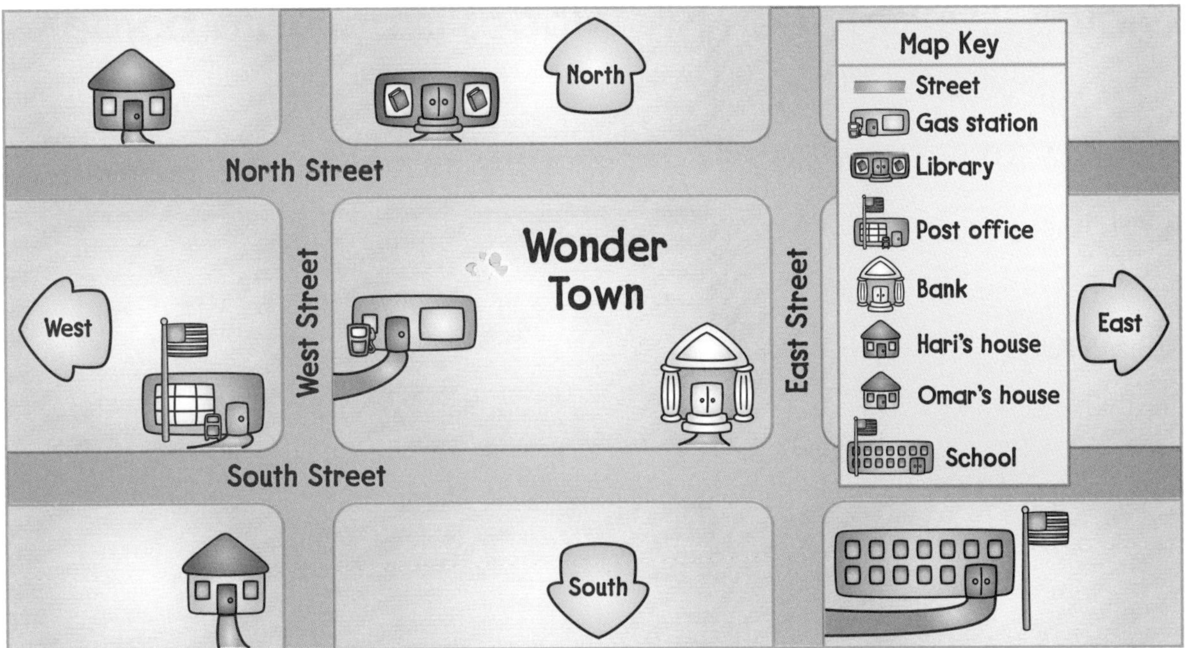

1. Start at Hari's house.
   Draw a line to show the route he can take to school.

2. On what street is the school? ____________________

3. Omar is Hari's new friend.
   Draw a line to show Omar's route to school.

4. Does Omar live east or
   west of the school? ____________________

5. Is the library north or
   south of the gas station? ____________________

Borders

Maps show where places begin and end.
A dividing line between two places is called a border.

Look at the fence in this photo. The fence shows where the border is.

Look at the line with dashes on this map. This line is a symbol. It stands for a border.

Maps show other kinds of borders, too. A river can be a border. So can a road. Draw an X on three kinds of borders on this map.

Name ____________________

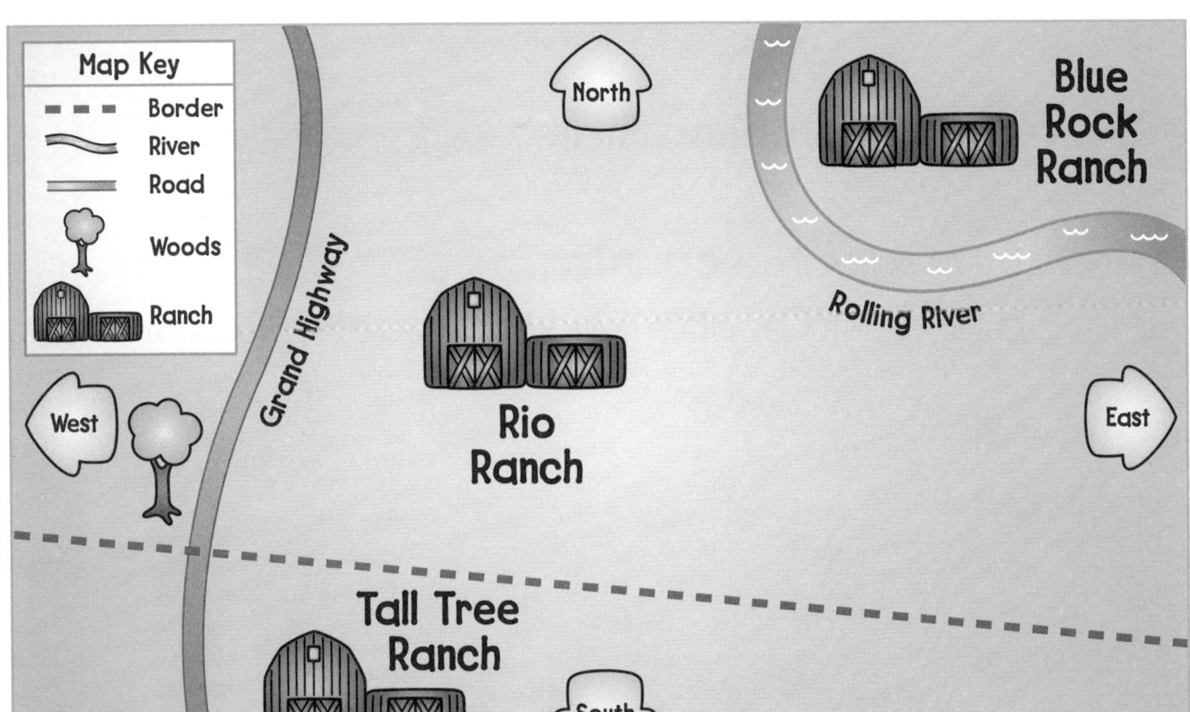

This map shows different borders.

1. This symbol - - - - - stands for a ____________________.

2. The border to the west of Rio Ranch is a ____________________.

3. What is the border between Rio Ranch and Blue Rock Ranch? ____________________

4. In which direction is Tall Tree Ranch from Rio Ranch? ____________________

5. Are the woods east or west of Rio Ranch? ____________________

Name ____________________ 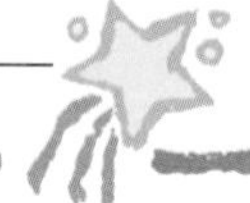

The United States

Here is a map of the United States.

The United States is a large **country**.
A country is a land and people who live there.

North
WASHINGTON
MONTANA
NORTH DAKOTA
MINNESOTA
OREGON
IDAHO
WISCONSIN
SOUTH DAKOTA
WYOMING
NEBRASKA
IOWA
ILLINOIS
NEVADA
UTAH
COLORADO
CALIFORNIA
KANSAS
MISSOURI
ARIZONA
OKLAHOMA
ARKANSAS
NEW MEXICO
West
TEXAS
LOUISIANA
ALASKA
HAWAII
South

Name ______________________________ 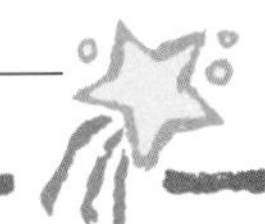

The United States has 50 states.
Each state is a part of the country.
The states are different shapes and sizes.

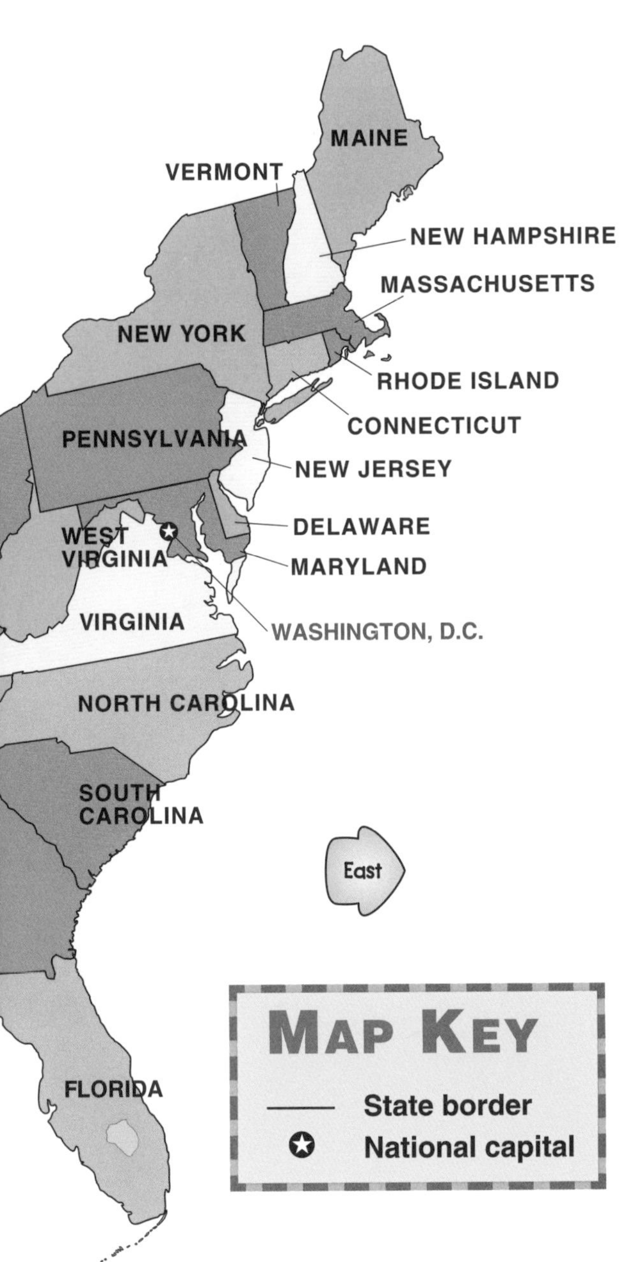

1. What does this symbol ——— mean?

   ____

2. What is your state?

   ____

3. How many states share a border with your state?

   ____

4. Name a state in the east.

   ____

5. Is Texas in the north or south?

   ____

6. Is Oregon in the west or east?

   ____

7. What state is south of Utah?

   ____

8. What state is west of Ohio?

   ____

Name ____________________

A State Map

This map shows the state of Indiana. Each state has a capital city.

A capital is the city where the leaders of the state work. The capital of Indiana is Indianapolis.

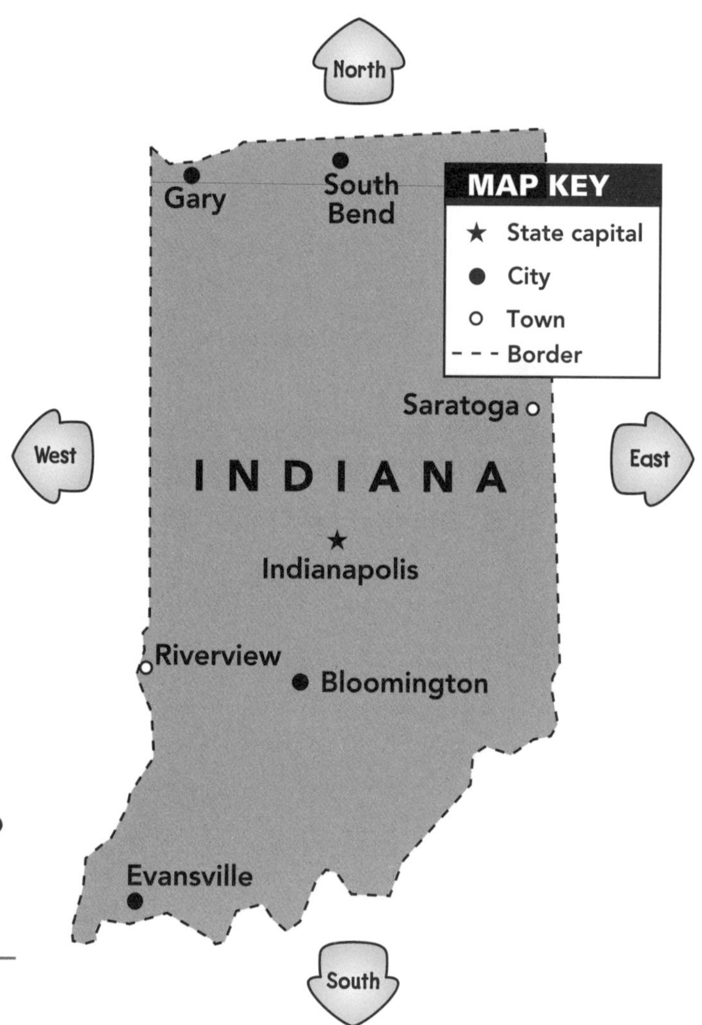

1. What does this symbol ★ stand for?

____

2. Is Evansville in the north or south of the state? ____________________

3. In what part of the state is South Bend? ____________________

4. Is Riverview in the west or the east part of the state? ____________________

This map shows where Indiana is in the United States.

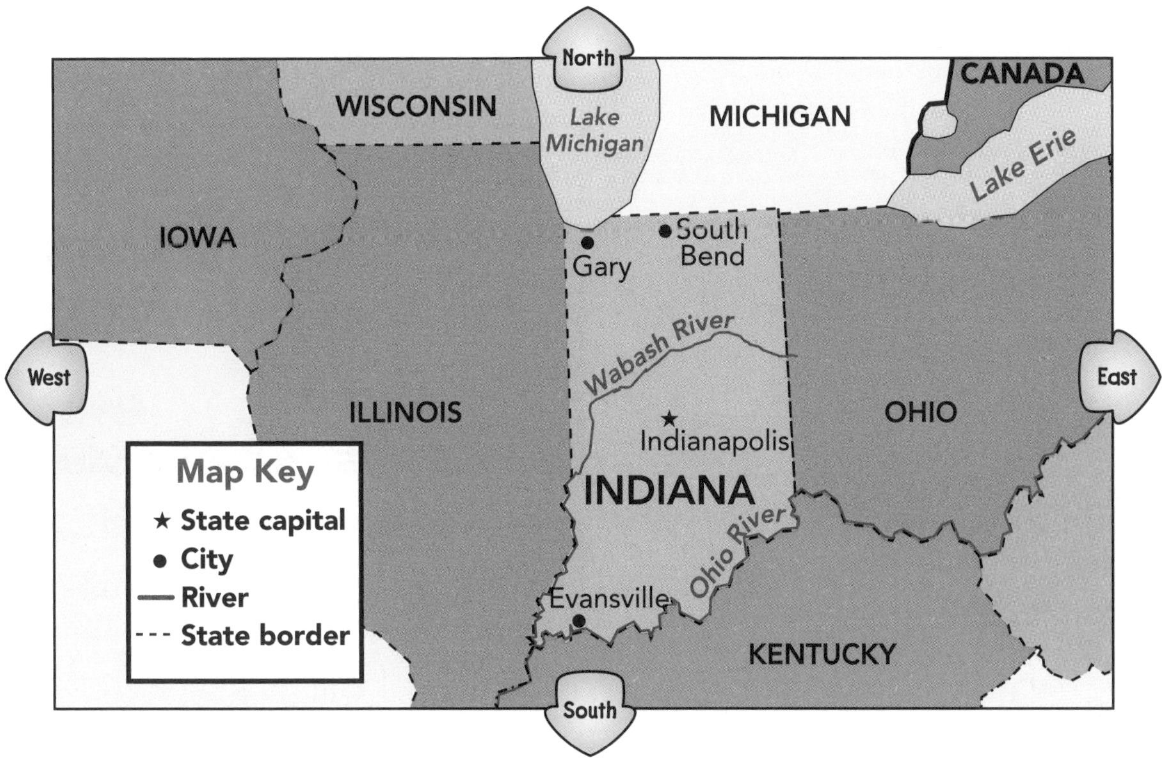

1. What does this symbol - - - - - - - - mean? ______________________

2. What river forms a border on the south of Indiana? ______________________

3. What river forms a border on the west of Indiana? ______________________

4. How many states share a border with Indiana? ______________________

5. What lake forms a border on the north of Indiana? ______________________

A City Map

The United States has a capital city.

It is Washington, D.C. The President of the United States lives and works there. So do other leaders of the country.

The President lives and works in the White House.

Washington, D.C., has many important buildings. You can see some of them on the map on page 291.

1. **Find the Washington Monument. Is it north or south of the White House?** ______________

2. **Find the U.S. Capitol. Trace a route on the map to the White House.**

3. **Find the National Gallery of Art. Is it east or west of the U.S. Capitol?** ______________

4. **Constitution Avenue runs from west to** ______________ **.**

5. **Name a museum you would like to visit.**

____

Name ____________________

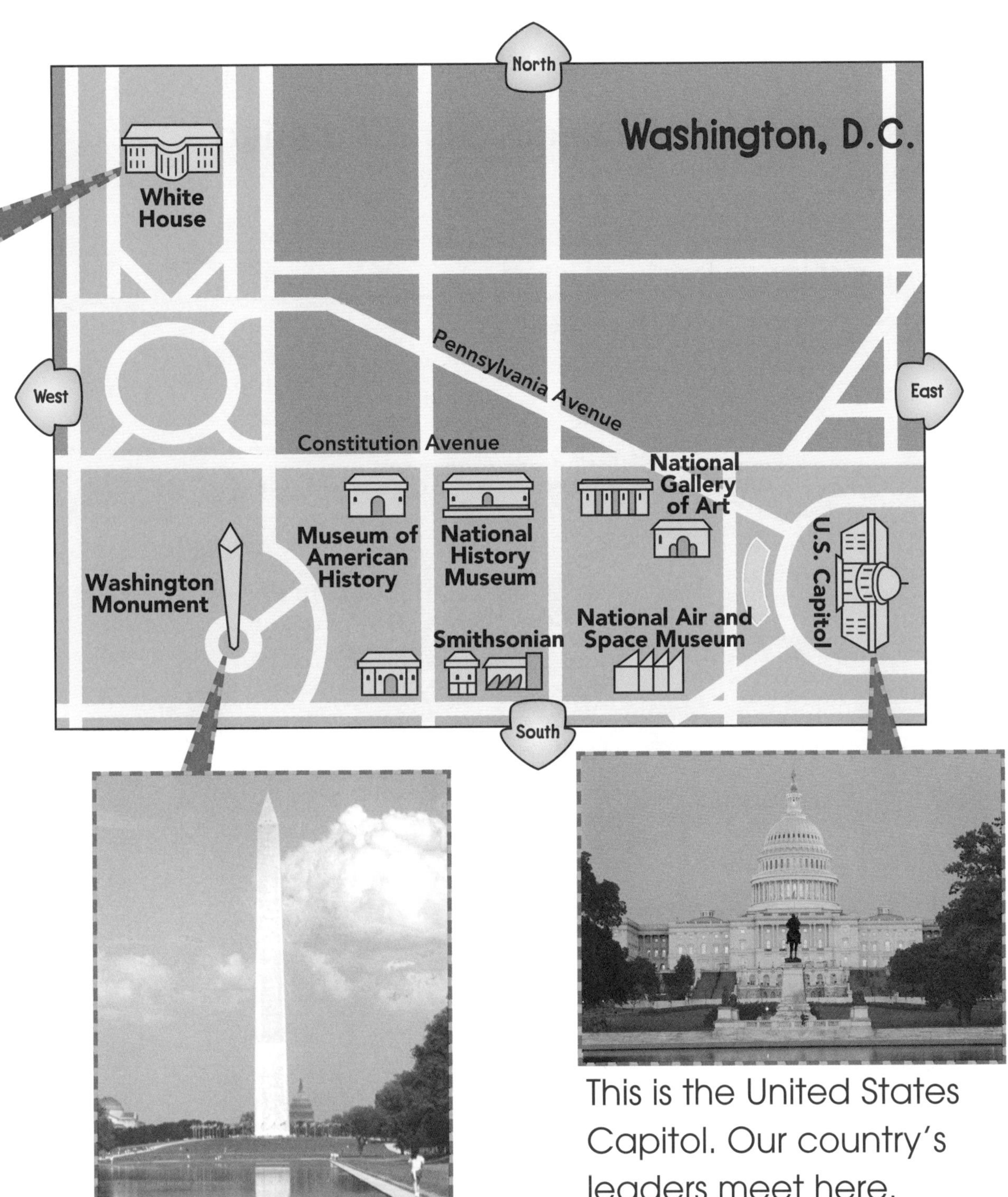

This is the United States Capitol. Our country's leaders meet here.

This is the Washington Monument. It honors George Washington. He was our first President.

North America

This map shows North America. North America is a continent.

A continent is a large body of land.
The United States is in North America.

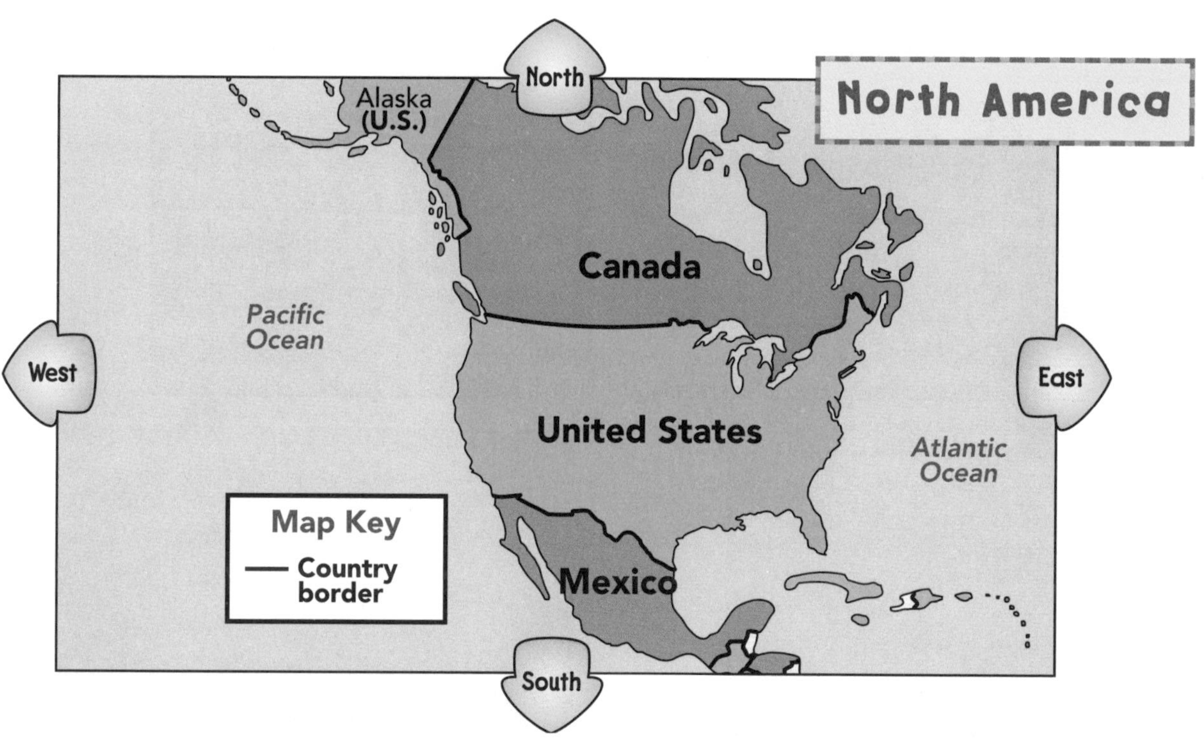

1. **What does the symbol ——— mean?** ______________

2. **What country is north of the United States?** ______________

3. **In which direction is Mexico from the United States?** ______________

Name ___________________________

Around the continents are Earth's oceans. An ocean is a very big body of salt water.

Earth has four oceans.
This map shows two of them.

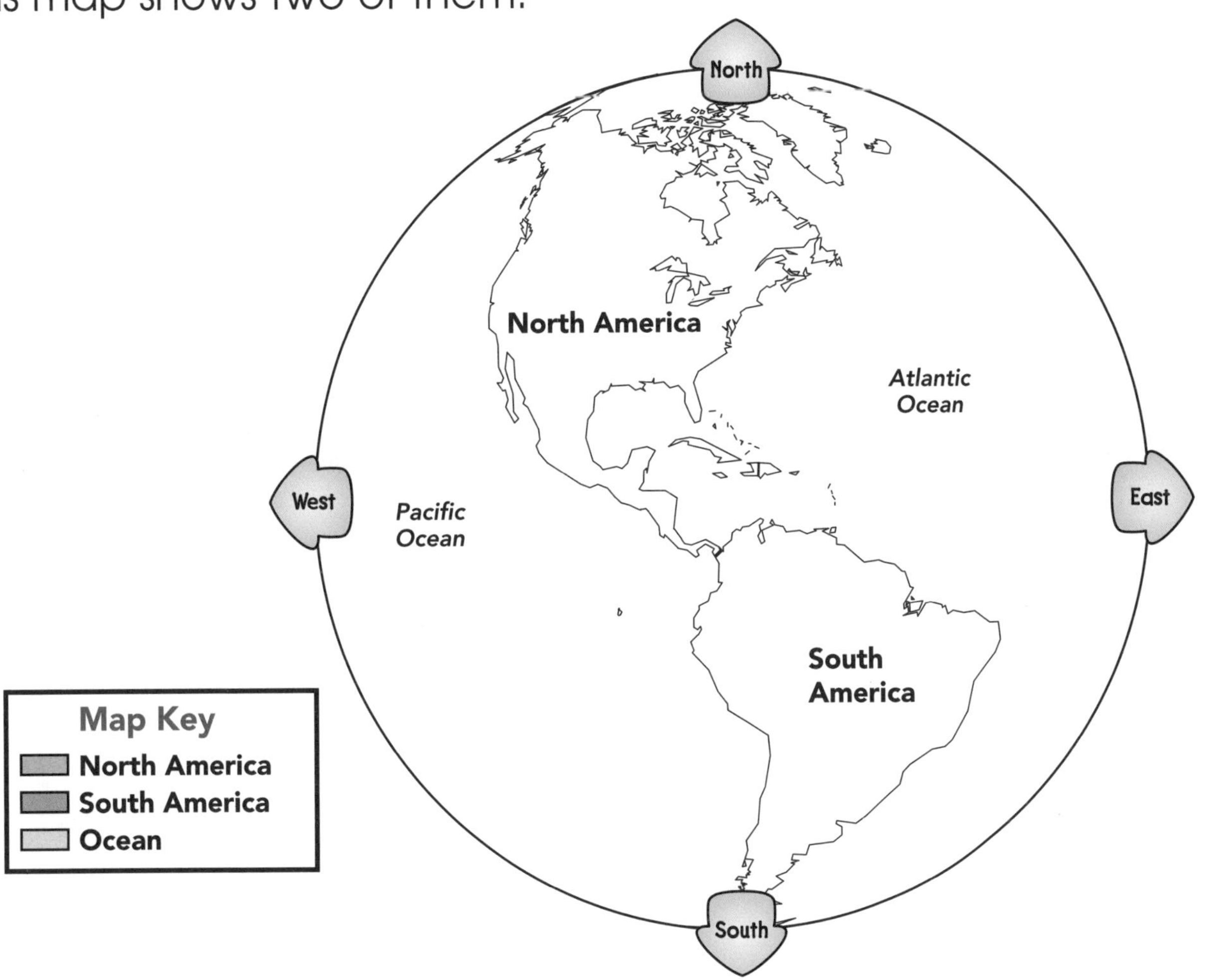

1. What ocean is to the east of North America? ___________________________

2. What ocean is to the west of North America? ___________________________

3. Color the map to match the map key.

A World Map

Remember, Earth is round like a ball. But you can only see one side of a ball at once.

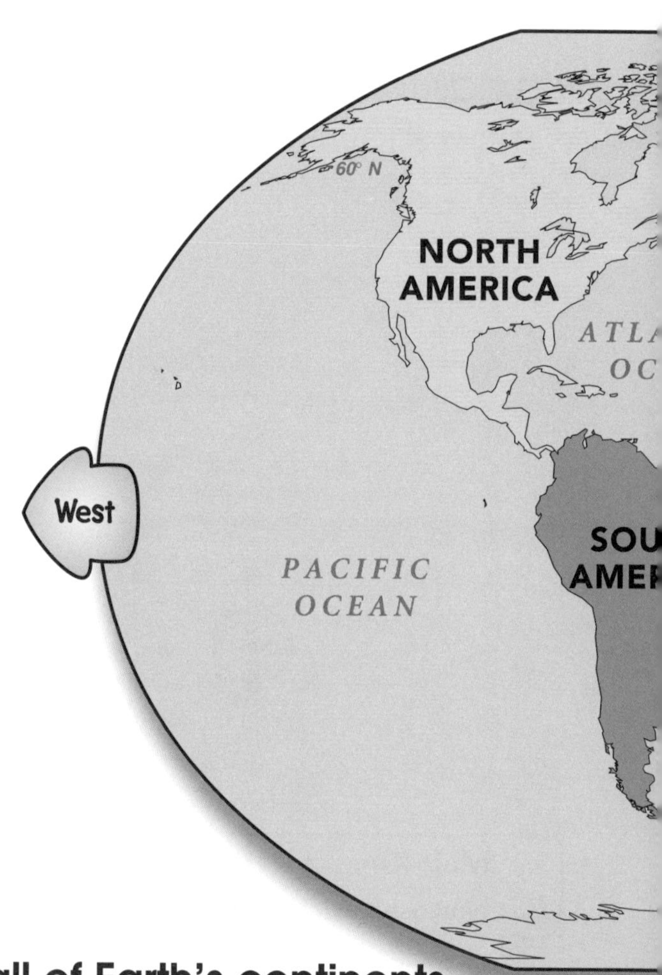

1. Here is a map of Earth. It shows all of Earth's continents. Count to find seven continents.

2. The map shows the four oceans of Earth, too. What are their names?

   ____________________ ____________________

   ____________________ ____________________

3. What continent is north of Africa? ____________________

Name ______________________________

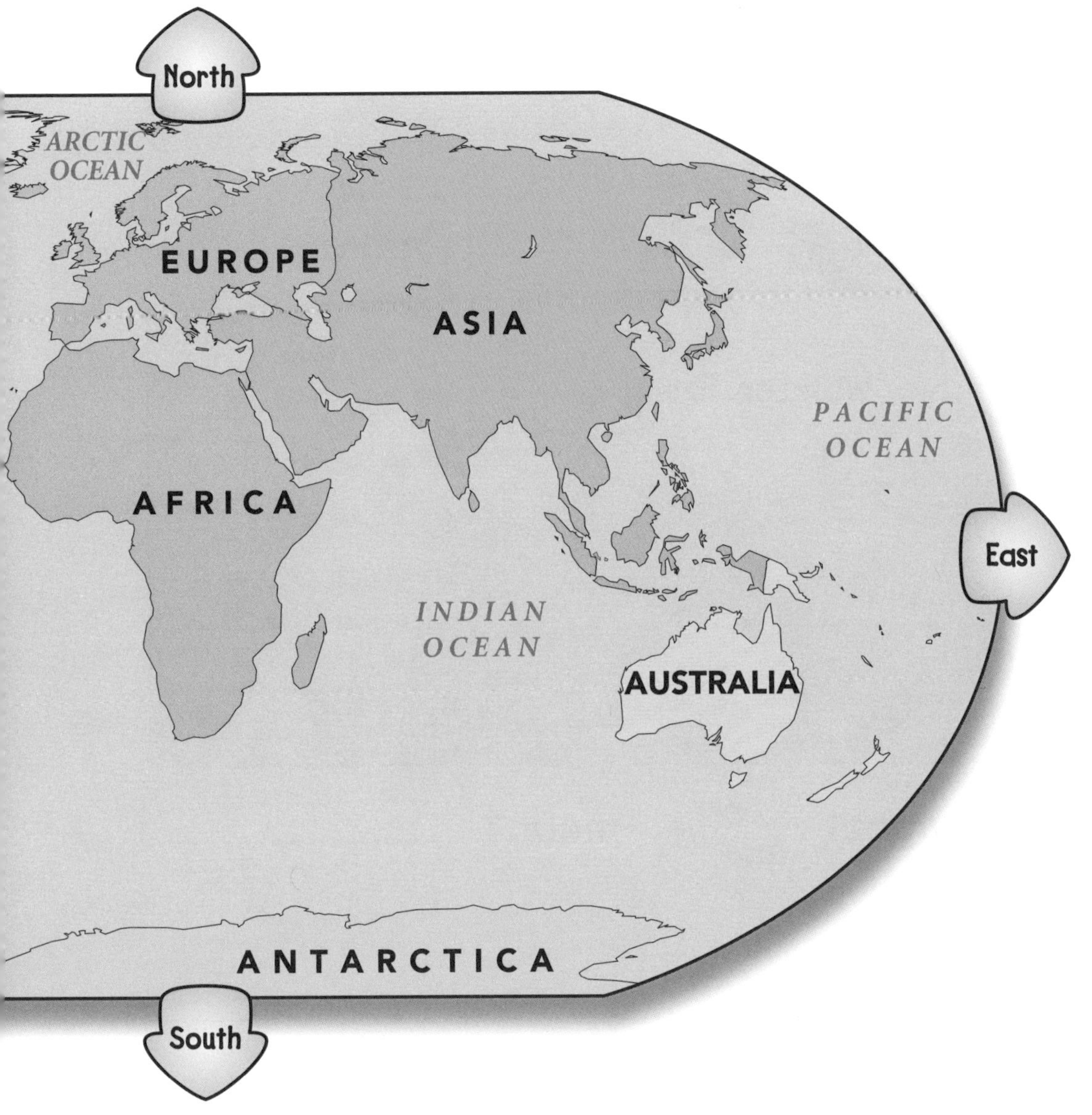

4. What continent is south of North America? ______________________________

5. What ocean is west of Australia? ______________________________

6. What ocean is in the north part of Earth? ______________________________

7. What continent is in the far south part of Earth? ______________________________

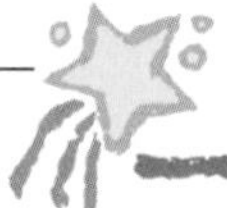

Map Review 1

Use the map to answer the questions.

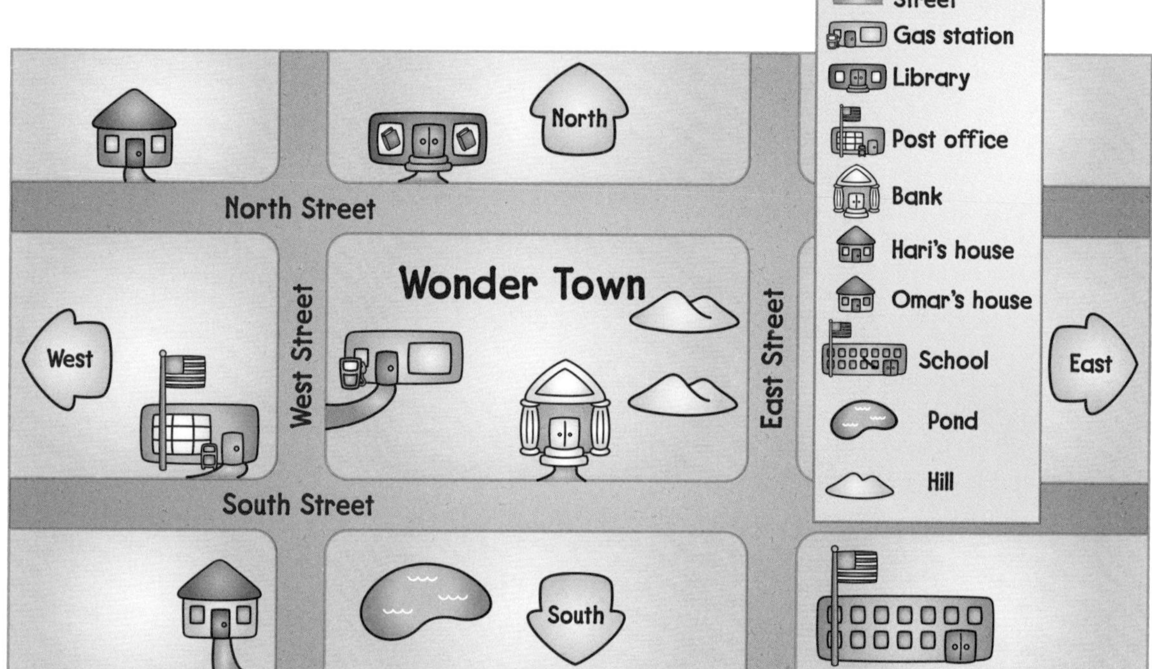

1. What does this symbol 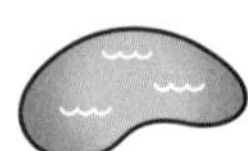 mean? ______________

2. What kind of land is to the east of the bank? ______________

3. On what street does Hari live? ______________

4. Draw a route from Hari's house to Omar's house.

5. Where can Hari mail a letter? ______________

6. Is Hari's house north or south of the school? ______________

Map Review 2

Use the map to answer the questions.

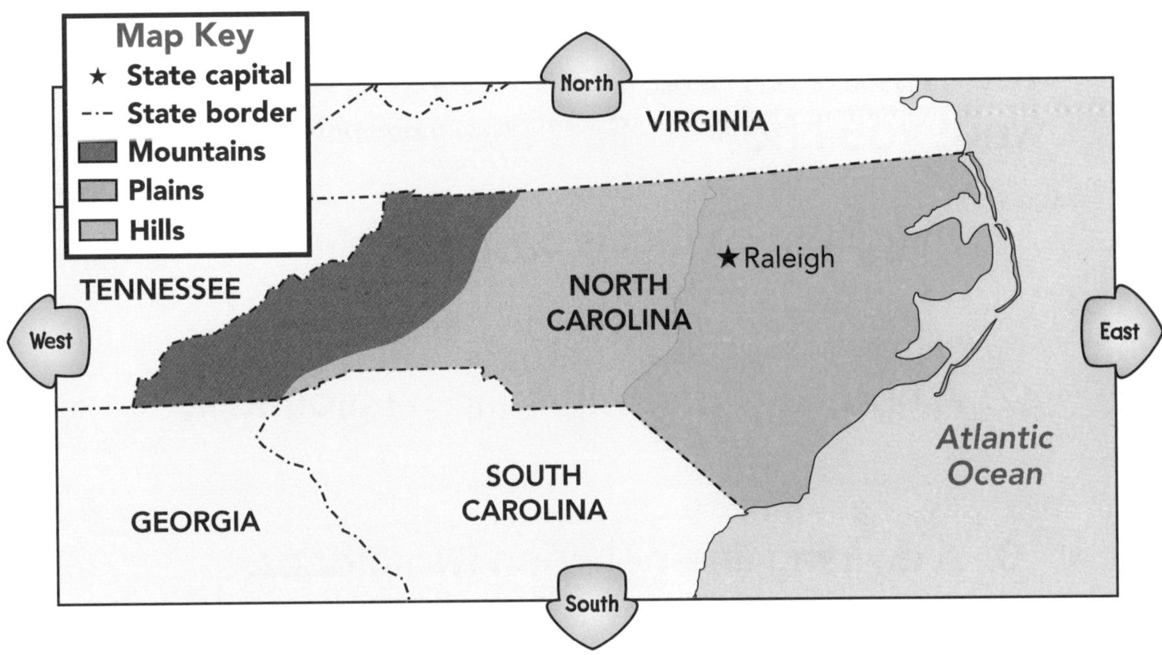

1. North Carolina is one of 50 ____________________.

2. The capital of North Carolina is ________________.

3. This symbol [ ] means ____________________.

4. North Carolina shares a border with ____________________ other states.

5. To the east of North Carolina is the ____________________.

6. Are the mountains in the east or west part of North Carolina? ____________________

Thinking About Maps

You have learned a lot about maps. Use what you know to find the secret words.

1. The direction that is opposite of north.

   ___ ___ ___ ___ ___
   (7 under the 1st letter, 4 under the 4th letter)

2. A body of water with land all around it.

   ___ ___ ___ ___
   (9 under the 2nd letter, 5 under the 4th letter)

3. A dividing line between two places.

   ___ ___ ___ ___ ___ ___
   (6 under the 4th letter)

4. A drawing that stands for something real.

   ___ ___ ___ ___ ___ ___
   (12 under the 1st letter)

5. Very high land.

   ___ ___ ___ ___ ___ ___ ___ ___
   (1 under the 3rd letter, 8 under the 5th letter, 3 under the 7th letter, 2 under the 8th letter)

6. A way to go from one place to another.

   ___ ___ ___ ___ ___
   (10 under the 4th letter, 11 under the 5th letter)

Now, can you figure out the secret words?

___	___	___	___	___	___		___	___	___	___	___	___
1	2	3	4	5	6		7	8	9	10	11	12

Glossary

border	A border is a dividing line between two places.
capital	A capital is a city where government leaders work.
continent	A continent is a large body of land. North America is a continent.
country	A country is a land and the people who live there.
direction	A direction tells where something is. The four main directions are north, south, east, and west.
east	East is one of the four main directions. East is the opposite of west.
Earth	Earth is the planet on which people live.
far	Far is a word that tells where things are. Far is the opposite of near.
globe	A globe is a model of Earth.
hill	A hill is land that is higher than a plain but not as high as a mountain.
lake	A lake is a body of water that has land all around it.
left	Left is a word that tells where things are. Left is the opposite of right.
map	A map is a drawing of a place from above. A map shows part or all of Earth.

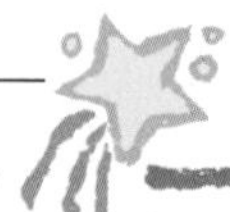

map key	A map key is a list of symbols used on a map. The map key tells what each symbol means.
mountain	A mountain is very high land.
near	Near is a word that tells where things are. Near is the opposite of far.
neighborhood	A neighborhood is a place where people live and work.
north	North is one of the four main directions. North is the direction toward the North Pole.
ocean	An ocean is a very large body of water. Earth has four oceans.
plain	A plain is flat land.
right	Right is a word that tells where things are. Right is the opposite of left.
river	A river is a body of water that flows across the land.
route	A route is a way to go from one place to another.
south	South is one of the four main directions. South is the direction toward the South Pole.
state	A state is part of the United States. There are 50 states.
symbol	A symbol is a drawing that stands for something real.
west	West is one of the four main directions. West is the opposite of east.

Scholastic Success With

ADDITION & SUBTRACTION

Clowning Around

Add. Color the picture using the color code.

Color Code

1	pink
2	white
3	black
4	brown
5	purple
6	green
7	blue
8	orange
9	yellow
10	red

2 + 3

3 + 3 | 1 + 0 | 4 + 2 | 0 + 1 | 5 + 1

4 + 1 =

6 + 2

3 + 5

2 + 1

3 + 0

7 + 0 =

5 + 5 =

6 + 1 =

1 + 1

7 + 3 =

3 + 1 =

Lovely Ladybugs

Write a number sentence to show how many spots each ladybug has.

Color the ladybug with the greatest number of spots red.
Color the ladybug with the least number of spots blue.

Beautiful Bouquets

Look at the number on each bow. Draw more flowers to match the number written on the bow.

7

10

4

6

9

5

8

3

Color the bows with an even number yellow.
Color the bows with an odd number purple.

Name ______________________________________

Telephone Math

What kind of phone never rings? ______________________

To find out, solve the addition problems. Then use the code on the telephone to replace your answers with letters. The first one has been done for you.

$$\begin{array}{r} 6 \\ +\,2 \\ \hline 8 \end{array}$$ A

$$\begin{array}{r} 5 \\ +\,1 \\ \hline \end{array}$$ ______

$$\begin{array}{r} 4 \\ +\,4 \\ \hline \end{array}$$ ______

$$\begin{array}{r} 3 \\ +\,6 \\ \hline \end{array}$$ ______

$$\begin{array}{r} 3 \\ +\,0 \\ \hline \end{array}$$ ______

$$\begin{array}{r} 3 \\ +\,4 \\ \hline \end{array}$$ ______

$$\begin{array}{r} 2 \\ +\,2 \\ \hline \end{array}$$ ______

$$\begin{array}{r} 2 \\ +\,1 \\ \hline \end{array}$$ ______

$$\begin{array}{r} 1 \\ +\,1 \\ \hline \end{array}$$ ______

$$\begin{array}{r} 0 \\ +\,1 \\ \hline \end{array}$$ ______

Write your telephone number in letters using the phone code above.

____

High Flyer

Do the subtraction problems.

If the answer is 1 or 2, color the shape red.
If the answer is 3 or 4, color the shape blue.
If the answer is 5 or 6, color the shape yellow.
If the answer is 7 or 8, color the shape green.
If the answer is 9, color the shape black.
Color the other shapes the colors of your choice.

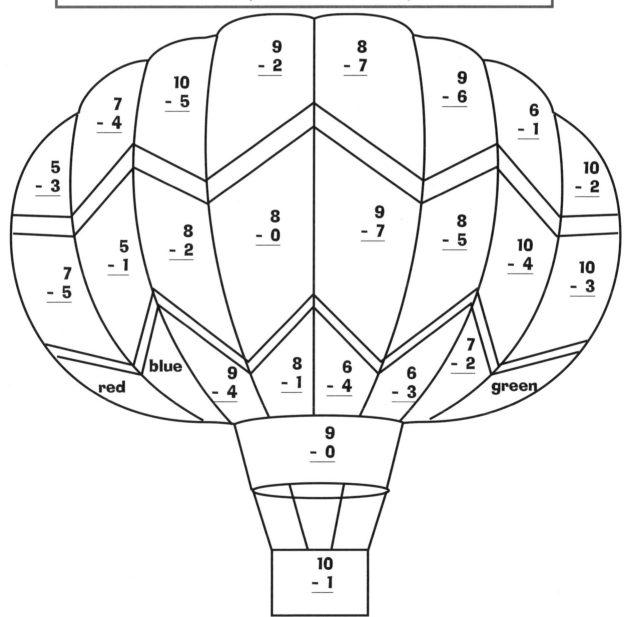

Name ____________________

Juggling Act

Cross out. Write how many are left.

$3 - 1 =$ 2

$4 - 2 =$ ____

$7 - 4 =$ ____

$9 - 6 =$ ____

$5 - 3 =$ ____

$6 - 5 =$ ____

Name ______________________________

Ocean Life

Use the math picture on page 309 to count and write the number in each box. Subtract the numbers.

1.  $\square$ − $\square$ = $\square$

2.  $\square$ − $\square$ = $\square$

3.  $\square$ − $\square$ = $\square$

4.  $\square$ − $\square$ = $\square$

5.  $\square$ − $\square$ = $\square$

6.  $\square$ − $\square$ = $\square$

7. 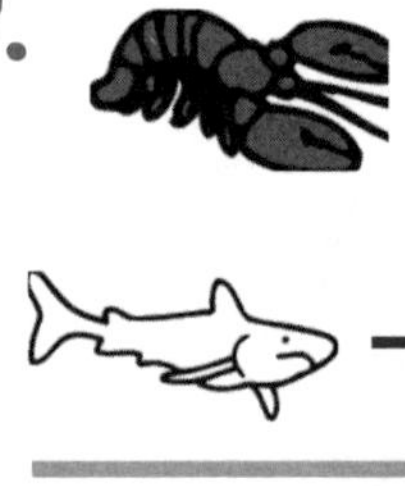 $\square$ − $\square$ = $\square$

8. 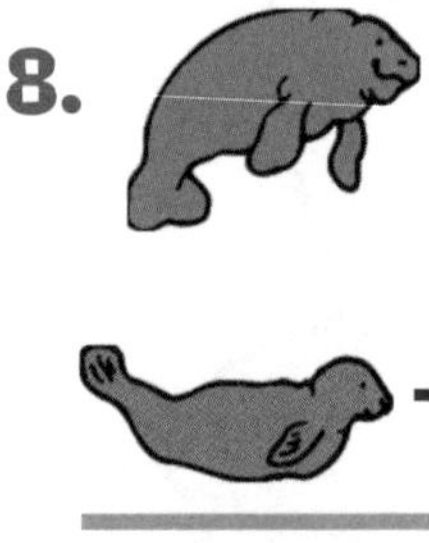 $\square$ − $\square$ = $\square$

9.  $\square$ − $\square$ = $\square$

Name ___________________________

Coloring Key

dark blue

pink

dark gray

light gray

light blue

dark brown

white

brown

peach

black

Trucking Along

Subtract. Color the picture using the color code.

Color Code

0	white
1	brown
2	black
3	green
4	purple
5	orange
6	yellow
7	blue
8	red

Night Lights

Subtract. Connect the dots from greatest to least.

10 – 3 = ☐

9 – 1 = ☐

8 – 2 = ☐

10 – 1 = ☐

9 – 4 = ☐

10 – 0 = ☐

7 – 3 = ☐

5 – 3 = ☐

6 – 5 = ☐

8 – 5 = ☐

Subtract. Connect the dots from least to greatest.

10 – 0 = ☐

9 – 8 = ☐

7 – 5 = ☐

10 – 1 = ☐

10 – 7 = ☐

10 – 2 = ☐

The top picture gives off its own light. Color this picture orange. The bottom picture reflects light from the sun. Color this picture yellow.

7 – 0 = ☐

6 – 2 = ☐

9 – 3 = ☐

9 – 4 = ☐

Name ______________________________

Hop to It: Add and Subtract

Add or subtract. Trace the number line with your finger to check your work.

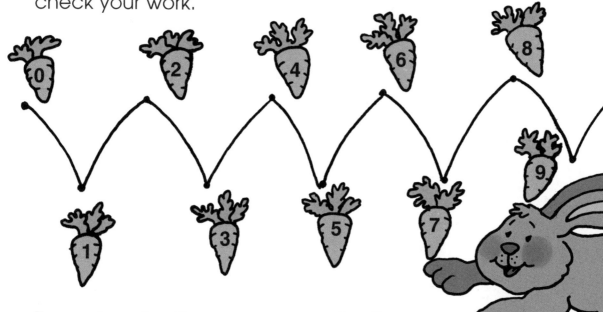

Examples: **4 + 5 =** _____ **4 – 2 =** _____

Start on **4**. Start on **4**.

Move **5**  right. Move **2** left.

7 – 3 = _____	**9 – 6 =** _____	**2 + 0 =** _____
5 + 5 = _____	**8 – 7 =** _____	**4 + 3 =** _____
10 – 4 = _____	**6 + 2 =** _____	**7 – 2 =** _____

Circle the answer to each question.

What direction did  **move to add? left or right**

What direction did move to subtract? left or right

Name ____________________

Mitten Matchup

Add or subtract. Draw a line to match mittens with the same answer.

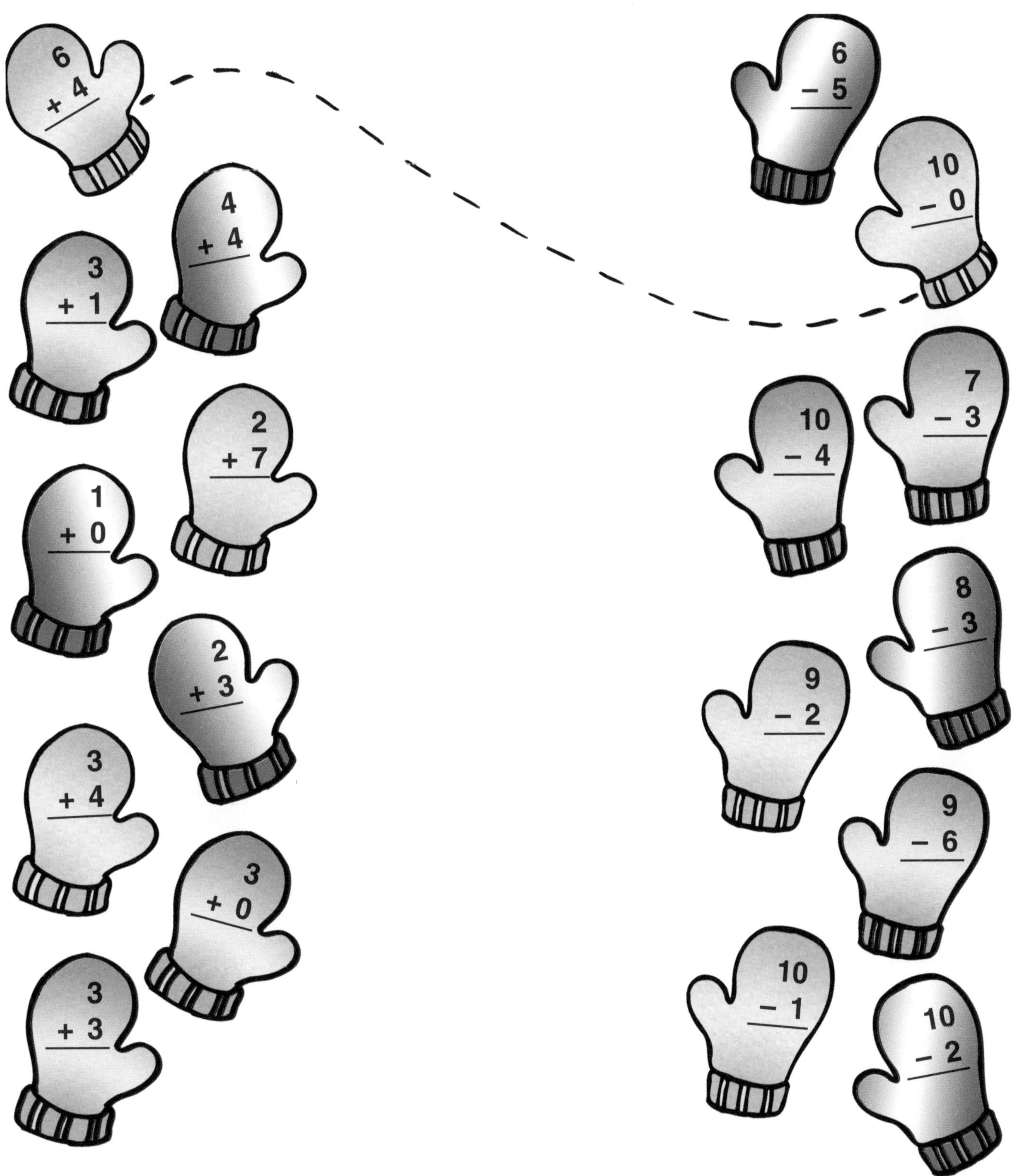

Blast Off

Add or subtract. Then use the code to answer the riddle below.

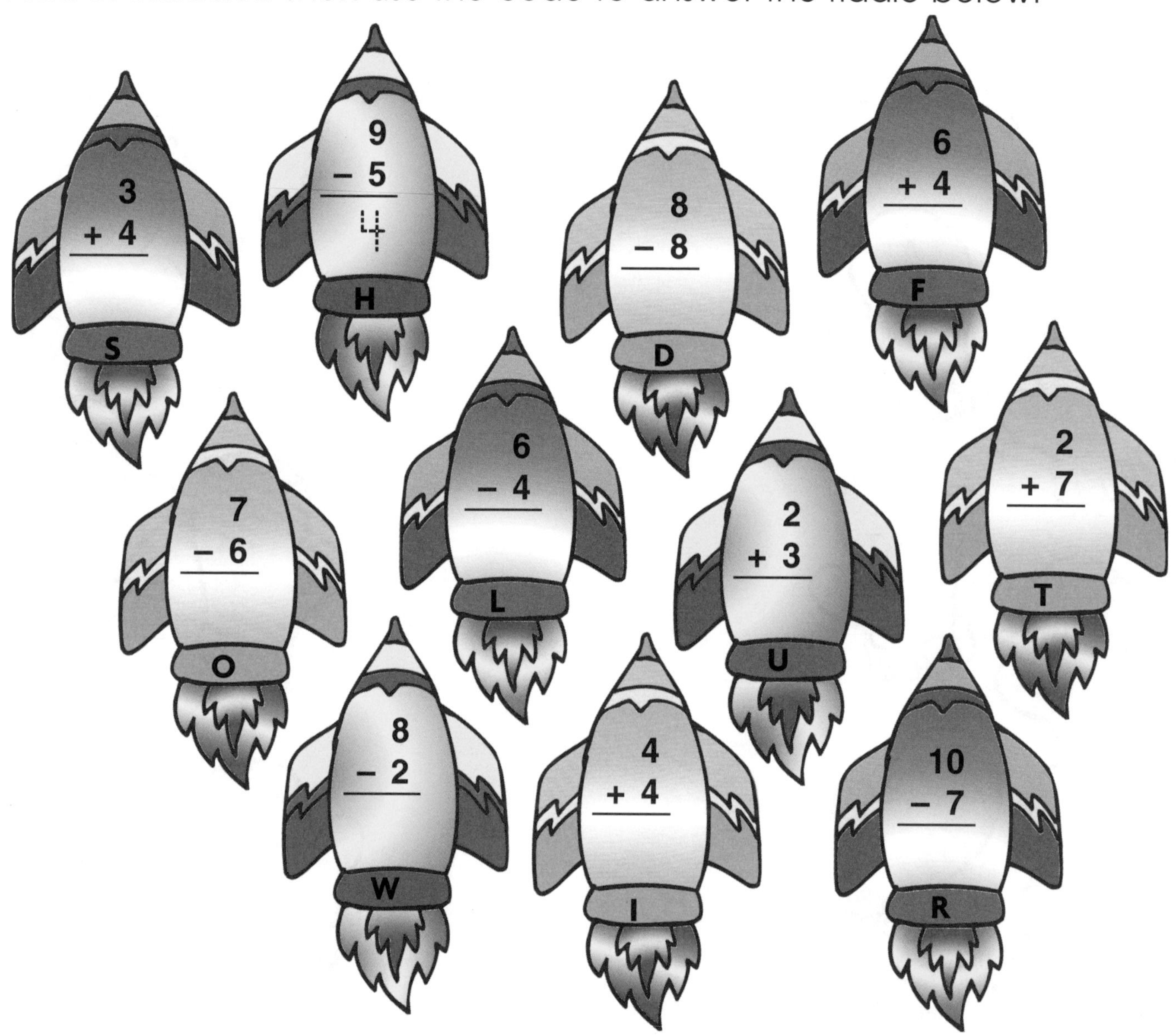

How is an astronaut's job unlike any other job?

___ ___' ___   ___ ___ ___   ___ ___
8 9 7   1 5 9   1 10

___ ___ ___ ___   ___ ___ ___ ___ ___!
9 4 8 7   6 1 3 2 0

Name ______________________________

Adding/subtracting through 10—bar graph

Out on the Town

Color a box on the graph for each item in the picture.

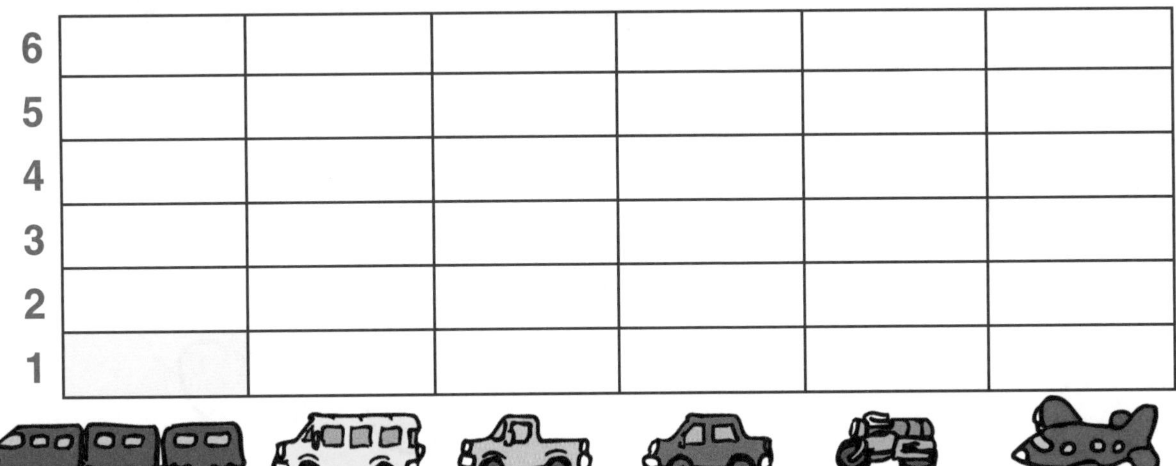

A. How many  and  altogether? 6 + 2 = 8

B. How many  and  in all? ____ + / − ____ = ____

C. How many more  than  ? ____ + / − ____ = ____

Name ____________________

Shapes on a Snake

Add or subtract.

A. 6 + 4 = 10

B. – = ____

C. – = ____

D. + = ____

E. + = ____

F. + = ____

G. + = ____

H. + = ____

I. – = ____

J. – = ____

Name ______________________

Planes . . . Trains . . .

Add or subtract.

A. There are **7** cars in the parking lot. Then **3** more cars park there, too. How many cars are there in all in the lot?

7 (+/−) 3 = 10 cars

B. There are **7** boxes on the truck. Then **4** boxes fall on the street. How many boxes are left on the truck?

____ +/− ____ = ____ boxes

C. There are **10** planes waiting on the runway. Then **6** planes take off. How many planes are left on the runway?

____ +/− ____ = ____ planes

D. There are **8** girls and **2** boys on the bus. How many more girls than boys are on the bus?

____ +/− ____ = ____ more girls

E. There are **5** people in the first car and **4** people in the second car. How many people in all?

____ +/− ____ = ____ people

Name ______________________________

Slice It Up

Add. Color the picture using the color code.

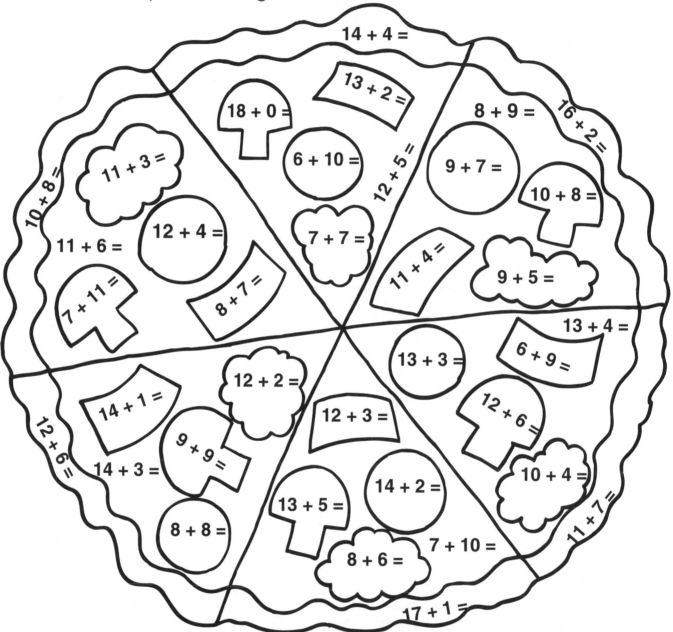

Color Code	brown	green	red	yellow	tan
	14	15	16	17	18

How many different ways can you make a sum of 10? Show your work on another piece of paper.

Leap on Over

Add. To show the frog's path across the pond, color each lily pad green if the sum is greater than 10.

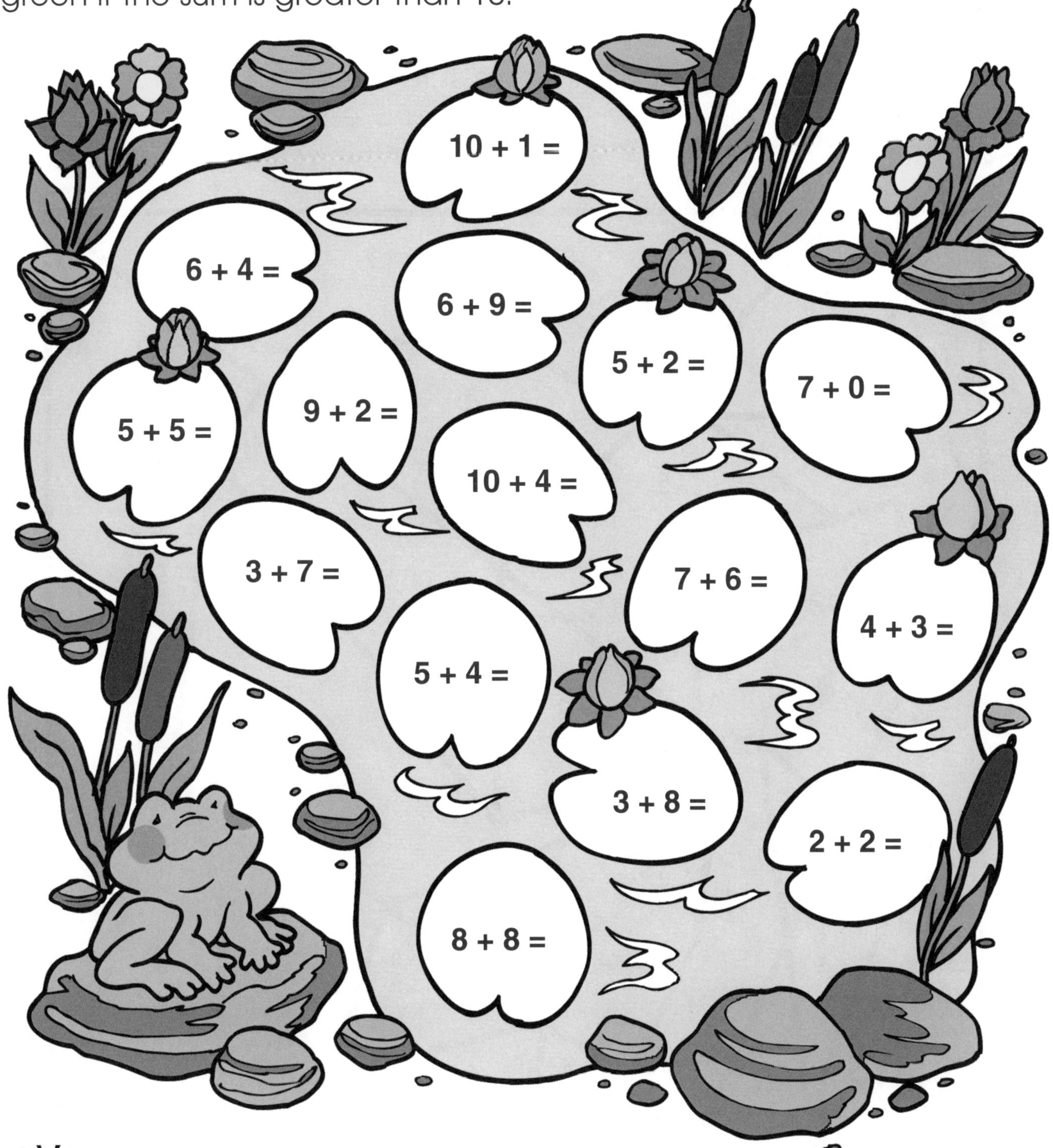

10 + 1 =

6 + 4 =

6 + 9 =

5 + 2 =

7 + 0 =

5 + 5 =

9 + 2 =

10 + 4 =

3 + 7 =

7 + 6 =

4 + 3 =

5 + 4 =

3 + 8 =

2 + 2 =

8 + 8 =

How many leaps did the frog take across the pond? ______

Name ______________________________  **Adding to 18**

Animal Mystery

What kind of animal always carries a trunk?

____

To find out, solve the addition problems. If the answer is greater than 9, color the shape yellow. If the answer is less than 10, color the shape gray.

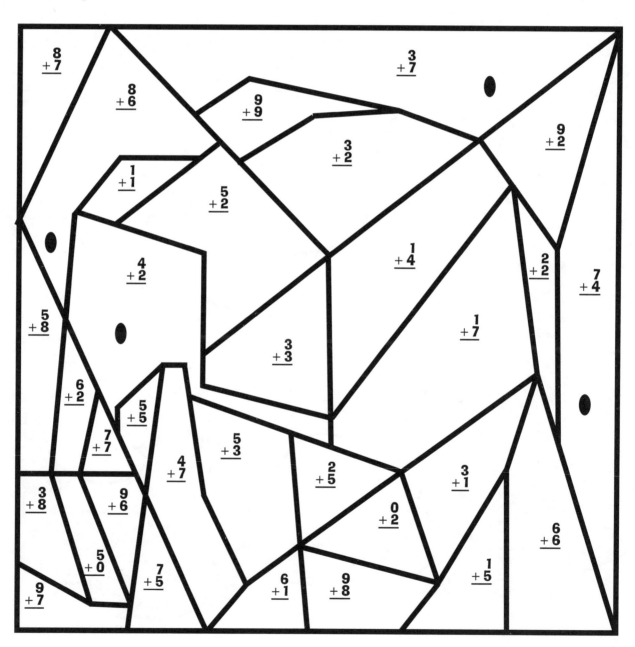

8 + 7

3 + 7

8 + 6

9 + 9

9 + 2

3 + 2

1 + 1

5 + 2

4 + 2

1 + 4

2 + 2

7 + 4

5 + 8

1 + 7

3 + 3

6 + 2

5 + 5

7 + 7

5 + 3

4 + 7

2 + 5

3 + 1

3 + 8

9 + 6

0 + 2

6 + 6

5 + 0

7 + 5

6 + 1

9 + 8

1 + 5

9 + 7

Name ____________________

Scarecrow Sam

Why doesn't Scarecrow Sam tell secrets when he is near Farmer Joe's bean patch? ____________________

To find out the answer, add the numbers. Circle the pumpkins that have sums of 14, and write the letters that appear inside those pumpkins in the boxes below.

1. $4 + 2$ **G**	2. $7 + 7$ **B**	3. $9 + 5$ **E**	
4. $10 + 4$ **A**	5. $4 + 8$ **R**	6. $6 + 8$ **N**	
7. $11 + 3$ **S**	8. $14 + 0$ **T**	9. $7 + 2$ **P**	10. $13 + 1$ **A**
11. $5 + 8$ **S**	12. $12 + 2$ **L**	13. $7 + 4$ **H**	14. $5 + 9$ **K**

Name ______________________________

Flying High

Add down and across to find the missing number.

A.

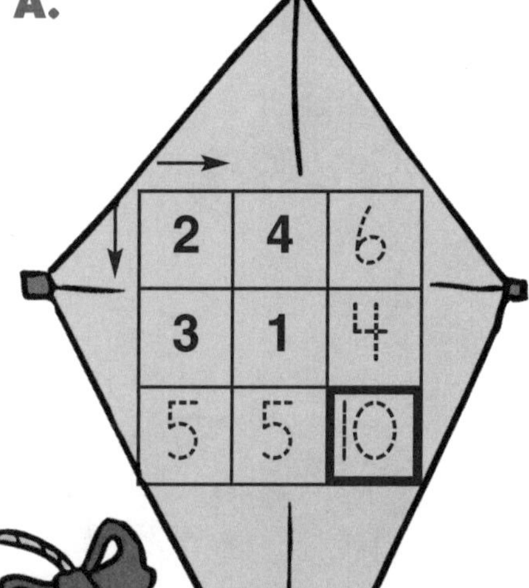

2	4	6
3	1	4
5	5	10

B.

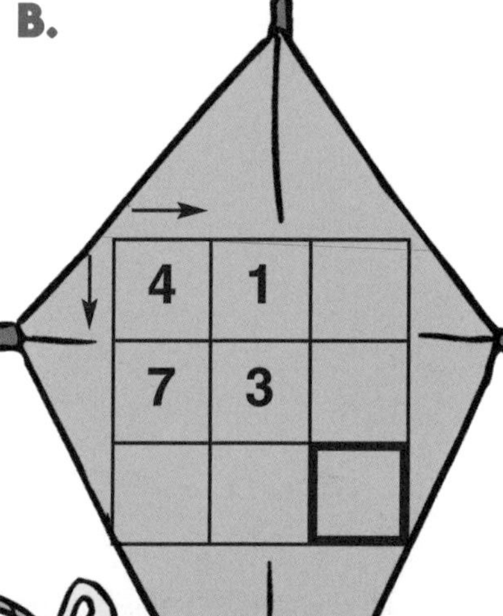

4	1	
7	3	

C.

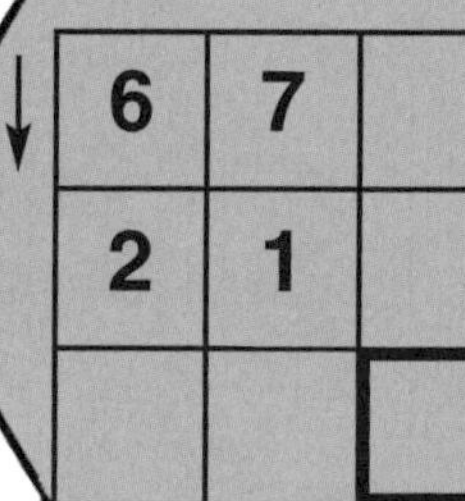

6	7	
2	1	

D.

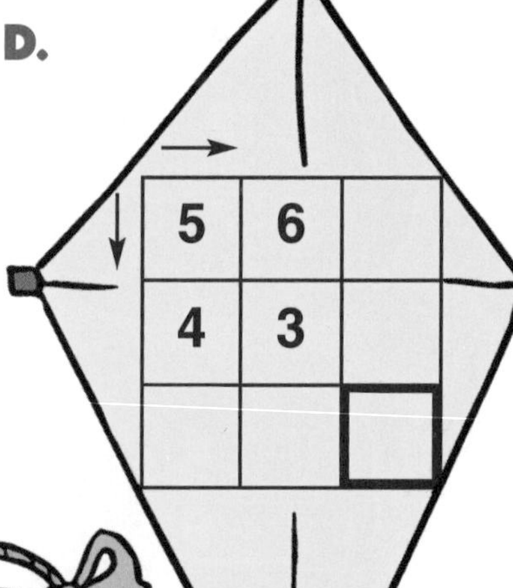

5	6	
4	3	

E.

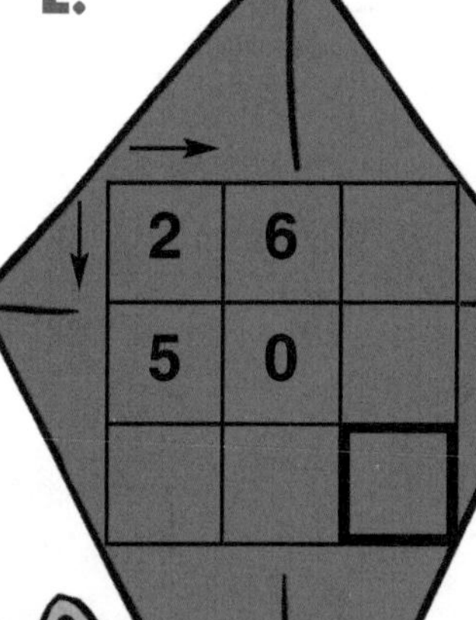

2	6	
5	0	

F.

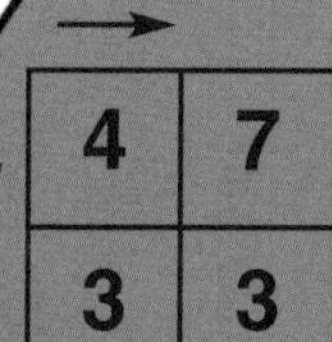
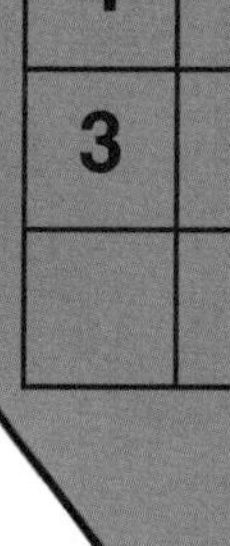

4	7	
3	3	

Double Dips

Write the doubles that equal the number on the cone.

Circle the answer.

When adding doubles, the sum will always be: even odd

Name ______________________

Not Far From Home

Start at [house] Write the number of steps. Add.

steps to + steps home = _____ steps

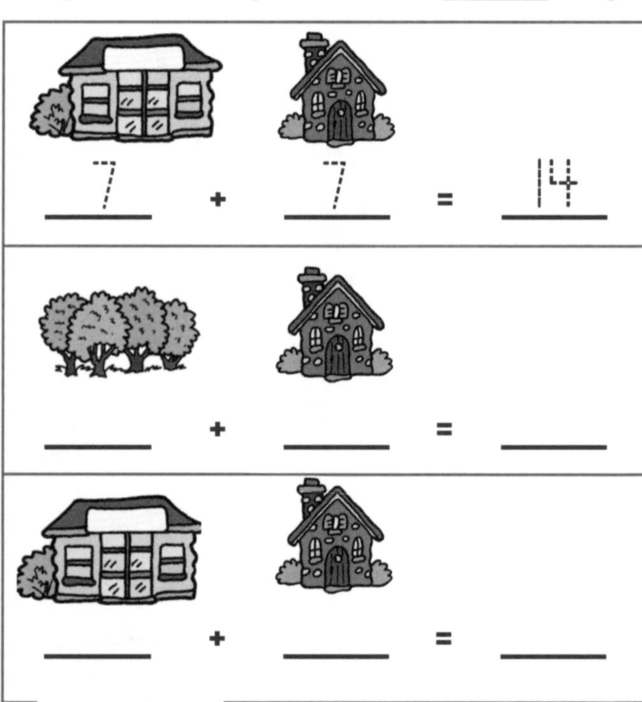

7 + 7 = 14

___ + ___ = ___

___ + ___ = ___

___ + ___ = ___

steps to + steps home = _____ steps

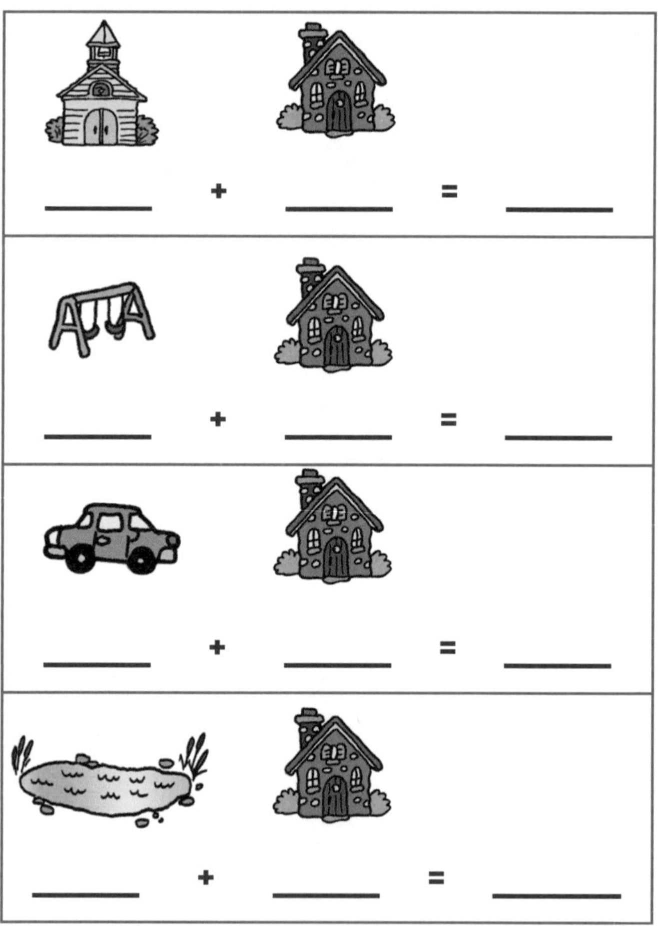

___ + ___ = ___

___ + ___ = ___

___ + ___ = ___

___ + ___ = ___

Break the Code

Subtract.

A. 6 − 2 =

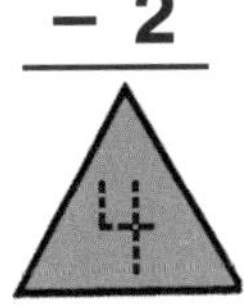

B. 13 − 7 =

C. 17 − 7 =

D. 18 − 9 =

E. 15 − 8 =

F. 11 − 9 =

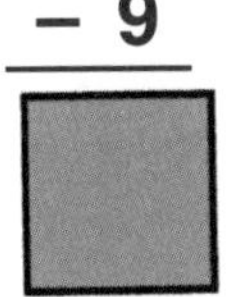

G. 9 − 4 =

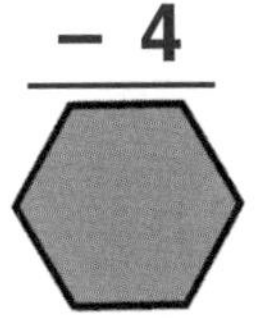

H. 14 − 6 =

I. 11 − 8 =

J. 7 − 6 =

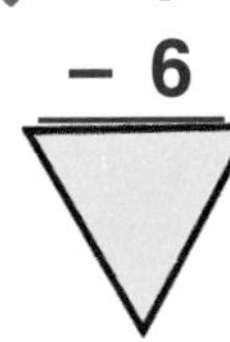

Use the answers above to solve each problem.

K.

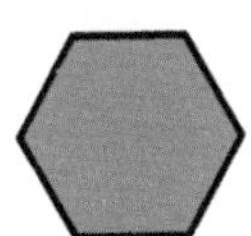

−

L.

−

M.

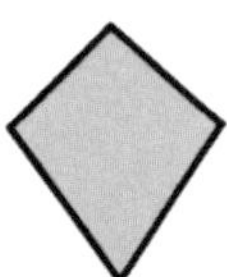

−

N.

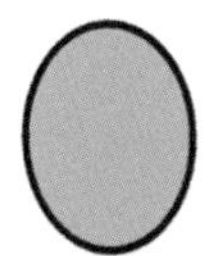

−

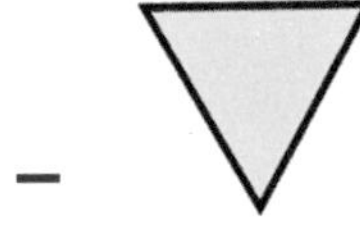

O.

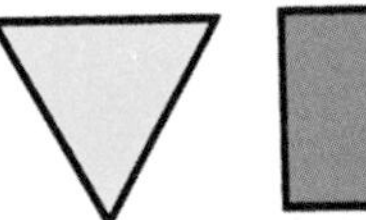

−

P.

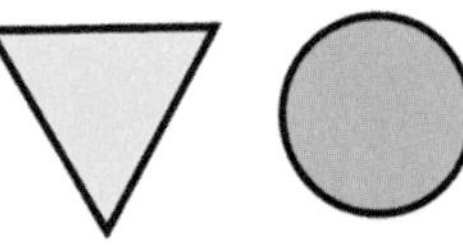

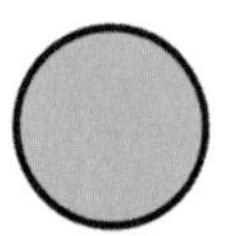

−

Q.

−

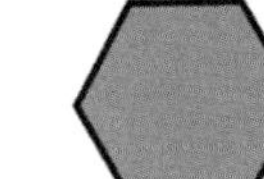

Name ______________________________________ 

The Big Search

Subtract. Circle the difference.

11 – 7 = five three four	**14 – 9 =** nine one five
13 – 6 = six nine seven	**16 – 5 =** twelve thirteen eleven
18 – 9 = eleven ten nine	**17 – 11 =** seven six ten
15 – 5 = ten seven five	**12 – 9 =** three two four
12 – 4 = six eight nine	**11 – 9 =** three five two

Find each circled number in the word puzzle. Look → and ↓.

f	o	u	r	h	i	o	n	e	g	s	k	m
i	f	o	n	t	g	y	f	a	f	u	e	z
f	t	l	u	e	j	s	i	x	s	b	x	t
t	t	w	e	l	v	e	v	k	s	t	l	h
e	p	n	i	n	e	w	e	j	e	r	t	i
e	d	n	g	q	i	h	r	y	v	a	q	r
n	v	h	h	o	t	h	r	e	e	c	s	t
d	m	k	t	c	w	b	t	e	n	t	r	e
x	d	i	p	g	o	a	c	p	f	i	s	e
c	e	l	e	v	e	n	a	b	z	o	v	n
b	w	u	d	i	f	f	e	r	e	n	c	e

See if you can find these number words: twelve, fifteen, thirteen, subtraction, difference.

Race Through the Facts

Add or subtract. The race car that ends with the highest number wins the race!

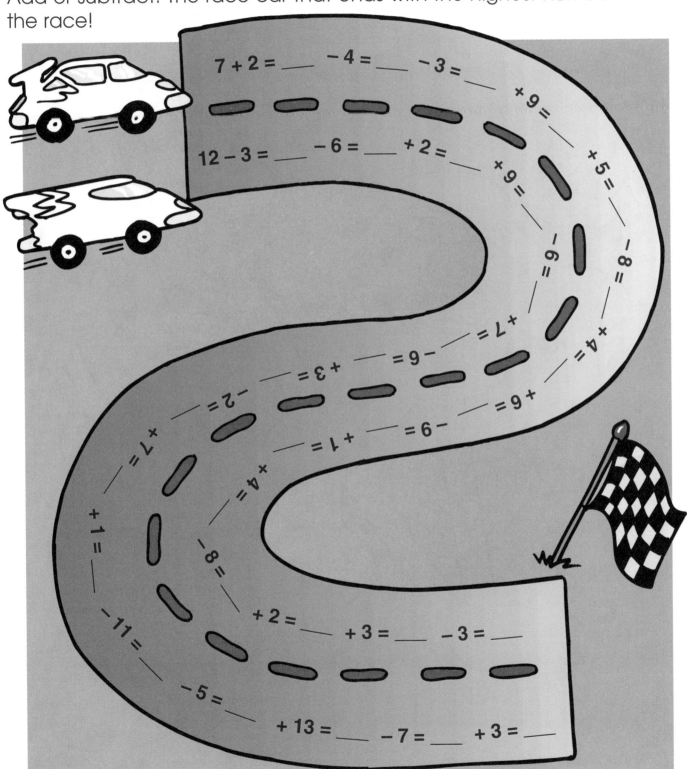

7 + 2 = ___ − 4 = ___ − 3 = ___ + 9 = ___ + 5 = ___ − 8 = ___ + 4 = ___ + 9 = ___ − 9 = ___ + 1 = ___ + 4 = ___ − 8 = ___ + 2 = ___ + 3 = ___ − 3 = ___

12 − 3 = ___ − 6 = ___ + 2 = ___ + 9 = ___ − 9 = ___ + 7 = ___ − 9 = ___ + 3 = ___ − 2 = ___ + 7 = ___ + 1 = ___ − 11 = ___ − 5 = ___ + 13 = ___ − 7 = ___ + 3 = ___

Color the winning race car blue.

Name ____________________

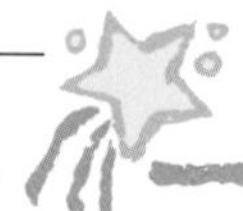

Little Snacks

Add or subtract. Then follow the maze through the even answers.

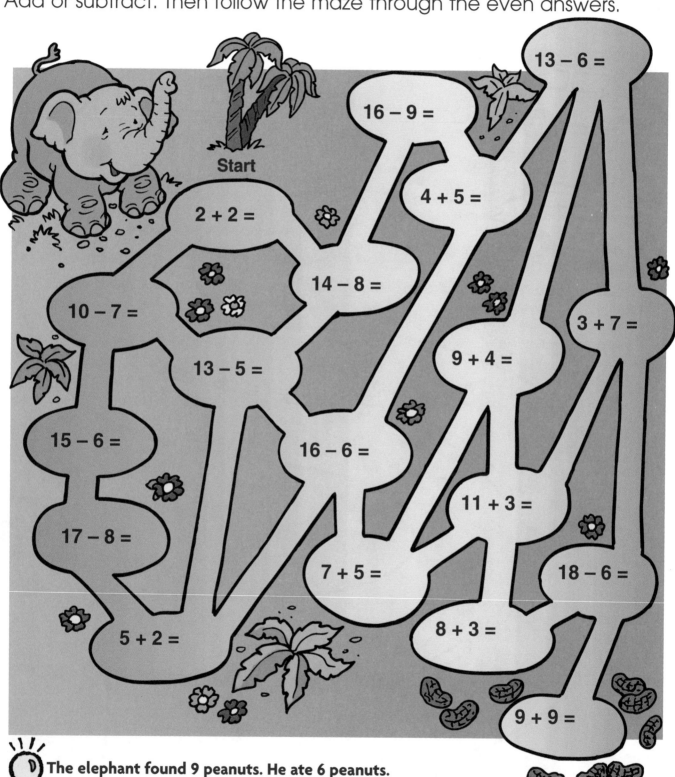

Start

2 + 2 =

14 − 8 =

10 − 7 =

13 − 5 =

15 − 6 =

16 − 6 =

17 − 8 =

5 + 2 =

16 − 9 =

4 + 5 =

9 + 4 =

11 + 3 =

7 + 5 =

8 + 3 =

13 − 6 =

3 + 7 =

18 − 6 =

9 + 9 =

The elephant found 9 peanuts. He ate 6 peanuts.
How many peanuts are left? ______

Name ______________________________

Flying Families

Fill in the missing number for each family. Use the numbers from the box.

9	12	15	8	10
6	4	7	5	11	2

Fill in the families with twins.

3 3
6

14

18

10

16

Name ______________________________

Colorful Flowers

Color a box on the graph for each item in the picture.

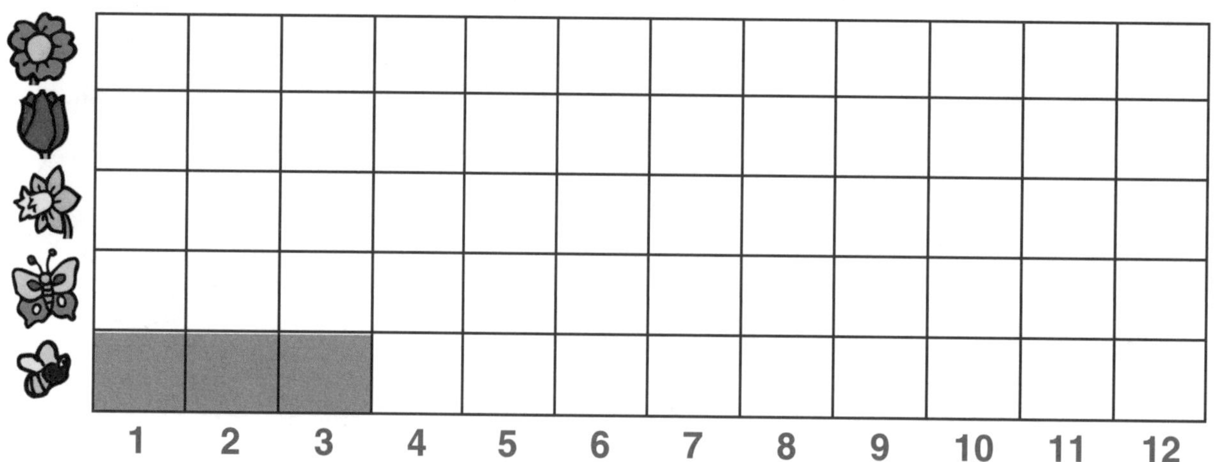

A. Which flower is found the most?  

B. How many  and altogether? ______ + ______ = ______

C. How many more  than  ? ______ - ______ = ______

D. How many insects in all? ______ + ______ = ______

E. How many more  than ? ______ - ______ = ______

F. How many  and  altogether? ______ + ______ = ______

Name ____________________

A Nutty Bunch

Add or subtract. Color the nut brown if the answer matches the squirrel.

Create a nutty bunch.

Name ____

Penguin Parade

Add or subtract. Write the pattern on the flag.

Flag						
−1	5 + 7	8 + 3	15 − 5	18 − 9	11 − 3	12 − 5
	9 − 7	12 − 8	5 + 1	16 − 8	13 − 3	7 + 5
	12 − 9	11 − 5	13 − 4	7 + 5	18 − 3	11 + 7
	15 − 2	4 + 7	12 − 3	12 − 5	8 − 3	12 − 9

Name ______________________________

A Perfect Strike

Fill in the missing number.

Find three different ways to make 8 with 3 numbers.

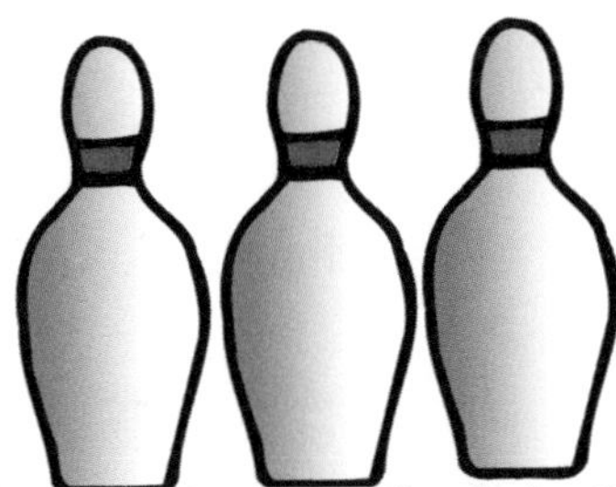

Name ______________________________

What a Treat!

Find the number in the mouse and cheese. ☐

Find the sum of the numbers in the cheese.

_____ + _____ + _____ = _____

Find the sum of the numbers in the mouse.

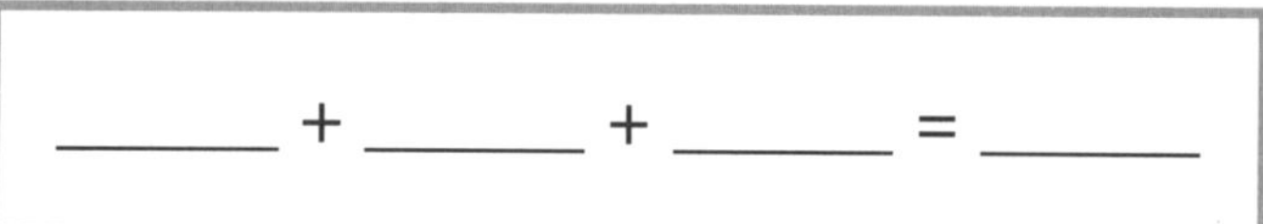

_____ + _____ + _____ = _____

Find the number in the rabbit and carrot. ☐

Find the sum of the largest number in the rabbit and the smallest number in the carrot.

_____ + _____ = _____

Find the difference between the largest and smallest number in the carrot.

_____ - _____ = _____

Find the sum of all the numbers in the mouse and cheese.

_____ + _____ + _____ + _____ + _____ = _____

Find the sum of all the numbers in the rabbit and carrot.

_____ + _____ + _____ + _____ + _____ = _____

Name ______________________________

Where's the Beach?

Add. To find the path to the beach, color each box with an odd answer yellow.

	14 + 3	34 + 2	81 + 3	
76 + 2	25 + 4	56 + 3	11 + 3	40 + 8
87 + 1	22 + 2	32 + 3	65 + 1	93 + 5
10 + 8	41 + 2	70 + 7	32 + 6	84 + 4
73 + 5	63 + 2	55 + 1	41 + 5	23 + 3
	98 + 1	53 + 4	82 + 5	

Name ______________________________

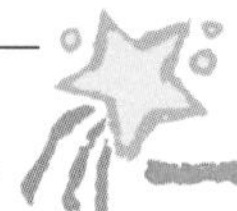

By the Seashore

Use the code below to write each missing number. Add.

93	82	14	21	53
+ 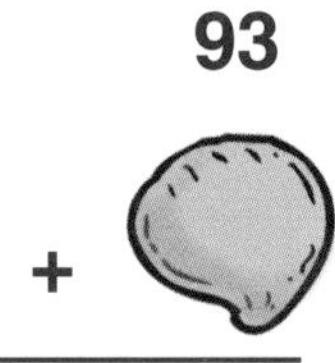	+	+ 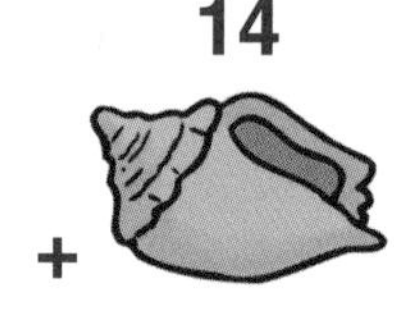	+ 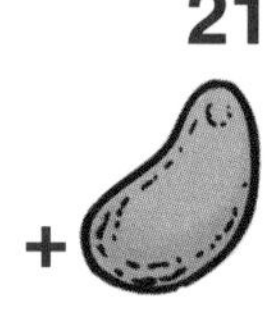	+

45	73	36	61	32
+	+ 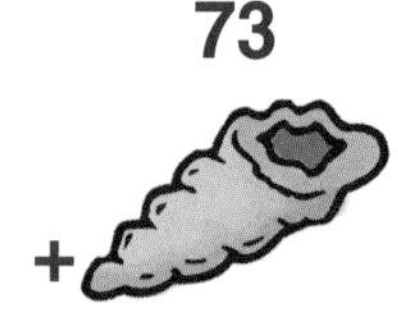	+ 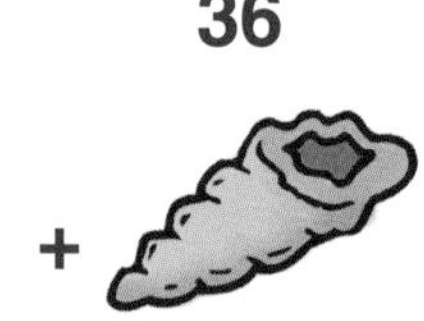	+ 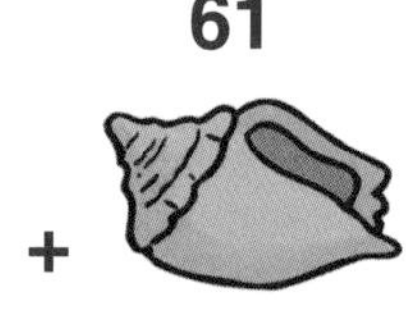	+

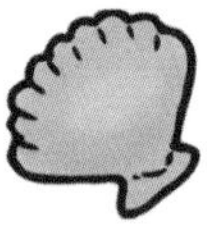

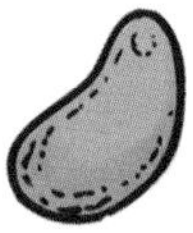

Find the sum for all the shells. _____ + _____ + _____ + _____ + _____ = _____

Name ______________________________

Sail Away

Finish each addition sentence. Add.

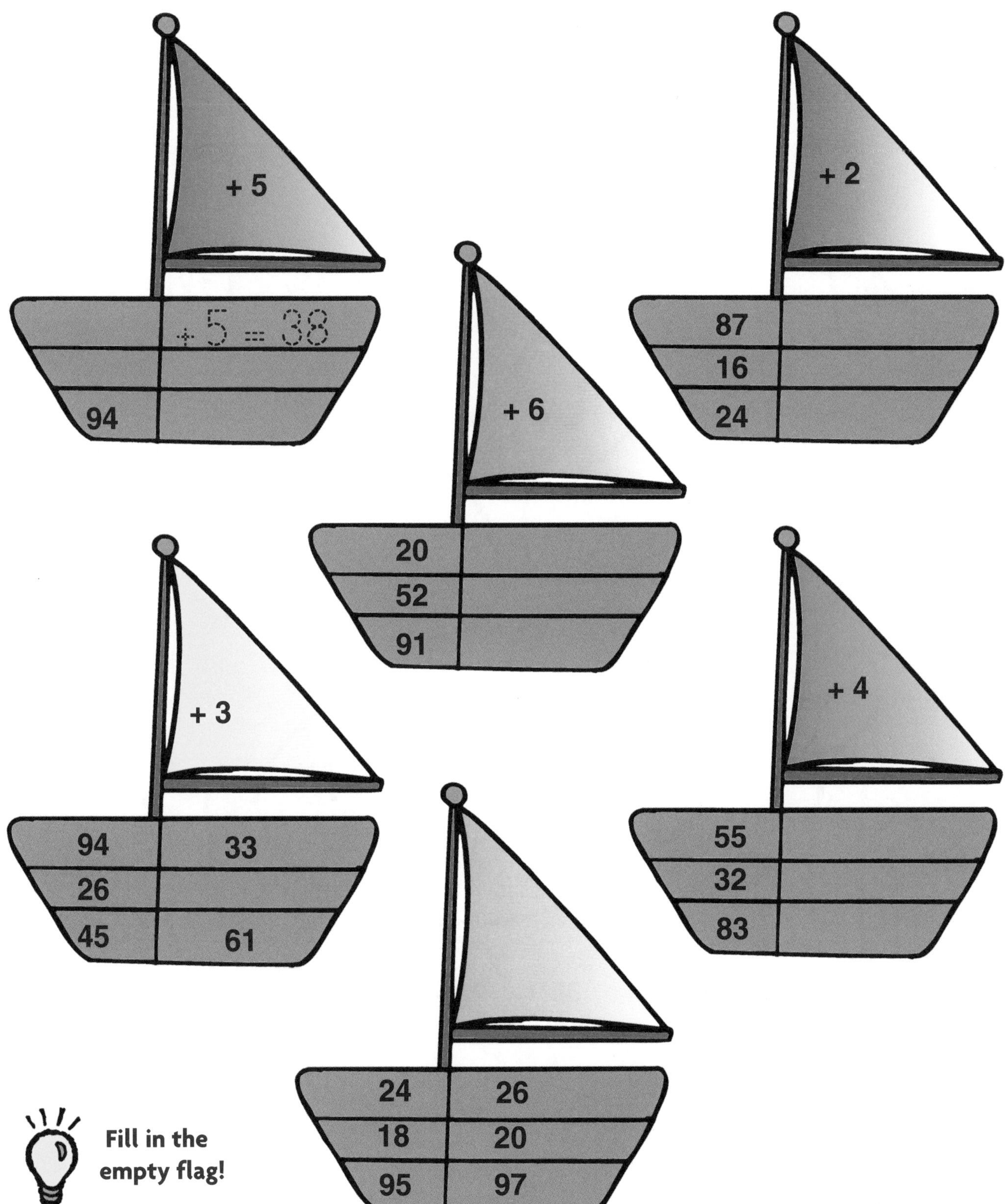

Fill in the empty flag!

Name ___________________________

Dino-Math

Subtract. Color the picture using the color code.

Color Code

16	red
22	orange
34	purple
57	blue
73	yellow
85	green

Name ______________________________

Number Buddies

Subtract. Remember: the largest number always goes on top!

Fill in each missing number.

39

35

27

20

88

83

Name ______________________________________

Treasure Island

Subtract.

43 − 1	95 − 5	79 − 3	36 − 4	89 − 7	66 − 3	83 − 2
59 − 9	37 − 2	24 − 3	27 − 6	42 − 1	90 − 0	55 − 2
33 − 3	84 − 4	28 − 8	71 − 1	62 − 2	68 − 3	77 − 3

Use the clues to find the gold, the ship, and the treasure in the boxes above.

The difference is greater than **50** and less than **55**. Color the box with the gold yellow.

The difference is greater than **30** and less than **35**. Color the box with the ship orange.

The difference is greater than **70** and less than **75**. Color the box with the treasure red.

Riding on Air

Add. Color the picture using the color code.

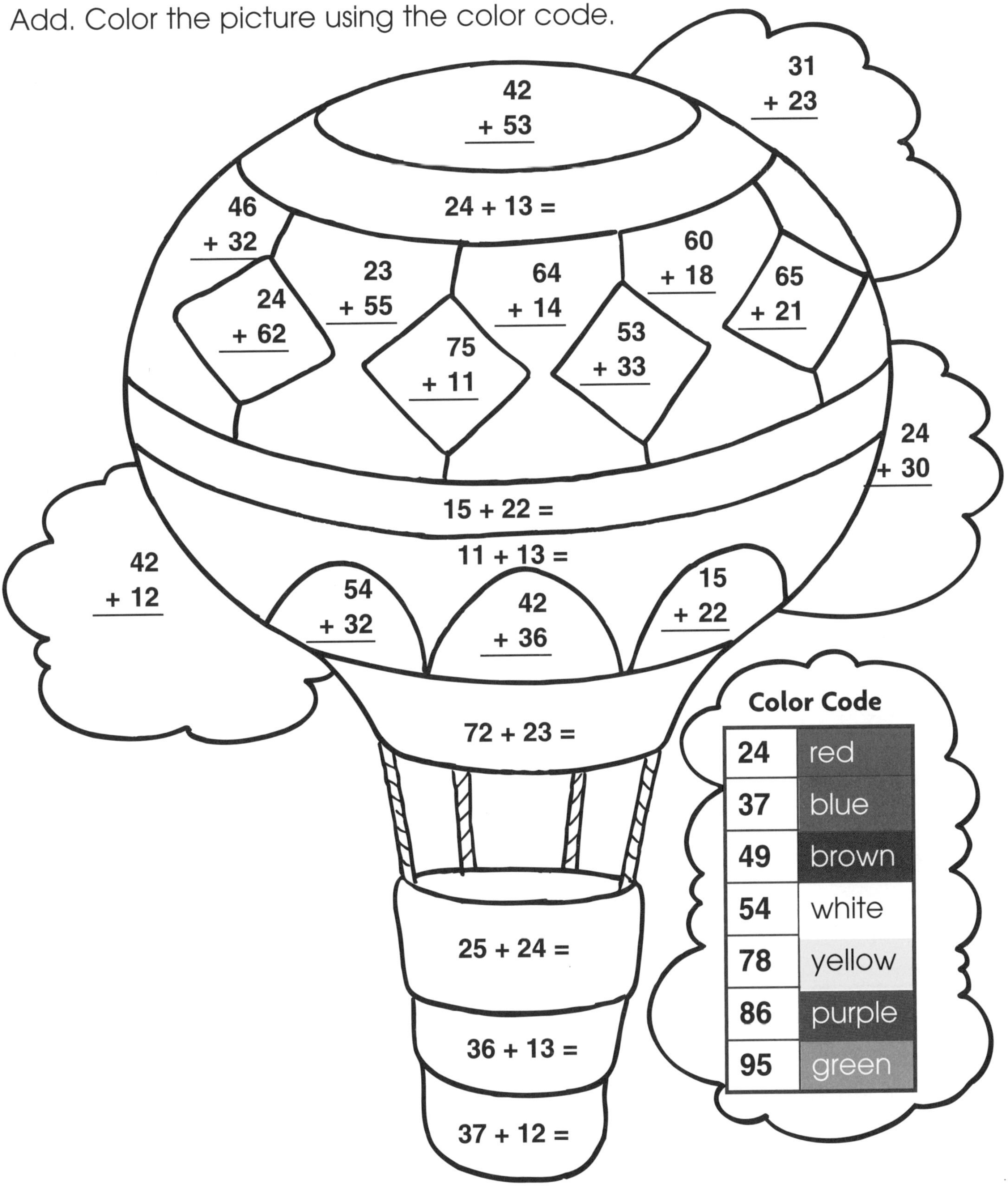

Color Code

24	red
37	blue
49	brown
54	white
78	yellow
86	purple
95	green

Name ________________________________

Number Puzzler

Can you spell 80 in two letters?

To find out how, do the addition problems. If the answer is even, shade the square. If your answers are correct, the shaded squares will spell the answer.

<table>
<tr><td>12
+ 13</td><td>24
+ 34</td><td>22
+ 21</td><td>77
+ 22</td><td>35
+ 43</td><td>52
+ 12</td><td>40
+ 52</td></tr>
<tr><td>11
+ 31</td><td>30
+ 39</td><td>46
+ 52</td><td>15
+ 12</td><td>10
+ 71</td><td>63
+ 11</td><td>13
+ 80</td></tr>
<tr><td>36
+ 32</td><td>30
+ 10</td><td>11
+ 11</td><td>15
+ 4</td><td>20
+ 21</td><td>15
+ 11</td><td>22
+ 33</td></tr>
<tr><td>14
+ 14</td><td>13
+ 16</td><td>10
+ 20</td><td>14
+ 25</td><td>11
+ 20</td><td>15
+ 21</td><td>20
+ 31</td></tr>
<tr><td>36
+ 52</td><td>21
+ 32</td><td>10
+ 50</td><td>44
+ 41</td><td>24
+ 43</td><td>31
+ 21</td><td>13
+ 82</td></tr>
</table>

Color the Sunflower

Do the addition problems in the sunflower picture below. Then use the Color Key to tell you what color to make each answer.

Extra: Write your age on four flashcards, and then add a 6, 7, 8, and 9 to each of the cards. Practice the answers with a friend.

Color Key

56 = green

68 = orange

89 = yellow

97 = blue

32 + 24

16 + 40

77 + 12

54 + 14

34 + 34

53 + 36

26 + 63

23 + 45

35 + 62

38 + 30

22 + 67

47 + 42

51 + 17

46 + 22

71 + 18

33 + 23

44 + 12

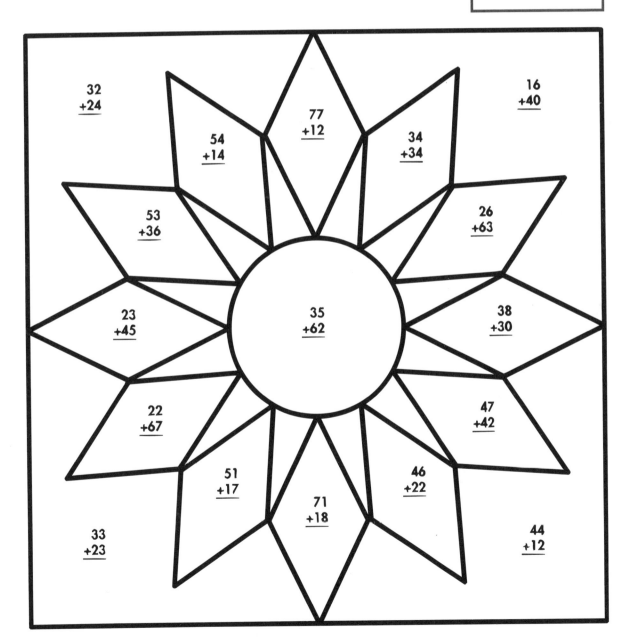

Roger the Rooster

Why did Roger the Rooster decide not to get in a barnyard fight?

____

To find out, add the numbers and shade the blocks as described below.

Shade the squares in row 1 that contain answers less than 25.
Shade the squares in row 2 that contain odd-numbered answers.
Shade the squares in row 3 that contain answers greater than 35.
Shade the squares in row 4 that contain even-numbered answers.
Shade the squares in row 5 that contain answers that end in zero.

13 + 11 H	26 + 33 Y	16 + 31 O	10 + 12 E	64 + 24 U
20 + 15 W	71 + 12 A	25 + 21 W	51 + 10 S	22 + 16 O
22 + 10 L	14 + 14 C	20 + 10 E	25 + 31 A	21 + 3 L
42 + 30 C	13 + 43 H	54 + 15 F	21 + 61 I	61 + 33 C
10 + 30 K	20 + 30 E	16 + 32 J	71 + 23 S	70 + 20 N

Name ________________________________

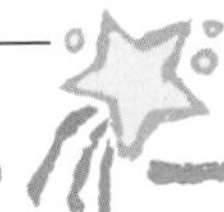

Baseball Puzzle

What animal can always be found at a baseball game?

____

To find out, do the subtraction problems. If the answer is greater than 9, color the shapes black. If the answer is less than 10, color the shapes red.

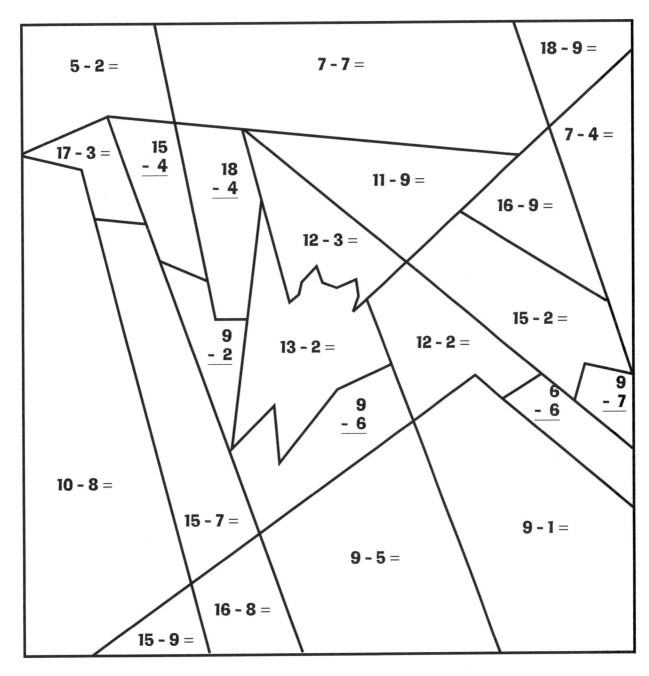

5 - 2 =

7 - 7 =

18 - 9 =

17 - 3 =

15 - 4 =

18 - 4 =

11 - 9 =

7 - 4 =

16 - 9 =

12 - 3 =

15 - 2 =

9 - 2 =

13 - 2 =

12 - 2 =

9 - 6 =

6 - 6 =

9 - 7 =

10 - 8 =

15 - 7 =

9 - 1 =

9 - 5 =

16 - 8 =

15 - 9 =

Name ______________________________

Color the Bowtie

Do the subtraction problems in the picture below. Then use the Color Key to tell you what color to make each answer.

Extra: On the back of this sheet of paper, draw a picture of four of your friends or family members. Give each one a bowtie!

Color Key
14 = red
26 = purple
33 = blue
47 = yellow
63 = green

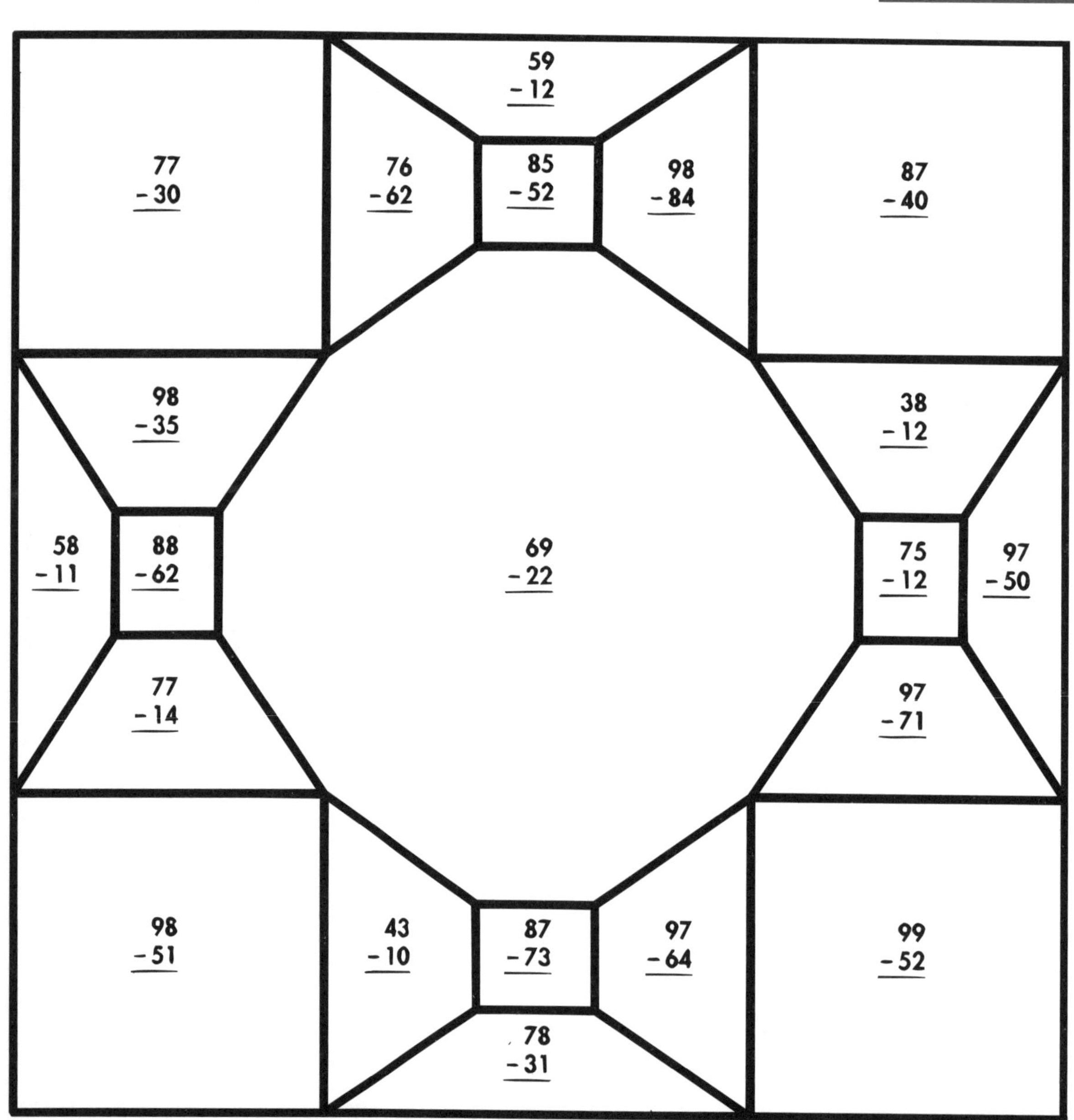

Name ____ 

Detective Work

Use the code to help Detective Dave discover the secret phone number. The first problem has been done for you.

1	2	3
4	5	6
7	8	9

1. 7 − 1 = 6

2. − = ____

3. − = ____

4. 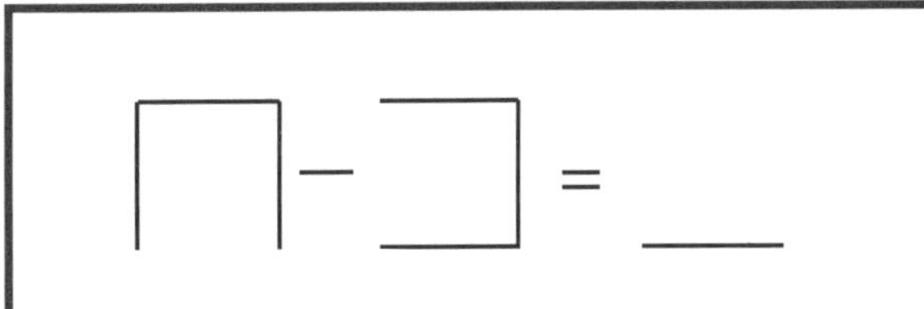
− = ____

5. − = ____

6. 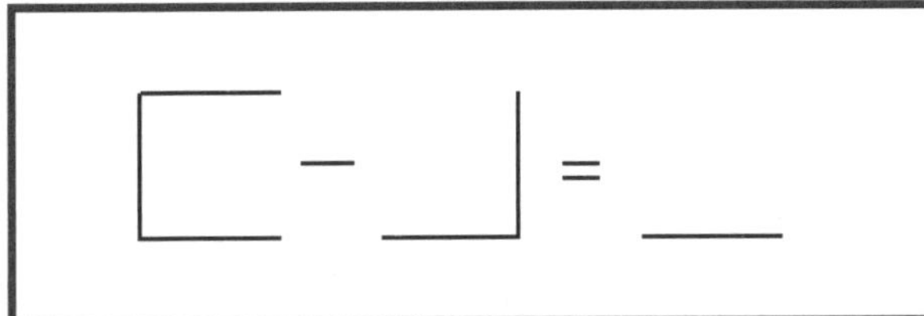
− = ____

7. − = ____

The phone number is:

___ ___ ___ - ___ ___ ___ ___

Name ______________________________

Have a Ball

Subtract.

$$\begin{array}{r} 39 \\ -\ 12 \\ \hline \end{array} \quad \begin{array}{r} 97 \\ -\ 23 \\ \hline \end{array} \quad \begin{array}{r} 59 \\ -\ 18 \\ \hline \end{array} \quad \begin{array}{r} 77 \\ -\ 12 \\ \hline \end{array}$$

$$\begin{array}{r} 79 \\ -\ 52 \\ \hline \end{array} \quad \begin{array}{r} 81 \\ -\ 11 \\ \hline \end{array} \quad \begin{array}{r} 88 \\ -\ 46 \\ \hline \end{array} \quad \begin{array}{r} 63 \\ -\ 10 \\ \hline \end{array}$$

$$\begin{array}{r} 58 \\ -\ 43 \\ \hline \end{array} \quad \begin{array}{r} 46 \\ -\ 23 \\ \hline \end{array} \quad \begin{array}{r} 35 \\ -\ 24 \\ \hline \end{array} \quad \begin{array}{r} 68 \\ -\ 35 \\ \hline \end{array}$$

$$\begin{array}{r} 32 \\ -\ 12 \\ \hline \end{array} \quad \begin{array}{r} 74 \\ -\ 72 \\ \hline \end{array} \quad \begin{array}{r} 69 \\ -\ 54 \\ \hline \end{array} \quad \begin{array}{r} 83 \\ -\ 52 \\ \hline \end{array}$$

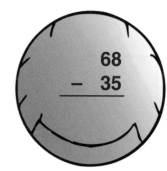

The Rams scored 49 points in the football game. The Bears scored 27 points. How many more points did the Rams score than the Bears? ______

Opposites Attract

Add or subtract. Connect the magnets that have the same answer.

$$\begin{array}{r} 42 \\ +\ 33 \\ \hline \end{array}$$

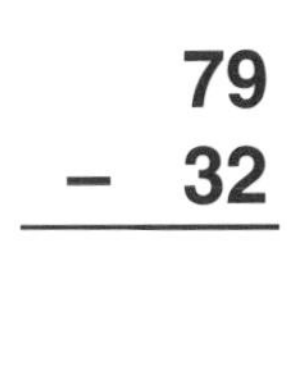

$$\begin{array}{r} 79 \\ -\ 32 \\ \hline \end{array}$$

$$\begin{array}{r} 32 \\ +\ 54 \\ \hline \end{array}$$

$$\begin{array}{r} 99 \\ -\ 24 \\ \hline \end{array}$$

$$\begin{array}{r} 35 \\ +\ 12 \\ \hline \end{array}$$

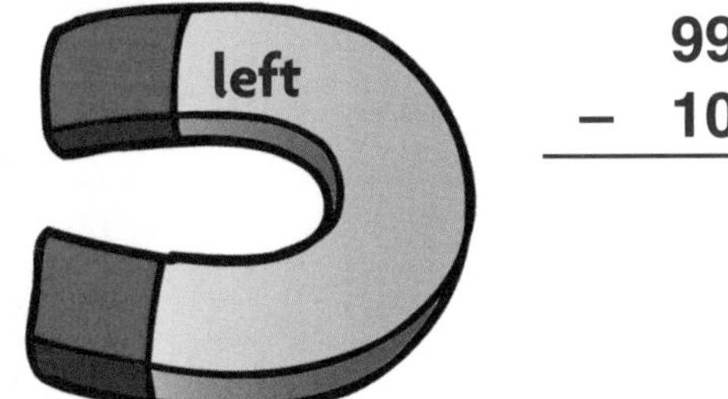

$$\begin{array}{r} 99 \\ -\ 10 \\ \hline \end{array}$$

$$\begin{array}{r} 13 \\ +\ 10 \\ \hline \end{array}$$

$$\begin{array}{r} 98 \\ -\ 12 \\ \hline \end{array}$$

$$\begin{array}{r} 37 \\ +\ 52 \\ \hline \end{array}$$

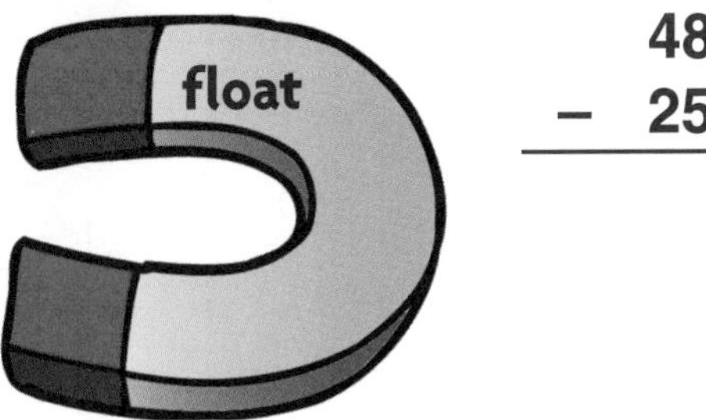

$$\begin{array}{r} 48 \\ -\ 25 \\ \hline \end{array}$$

On another piece of paper, write an addition and subtraction problem which have the same answer.

Name ___________________________

How Much Money?

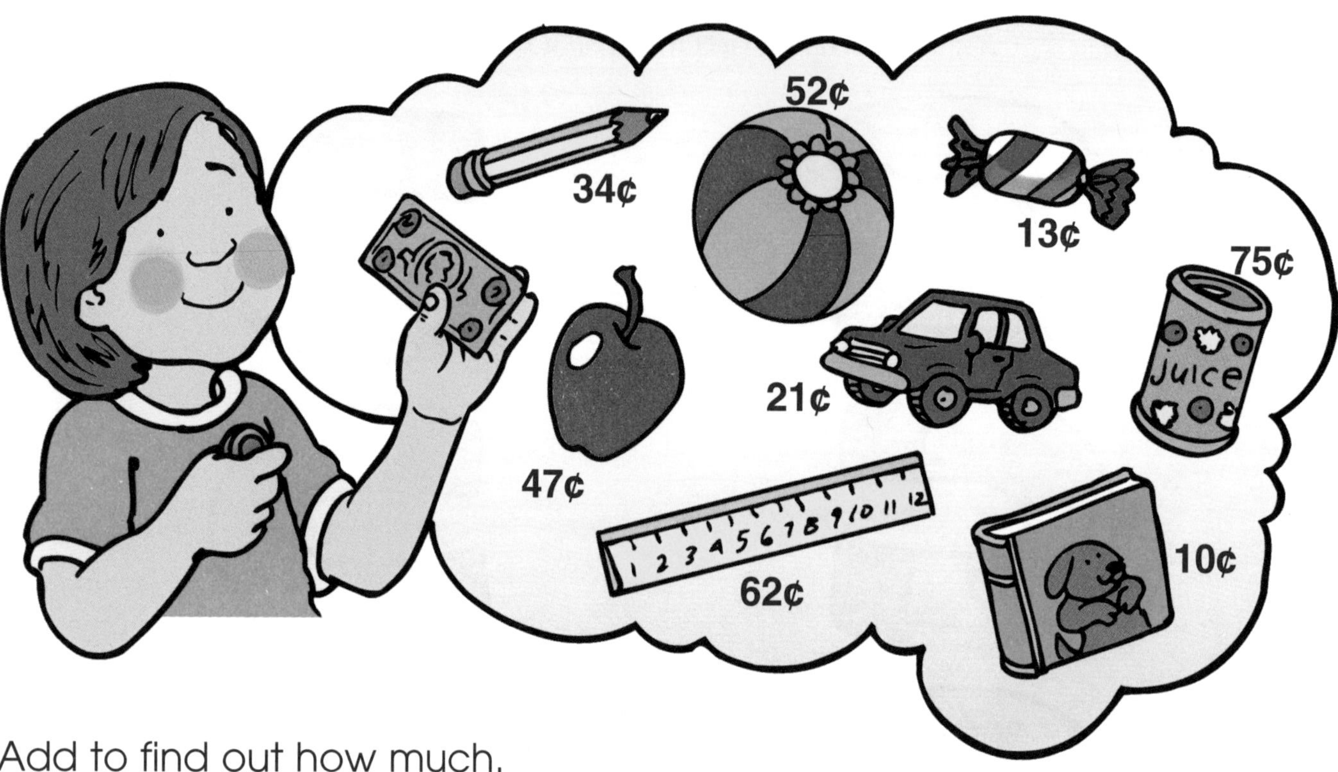

Add to find out how much.

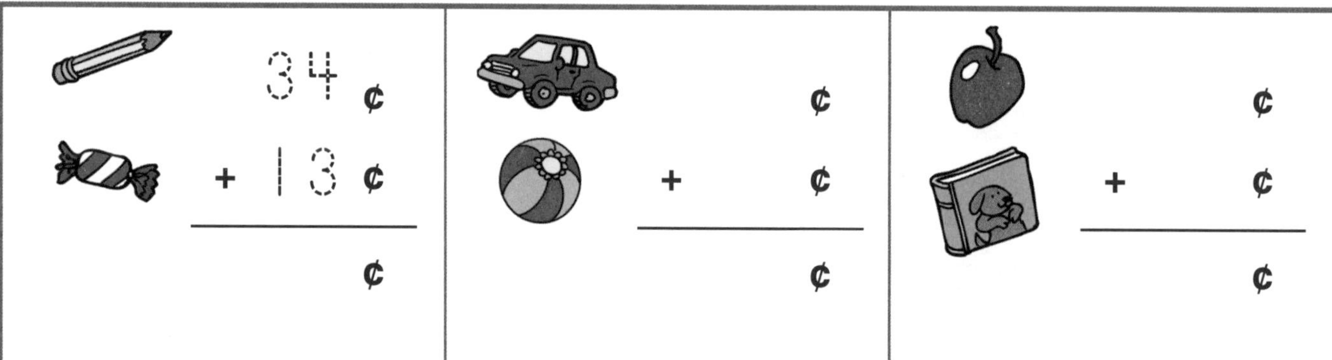

Subtract to find out how much.

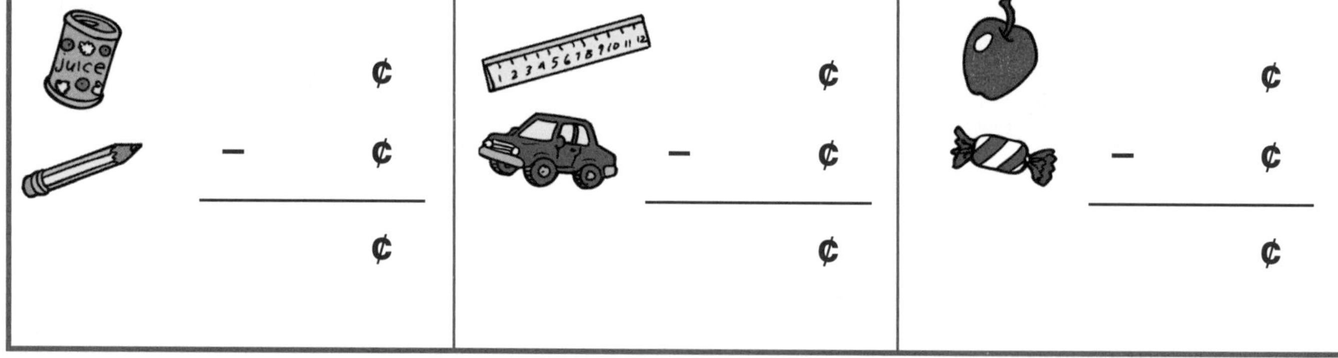

Name ______________________________

Snuggle Up With a Book

Day of the Week	Reading Minutes
Sunday	97
Monday	28
Tuesday	73
Wednesday	44
Thursday	51
Friday	45
Saturday	80

Use the chart to answer the questions.

A. What day did Alex read for the longest time?

____

B. How many minutes did Alex read on Wednesday and Friday? ______ minutes

C. What day did Alex read for the shortest time?

____

D. How many more minutes did Alex read on Sunday than Tuesday? ______ minutes

E. How many minutes did Alex read on Monday and Thursday? ______ minutes

F. How many more minutes did Alex read on Tuesday than Thursday? ______ minutes

One hour is 60 minutes. On what days did Alex read longer than one hour?

__________________, __________________, __________________

Name ____________________

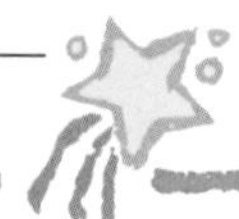

Let the Sun Shine

Add or subtract. Then use the code to fill in the letters to finish each sun fact.

13	26	34	42	57	63	71	76	85	88
f	a	s	g	r	e	l	h	t	i

$13 + 21 =$ ___ $32 + 53 =$ ___ $57 - 31 =$ ___ $89 - 32 =$ ___

The sun is a ___ ___ ___ ___.

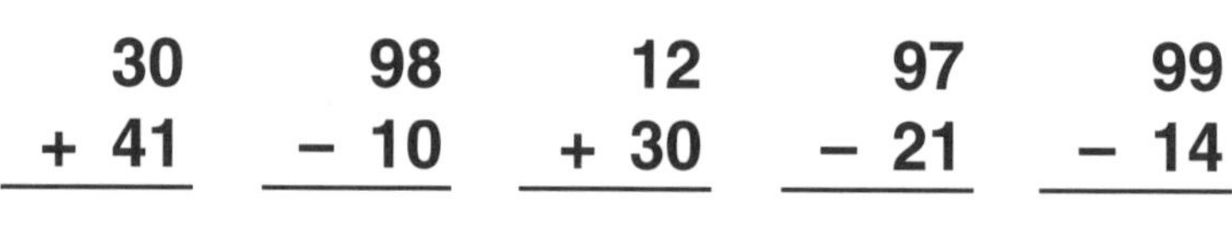

$30 + 41 =$ ___ $98 - 10 =$ ___ $12 + 30 =$ ___ $97 - 21 =$ ___ $99 - 14 =$ ___

The sun gives ___ ___ ___ ___ ___ and

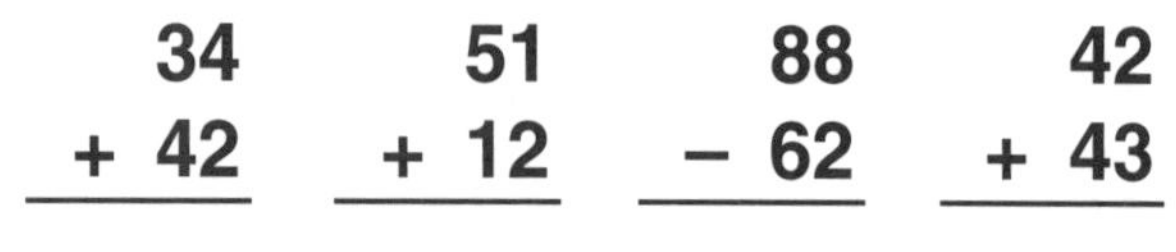

$34 + 42 =$ ___ $51 + 12 =$ ___ $88 - 62 =$ ___ $42 + 43 =$ ___

___ ___ ___ ___ to Earth.

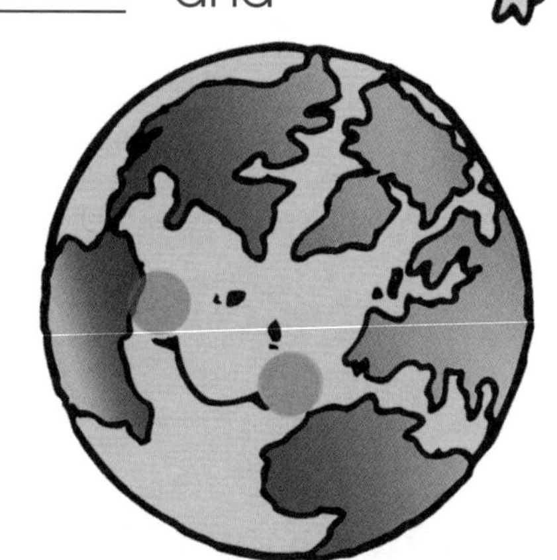

$88 - 17 =$ ___ $56 + 32 =$ ___ $49 - 36 =$ ___ $30 + 33 =$ ___

Without the sun, there would be no ___ ___ ___ ___.

Name ______________________

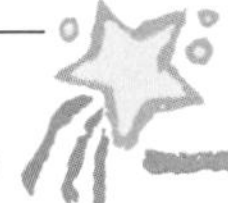

Animal Surprises

Add or subtract. Match the answer to the animal fact.

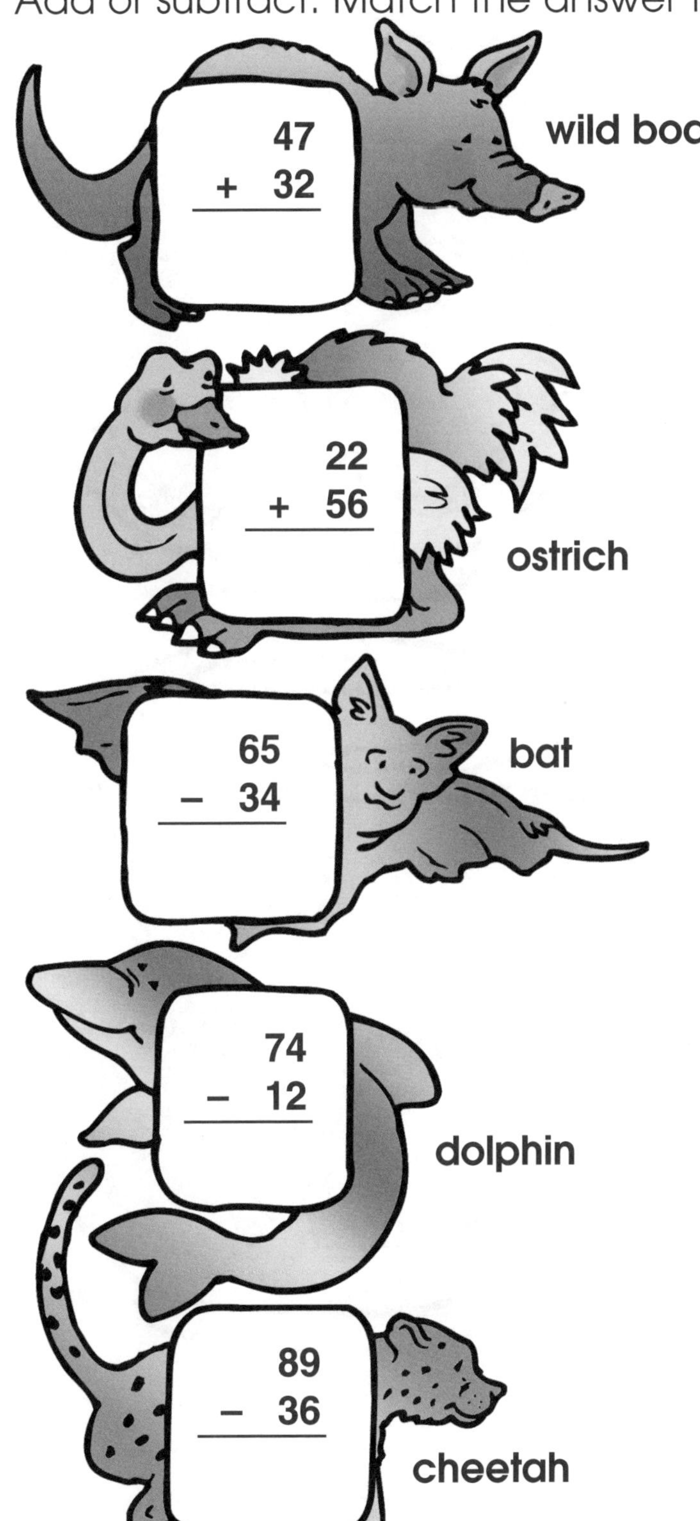

(31) I am the only mammal that can fly.

(78) I am a large bird, but I cannot fly.

(79) I can weigh over 250 pounds.

(53) I am the fastest of all animals.

(62) I swim like a fish, but I am really a mammal.

Name ______________________________

Fishbowl

Add or subtract. Circle the fish that does not belong with the family. Hint: Look at the tens place.

Make another family with 7 in the tens place.

Scholastic Success With

MATH

Name ______________________________

Color the Basket

Count the number of dots or triangles in each shape. Then use the Color Key to tell you what color to make each shape. (For example, a shape with 7 dots will be colored green.)

Extra: On the back of this sheet of paper, draw a basket filled with six things you would carry in it.

Color Key
6 = yellow
7 = green
8 = brown
9 = red
10 = green

Number User

I use numbers to tell about myself.

1. ______________________
MY STREET NUMBER

2. ______________________
MY ZIP CODE

3. ______________________
MY TELEPHONE NUMBER

4. ______________________
MY BIRTHDAY

5. ______________________
MY AGE

6. ______________________
MY HEIGHT AND WEIGHT

7. ______________________
NUMBER OF PEOPLE IN MY FAMILY

I CAN COUNT UP TO

8. ______________________

Name ______________________________________

Frog School

At Frog School, Croaker Frog and his friends sit on lily pads.

Are there enough lily pads for all the frogs in Croaker's class?
Yes ____ No ____

Draw lines to match the frogs with the lily pads.

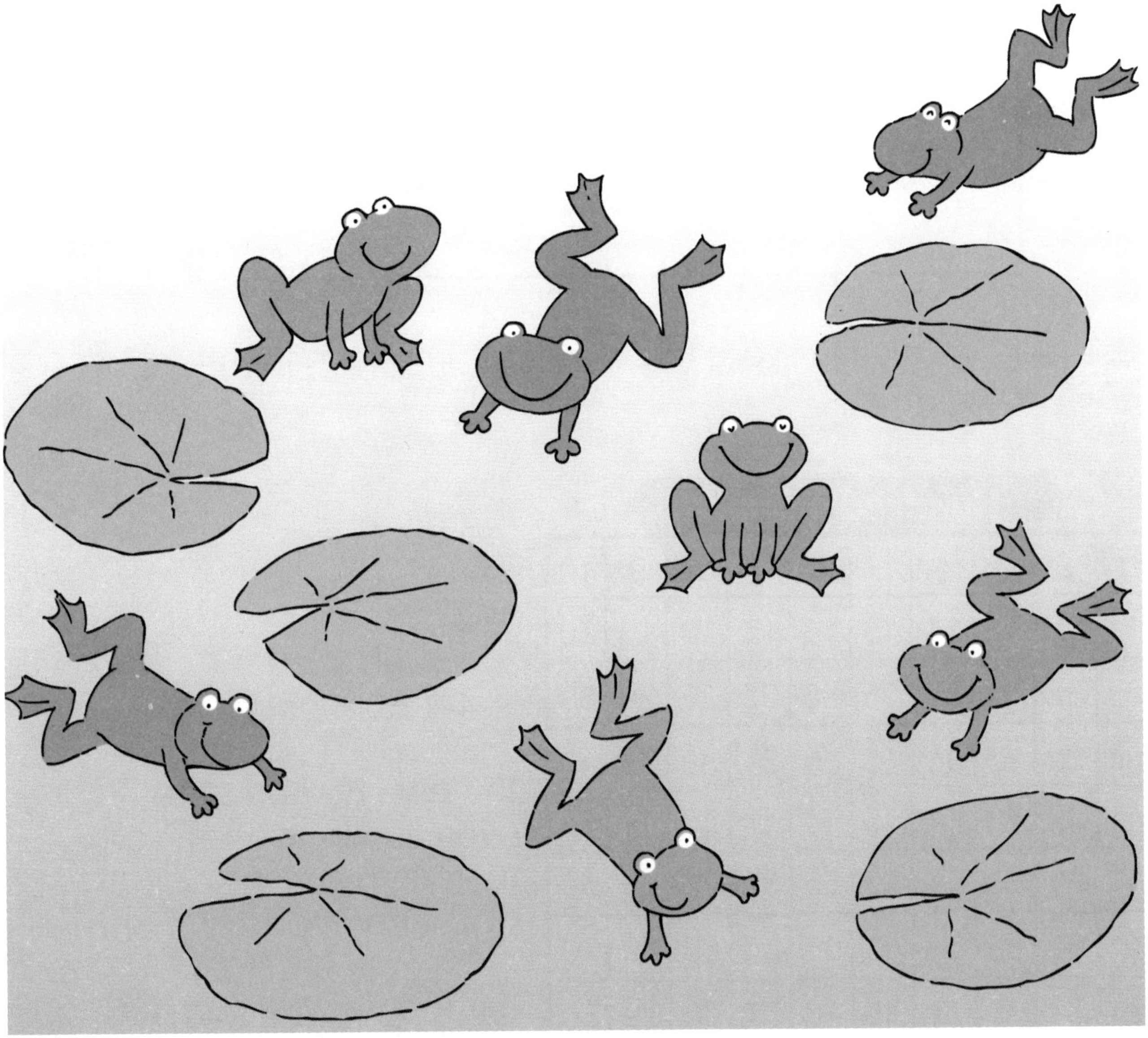

How many frogs need lily pads? ___________.

Name ______________________________

Odd and Even Patterns

A pattern can have two things repeating. This is called an "AB" pattern.

1. Look around the classroom. What "AB" patterns do you see? Draw one "AB" pattern in the box.

2. Use red and blue crayons to color the numbers in the chart using an "AB" pattern.

Hundred's Chart

1	2	3	4	5	6	7	8	9	10
11	12	13	14	15	16	17	18	19	20
21	22	23	24	25	26	27	28	29	30
31	32	33	34	35	36	37	38	39	40
41	42	43	44	45	46	47	48	49	50
51	52	53	54	55	56	57	58	59	60
61	62	63	64	65	66	67	68	69	70
71	72	73	74	75	76	77	78	79	80
81	82	83	84	85	86	87	88	89	90
91	92	93	94	95	96	97	98	99	100

Use this rule:
1 = red
2 = blue
3 = red
4 = blue, and so on

The blue numbers are **even numbers**. They can be split evenly into 2 whole numbers.

The red numbers are **odd numbers**. They cannot be split evenly into 2 whole numbers.

Name ____________________________________ 

Classroom Garage Sale

Tolu's class did some spring cleaning. Then they had a garage sale. They sorted the things they were selling. Sort these objects into like groups. Draw the items of each group on one of the tables below.

______________________ ______________________ ______________________

Below each table, write a label for the group.

Flowers in a Pot

Count the dots in the boxes. Then color the matching number word.

five
two
three
two
four
two
one
one
one
one
one
five

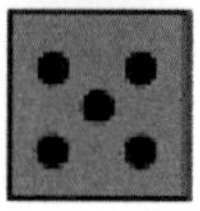

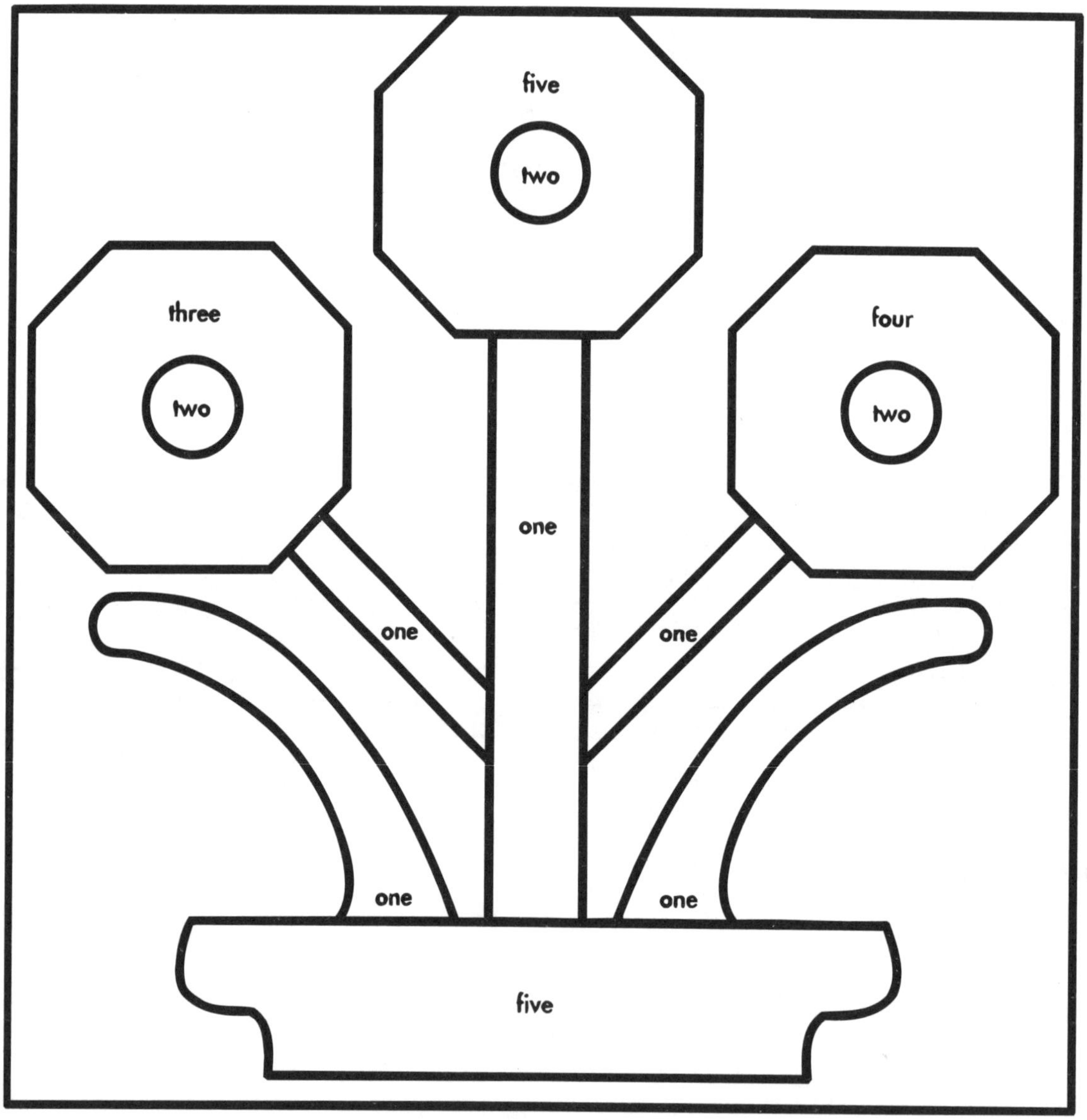

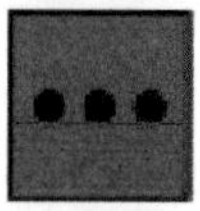

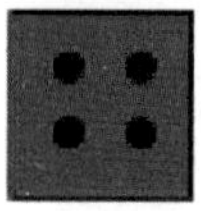

Use bright colors to draw a pot of flowers on another sheet of paper.

Sign Shape

Street signs come in different shapes. Use string to form the shapes below. Work with a partner. Answer the questions below about the shapes, too.

What shape is this sign? ________________

How many sides does it have? ________

What shape is this sign? ________________

How many sides does it have? ________

What shape is this sign? ________________

How many sides does it have? ________

What shape is this sign? ________________

How many sides does it have? ________

Bird Feeder Geometry

It's spring! The birds are coming back. Kwaku and his mother made two bird feeders.

What shapes can you find on their feeders? Write your ideas on the lines. ______________________________

____

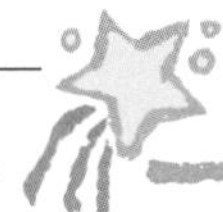

Shape Study

"Symmetry" exists when the two halves of something are mirror images of each other.

Look at the pictures below. Color those that show symmetry. (Hint: Imagine the pictures are folded on the dotted lines.)

Complete the drawings below. Connect the dots to show the other half. (Hint: The pictures are symmetrical!)

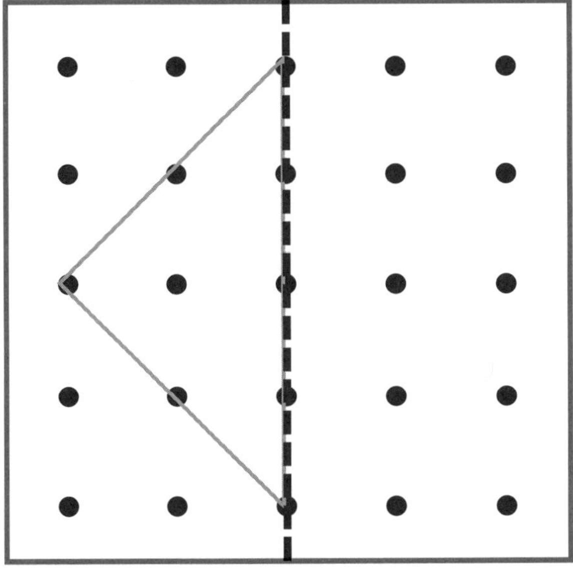

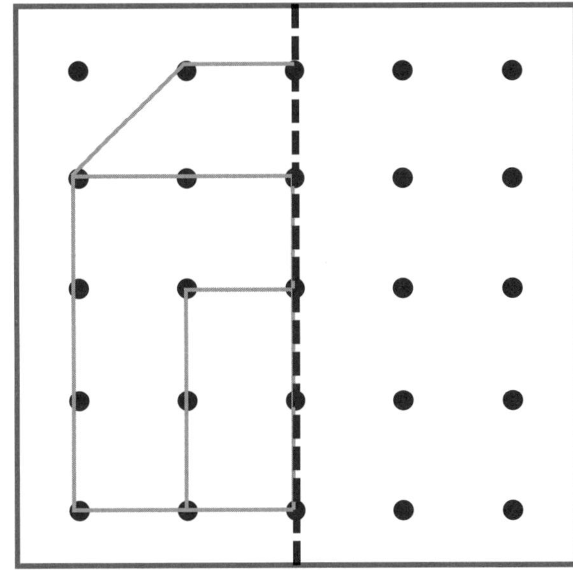

Name ______________________________

Patterns, number sense

Picking Out Patterns

On the 100th day of school, everyone in Pat's class picked out patterns on the 100 Chart. Look at the chart below.

1	2	3	4	5	6	7	8	9	10
11	12	13	14	15	16	17	18	19	20
21	22	23	24	25	26	27	28	29	30
31	32	33	34	35	36	37	38	39	40
41	42	43	44	45	46	47	48	49	50
51	52	53	54	55	56	57	58	59	60
61	62	63	64	65	66	67	68	69	70
71	72	73	74	75	76	77	78	79	80
81	82	83	84	85	86	87	88	89	90
91	92	93	94	95	96	97	98	99	100

Find and finish the pattern starting with 2, 12, 22

____

Find and finish the pattern starting with 100, 90, 80

____

Find and finish the pattern starting with 97, 87, 77

____

Find and finish the pattern starting with 11, 22, 33

____

Name ________________________________ 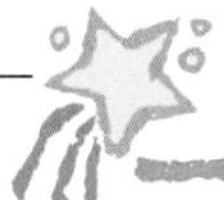

Mystery Critter

I climb up the side of walls and never fall.
I am a fast runner and have a very long tail. Who am I? ________

To find out, connect the numbers in order from 20 to 68.

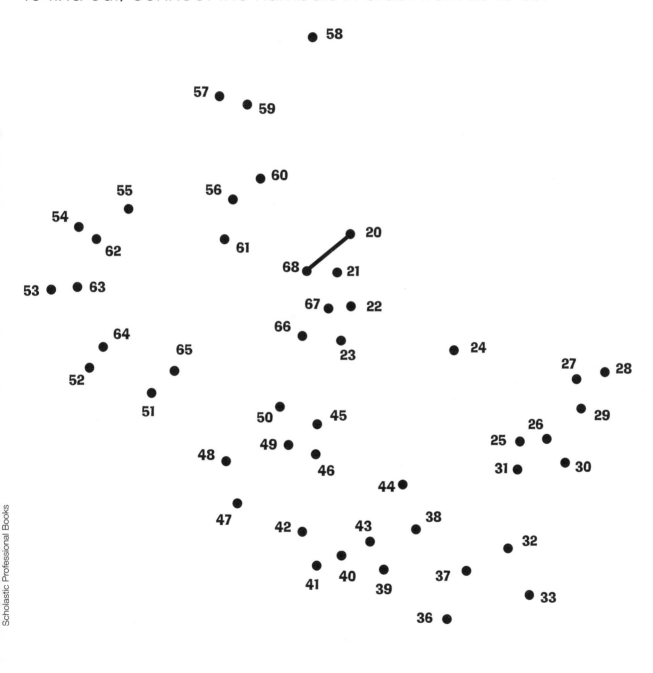

Snowflakes on Mittens

Estimate how many snowflakes are on each mitten.
For the first mitten, skip count by 2s to find out.
(You can circle groups of 2.)
For the second mitten, skip count by 5s to check your answer.
(You can circle groups of 5.)

Would snowflakes really wait for you to count?
Explain your answer:

Name ____________________  **Skip counting with fives**

Patterns of Five

Look at the number chart below. Starting with 1, count 5 squares. Color in the fifth square. Then count 5 more squares and color in the fifth square. Keep going until you reach 100.

Hundred's Chart

1	2	3	4	5	6	7	8	9	10
11	12	13	14	15	16	17	18	19	20
21	22	23	24	25	26	27	28	29	30
31	32	33	34	35	36	37	38	39	40
41	42	43	44	45	46	47	48	49	50
51	52	53	54	55	56	57	58	59	60
61	62	63	64	65	66	67	68	69	70
71	72	73	74	75	76	77	78	79	80
81	82	83	84	85	86	87	88	89	90
91	92	93	94	95	96	97	98	99	100

Tally marks can be arranged in groups of five, like this: 𝍸 𝍸 𝍸
Then you can count by fives.

Count how many girls and boys are in your class. Draw tally marks in groups of five.

Girls: ____________________ Boys: ____________________

Now count the total number. Write the totals here:

Girls: ____________________ Boys: ____________________

Ladybug Dots

Every year, ladybugs hibernate when the weather gets cool. Count the dots on each ladybug wing. Then write an equation to show the total number of dots each ladybug has. The first one has been done for you.

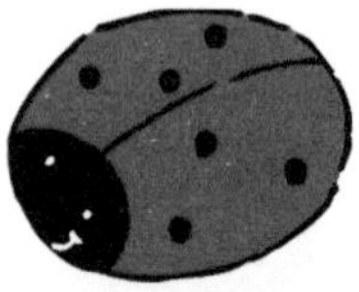

3 + **3** = **6**

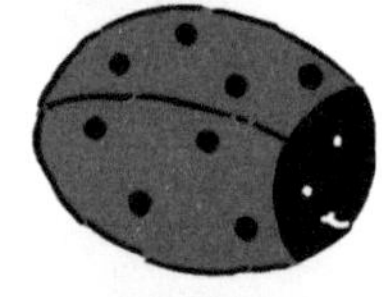

______ + ______ = ______

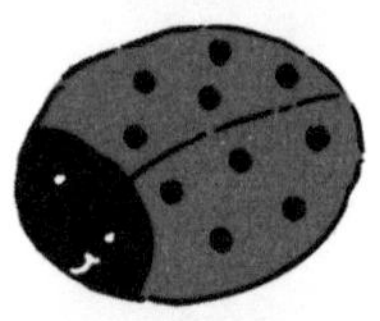

______ + ______ = ______

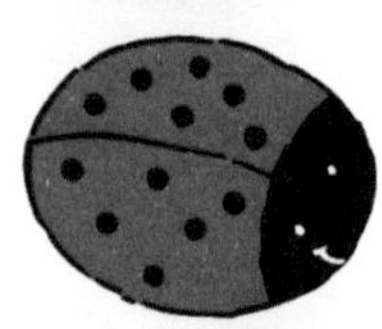

______ + ______ = ______

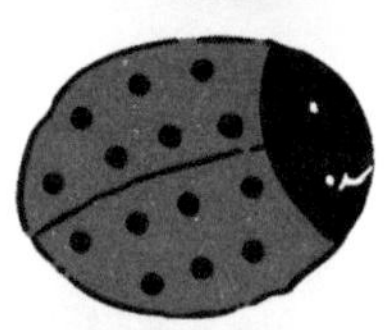

______ + ______ = ______

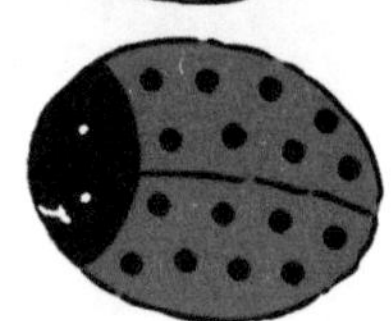

______ + ______ = ______

Write the sums in order, from lowest to highest.

______ ______ ______ ______ ______

What pattern do you see?

____

Pattern Block Design

How many total pieces are in this pattern block design?

2 + **2** + **1**= ______

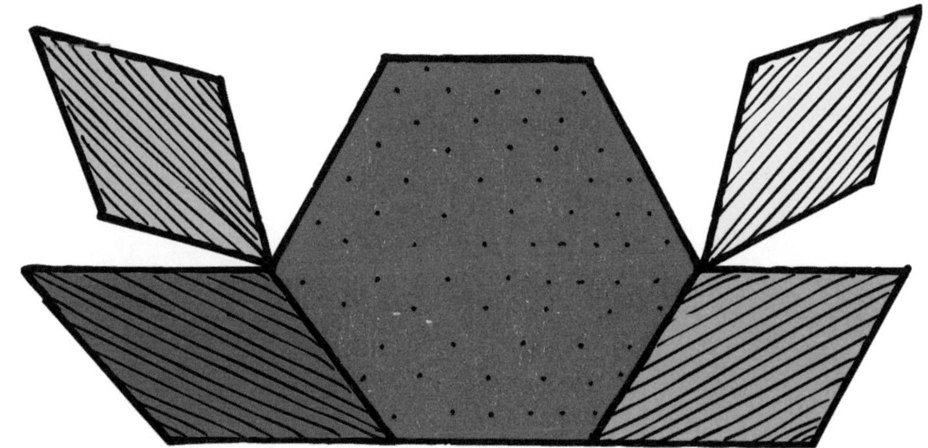

Now make your own design by drawing 5 pattern blocks. Connect the blocks to form a pattern different from the one above. You may want to use a block pattern more than once.

Write an equation to show how many of each shape you used.

Equation: ____________________

Name ______________________

Coin-Toss Subtraction

Toss 3 coins. Write "H" for heads or "T" for tails in the circles below to show how the coins landed. Then finish each sentence to tell about your toss. Write a subtraction equation to show your toss, too. Write the number of heads first. We did the first one for you. Try it three times.

(H) (H) (T) There are ___more___ heads than tails.
(more/fewer)

Subtraction equation: ___3 coins___ - ___2 heads___ = ___1 tail___

( ) ( ) ( ) There are __________ heads than tails.
(more/fewer)

Subtraction equation: __________ - __________ = __________

( ) ( ) ( ) There are __________ heads than tails.
(more/fewer)

Subtraction equation: __________ - __________ = __________

( ) ( ) ( ) There are __________ heads than tails.
(more/fewer)

Subtraction equation: __________ - __________ = __________

Name ______________________

What's Your Story?

Look at the equation below.

$3 + 3 = 6$

Make up a story to go with the equation.

Draw a picture in the box to go with your story.

Now write about your picture on the lines below.

____

____

____

____

____

Coin-Toss Addition

Toss 6 coins. Write "H" for heads or "T" for tails in the circles below to show your toss. Then write the addition equation. Write the number of "heads" first. We did the first one for you. Try it five times.

(H) (H) (H) (H) (T) (T) Equation: **4 + 2 = 6**

( ) ( ) ( ) ( ) ( ) ( ) Equation: ____________

( ) ( ) ( ) ( ) ( ) ( ) Equation: ____________

( ) ( ) ( ) ( ) ( ) ( ) Equation: ____________

( ) ( ) ( ) ( ) ( ) ( ) Equation: ____________

( ) ( ) ( ) ( ) ( ) ( ) Equation: ____________

Name ____ 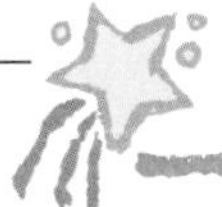

Time to Get Up!

Twenty animals were hibernating near Sleepy Pond.
5 of them woke up. Color 5 animals below.

How many are still sleeping? ________________________

A week later, 7 more woke up. Color 7 other animals.

How many are still sleeping? ________________________

Name ______________________________

Money Matters

Alex asked his little brother Billy to trade piggy banks.

Alex's bank has these coins:

Billy's has these coins:

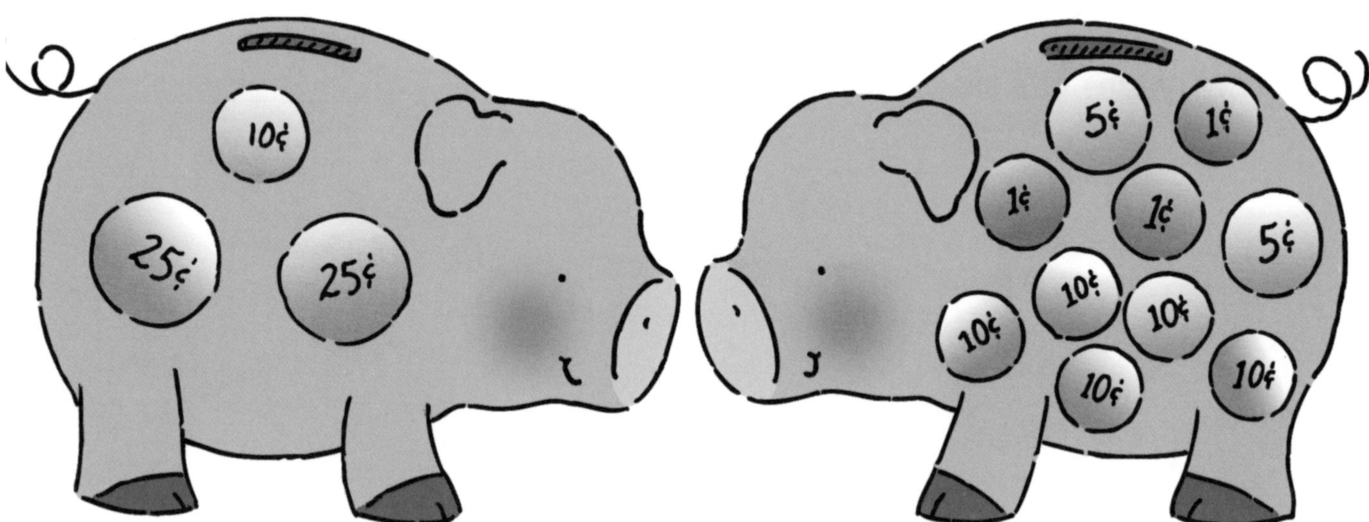

Do you think this is a fair trade? ______________________________

Test your answer:

Add up Alex's coins: ______________________________

Add up Billy's coins: ______________________________

Write the totals in this Greater Than/Less Than equation:

______________________ > ______________________

Who has more money? ______________________________

The Truth About the Tooth Fairy

Look at Ali Gator's teeth.

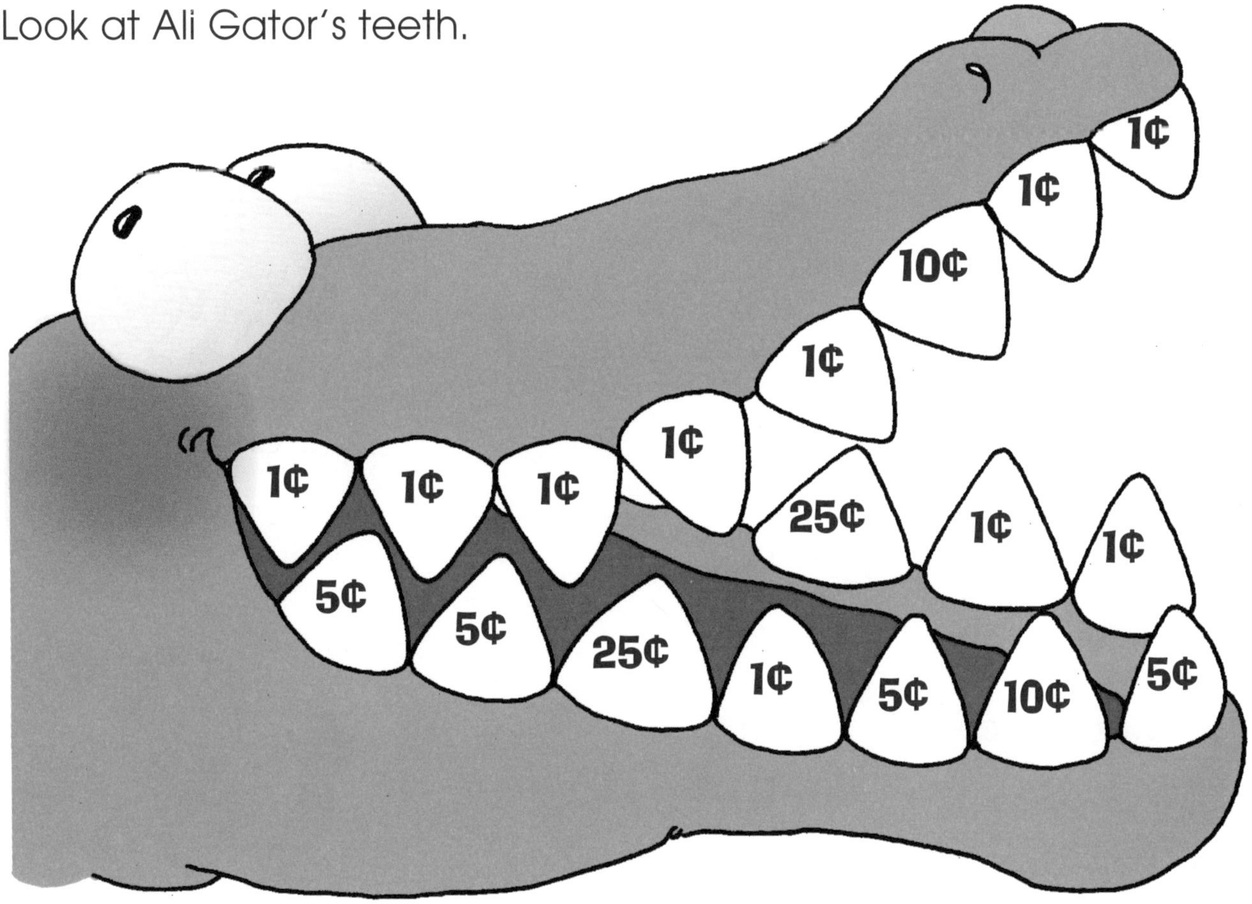

	How many teeth?	How much money in all?	
1. How many 1¢?	☐	☐	cents
2. How many 5¢?	☐	☐	cents
3. How many 10¢?	☐	☐	cents
4. How many 25¢?	☐	☐	cents

Measuring Up

People didn't always measure with rulers. Long ago, Egyptians and other peoples measured objects with body parts. Try it!

A "digit" is the width of your middle finger at the top joint where it bends.

How many digits long is:

a pair of scissors? ________________________

a math book? ________________________

a crayon? ________________________

A "palm" is the width of your palm.

How many palms long is:

a telephone book? ________________________

your desk? ________________________

a ruler? ________________________

A "span" is the length from the tip of your pinkie to the tip of your thumb when your hand is wide open.

How many spans long is:

a broom handle? ________________________

a table? ________________________

a door? ________________________

Name ______________________________ 

Penguin Family on Parade

The penguin family is part of the winter parade. They need to line up from shortest to tallest. Give them a hand! Use a ruler to measure each penguin. Label each penguin with its height. Then write the name of each penguin in size order, from smallest to tallest.

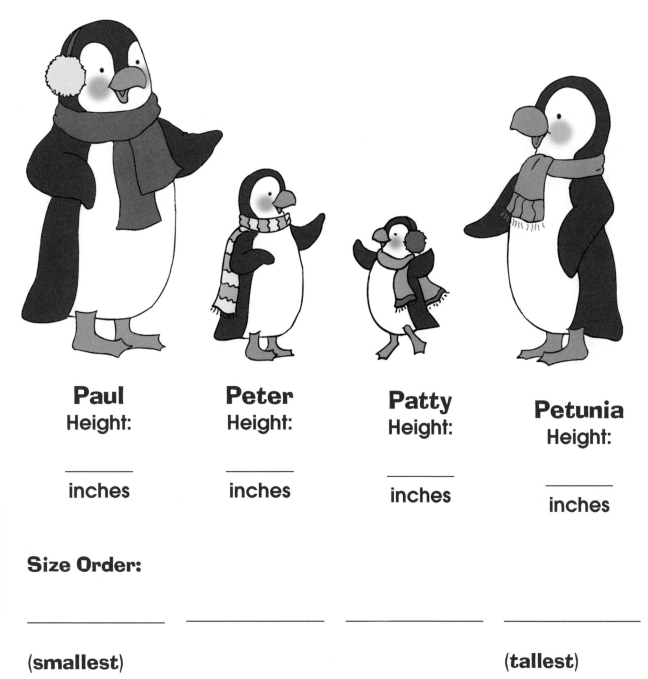

Paul	**Peter**	**Patty**	**Petunia**
Height:	**Height:**	**Height:**	**Height:**
______ **inches**	______ **inches**	______ **inches**	______ **inches**

Size Order:

______________ ______________ ______________ ______________

(smallest) **(tallest)**

Look and Learn

Look at each picture. Estimate how long you think it is. Then measure each picture with a ruler. Write the actual length in inches.

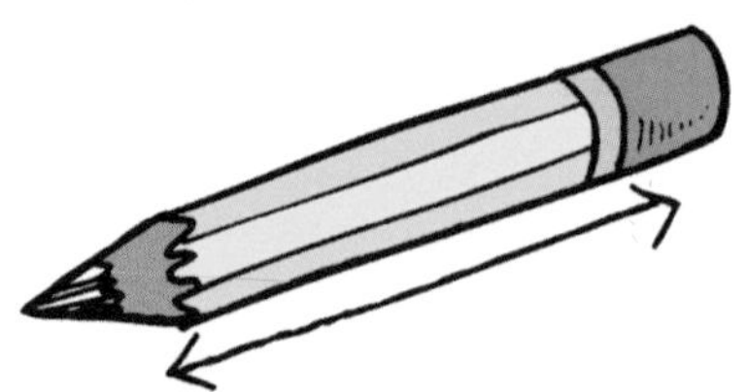

Estimate: __________ **inches**
Actual: ___________ **inches**

Estimate: __________ **inches**
Actual: ___________ **inches**

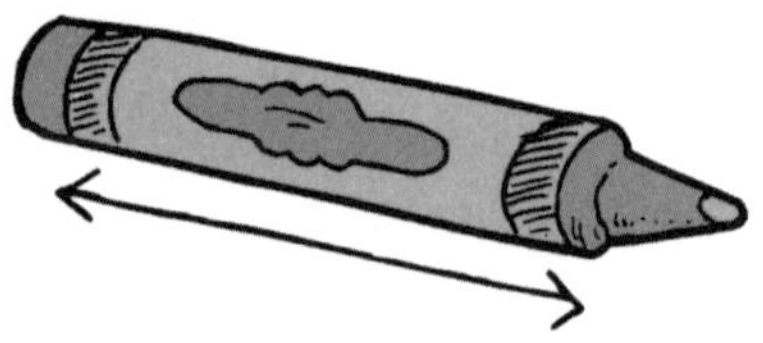

Estimate: __________ **inches**
Actual: ___________ **inches**

Estimate: __________ **inches**
Actual: ___________ **inches**

Practice measuring other things in the room with a ruler.

Turn Up the Volume

How many quarts equal 1 gallon? Find out! Fill a quart container with water. Pour it into a gallon container. Keep doing it until the gallon is full. Color the correct number of quarts below. Write the numeral on the line: **1 gallon = ____________ quarts.**

Now try it with other containers, too.

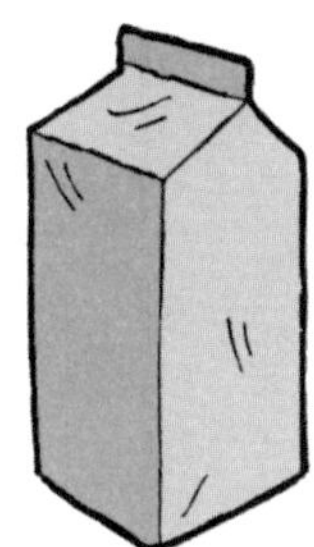

1 quart = ____________ pints

1 pint = ____________ cups

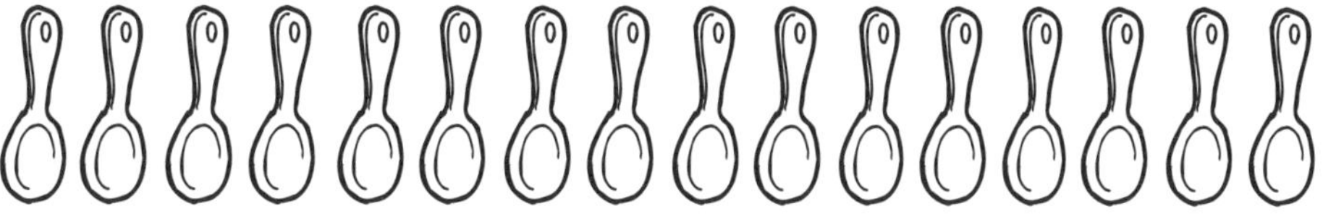

1 cup = ____________ tablespoons

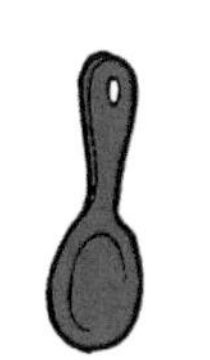

1 tablespoon = __________ teaspoons

Adding Sides

Use the inch side of a ruler and measure each side of each rectangle. Write the inches in the spaces below. Then add up all the sides to find the perimeter, or distance, around each rectangle.

___ + ___ + ___ + ___ = ____ **inches**

___ + ___ + ___ + ___ = ____ **inches**

___ + ___ + ___ + ___ = ____ **inches**

Name ________________________________

Centimeters

Things can be measured using centimeters. Get a ruler that measures in centimeters. Measure the pictures of the objects below.

book	book
Out Came The Sun	By The River
_____ centimeters	_____ centimeters
straw	**marker**
_____ centimeters	_____ centimeters
5 cubes	**10 cubes**
_____ centimeters	_____ centimeters
shoe	**hand**
_____ centimeters	_____ centimeters

Five Senses

We learn about the world by using our 5 senses. The 5 senses are seeing, hearing, smelling, touching, and tasting.
Look at the pictures on the left side of the graph. Think about which of your senses you use to learn about it. Draw a checkmark in the box to show the senses used. (Hint: You might use more than one.)

	See	Hear	Smell	Touch	Taste

Now graph how many senses you used for each object.

5					
4					
3					
2					
1					

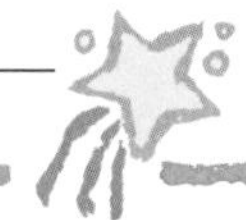

Rainbow Graph

Which color of the rainbow is your favorite? Color in the box for your favorite color. Have 5 classmates color the boxes to show their favorite colors, too.

Which color is liked the most? ______________________

Which color is liked the least? ______________________

Are any colors tied? ______________________

Which ones? ______________________

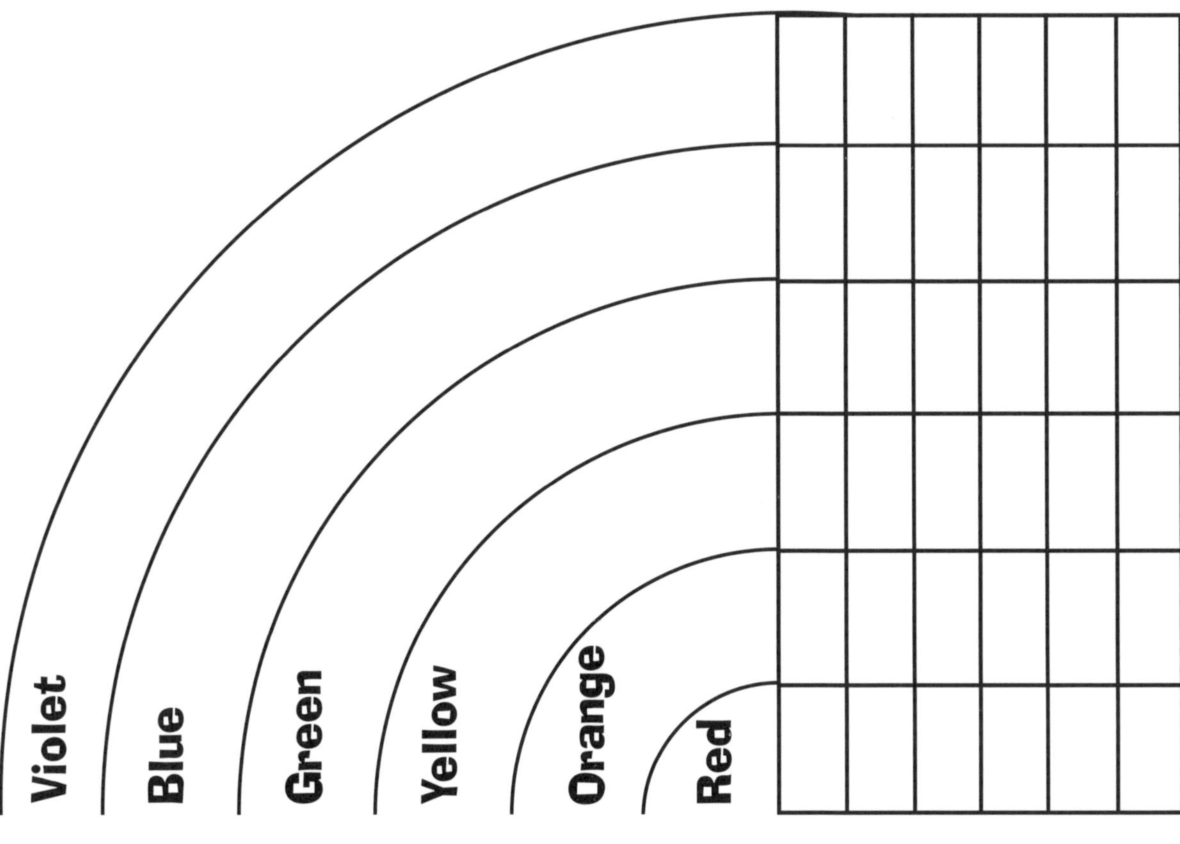

School Supplies

1. Find each letter and number pair on the graph.
2. Color a yellow square for each pair.
3. What picture did you make?

____

	Across	Up
1.	C	4
2.	C	5
3.	D	4
4.	D	5
5.	E	4
6.	E	5
7.	F	4

	Across	Up
8.	F	5
9.	G	4
10.	G	5
11.	H	4
12.	H	5
13.	I	4
14.	I	5

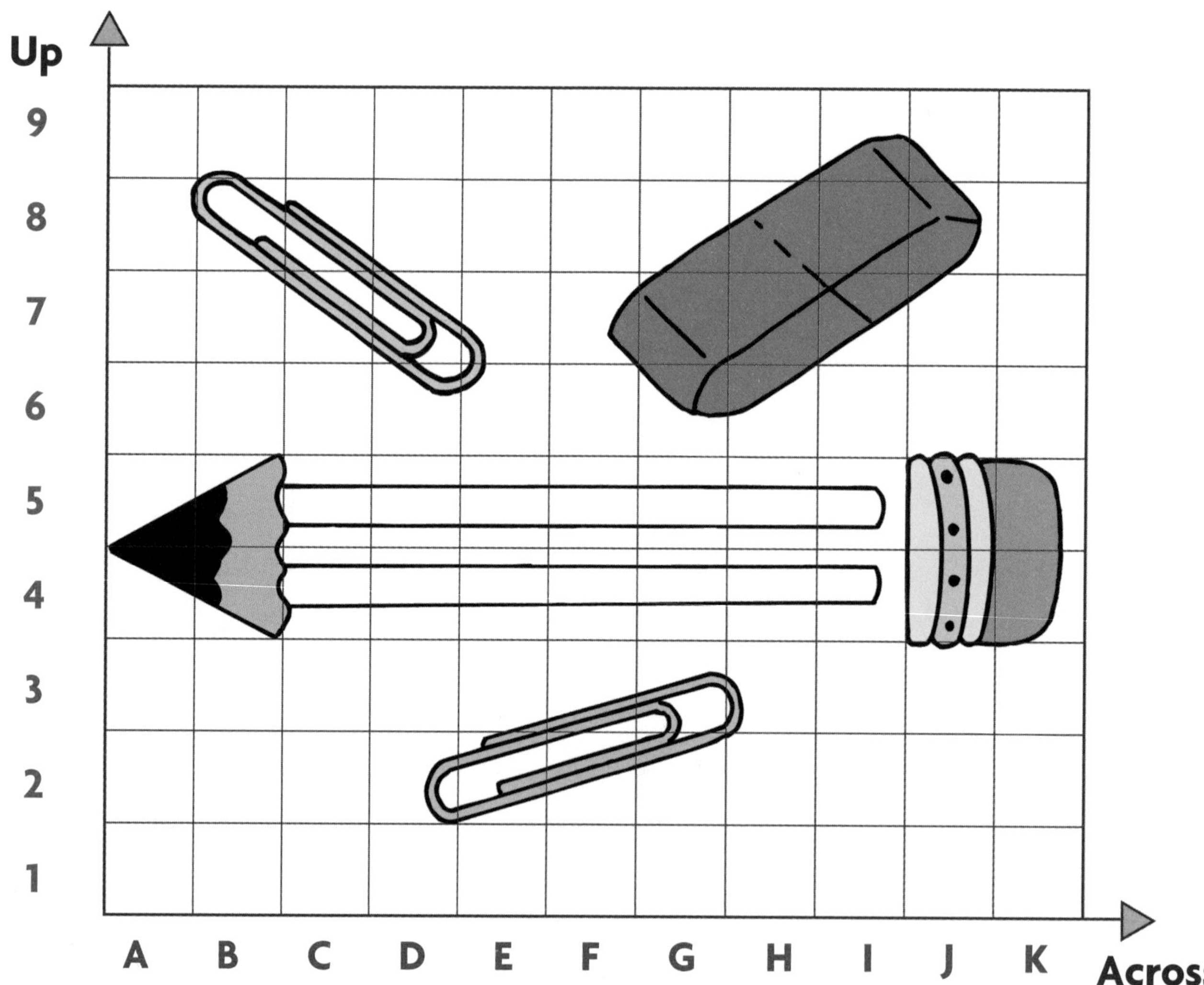

Surprises!

1. Find each number pair on the graph. Make a dot for each.
2. Connect the dots in the order that you make them.
3. What picture did you make?

____

	Across	Up
1.	9	2
2.	7	4
3.	8	4
4.	6	6
5.	7	6
6.	5	8
7.	3	6
8.	4	6
9.	2	4
10.	3	4
11.	1	2

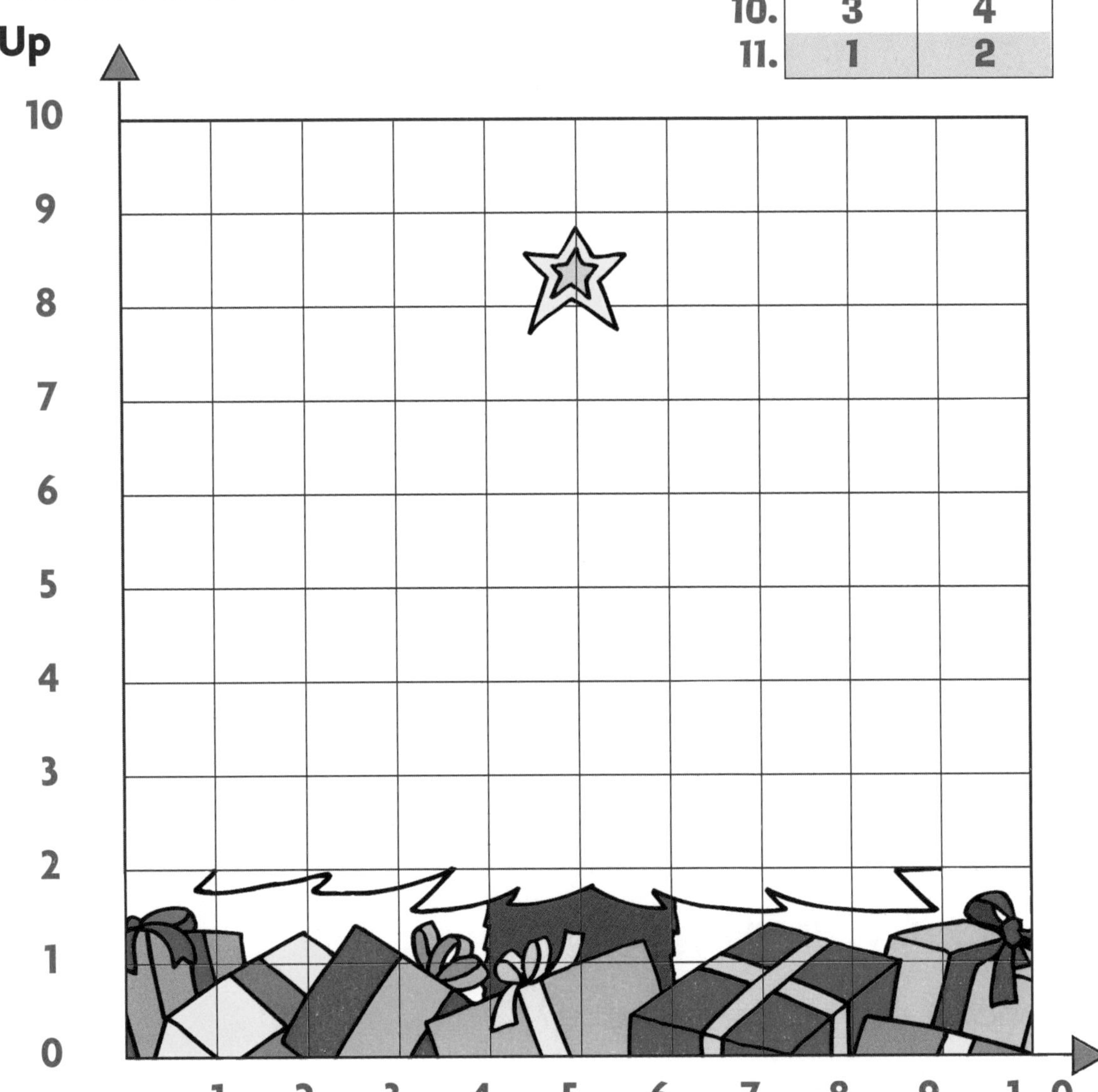

Name ______________________________ 

December Weather

In December, Mrs. Monroe's class drew the weather on a calendar. Each kind of weather has a picture:

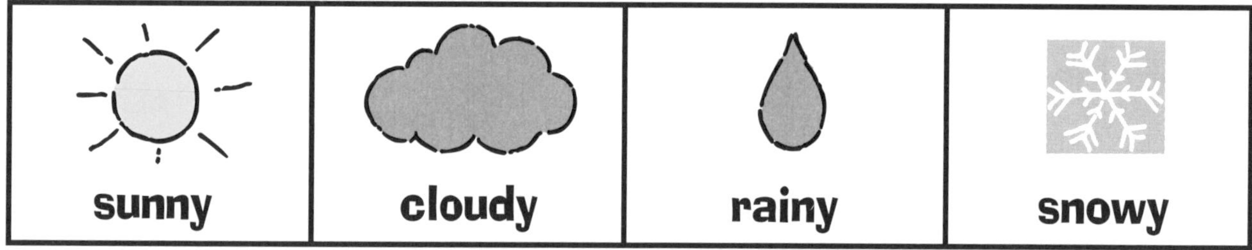

Look at the calendar. Answer the questions below.

December

SUN.	MON.	TUES.	WED.	THURS.	FRI.	SAT
	1	2	3	4	5	6
7	8	9	10	11	12	13
14	15	16	17	18	19	20
21	22	23	24	25	26	27
28	29	30	31			

How many sunny days did they have? ______________

How many cloudy days did they have? ______________

How many rainy days did they have? ______________

How many snowy days did they have? ______________

Which kind of weather did they have the most? ______________

Name ______________________________

Fun With Fractions

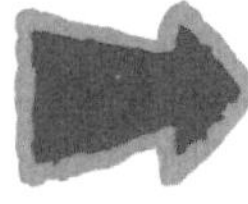

A fraction is a part of a whole.

The shapes below are split into parts, or fractions.
Color only the shapes that are split into equal parts (equal fractions).

1

2

3

4

5

6

7

8

Parts to Color

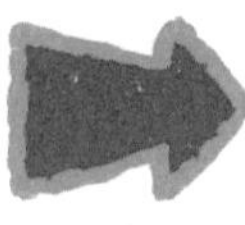

A fraction has two numbers. The top number will tell you how many parts to color. The bottom number tells you how many parts there are.

Color 1/5 of the circle.

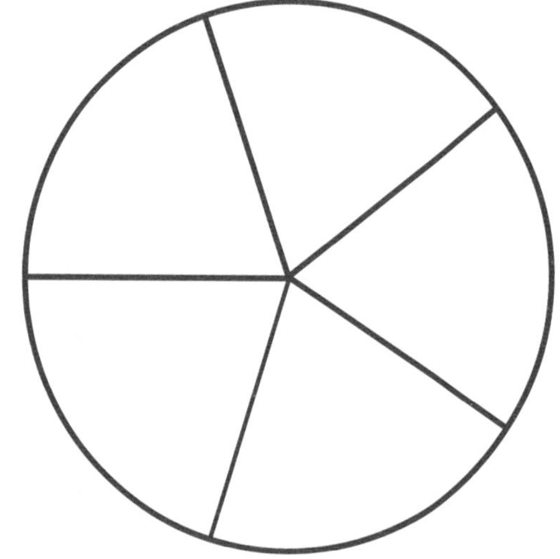

Color 4/5 of the rectangle.

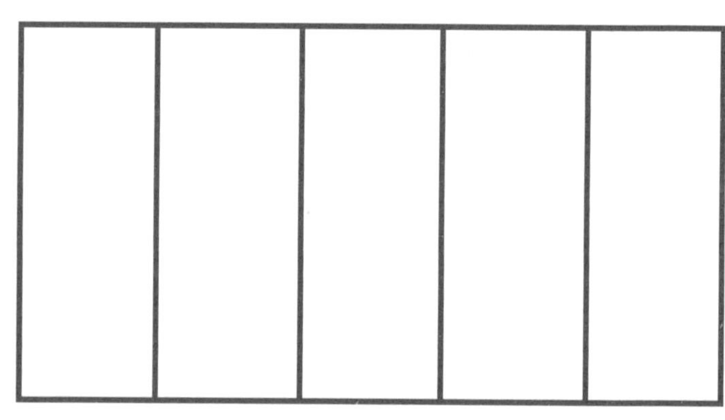

Color 3/5 of the ants.

Color 2/5 of the spiders.

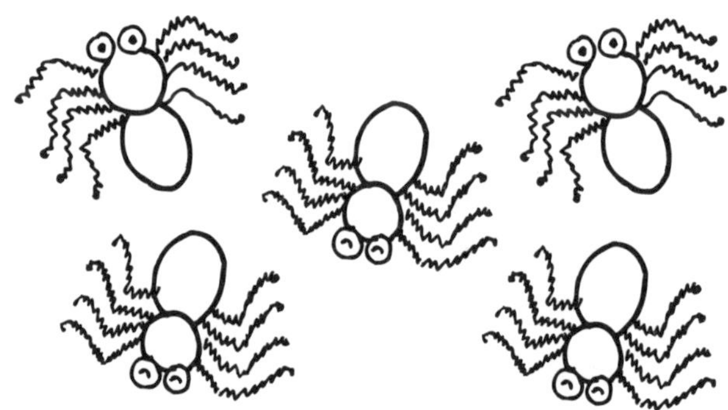

Color 0/5 of the bees.

Color 5/5 of the worms.

More Parts to Color

A fraction has two numbers. The top number will tell you how many parts to color. The bottom number tells you how many parts there are.

Color 1/8 of the circle.

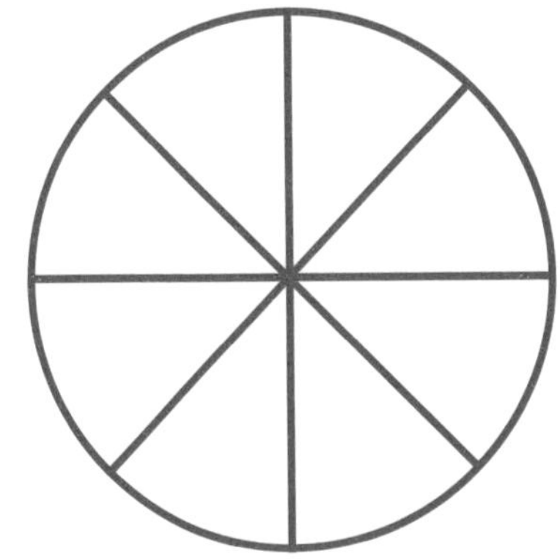

Color 6/8 of the rectangle.

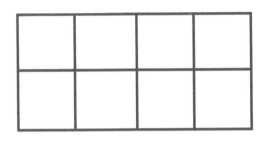

Color 4/8 of the suns.

Color 8/8 of the stars.

Color 2/8 of the moons.

Color 3/8 of the planets.

Clock Work

Draw the hands on the clock so it shows 2:00.

Draw the hands on the clock so it shows 3:00.

Draw the hands on the clock so it shows 4:00.

Draw the hands on the clock so it shows 5:00.

What do you do at 2:00 in the afternoon?

Write about it on the lines below.

____

____

More Clock Work

Draw the hands on the clock so it shows 3:00.	Draw the hands on the clock so it shows 6:00.

Draw the hands on the clock so it shows 9:00.	Draw the hands on the clock so it shows 12:00.

What do you do at 3:00 in the afternoon?

Write about it on the lines below.

____

____

Even More Clock Work

Draw the hands on the clock so it shows 4:00.

Draw the hands on the clock so it shows 4:30.

What do you do at 4:00 in the afternoon?

Write about it on the line below.

____

Draw the hands on the clock so it shows 6:00.

Draw the hands on the clock so it shows 6:30.

What do you do at 6:00 in the evening?

Write about it on the line below.

____

About Time

Why do we need to know how to tell time? List your ideas below.

____

____

____

____

How Long Is a Minute?

Think about how much you can do in one minute.
Write your estimates in the Prediction column. Then time yourself.
Write the actual number in the Result column.

Prediction: In One Minute I Can	Result
Jump rope _____ times.	
Write the numbers 1 to _____ .	
Say the names of _____ animals.	

Answer Key

READING COMPREHENSION

Page 12
1. a good reader; 2. looks at the picture; 3. the title; 4. the words

Page 13
Main idea: Trucks do important work.

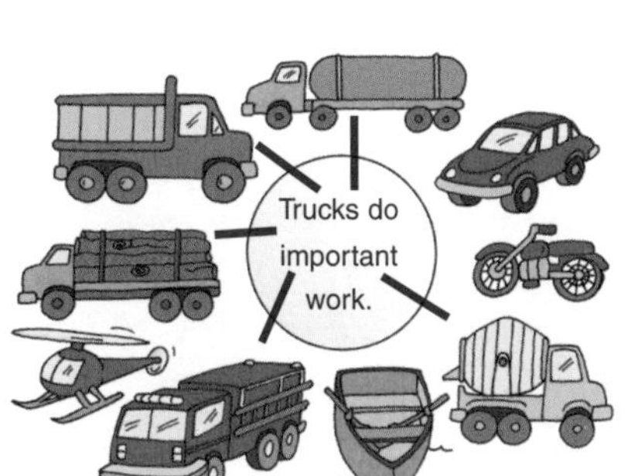

Page 14
Main idea: Clowns can do funny tricks.

Page 15
KATE: Names have special meanings.

Casey means brave.
George means farmer.
Sarah means princess.

Page 16

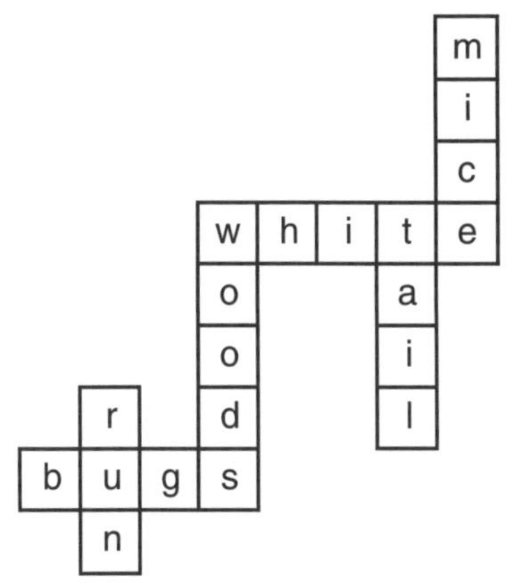

Page 17

1. in reading class; 2. camping

Page 18
Kelly packed pajamas, shirt, shorts, toothbrush, toothpaste, hairbrush, swimsuit, pillow, storybooks, sunglasses. Compound words: grandmother, suitcase, toothbrush, toothpaste, hairbrush, swimsuit, storybooks, sunglasses

Page 19
1. Texas; 2. oil; 3. President; 4. wife; 5. Jenna

His cat's name is INDIA.

Page 20
Make-believe: ketchup bottles and a watermelon bowling, a talking milk jug, dancing bananas, chicken wings that can fly all by themselves, laughing soup cans, dancing carrots

Page 21
Facts: Clouds float in the sky. Clouds are made of tiny drops of water. Fog is a cloud on the ground. (All others are make-believe.)

Page 22
Make-believe: pig, goat and sheep, horses, pizza and hamburgers, mouse and table, golden eggs, crickets (The others are real.)

Page 23
5, 1; 4, 3, 2

Tara bought pencils, scissors, glue, and crayons.

Page 24
6, 4, 2; 3, 1, 5

LEARN TO DIVE

Page 25
1. Each star should be outlined in blue and colored red inside. 2. One moon should be yellow and one orange. 3. A face should be drawn on each sun. 4. 3; 5. 2; 6. 4; 7. 3 + 2 + 4 = 9; 8. stars moon

Page 26

1. 

2. 

3. 

4. 

5. 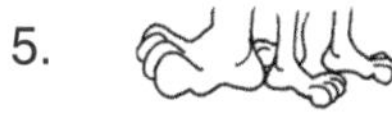

6 

Page 27

The pictures that do not belong are bike, telephone, snowman, pumpkin, skates, and frog. (The other pictures should be colored.)

2. hot, cold; 3. up, down; 4. starfish; 5. yellow

Page 28
IT WAS A FLYING CARPET. No

Page 29
1. true; 2. false; 3. false; 4. true; 5. true

Page 30
The children's pictures should include everything described in the sentences.

Page 31
The children should have added these things to the picture: black clouds, lightning striking the tallest tree, the word "Moo" in a bubble above a cow, rain, a mud puddle by the barn door, hay blowing out of the barn window.

Page 32
1. penguin; 2. baby; 3. octopus; 4. ant; 5. grandmother; 6. bear; 7. firefighter

Page 33
1. chickenpox; 2. James scratched them. 3. 9; 4. She got chickenpox, too.

Page 34

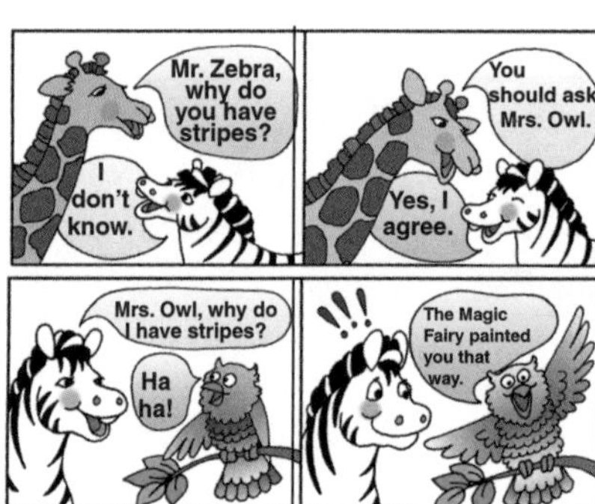

Page 35

Bacon and eggs do not belong.

Page 36
Sandie's Shoe Store: sandals, boots, sneakers, high heels; Movie Town Cinema: tickets, popcorn, big screen, candy; Pepe's Mexican Food: tacos, burrito, beans, peppers; Gale's Gardening Goodies: tulip bulbs, fertilizer, gardening gloves, pots

Page 37
Meats: ham, chicken, roast; Dairy: milk, cheese, yogurt; Bread: rolls, bagels, biscuits; Fruits and Vegetables: carrots, corn, apples

Page 38

Page 39

He knew he had to do the right thing.

Page 40
FAST FOOD, FLOWER BED

Page 41

They are in the first grade.

Page 42
1. Juan's dad; 2. Juan's dad; 3. both; 4. Ann's dad; 5. both; 6. Ann's dad; 7. Juan's dad; 8. both; 9. Ann's dad; 10. both

Page 43

1.

2.

3.

Page 44
1. an arm like a paddle; 2. not dangerous; 3. slap at; 4. lose; 5. hide in the ground

Page 45
1. a small city; 2. little furry animals; 3. tunnels; 4. rooms; 5. pests

Page 46
1. Sandy used lanterns at night because the cabin had no electricity. 2. Sandy and Austin bathed in a stream because the cabin had no running water. 3. Sandy felt better about missing Kendra because she talked to her on the cell phone. 4. Sandy's dad could not call his office because the cell phone was dead.

Page 47
1. The worms got tangled up when they danced. 2. They were tied in a knot so they got married.

Page 48
1. E; 2. B; 3. D; 4. F; 5. A; 6. C.

Page 49

The children's pictures should show a crown on Margie's arm, a shoe on her head, different colors on each fingernail, a red nose, a fork in her hair, and a purple belt around her knees.

6. the way she dresses; 7. He wears his clothes backward.

Page 50
1. happy; 2. worried; 3. silly; 4. sad; 5. scared; 6. surprised

Page 51
1. green; 2. red; 3. red; 4. yellow; 5. red; 6. yellow; 7. green

Page 52
Picture: rainbow 1. appear; 2. gold; Picture: airplane 3. high; 4. again; 5. bee

Page 53
2. Don't be greedy. Be happy with what you have. Picture answers: dog, meat, bridge

Page 54

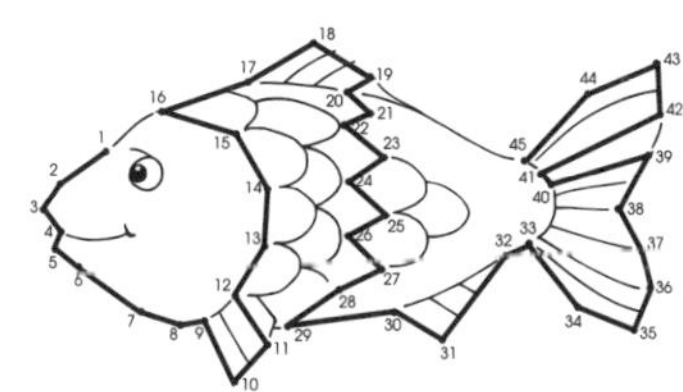

1. sharing 2. Marcus Pfister

TESTS: READING

Pages 57-60

TEST 1

A. Phonic Analysis: Consonants and Vowels

Sample: sun

1. bed   2. cat   3. dog
4. rug   5. sock

B. Vocabulary: Picture-Word Match

Sample: can

1. pig   2. run   3. car

C. High-Frequency Word Match

Sample: and

1. my   2. will   3. sad

D. Grammar, Usage, and Mechanic's

Sample: My bike is red.

1. I like to run.
2. Did you see it?
3. They sit on the mat.

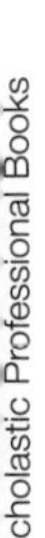

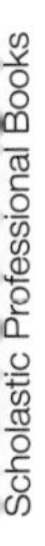

E. Reading Sentences
Sample: A girl sits.
1. The cat plays.
2. The book is on the desk.
3. She has a rabbit.
4. The dog sits on a hill.

F. Story Comprehension
1. dog
2. Rags the Dog
3. play

Pages 61-64

Test 2

A. Phonic Analysis: Consonants
Sample: bat
1. pot 2. fox 3. bell
4. bus 5. bug

B. Phonic Analysis: Vowels
Sample: cap
1. mop 2. pig 3. sun
4. duck 5. ten

C. High-Frequency Word Match
Sample: and
1. it 2. she 3. was
4. that 5. they

D. Vocabulary: Picture-Word Match
Sample: hat
1. bag 2. top 3. pen
4. fan 5. sock

E. Grammar, Usage, and Mechanics
Sample: The boy is happy.
1. She saw a duck.
2. Look at him run!
3. Where will I go?

F. Story Comprehension
1. a pig
2. Ted's Pig
3. Answers will vary.

Pages 65-68

Test 3

A. Phonic Analysis: Consonants
Sample: sun
1. ball 2. rug 3. flag
4. pen 5. truck

B. Phonic Analysis: Vowels
Sample: fish
1. bus 2. hat 3. frog
4. nest 5. cake

C. High-Frequency Word Match
Sample: is
1. for 2. he 3. you
4. said 5. them

D. Vocabulary: Picture-Word Match
Sample: bird
1. bat 2. dog 3. feet
4. hand 5. clock

E. Grammar, Usage, and Mechanics
Sample: The girl can jump.
1. The boy ran fast.
2. Look at me!
3. Where will I walk?

F. Story Comprehension
1.a kite
2. Kim's Kite
3. Answers will vary.

Pages 69-72

Test 4

A. Phonic Analysis: Consonants
Sample: dog
1. bat 2. fan 3. tree
4. moon 5. fish

B. Phonic Analysis: Vowels
Sample:sun
1.map 2.web 3.fox
4.pig 5.cake

C. High-Frequency Word Match
Sample: and
1. for 2. she 3. how
4. can 5. then

D. Vocabulary: Picture-Word Match
Sample: pen
1. hat 2. frog 3. bus
4. feet 5. bike

E. Grammar, Usage, and Mechanics
Sample: The
1. She
2. They
3. out!
4. day?
5. Amy.
6. I
7. We
8. his
9. Anna and Tim

F. Story Comprehension
1. a cat
2. string
3. Nate's Cat
4. Answers will vary

.

Pages 73-76

Test 5

A. Phonic Analysis: Consonants
Sample: baby
1. sheep 2. bath 3. snail
4. tree 5. frog

B. Phonic Analysis: Vowels
Sample: car
1. spoon 2. legs
3. puppies 4. boy 5. milk

C. High-Frequency Word Match
Sample: is
1. to 2. said 3. hello
4. best 5. smell

D. Vocabulary: Picture-Word Match
Sample: ant
1. wet 2. dish 3. saw
4. bug 5. cake

E. Grammar, Usage, and Mechanics
Sample: is
1. I
2.The
3. me!
4. Nan and Nell
5. you
6. We
7. They
8. Joey.
9. She

F. Story Comprehension
1. goldfish
2. Goldie and Finny
3. bowl

Pages 77-80

Test 6

A. Phonic Analysis: Consonants
Sample: bag
1. mop 2. cheese 3. ten
4. fish 5. train

B. Phonic Analysis: Vowels
Sample: sun
1. six 2. cat 3. boat
4. teeth 5. foot

C. High-Frequency Word Match
Sample: me
1. is 2. said 3. where

D. Grammar, Usage, and Mechanics
Sample: The dog is furry.
1. He didn't like it.
2. Can you run fast?
3. Where can I play?

E. Reading Sentences
Sample: A boy runs.
1. She put the sock in the box.
2. The nest has ten eggs.
3. She plays on the swing.
4. The truck can go fast.

F. Story Comprehension
1. read
2. Books Tom Reads
3. animals
4. Pet Rabbits

Pages 81-84

Test 7

A. Phonic Analysis: Consonants
Sample: fish
1. pen 2. broom 3. nest
4. truck 5.cheese

B. Phonic Analysis: Vowels
Sample: bat
1. ten 2. house 3. leaf
4. book 5. plane

C. High-Frequency Word Match
Sample: and
1. has 2. come 3. what

D. Grammar, Usage, and Mechanics
Sample: The cat sleeps.
1. Why can't we go?
2. They play all day.
3. Can Sam sit with us?

E. Reading Sentences
Sample: The boy kicks the ball.
1. The duck swims in the pond.
2. She rides her bike.
3. The leaf fell off the branch.
4. He can see the cow.

F. Story Comprehension
1. The Wind.
2. to fly a kite
3. seeds grow
4. blow away a leaf

Pages 85-88

Test 8

A. Phonic Analysis: Consonants
Sample: desk
1. pan 2. tree 3. ship
4. clock 5. hand

B. Phonic Analysis
Sample: net
1. cup 2. moon 3. cloud
4. boat 5. rake

C. Vocabulary: Picture-Word Match
Sample: fish
1. bed 2. nest 3. plane
4. coat 5. kite

D. High-Frequency Word Match
Sample: in
1. him 2. then 3. says
4. our 5. what

E. Grammar, Usage and Mechanics
Sample: He rides in a plane.
1. She runs very fast.
2. Where are my socks?
3. We play with the dog.

F. Story Comprehension
1. Rabbits
2. hear sounds from far away
3. in holes in the ground and in people's homes
4. Answers will vary.

Pages 89-92

Test 9

A. Phonic Analysis: Consonants
Sample: dress
1. train 2. flag 3. lamp
4. desk 5. spoon

B. Phonic Analysis: Vowels
Sample: fox
1. bell 2. gate 3. hose
4. teeth 5. leaf

C. High-Frequency Word Match
Sample: her
1. very 2. some 3. there
4. which 5. because

D. Vocabulary: Picture-Word Match
Sample: frog
1. kite 2. fish 3. plane
4. cupcake 5. butterfly

E. Grammar, Usage, and Mechanics
Sample: We
1. jump. 2. Dr. Jones 3. I
4. New York 5. rides

F. Story Comprehension
1. Jane Goodall
2. Africa
3. 3 years old
4.Answers will vary

Pages 93-96

Test 10

A. Phonic Analysis: Consonants
Sample: dog
1. six 2. tree 3. top
4. fan 5. ship

B. Phonic Analysis: Vowels
Sample: hat
1. sock 2. sun 3. coat
4. train 5. bike

C. High Frequency Word Match
Sample: the
1. is 2. have 3. said

D. Grammar, Usage, and Mechanics
Sample: The boy is happy.
1. She can't help us.
2. Can we play ball?
3. Where will I go?

E. Reading Sentences
Sample: A girl runs.
1. He walks the dog.
2. I can sit next to you.
3. The man has a big hat.
4. I like to play games.

F. Story Comprehension
1. dogs and cats
2. Good Pets
3. run and jump

Pages 97-100

Test 11

A. Phonic Analysis: Consonants
Sample: door
1. plant 2. twelve
3. thumb 4. sneakers
5. bench

B. Phonic Analysis: Vowels
Sample: girl
1. mouse 2. game
3. button 4. skates 5. egg

C. High-Frequency Word Match
Sample: send
1. that 2. like 3. sit
4. of 5. book

D. Vocabulary: Picture-Word Match
Sample: jump
1. brush 2. friends 3. pants
4. dollar 5. nine

E. Grammar, Usage, and Mechanics
Sample: eats
1. My 2. lives 3. is
4. Do 5. have 6. They

F. Story Comprehension
1. Baby Penguins
2. three days
3. the mother and father
4. Answers will vary.

GRAMMAR

Page 148
1. The 2. The 3. The 4. The

Page 149
1. The cat sat. 2. The dog sat.
3. I see the cat. 4. I can see.

Page 150
1. The 2. My 3. Jan 4. I 5. Ants

Page 151
1. I see Jan. 2. I go with Jan.
3. We see Dan.
4. I go with Dan and Jan.
5. school. 6. school.

Page 152
1. Dan is in the cab.
2. The cat is in the cab.
3. Mom is in the cab.
4. We see Dan and Mom.
5. van. 6. red.

Page 153
1. The cat is on the mat.
2. The rat is on the mop.
3. The rat sees the cat.
4. The rat can hop.
5. The cat and rat sit.

Page 154
1. (I) like to hop.
2. Pam and (I) like to hop.
3. (I) can hop to Mom.
4. Mom and (I) can hop.
5. Answers will vary.

Page 155
1. I 2. I 3. I 4. I 5. Answers will vary.

Page 156
1. I sit on a mat. 2. Pam and I like cats. 3. I see the van. 4. I like jam. 5. I like to nap.

Page 157
1. Pam 2. Dan 3. The cat
4. The van
5. Jan is hot.
6. The hat is on top.
7. The man sat.

Page 158
1. Bill paints. 2. Tom likes to read.
3. Pat plants flowers.
4. Answers will vary.

Page 159
1. The cat sits on a mat. 2. Pam and Dan like jam. 3. I see Mom. 4. I like my hat. 5. Ben can hop.

Page 160
1. I 2. Pam 3. We 4. We
1. I like dots.
2. Pam likes dots.
3. We like hats.
4. We like hats with dots.

Page 161
1. I like cats. 2. I see a man.
3. We go to school

Page 162
1. I see red dots. 2. Dan is in a big van. 3. The cat is fat. 4. We like the hat. 5. Ben likes jam.

Page 163
1.(?) 2.(?) 3.(?) 4.(?)
5. Answers will vary.
6. Answers will vary.

Page 164
1. Who hid the cat(?)
2. Can the cat see the rat (?)
4. Can the van go(?)
5. (Can we sit in the van?)
6. (Can Dan nap in the van?)

Page 165
1. Who hid my hat?
2. Did the hat have dots?
3. Did Jan like my hat?
4. Can you see the hat?
5. Dan has the hat?

Page 166
1. pig 2. pan 3. Pam 4. hill
5. The sun is hot.
6. Sam ran and ran.
7. Is the cat fat?

Page 167
1. Al, van 2. cat, mat 3. Pat, hill
4. Dan, Jan

Page 168
1. c. 2. b 3. b 4. a 5. c

Page 169
1.(H)ill(P)ark 2.(P)am 3.(D)on
4.(F)rog (L)ake 5. Answers will vary.

Page 170
1.(Pam) 2. (Ant Hill) 3. (Ron)
4. (Bat Lake) 5.(Spot) 6.(Hill Street)

Page 171
1. Don 2. Pig Hill 3. Jam Street
4. Jan 5. Ham Lake

Page 172
1. sits 2. ran 3. hid 4. naps 5. run
6. see

Page 173
1. see 2. sits 3. mops 4. run
5. hops

Page 174
1. b 2. a 3. c 4. c 5. a

Page 175
1. big 2. fast 3. bad 4. fat
5. fat 6. little

Page 176
1. little, fast
2. hot, big
3. It is fat.
4. They are little.

Page 177
1. silly 2. bad 3. black 4. big
5. green

Page 178
1. I. 2. T. 3. H. 4. T.
5. I can fill the basket.
6. Can you get the mop?
7. We can clean.

Page 179
1. She has a mop.
2. The dog is on top.
3. Dan gets the hats.
4. Ron can clean spots.
5. Put it in the pot.
6. Is it in the pan?

Page 180
1. You can get it.
2. The basket is big.
3. The hat is in the basket.
4. A cat can not go in it.
5. We can fill the basket.

Page 181
1. Help! The rat is on top!
2. Get the cat!
3. This cat is bad!
4. Uh-oh! The cat is wet!
5. Oh my! Get the dog!
6. Oh! The dog runs!

Page 182
1. Run to the show!
2. Oh my, I'm very late!
3. What a great show!
4. Watch out, the floor is wet!
5. Wow, we had lots of fun!

Page 183
1. Yes! The cow can kick!
2. That cat is bad!
3. That rat runs fast!
4. Oh no! A frog is in my house!
5. The pot is hot!

Page 184
1. hats 2. eggs 3. girls 4. cats
5. mugs 6. hands

Page 185
1. Jan has her mittens.
2. She will run up hills.
3. Jan runs with her dogs.
4. The dogs can jump.
5. cats 6. socks

Page 186
1. hands 2. pots 3. dogs 4. ants
5. frogs

Page 187
1. sits 2. sees 3. digs 4. naps
5. sees 6. run

Page 188
1. play 2. dance 3. talk 4. run

Page 189
1. sits 2. naps 3. hops
4. digs 5. ran

Page 190
1. school 2. ball 3. girl 4. friends
Person: girl Place: school
Thing: ball

Page 191
1. Run and kick in the park.
2. Kick with a foot.
3. Kick the ball.
4. The girl will run to get it.

5. Kick it to the net.

Page 192
1. park 2. girl 3. ball 4. friend
5. net

Page 193
1. The king is sad.
2. Let's bake him a cake.
3. Tell the king to come.
4. Let's eat the cake.
The king eats.

Page 194
1. This bear likes snow.
2. The water is cold.
3. The bear runs fast.
4. Two bears play.

Page 195
1. Pam will bake a cake.
2. Pam will see the king.
3. The king has a duck.
4. The duck is in the lake.
5. The king will eat cake.

Page 196
circle: What, See, Night, The, Light, Moon, See, Many, Stars, The, Sun, Moon

Answers will vary.

Page 197
1. look, stars 2. the, moon, shines, night 3. we, see, planets 4. many, moons, shine 5. night, day 6. The Sun in the Sky 7. See the Stars!

Page 198
1. Where is the Sun? 2. Many Cats to See 3. Day and Night 4. How Many Pigs? 5. The Big, Bad Wolf

Page 199
1. pot 2. pan 3. top 4. Jim
5. The pot is hot. __
6. See the pan? ____
7. Jim is fast. ________

Page 200
1. Jan, van 2. van 3. van, hill
4. Dan, Jan 5. answers will vary

Page 201
1. pans 2. Jim 3. cat 4. rat 5. cat

Page 202
1. is 2. were 3. was 4. are 5. now
6. in the past 7. now

Page 203
1. are, now 2. is, now 3. was, past
4. is, now 5. were, past

Page 204
1. was 2. were 3. are 4. is 5. are

Page 205
1. The, Gruff 2. They, Troll 3. His, Nosey 4. He 5. Dan and Pam like the play. Names a person, place, or thing. 6. They will read it to Jim.

First word in a sentence.

Page 206
1. Raul 2. Mrs. Chin 3. Sue
4. Lee Park

Page 207
1. I 2. Ron 3. Gruff 4. Troll
5. Nosey

WRITING

Page 210

The	For	That	with	know	but
here	on	When	Have	next	we
as	after	good	Make	there	see
Go	Look	Are	Could	is	why
This	who	said	in	come	them
Has	Name	Before	Her	Where	The

Page 211
1. The mouse; 2. He finds; 3. He eats; 4. Then he; 5. Oh no!; 6. The mouse

Page 212
1. We read; 2. Then we; 3. My bed; 4. My cat; 5. The sky; 6. My eyes

Page 213
1. My dog; 2. She must; 3. Maybe she; 4. Sometimes she; 5. I think

Page 214
Check that the child has added a period to the end of each sentence.

Page 215
Check that the child has added a period to the end of each sentence.

Page 216
1. Frogs and toads lay eggs. 2. The eggs are in the water. 3. Tadpoles hatch from the eggs. 4. The tadpoles grow legs. 5. The tadpoles lose their tails.

Page 217
1. Tadpoles become frogs or toads. 2. Frogs live near water. 3. Toads live under bushes. 4. Frogs have wet skin. 5. Toads have bumpy skin.

Page 218
The following sentences should be colored red: This is a flag., The flag has stars., The stars are white., The stripes are red., The stripes are white., The flag has a blue part., There are 50 stars.; The rest are not sentences and should be colored white.

Page 219

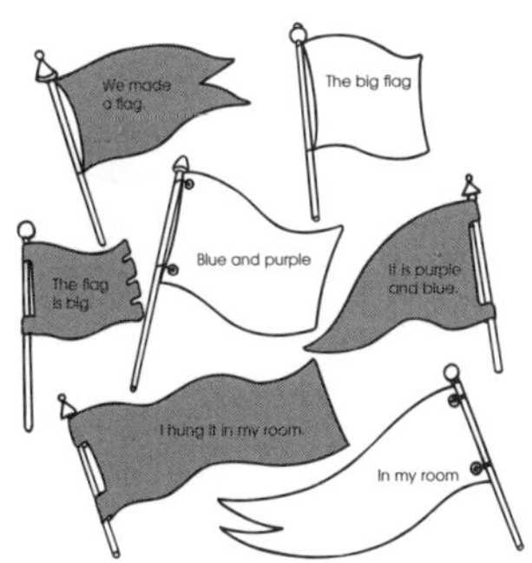
We made a flag.
The big flag
Blue and purple
It is purple and blue.
The flag is big.
I hung it in my room.
In my room

Page 220
Five boats are sailing.; We have four buckets.

Page 221
A jaguar is hiding.; Some butterflies are blue.; Frogs jump in the water.; Green snakes hang from trees.; The trees grow very tall.

Page 222
The snakes on the left side of the page should have been colored.

Page 223
1. The blue snake;
2. The yellow snake;
3. The green snake;
4. The brown snake;
5. The red snake; 6. The purple snake; 7. The black snake; 8. The orange snake

Page 224
Sentences will vary.

Page 225
Sentences will vary.

Page 226
Sentences will vary.

Page 227
Sentences will vary.

Page 228
The bones on the right side of the page should have been colored.

Page 229
1. is jumping.; 2. is barking.; 3. is eating.; 4. is sleeping.

Page 230
Sentences will vary.

Page 231
Answers will vary.

Page 232
Sentences will vary.

Page 233
Sentences will vary.

Page 234
Pictures will vary.

Page 235
Answers will vary.

Page 236
1. long ago; 2. yesterday; 3. in winter; 4. today; 5. in the fall; 6. last night; 7. all day; 8. at noon; 9. yesterday; 10. on Thanksgiving Day; 11. this morning; 12. Tomorrow

Page 237
Sentences will vary.

Page 238
Answers will vary.

Page 239
Sentences will vary.

Page 240
Sentences will vary.

Page 241
Sentences will vary.

Page 242
kitten, bat, cracker, ball

Page 243
sweet, red, smooth; bumpy, salty, crunchy,; small, squeaky, furry

Page 244
Adjectives will vary.

Page 245
Sentences will vary.

Page 246
Sentences will vary.

Page 247
Sentences will vary.

Page 248
Sentences will vary.

Page 249
Sentences will vary.

Page 250
My Space Friend; A Big Beak; The Big Win; A Knight's Tale

Page 251
Stories will vary.

Page 252
Sentences will vary.

Page 253
Sentences and pictures will vary.

MAPS

Page 256
1. yes
2. yes
3. yes
4. no
5. swimming pool; car; lawn

Page 257
Child should color answers on map.

Page 258
4. truck
5. yes

Page 259
Child should color answers on map.

Page 261
1. far
2. near
3. above

Pages 262–263
1. yes
2. yes
3. no
4. yes
5. school
6. flower shop
7. Map 3
8. Map 1

Page 264
1. round
2. people, animals, plants
3. Drawings will vary.

Page 265
1. blue, green, orange, yellow, purple, red
2. blue
3. smaller

Page 266
1. south
2. east

Page 267
1. east
2. north
3. west
4. south

Page 268
1. north
2. east
3. north
4. west

Page 269
1–4 Line begins at gate, runs north to popcorn, west to Ferris wheel, east to face painting, west to popcorn and north to arcade.
5. south

Page 270
1. c.
2. a.
3. d.
4. b.

Page 271
1. tree
2. airplane
3. railroad track
4. beach umbrella

Page 272
1. garden
2. road
3. house
4. stable

Page 273
1. south
2. sheep
3. west
4. Tree symbol should be drawn for forest.

Pages 274–275
1. mountain
2. plain
3. hill
4. river
5. mountain
6. hill
7. lake

Page 276
1–4 Child should write answers on picture.

Page 277
1. plain
2. east
3. west
4. Answers will vary.

Page 278
1. hill
2. campground
3. picnic table
4. river or lake
5. west

Page 279
1. Doony Park
2. snack stand
3. a fountain
4. dog run
5. playground
6. west

Page 280
1. school
2. apartment
3. store
4. house
5. Drawings will vary.

Page 281
1. school
2. Spring Street
3. Summer Street
4. west

Page 282
1. South Street
2. West Street
3. North Street
4. South Street

Page 283
1. Routes will vary.
2. East Street
4. west
5. north

Page 285
1. border
2. road
3. a river
4. south
5. west

Page 287
1. state border
2. Answers will vary.
3. Answers will vary.
4. Answers will vary.
5. south
6. west
7. Arizona
8. Indiana

Page 288
1. state capital
2. south
3. north
4. west

Page 289
1. state border
2. Ohio River
3. Wabash River
4. four
5. Lake Michigan

Page 290
1. south
2. Answers will vary.
3. west
4. east
5. Answers will vary.

Page 292
1. country border
2. Canada
3. south

Page 293
1. Atlantic Ocean
2. Pacific Ocean

Pages 294–295
2. Atlantic, Pacific, Arctic, Indian
3. Europe
4. South America
5. Indian Ocean
6. Arctic Ocean
7. Antarctica

Page 296
1. pond
2. hill
3. North Street
4. Routes will vary.
5. post office on South Street
6. north

Page 297
1. states
2. Raleigh
3. plains
4. four
5. Atlantic Ocean
6. west

Page 298
1. south
2. lake
3. border
4. symbol
5. mountain
6. route

Secret Words:
United States

ADDITION & SUBTRACTION

Page 302

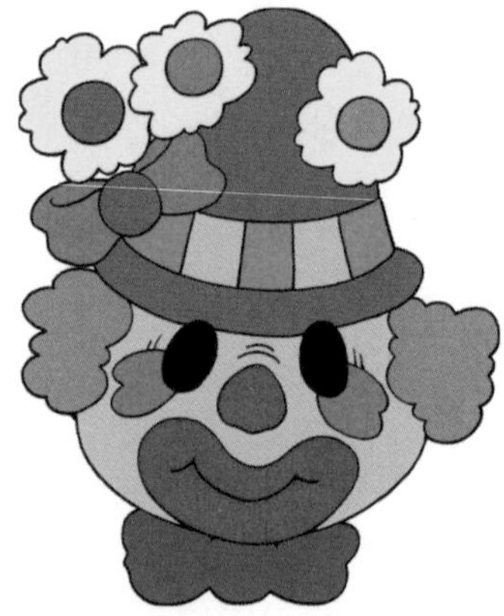

Check child's coloring.

Page 303
1 + 2 = 3, 2 + 3 = 5, 7 + 3 = 10; 3 + 4 = 7, 1 + 0 = 1, 3 + 2 = 5; 1 + 1 = 2, 4 + 4 = 8; 1 + 3 = 4; The ladybug with 10 spots should be colored red. The ladybug with 1 spot should be colored blue.

Page 304
Check that the child has drawn the correct number of flowers. 7: needs 3, 10: needs 5, 4: needs 1; 6: needs 2, 9: needs 5; 5: needs 3, 8: needs 4, 3: needs 2; Color the bows with the numbers 4, 6, 8, and 10 yellow. Color the bows with 3, 5, 7, and 9 purple.

Page 305
A SAXOPHONE

6 + 2 = 8; 5 + 1 = 6; 4 + 4 = 8

3 + 6 = 9; 3 + 0 = 3; 3 + 4 = 7

2 + 2 = 4; 2 + 1 = 3; 1 + 1 = 2

0 + 1 = 1

Page 306
5 – 3 = 2; 7 – 4 = 3; 10 – 5 = 5; 9 – 2 = 7; 8 – 7 = 1; 9 – 6 = 3; 6 – 1 = 5; 10 – 2 = 8; 7 – 5 = 2; 5 – 1 = 4; 8 – 2 = 6; 8 – 0 = 8; 9 – 7 = 2; 8 – 5 = 3; 10 – 4 = 6; 10 – 3 = 7; 9 – 4 = 5; 8 – 1 = 7; 6 – 4 = 2; 6 – 3 = 3;

7 – 2 = 5; 9 – 0 = 9; 10 – 1 = 9

Page 307
2, 3, 2; 3, 2, 1

Pages 308–309
1. 9 – 4 = 5; 2. 8 – 1 = 7;

3. 10 – 3 = 7; 4. 8 – 6 = 2;

5. 7 – 2 = 5; 6. 8 – 4 = 4

7. 10 – 4 = 6; 8. 8 – 2 = 6;

9. 9 – 6 = 3

Page 310

Page 311

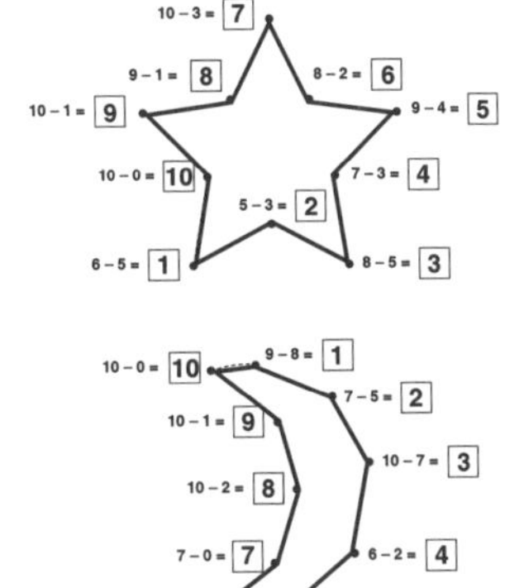

Page 312
4, 3, 2; 10, 1, 7; 6, 8, 5; The rabbit moved right to add. The rabbit moved left to subtract.

Page 313

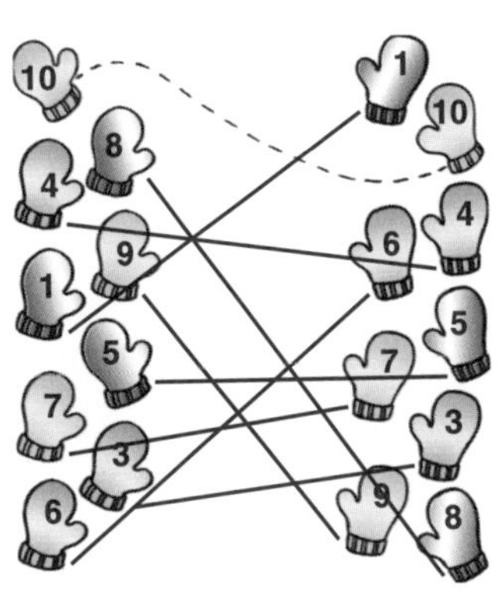

Page 314

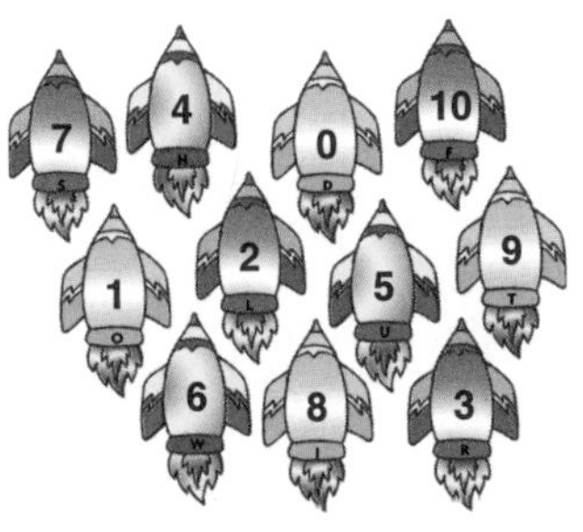

IT'S OUT OF THIS WORLD!

Page 315

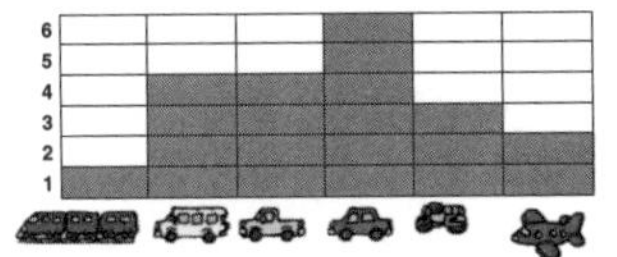

A. 6 + 2 = 8; B. 3 + 1 = 4;
C. 6 – 4 = 2

Page 316
A. 6 + 4 = 10; B. 10 – 5 = 5; C. 9 – 2 = 7; D. 4 + 6 = 10; E. 7 + 2 = 9; F. 2 + 3 = 5; G. 5 + 3 = 8; H. 6 + 4 = 10; I. 8 – 7 = 1; J. 10 – 3 = 7

Page 317
A. 7 + 3 = 10; B. 7 – 4 = 3; C. 10 – 6 = 4; D. 8 – 2 = 6; E. 5 + 4 = 9

Page 318

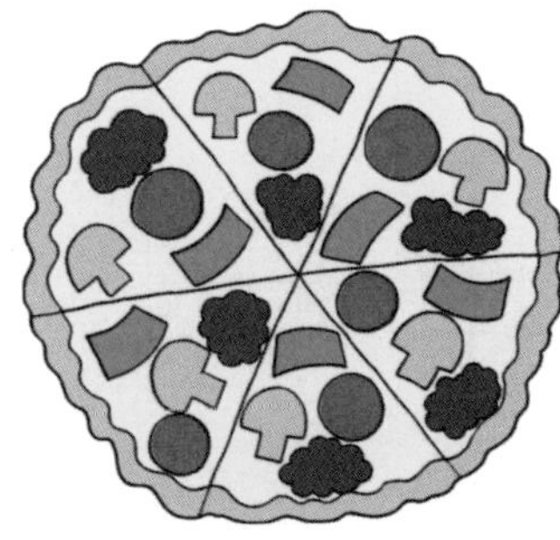

Check child's coloring.
11 ways; 0 + 10 = 10, 1 + 9 = 10, 2 + 8 = 10, 3 + 7 = 10, 4 + 6 = 10, 5 + 5 = 10, 6 + 4 = 10, 7 + 3 = 10, 8 + 2 = 10, 9 + 1 = 10, 0 + 10 = 10

Page 319

7 leaps

Page 320

8 + 7 = 15; 3 + 7 = 10; 8 + 6 = 14; 9 + 9 = 18; 1 + 1 = 2; 5 + 2 = 7; 3 + 2 = 5; 9 + 2 = 11; 4 + 2 = 6; 1 + 4 = 5; 2 + 2 = 4; 7 + 4 = 11; 5 + 8 = 13; 6 + 2 = 8; 7 + 7 = 14; 5 + 5 = 10; 4 + 7 = 11; 3 + 3 = 6; 1 + 7 = 8; 3 + 8 = 11; 5 + 0 = 5; 9 + 6 = 15; 5 + 3 = 8; 2 + 5 = 7; 0 + 2 = 2; 3 + 1 = 4; 9 + 7 = 16; 7 + 5 = 12; 6 + 1 = 7; 9 + 8 = 17; 1 + 5 = 6; 6 + 6 = 12

Page 321

Beans talk.

4 + 2 = 6; 7 + 7 = 14; 9 + 5 = 14

10 + 4 = 14; 4 + 8 = 12; 6 + 8 = 14

11 + 3 = 14; 14 + 0 = 14; 7 + 2 = 9

13 + 1 = 14; 5 + 8 = 13; 12 + 2 = 14

7 + 4 = 11; 5 + 9 = 14

Page 322

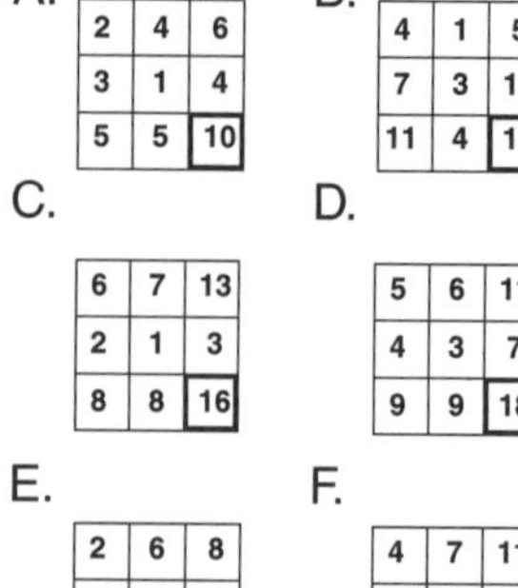

A.

2	4	6
3	1	4
5	5	10

B.

4	1	5
7	3	10
11	4	15

C.

6	7	13
2	1	3
8	8	16

D.

5	6	11
4	3	7
9	9	18

E.

2	6	8
5	0	5
7	6	13

F.

4	7	11
3	3	6
7	10	17

Page 323

8, 8; 4, 4; 6, 6; 8, 8; 1, 1; 3, 3; 9, 9; 2, 2; 5, 5; 7, 7; even

Page 324

7 + 7 = 14, 5 + 5 = 10, 8 + 8 = 16, 6 + 6 = 12; 9 + 9 = 18, 3 + 3 = 6, 2 + 2 = 4; 4 + 4 = 8

Page 325

A. 4; B. 6; C. 10; D. 9; E. 7; F. 2; G. 5; H. 8; I. 3; J. 1; K. 5 – 2 = 3; L. 9 – 3 = 6; M. 7 – 5 = 2; N. 8 – 1 = 7; O. 12 – 6 = 6; P. 16 – 8 = 8; Q. 14 – 5 = 9

Page 326

four, five; seven, eleven; nine, six; ten, three; eight, two

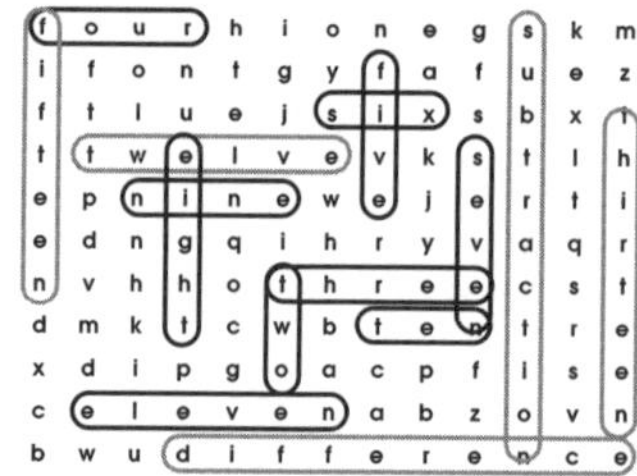

Page 327

7 + 2 = **9** – 4 = **5** – 3 = **2** + 9 = **11** + 5 = **16** – 8 = **8** + 4 = **12** + 6 = **18** – 9 = **9** + 1 = **10** + 4 = **14** – 8 = **6** + 2 = **8** + 3 = **11** – 3 = **8**; 12 – 3 = **9** – 6 = **3** + 2 = **5** + 9 = **14** – 6 = **8** + 7 = **15** – 6 = **9** + 3 = **12** – 2 = **10** + 7 = **17** + 1 = **18** – 11 = **7** – 5 = **2** + 13 = **15** – 7 = **8** + 3 = **11**; Color the bottom car blue.

Page 328

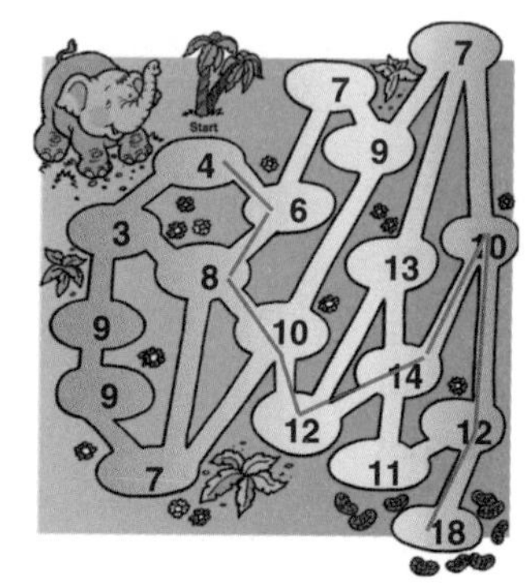

3 peanuts

Page 329

3, 3; 7, 7; 9, 9; 5, 5; 8, 8

Page 330

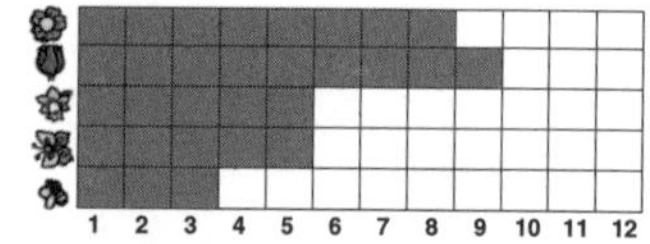

A. First flower should be circled.
B. 8 + 9 = 17; C. 5 – 5 = 0;
D. 5 + 3 = 8; E. 5 – 3 = 2;
F. 9 + 5 = 14

Page 331

A. 13, 12, 13, 13; B. 12, 11, 11, 11; C. 17, 15, 15, 17; D. 14, 14, 14, 16

Check child's coloring.

Page 332

- 1; 12, 11, 10, 9, 8, 7
+2; 2, 4, 6, 8, 10, 12
+3; 3, 6, 9, 12, 15, 18
-2; 13, 11, 9, 7, 5, 3

Page 333
2, 4, 2; 3, 5, 4; 6, 4, 10;
Answers will vary.

Page 334
5; 3 + 2 + 5 = 10; 4 + 5 + 7 = 16; 6; 7 + 2 = 9; 6 – 2 = 4; 7 + 4 + 5 + 3 + 2 = 21; 1 + 7 + 6 + 3 + 2 = 19

Page 335

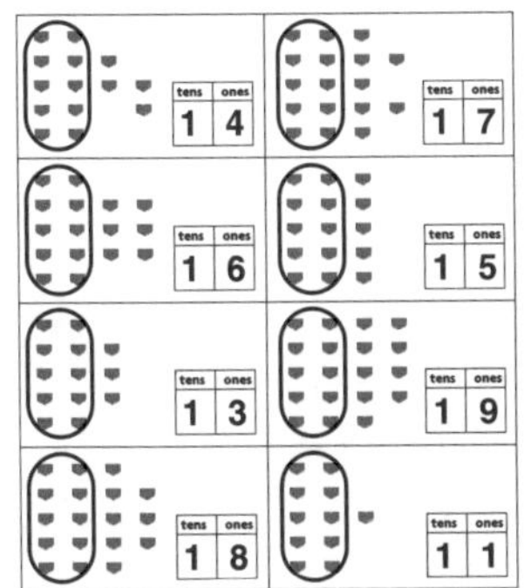

Page 336

Check child's coloring.; 14 days

Page 337

	17	36	84	
78	29	59	14	48
88	24	35	66	98
18	43	77	38	88
78	65	56	46	26
	99	57	87	

Page 338
93 + 6 = 99, 82 + 4 = 86, 14 + 5 = 19, 21 + 7 = 28, 53 + 6 = 59; 45 + 4 = 49, 73 + 3 = 76, 36 + 3 = 39, 61 + 5 = 66, 32 + 7 = 39; 4 + 7 + 5 + 3 + 6 = 25

Page 339

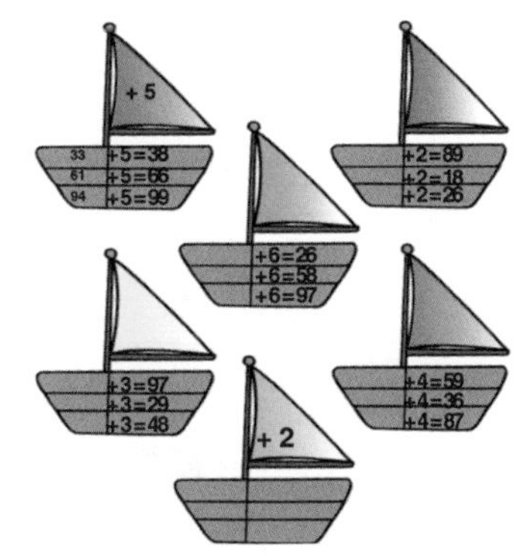

Page 340

Check child's coloring.

Page 341
A. 39 – 7 = 32; B. 54 – 1 = 53; C. 87 – 6 = 81;
D. 73 – 3 = 70; E. 25 – 4 = 21; F. 42 – 2 = 40;
G. 98 – 7 = 91; H. 66 – 5 = 61;
4, 7, 5

Page 342
42, 90, 76, 32, 82, 63, 81; 50, 35, 21, 21, 41, 90, 53; 30, 80, 20, 70, 60, 65, 74; The box with 53 should be colored yellow. The box with 32 should be colored orange. The box with 74 should be colored red.

Page 343

Check child's coloring.

Page 344
AT
12 + 13 = 25; 24 + 34 = 58;
22 + 21 = 43; 77 + 22 = 99;
35 + 43 = 78; 52 + 12 = 64
40 + 52 = 92; 11 + 31 = 42;
30 + 39 = 69; 46 + 52 = 98;
15 + 12 = 27; 10 + 71 = 81;
63 + 11 = 74; 13 + 80 = 93;
36 + 32 = 68; 30 + 10 = 40;
11 + 11 = 22; 15 + 4 = 19
20 + 21 = 41; 15 + 11 = 26;
22 + 33 = 55; 14 + 14 = 28;
13 + 16 = 29; 10 + 20 = 30;
14 + 25 = 39; 11 + 20 = 31;
15 + 21 = 36; 20 + 31 = 51;
36 + 52 = 88; 21 + 32 = 53;
10 + 50 = 60; 44 + 41 = 85;
24 + 43 = 67; 31 + 21 = 52;
13 + 82 = 95;

Page 345
32 + 24 = 56; 16 + 40 = 56;
54 + 14 = 68; 77 + 12 = 89;
34 + 34 = 68; 53 + 36 = 89;
26 + 63 = 89; 23 + 45 = 68;
35 + 62 = 97; 38 + 30 = 68;
22 + 67 = 89; 47 + 42 = 89

Page 346
HE WAS A CHICKEN.

13 + 11 = 24; 26 + 33 = 59;
16 + 31 = 47; 10 + 12 = 22;
64 + 24 = 88; 20 + 15 = 35;
71 + 12 = 83; 25 + 21 = 46;
51 + 10 = 61; 22 + 16 = 38;
22 + 10 = 32; 14 + 14 = 28;
20 + 10 = 30; 25 + 31 = 56;
21 + 3 = 24; 42 + 30 = 72;
13 + 43 = 56; 54 + 15 = 69;
21 + 61 = 82; 61 + 33 = 94;
10 + 30 = 40; 20 + 30 = 50;
16 + 32 = 48; 71 + 23 = 94;
70 + 20 = 90

Page 347
A BAT

5 – 2 = 3; 7 – 7 = 0; 18 – 9 = 9;
17 – 3 = 14; 15 – 4 = 11;
18 – 4 = 14; 12 – 3 = 9;
11 – 9 = 2; 16 – 9 = 7; 7 – 4 = 3;
10 – 8 = 2; 15 – 7 = 8; 9 – 2 = 7;
13 – 2 = 11; 12 – 2 = 10;
15 – 2 = 13; 9 – 6 = 3; 6 – 6 = 0;
9 – 7 = 2; 15 – 9 = 6; 16 – 8 = 8;
9 – 5 = 4; 9 – 1 = 8

Page 348
77 – 30 = 47; 76 – 62 = 14;
59 – 12 = 47; 85 – 52 = 33;
98 – 84 = 14; 87 – 40 = 47;
98 – 35 = 63; 58 – 11 = 47;
88 – 62 = 26; 77 – 14 = 63;
69 – 22 = 47; 38 – 12 = 26;
75 – 12 = 63; 97 – 71 = 26;
97 – 50 = 47; 98 – 51 = 47;
43 – 10 = 33; 87 – 73 = 14;
78 – 31 = 47; 97 – 64 = 33;
99 – 52 = 47

Page 349
1. 7 – 1 = 6; 2. 9 – 2 = 7;
3. 3 – 2 = 1; 4. 8 – 4 = 4,
5. 5 – 5 = 0; 6. 6 – 1 = 5;
7. 8 – 2 = 6

The phone number is 671-4056.

Page 350
27, 74, 41, 65; 27, 70, 42, 53; 15, 23, 11, 33; 20, 2, 15, 31; 22

Page 351

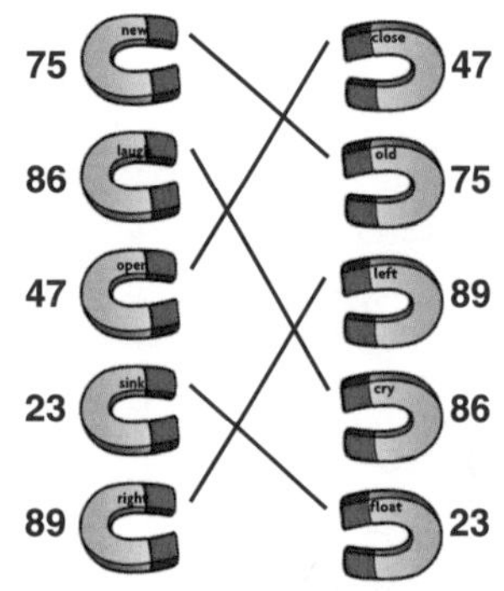

Answers will vary.

Page 352
34 + 13 = 47, 21 + 52 = 73, 47 + 10 = 57; 75 – 34 = 41, 62 – 21 = 41, 47 – 13 = 34

Page 353
A. Sunday; B. 89;
C. Monday; D. 24; E. 79; F. 22;
Sunday, Tuesday, Saturday

Page 354
34, 85, 26, 57; star; 71, 88, 42, 76, 85; light; 76, 63, 26, 85; heat; 71, 88, 13, 63; life

Page 355

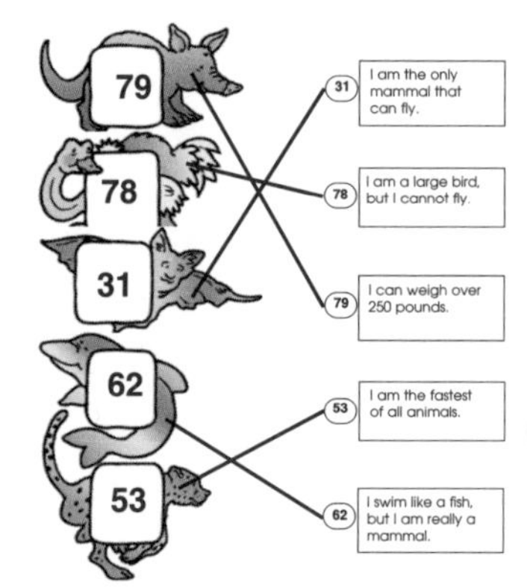

Page 356

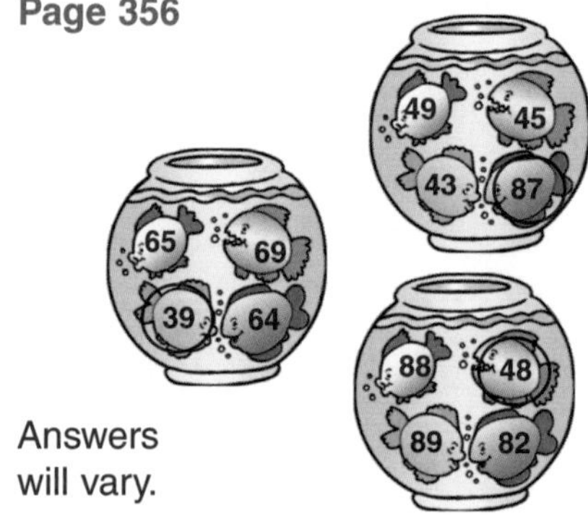

Answers will vary.

MATH

Page 359
Check child's picture to make sure each shape has the correct color:

6 = yellow;
7 = green;
8 = brown;
9 = red;
10 = green.

Page 360
Answers will vary, but check to make sure that child has supplied correct numbers for each category.

Page 361
Check to make sure that child has drawn lines from five different frogs to the lily pads.

Extra: 2

Page 362

1. Answers will vary.
2. Numbers will be colored in using an AB pattern ofred and blue.

Page 363

Possible groups

Balls: soccer ball, basketball, rubber ball

Winter clothes: scarf, hat, boots

Art supplies: paint, paintbrush, crayon

Page 364

Check child's picture to make sure that each shape has the correct color:

one = green;

two = yellow;

three = red;

four = purple;

five = blue.

Page 365

Yield sign: triangle, 3

Caution sign: diamond, 4

Speed-limit sign: rectangle, 4

Stop sign: octagon, 8

Page 366

Left birdhouse: cube, octagon, hexagon, rectangle, square, rectangle solid

Right birdhouse: cylinder, triangle, circle, rectangle

Page 367

Color the first butterfly, the second heart, the lightbulb, and the snowflake; drawings should show the other halves.

Page 368

1. 32, 42, 52, 62, 72, 82, 92
2. 70, 60, 50, 40, 30, 20, 10
3. 67, 57, 47, 37, 27, 17, 7
4. 44, 55, 66, 77, 88, 99

Page 369

A salamander

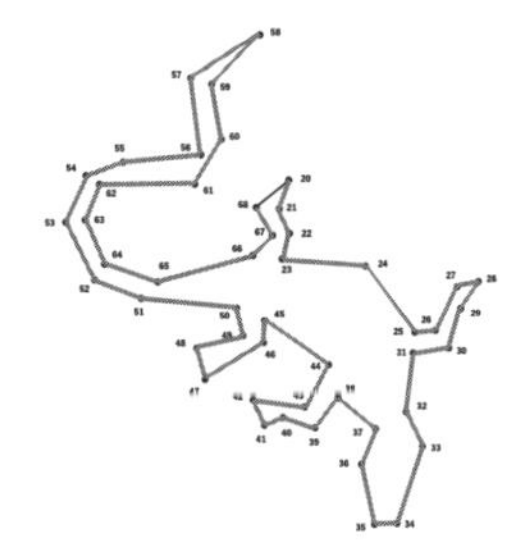

Page 370

Estimates will vary. 2, 4, 6, 8, 10, 12, 14, 16, 18, 20, 5, 10, 15, 20

Extra: No. Snowflakes would melt before you could count them.

Page 371

1	2	3	4	5	6	7	8	9	10
11	12	13	14	15	16	17	18	19	20
21	22	23	24	25	26	27	28	29	30
31	32	33	34	35	36	37	38	39	40
41	42	43	44	45	46	47	48	49	50
51	52	53	54	55	56	57	58	59	60
61	62	63	64	65	66	67	68	69	70
71	72	73	74	75	76	77	78	79	80
81	82	83	84	85	86	87	88	89	90
91	92	93	94	95	96	97	98	99	100

Answers will vary.

Page 372

4 + 4 = 8

5 + 5 = 10

6 + 6 = 12

7 + 7 = 14

8 + 8 = 16

Extra: 6, 8, 10, 12, 14, 16

Pattern: Count by 2s, even numbers, doubling

Page 373

5

Child's patterns and equations will vary.

Page 374

Answers will vary.

Page 375

Answers will vary.

Page 376

Answers will vary.

Page 377

15; 8

Page 378

Alex's coins: 5¢ + 25¢ + 10¢ = 60 ¢

Billy's coins: 10¢ + 10¢ + 10¢ + 10¢ + 10¢ + 5¢ + 5¢ + 1¢ + 1¢ + 1¢ = 63¢

63¢ > 60¢ Billy has more money.

Page 379

1¢: 10 coins for 10¢

5¢: 4 coins for 20¢

10¢: 2 coins for 20¢

25¢: 2 coins for 50¢

Page 380

Answers will vary.

Page 381

3 1/2 inches, 2 inches, 1 1/2 inches, 3 inches

Patty, Peter, Petunia, Paul

Page 382

pencil: 2

lunchbox: 1

crayon: 2

notebook: 1

Page 383
1 gallon = 4 quarts
1 quart = 2 pints
1 pint = 2 cups
1 cup = 12 tablespoons
1 tablespoon = 3 teaspoons

Page 384
1 + 2 + 1 + 2 = 6 inches
2 + 3 + 2 + 3 = 10 inches
2 + 5 + 2 + 5 = 14 inches

Page 385
book height: 2 centimeters
book width: 3 centimeters
straw: 6 centimeters
marker: 4 centimeters
5 cubes: 4 centimeters
10 cubes: 8 centimeters
shoe: 5 centimeters
hand: 3 centimeters

Page 386
Answers will vary. The following is a likely answer. Check children's graphs to make sure that they correspond to the boxes checked.
chicken: see, hear, smell, touch
sun: see
lemonade: see, touch, taste
flowers: see, smell, touch
drums: see, hear, touch

Page 387
Answers will vary.

Page 388

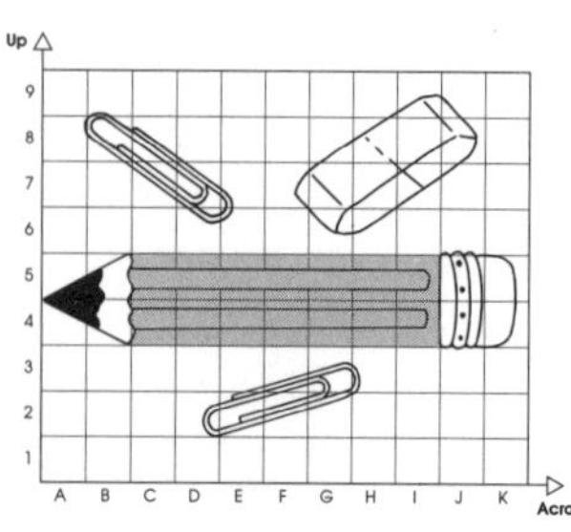

Page 389

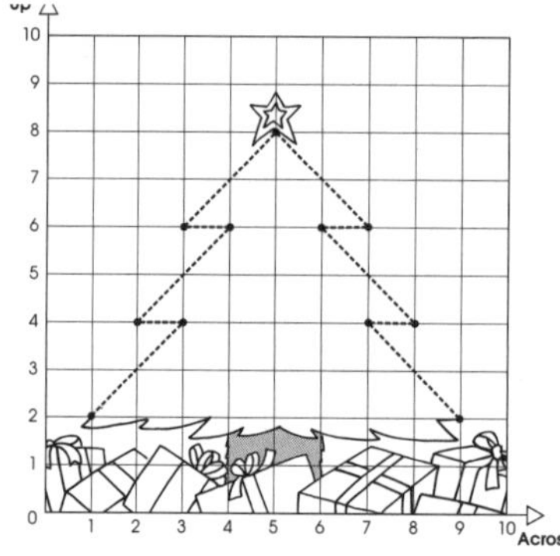

Page 390
Sunny days: 12
Cloudy days: 8
Rainy days: 5
Snowy days: 6

Page 391
Color shapes 1, 2, 5, 6, 7, and 8.

Page 392
1/5 of the circle, 4/5 of the rectangle, 3 ants, 2 spiders, 0 bees, 5 worms

Page 393
1/8 of the circle, 6/8 of the square, 4 suns, 8 stars,
2 moons, 3 planets

Page 394

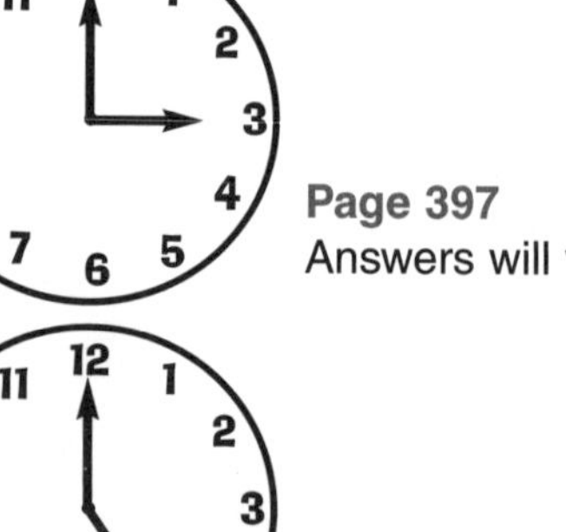

Page 395

Page 396

Page 397
Answers will vary.

To the companies dedicated to succeeding
through concurrent engineering
and to the product development teams
who enable that success.

"There is no greater challenge than to have someone relying upon you; no greater satisfaction than to vindicate this expectation."

—Kingman Brewster, president of Yale University

Contents

Preface

In the mid-1980s, several companies approached Mentor Graphics Corporation and asked for assistance in solving their time-to-market pressures. These companies wanted Mentor Graphics to participate in improving their performance by providing them with a cost-effective product development environment. These requests led the authors and others at Mentor Graphics to evaluate what would be needed to create a product development environment for the 1990s.

These evaluations indicate that increasing the number of tools and amount of data, without other changes, cannot break down the barriers to improved productivity. The tools and data must be accompanied by new product development processes that meet the requirements of the market and current technologies. These processes, along with the tools, data, and employees who use them, must exist in a product development environment shaped by the philosophy and methodology of concurrent engineering.

This book describes the concurrent engineering environment necessary for developing electronic, software, mechanical, and system products in the 1990s. It is written for today's decision makers who must communicate their company's vision for tomorrow. If you are one of those decision makers, you are a manager of change, and concurrent engineering methods will enable you to reshape your company's product development environment into the concurrent engineering environment your company needs now and in the future.

Acknowledgments

Writing a book about concurrent engineering involves, by necessity, a concurrent approach. Many individuals joined together, forming a "mixed-discipline team" that provided research background for the book. Charlie Sorgie brought his experience in systems engineering. Dr. Geoff Bunza, Dr. Dave Ullman, Dr. Ed Thompson, and Dr. Jonathan Weiss brought experience with product development process issues. Darrel Baker and Tom Cyr brought experience in consulting and process assessment technology. Jose De Castro, Ken Salzberg, Bill Stevens, and Grant Vergottini brought experience in frameworks and automated concurrent engineering.

These individuals–the core team–initially struggled with deciding exactly what information the book should communicate. As with all mixed-discipline teams, we first had to define a common vocabulary and agree on a common purpose before we could agree on individual priorities. This process of collaborating to reach a consensus proved to be a valuable experience for everyone and yielded the results in this book.

After the core team prepared the initial drafts of the book, an impressive list of reviewers–the extended team–joined the project. If it's true that any book is only as good as its reviewers, then this should be an extraordinary book. Many thanks to:

❖ The CALS/CE Task Group: Larry Linton's Electronic Systems Subtask Group (including Jack Abramowitz, Stew Elder, Al Herner, Kathy Hutchison, Dennis Hoffman, Bill Vitaliano) and Yosef Haridm's Frameworks Subtask Group

❖ The Mentor Graphics review team: Dave Brinker, Rich Bruer, Tom Bruggere, Dave Chen, Bill Chown, Russ Henke, Nic Herriges, Gordon Hoffman, Paul Hofstadler, Peter Hoogerhuis, Wendy Hughson, Howard Ko, Gerry Langeler, Larry Loper, Berkeley Merchant, Hiroshi Okubo, Sam Pickens, Phil Robinson, Charlie Rosenthal, Rick Samco, Mike Stanbro, John Stedman, George Tice, Dave Van Vaerenewyck, and Dan Wick.

❖ The industry leaders who stepped forward to add great value: Andy Graham, CAD Framework Initiative; Don Hall and Lt. Col. Doug Webster, Office of the Secretary of Defense; Russ Hall, Logic Modeling Systems, Inc.; Dr. William Lattin, Logic Automation, Inc.; Naomi J. McAfee, Westinghouse Electric Corporation; Mitsuo Shimizu, Canon, Inc.; Dr. Paul Sullivan, Micro Electronics & Computer Technology Corp.; and Andrew Yskamp, Allied-Signal Aerospace Co.

Often unstated, but clearly important to the success of a team is the spirit of its members. Special thanks to Terry Barce, Diane Cain, Maxine Nelson, and Charla Netz for their cheerful support.

Any product development process can benefit from a process management facility that monitors and evaluates changes in the design. Throughout the development process of this book, we were grateful to our developmental editor, George Truett, who kept our wandering ideas focused, connected, and clearly stated.

Meeting the customer's expectations is ultimately the definition of good design. Many thanks for the creative direction and production efforts of the GRADY BRITTON BROWN team, especially Susan Brown and Wilbur Kauffman, for exceeding our expectations. Thanks also to Fred Ingram for capturing the essence of concurrent engineering in his cover and chapter divider art.

Introduction

Concurrent engineering isn't new. Many companies will argue that they have been practicing concurrent engineering for a long time, and to varying degrees, they are right.

Concurrent Engineering Time Line

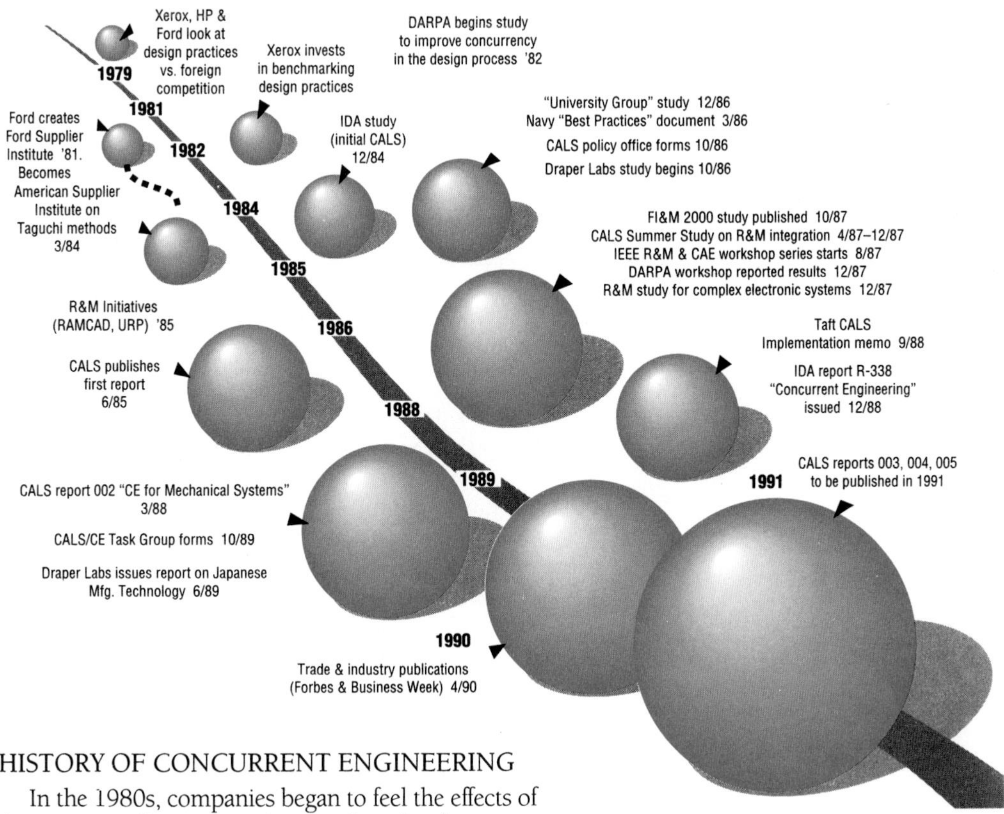

HISTORY OF CONCURRENT ENGINEERING

In the 1980s, companies began to feel the effects of three major influences on their product development:

- Newer and innovative technologies
- Increasing product complexities
- Larger organizations

Companies were forced to look for new product development methods. One of the most significant events in the concurrent engineering time line took place in 1982, when the Defense Advanced Research Projects Agency (DARPA) began a study to look for ways to improve concurrency in the design process. Five years later, when the results of the DARPA study were released, they proved to be an important foundation on which other groups would base further study.

"Concurrent engineering is a systematic approach to the integrated, concurrent design of products and their related processes, including manufacture and support. This approach is intended to cause the developers, from the outset, to consider all elements of the product life cycle from concept through disposal, including quality, cost, schedule, and user requirements."

IDA Report R-338

In the summer of 1986, the Institute for Defense Analyses (IDA) Report R-338 coined the term concurrent engineering to explain the systematic method of concurrently designing both the product and its downstream production and support processes. The IDA Report provided the first definition of concurrent engineering.

This definition is now widely accepted. The IDA Report defined what concurrent engineering is—but how should a company implement it? How can a company create an environment that supports concurrent engineering?

First, you, as a manager of change in your company, must understand the necessity of concurrent engineering to survive global competition in the 1990s. You must understand the four key dimensions of a concurrent engineering environment and identify the appropriate approach for applying concurrent engineering to your company's product development process. And finally, you must consider the inevitable necessity of automating your company's concurrent engineering environment.

WHAT'S INSIDE

This book will guide you on your journey toward understanding what a concurrent engineering environment is and how to begin creating it in your company. Make no mistake about the importance of this journey: It is about the continued growth and prosperity of your company.

Chapter 1 looks at the five forces of change—technology, tools, tasks, talent, and time—in today's competitive global marketplace. You can use these as resources in a concurrent engineering environment. Then Chapter 2 defines the concurrent engineering environment in terms of its four key dimensions: organization, communication infrastructure, requirements, and product development. By understanding the need to balance these dimensions, you can apply a concurrent engineering approach to transform your current product development environment. To determine the right concurrent engineering approach for your company, Chapter 3 provides an assessment tool. And finally, Chapter 4 looks at automation and provides you with a five-phased plan for automating your concurrent engineering environment.

As you read this book, you will find that many of the examples in it reflect the experience of Mentor Graphics in working with the electronic design industry. However, the vision communicated by this book reaches far beyond the electronics industry. For any company in the world that develops a product, this vision of a concurrent engineering environment could represent a path toward continuing success.

A rose by any other name—

- ***team design***
- ***simultaneous engineering***
- ***produceability engineering***
- ***concurrent design***
- ***transition to manufacturing***
- ***integrated product development***

—is still concurrent engineering.

ONE

TODAY'S CHANGING PRODUCT DEVELOPMENT ENVIRONMENT.

TO BE A WINNER, YOUR

COMPANY MUST TRANSFORM

THE FIVE FORCES OF CHANGE—

TECHNOLOGY, TOOLS, TASKS,

TALENT, AND TIME—

INTO WELL-MANAGED RESOURCES

FOR PRODUCT DEVELOPMENT.

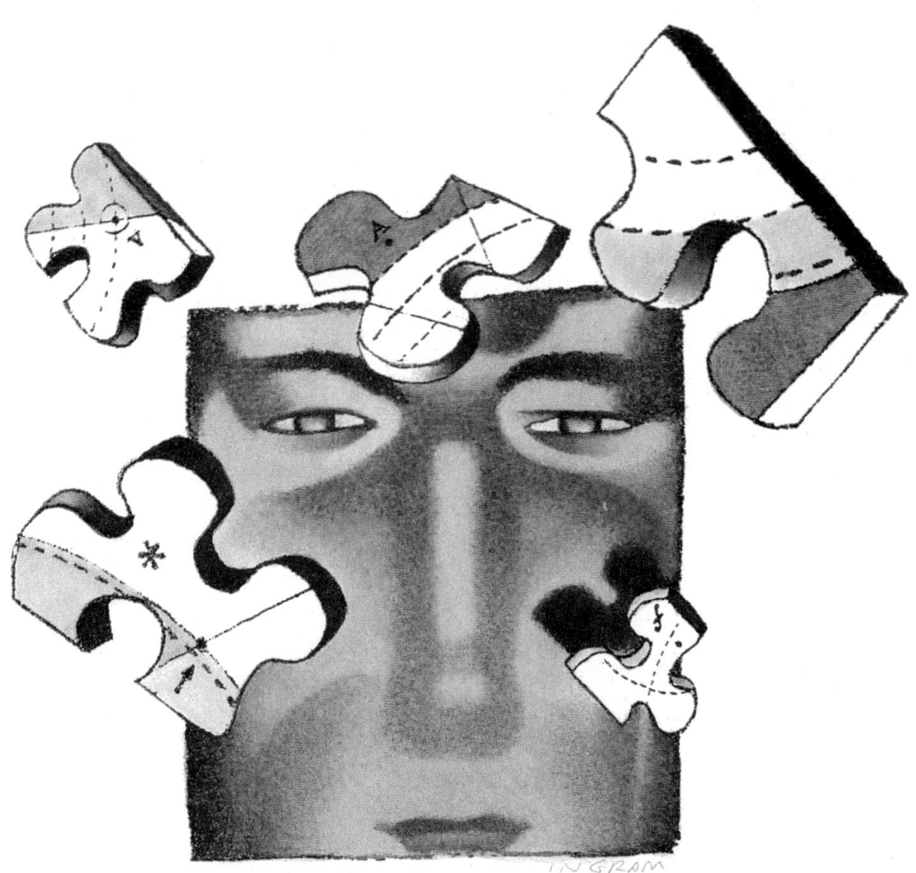

THE FIVE FORCES OF CHANGE

Today's Changing Product Development Environment

With the growth of multinational corporations, competition in the world marketplace is relentless. Those who can get the highest quality, price competitive product to market in the least time are going to be winners. Even small companies must understand this and be ready to participate in global markets to be successful.

In the 1950s and 1960s, United States industry dominated world technology with one innovation after another. Consumers bought "Made in the USA." That label meant a quality product with the latest technology, and it offered prestige.

In the 1970s and 1980s, companies around the world have competed for the business of the planet's consumers and have won much of it from US companies. Innovation alone has no longer been the guarantee of a successful product.

US companies did not mount an effective response to this challenge. They met the tide of lower-cost products by cutting prices and, inevitably, their own profit margins. They cut their work forces to beef up profits. And in many cases, they lost the employees needed to bring their products to market quickly.

This was the wrong strategy then and it's the wrong strategy now for any company that wants to compete in today's global economy.

In the 1990s, success will be the result of understanding customer needs, developing a product to meet those needs, bringing that product to market quickly at a fair value, and—most importantly—convincing the user that your product can improve their productivity, quality, and profitability.

Even if you agree with this general prescription for product success, it's ineffective without a more detailed knowledge of how to use and control the basic forces of change that affect product development: technology, tools, tasks, talent, and time. By not harnessing, directing, and efficiently applying any one of these forces, a company reduces its chance for success, whereas well-managed forces of change can become resources within a company.

These forces of change are at work in disturbing or stabilizing a specific company setting—the product development environment. This environment includes the people, concepts, and technologies necessary to design a product, manufacture it, and market it. By directing these forces toward productivity and immediate response to the competition, managers will be able to make the decisions that translate into a company's continuing survival and, better yet, growth.

So, consider these questions about how your company views and works with the five forces of change.

Technology. How successfully does your company take advantage of those technologies that are currently available? Are you a technology leader in your marketplace? Are the product interfaces built on industry standards? Do you have a long-range vision for your product that will guide the technology you use and develop? Are you developing technologies that will provide product leadership?

"Technology is the most subtle and most effective engineer of social change."

–Robert McIver,
Royal Bank of Canada

Tools. What are the best tools to use? What level of automation is required? What level of compatibility and integration is required? How well is your company managing the impact of new tools on your employees and their tasks? Are you actively working with other industry leaders and associations to standardize tool interfaces? What data is required by the tools and how will that data be managed?

Tasks. How are tasks defined, then divided up, and managed effectively—especially as they increase in complexity? Is the task process continually improved upon to achieve increasing levels of quality and productivity? Would the automation of tasks increase your efficiency?

Talent. How does your company get talented employees to work effectively, and of greater concern, how do you ensure a long-term supply of talent? Do you provide interesting and challenging jobs with continuing training and education? Do managers help to keep employees satisfied and empower them by relinquishing authority? Do managers understand and communicate the company's vision?

Time. How does your company shorten product time-to-market? How do you quickly introduce product improvements? What are the metrics for improving the product development cycle time?

Some aspects of these five forces can be managed by the strategy and organization within the product development environment. Other aspects are managed by your company's interaction with the resources outside this environment. And how you work with one of these forces affects what you do with another. For example, decisions about technologies impact the choice of tools. The tools you use may shorten the time to market. The way tasks are structured can affect how well you use the talent of your work force, what the quality of their research and development (R&D) is, and how much time it takes to do a task.

So the main thing to remember is that these forces not only exist in parallel, side by side, but also are fully integrated vertically and horizontally in the product development environment. They are part of the living corporate fabric that is being continually woven and repatterned so that a company can compete successfully. And the first thing to do is to understand these five forces of change so that by creative and effective management they can become valued resources.

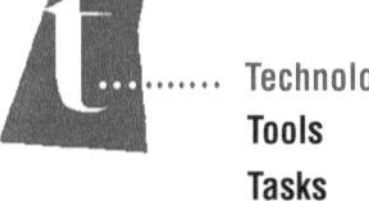

Technology
Tools
Tasks
Talent
Time

PROGRESSIVE AND COMPLEX TECHNOLOGY

In this century, the speed by which knowledge is applied to practical purposes is astounding, partly because a single human mind can no longer keep track of what's happening. When you step back into the history of a particular technology and trace its momentum and applications, it's easier to understand a company's frustration at the fast pace of technology. It seems that technology is out of control.

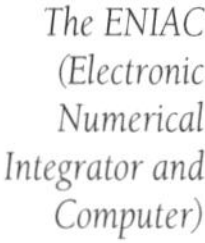

The ENIAC (Electronic Numerical Integrator and Computer)

As a concrete example of the result of many technologies—take a historical glance at how the technology of the electron tube has furthered the advance of other technologies over the last eight and a half decades.

In 1904, Dr. Fleming invented the electron tube. Early in 1946 the ENIAC (Electronic Numerical Integrator And Computer) computer had a population of 15,000 vacuum tubes over an area of 1500 square feet. This electronic dinosaur weighed 30 tons and failed every ten minutes or so. It was both marvelous and ready for extinction.

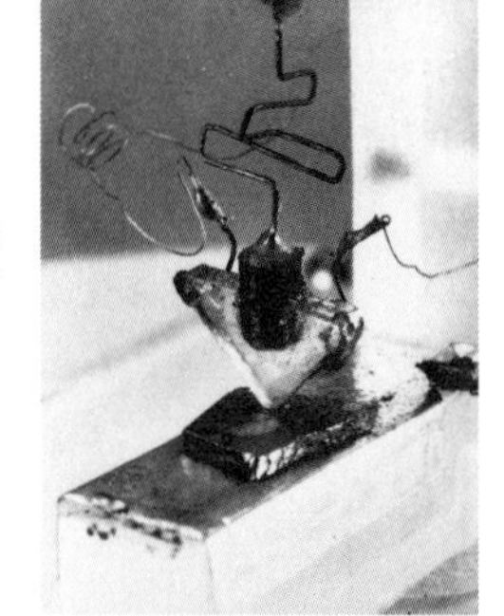

The first transistor

Two years later (late in 1947), Bardeen, Brattain, and Shockley compressed the function of the electron tube into a transistor. More versatile than the vacuum tubes before them, discrete transistors were joined together in a laboratory in 1959 by Jack Kilby of Texas Instruments to create the first integrated circuit.

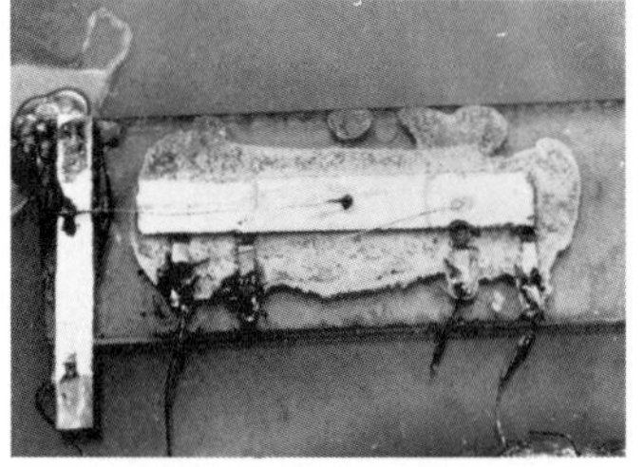

The first integrated circuit

Source: The Computer Museum, Boston, Mass.

The first microprocessors were introduced to the electronic marketplace in the 1970s. Intel Corporation introduced the 4004 in mid-1971, the 8008 in early 1973, and the 8080 in early 1974. Motorola introduced the 6800 during the latter part of 1974. All of these early microprocessors contained fewer than 30,000 transistors. In 1979, Motorola introduced the massive 68000 microprocessor with 68,000 transistors.

Eight years later in 1987, Intel introduced the 80386—a 275,000 transistor microprocessor. By 1989, one million transistor integrated circuits were sampled by both the Intel i486 and the i860. Early in 1990, the Motorola 68040 included as many as 1.2 million transistors.

Technologies that enabled more complex designs

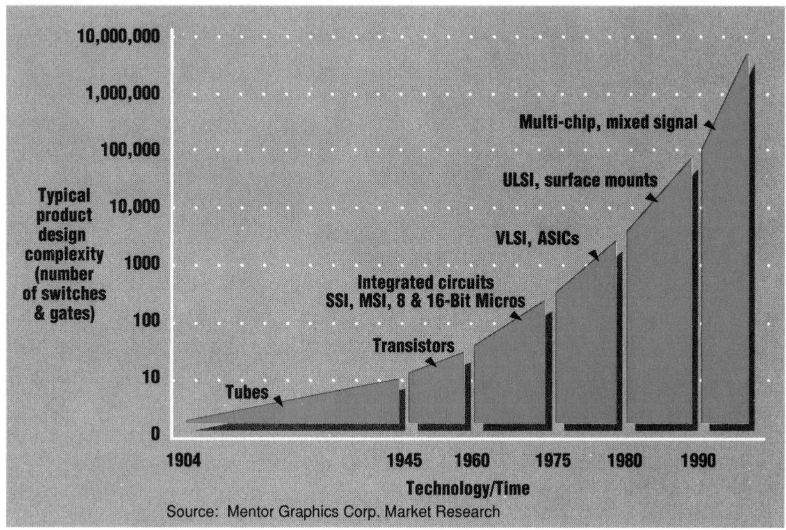

Our individual lives and our global economies are being changed continuously by new product innovations. Watches, calculators, pocket computers, voice-mail, automatic teller systems—all have moved us into the age of pushbutton information systems.

The technological trend toward processing and managing information on smaller, notebook-sized equipment has just begun. And the increasing number of high-tech tools, machines, and consumer products testifies to the proliferation of newer technologies and their increasing complexity.

THE EFFECT OF NEW TECHNOLOGIES

Because of this constant renewal of technologies, a single company rarely generates a unique technology from scratch. But a company can capture, represent, present, manipulate, reuse, and integrate information that will, in effect, generate a new technology that leads to new applications and products.

Yet many companies are unfortunate examples of having sophisticated product technologies, but remain unable to translate these technological advantages into an increasing share of the worldwide market. An oft-cited example is what has happened to the semiconductor market for companies in the United States.

For US companies, the share of the world semiconductor market dropped from 50 percent in 1984 to 34 percent in 1990 while the share for Japan's companies rose to more than 52 percent. US companies have virtually stopped selling dynamic random-access memory (DRAM) chips on the open market, and American makers of semiconductor manufacturing equipment are closing shop. Japanese companies are now dominant in these fields.

For US companies, the share of the world market for the consumer electronics products that incorporate a large fraction of semiconductors—products such as videocassette recorders, motor-driven 35 mm autofocus cameras, and compact disc players—has dropped to about 5 percent since 1975. The share for Japan's companies has risen from about 10 percent to more than 25 percent.

Some would argue that a company loses market share when research and development (R&D) is not adequately funded. Investment in basic research is essential for a company's long-term economic growth. While this is especially true in the fast-paced field of electronics, it does not apply to many companies in the United States. According to Derteuzos, Lester, and Solow in their book, *Made in America*, "Prowess in research does not lead automatically to commercial success. New ideas must be converted into products that customers want, when they want them, and before competitors can provide them, and the products must be made efficiently and well."

"Prowess in research does not lead automatically to commercial success."

–Derteuzos, Lester, and Solow

Total spending on research and development in the United States is significantly higher than that in any other country. The United States leads the world in the quantity and quality of theoretical and basic research. US researchers receive more US basic research patents than the rest of the world combined. Yet this lead often has not yielded commercially competitive products.

The causes can be blamed on the failure of many US companies to produce state-of-the-art processes for designing, manufacturing, marketing, and distributing their products. This failure results in technological discoveries that are not quickly transformed into high-quality, best-value products. In contrast, the authors of *Made in America* state that European and Asian companies "have focused on applied research and on product and process development. As a result, they have greatly shortened the time between discovery and commercialization."

The fruits of R&D—new product data, scientific insights, inventions, revolutionary prototypes—are easily disseminated across national borders. Increasingly, the winners in the competitive race are the companies that make use of those fruits most rapidly and comprehensively. Starting first in the development of a technology no longer means finishing first in the marketplace.

In today's world, you never know where a good technology or idea for one will come from. Yet not all companies get the product information they need for success. Some R&D departments still feel that "if it's not invented here, it's not worth doing." There is pointed inattention to what's happening with similar research elsewhere in the world. Many companies do not actively seek the product information that is readily available and that can help them with designing, manufacturing, and marketing a new technology.

Any company that embraces this narrow and limited attitude about outside R&D will only contribute to its growing decline of the world market share. Even retaining the technology and those innovative concepts and designs for future products no longer means holding the key to product success. Companies may need to change the way they view, choose, and use technologies in developing a product—for example, starting with a quality-first focus—so that technology enables them to stay on the road to success.

TECHNOLOGICAL HURDLES

It might be helpful to list three specific hurdles that a company must clear so that the technology that goes into a product is the very best and timely—now and for the future.

Hurdle 1: Creating a long-range global vision. A typical vision for many companies is the balance sheet for the next quarter, and that short-term focus on profits starts to drive every decision. Not clearing this hurdle causes companies to destroy the diversity that keeps a product development environment healthy. It causes companies to reduce R&D. Long-term activities such as information gathering, investing in education, and developing the potentials already in the work force are eliminated as too costly.

The long-term result for a visionless company is day-to-day crisis management, not sustained growth. Dissatisfied employees don't know how to contribute to the company's development because they have no overall or long-term vision that they can use to mold their ideas. Users find a product line that has inconsistent quality and no integration. The product lacks new technologies and therefore cannot sustain effective competition in the marketplace.

"Innovation without quality is mere novelty."

–*Glen W. Fortinberry, in* The Value Side of Productivity

A long-term vision must reach outside the company's environment. For example, because the students of today are the engineers of tomorrow, companies should consider the basic education of citizens to be an important way to participate and invest in the future.

Many educational and industrial experts write how science and math courses are necessary as part of the useful skills required in today's job force. At the same time, students' understanding of those subjects is less than stellar.

In any country and company, employees who are oblivious to the applicable skills from science and mathematics will be unable to absorb and assimilate new technological insights into existing or conceived products and processes. It's quite clear that the success of a company's investment in technology depends on the ability of employees to quickly learn new technologies. This makes it imperative that companies stress and promote useful skills that translate into a good foundation for the continued training of employees.

Hurdle 2: Integrating R&D with the total product development process. This hurdle is found both inside and outside of the product development environment of individual companies. The R&D organization often has little connection with a company's manufacturing or marketing functions. Too often, R&D launches a sophisticated product idea into the hands of design engineers with no real-world data that relates to testing, manufacturing, and marketing.

When R&D does not proceed simultaneously with engineering and the design of production processes, a new product development process is needed. R&D insights must be continuously available for use in the design and production process, and companies must provide a way to cycle new design and production insights back into R&D.

An idea from R&D should be like a wave that ripples through the product development environment, and as it reaches production, marketing, and other areas, that wave creates secondary waves of information that change the original wave. Actually, each person, each tool, and each area that lives in the product development environment is constantly generating waves of ideas and receiving them in return as transformed reflections. The most successful companies understand and nurture this process.

Consider the success of companies that are designing their own chips for the first time and putting application-specific integrated circuits (ASICs) on printed circuit boards. They understand that a change in technology affects more than just the engineers; it ripples downstream and affects processes and employees in such areas as documentation, purchasing, testing, and manufacturing. These companies may see an extension in the amount of time it takes to get the design done, but downstream benefits make up for the longer upstream time. Problems may include multiple sources for manufacturing the ASICs in case a foundry goes out of business or drops a particular ASIC technology, and these companies must now simulate the ASIC design to reduce the 50% failure rate of ASICs in a printed circuit board (PCB) prototype. But they are also seeing the benefits of the use of fewer parts and outside vendors, ease of assembly, reliability, lower overall product cost, easy to reuse ASICs, and higher net profits because of integrating R&D with the total product development process.

Hurdle 3: Overcoming the not-invented-here syndrome. This hurdle is a wall that prevents useful outside information from informing and stimulating the product development environment. Over time, this blunts a company's competitive edge.

A company that doesn't send its researchers, engineers, and technicians to conferences or trade shows or to visit global competitors raises this hurdle and makes it more difficult to overcome. This hurdle can be the reason that a company neglects the gathering of data on the results of government-funded research in other countries. It can mean a loss of valuable information that comes from reviewing technical and scientific journals and newspapers published throughout the world.

Each company needs a systematic approach to learn about and rapidly disseminate new technological insights—whether it is a breakthrough invention, a more efficient method of designing, manufacturing or assembling products, or a new way of organizing a system for managing information. Some companies clear this hurdle by using partnerships as a way to bring in outside technology. In a partnership, a company can contract to use the technology of another company and thereby eliminate the need to invent that technology.

Not clearing this hurdle also keeps world-wide industry standards from being developed and accepted. This lack of standards impedes the flow of information about technological developments—especially in such areas as software languages, operating systems, databases, and human and machine interfaces.

This hurdle can also exist outside a company, as in a country where defense-dominated funding can skew research priorities, limit the flow of information, and reduce the commercial benefits of research. While many defense technologies have civilian uses, certain barriers impede the transfer of technology from military to commercial applications. Much defense research is not accessible because it is classified. Also, military specifications call for higher performance—and higher prices—than civilian consumers need or want. A company in such a country needs to press for an ongoing review of military-funded research so that it can be used in the commercial sector as soon as possible.

Technology
Tools
Tasks
Talent
Time

AN UNENDING EVOLUTION OF TOOLS

The automobile employee turning a wrench, the electronics engineer wiring a test board—both are fast becoming images from the past. Robots tighten the bolts and manufacture and test products.

Old and outdated tools, which were new in the 1980s, are disappearing from the hands of employees. Endless hours of applying solder with a soldering iron have been replaced with a few taps on the keyboard of a computer. Tools are matching the evolution of technology.

For example, in 1980, a typical single-user workstation had a performance much less than a single mips (million instructions per second) and cost a fortune. Multi-user minicomputers had about 1 mips, but when shared by 5 to 15 designers, they

Tools are matching the evolution of technology

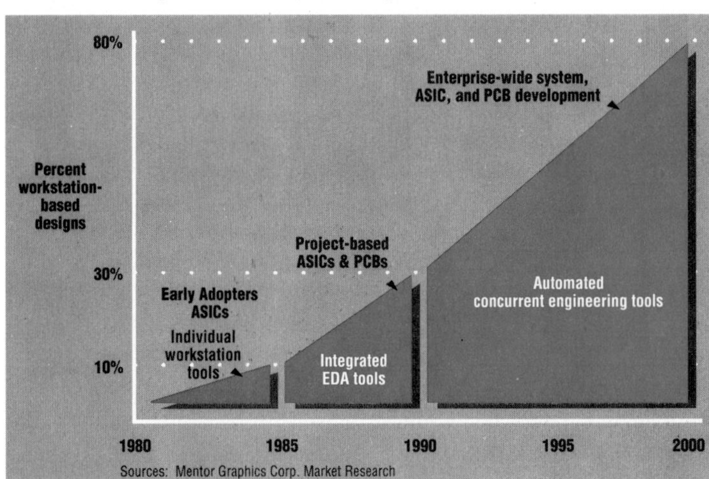

were no better than souped-up data entry systems. Today, the typical single-user workstation that boasts between 10 and 72 mips, with the typical workstation operating between 12 to 20 mips, will evolve in the 1990s to state-of-the-art workstations that operate well beyond 100 mips.

This evolution in design tools and technologies is necessary to keep up with the competitive demands for producing better products faster. As the figure on the preceeding page illustrates, the fastest growth in the electronic design automation (EDA) industry will be in the next ten years. In 1990, approximately 30% of all designs were created on EDA workstations, but it's estimated that in 1999, 80% of all designs will be created on workstations. The type of tools a company uses may be one indicator of how successful a company will be.

ISLANDS OF AUTOMATION

In the 1970s, because powerful computers were very expensive, companies set up various organizations, such as Engineering Services, to share this expense. These organizations established their own computing needs and capabilities and thus created environments of functional isolation.

In the 1980s, the introduction of the workstation dropped the price/performance ratio of computers. Companies could afford to put a computer on almost every person's desk. Different tools were developed depending on the job. The design of printed circuit boards (PCBs) required different tools than those for the design of integrated circuits (ICs).

But these powerful tools were still functionally isolated—islands of automation. The PCB tools and IC design tools couldn't share data. It resulted in the "sneaker-net" approach to

From islands of automation to interoperable systems

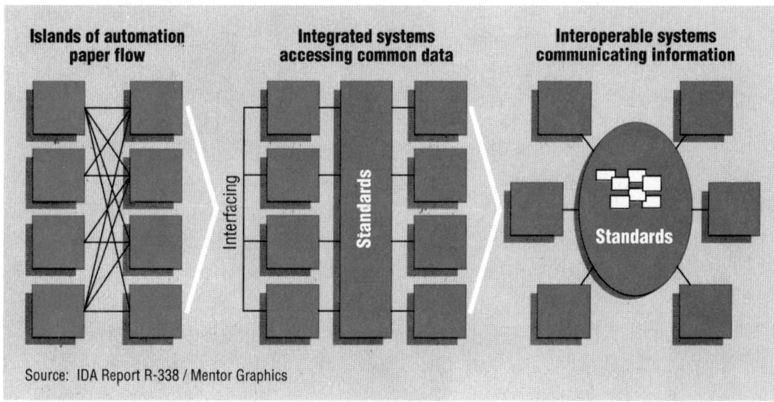

integrating tools and information. To provide integration between computers, you had to collect data from one computer, put it on mag tape or on a floppy disk, walk it over to another, transfer the data to a file, then translate the data into the format required for a specific tool to read. Advanced variations of this approach include custom or standard interfaces as part of each tool to ease the transfer of information. For instance, this method of data translation and integration may use a local area network for the transfer of files from one computer to another in a standardized format.

Now these islands of automation are beginning to disappear as other systems evolve. The "multi-window" approach is typical of how many of today's tools can use data directly from each other. Two or more tools may reside on the same computer at the same time and present their information in windows, which allows the user to copy data from the window of one tool and paste it into the window of another tool.

The ultimate enabler of tool and data integration is the interoperable approach, where multiple tools have access to the original data, not copies of the data. And when you make a change to data in one tool, the change automatically occurs in the data used by all other tools. These tools can reside both on single computers and be shared through a network. To have integrated tools is important, but so is the level of integration. Without integration or interoperability, you create barriers where people have to re-enter data at various stages in the process.

The growing use of tools with efficient, standardized interfaces gets the job done without losing time, without making many false starts, and without repeating work that has been done before. And as the product development environment becomes ever more complicated, the future of communicating information will be based on interoperable tools that are interactively linked in a standardized data management system.

NEW TOOLS CAN CHANGE JOB RESPONSIBILITIES

The demand for new tools creates new technologies. But sometimes companies are reluctant to invest in new tools because of the hidden costs of retraining as well as reshuffling jobs. Simply put, the change does not feel like a process, just an upheaval with no goal in sight.

It's true that the evolution in tools means a change in job responsibility for many employees. A tool itself, given its capabilities and limitations, can help an employee concentrate on a particular area or diversify a job to include more tasks in a process.

For example, the design engineer is now taking on what the layout engineer and what the test engineer used to do. But layout engineers haven't lost their jobs—they are taking on new responsibilities, too. They must now think about various trade-offs, such as thermal considerations and mechanical interference, and still provide expertise to the component placement and routing process.

Sometimes the employees are not prepared for this change, and sometimes this kind of change happens even though it was not planned. A shortage in the marketplace for a particular skill can cause you to buy tools that expand the skills of other employees to fill the gap. For example, right now in the United States there are around 400,000 design engineers and only 12,000 layout engineers. By necessity, the design engineers are doing the work of the layout engineers—when they have the right tools to extend their skills.

How employees approach the need for being flexible about their jobs depends on the atmosphere in the product development environment.

- Are employees aware of their roles in a product's development?
- Is initiative rewarded?
- Is their training adequate and positive?
- Are new skills and responsibilities rewarded?
- Do employees get the tools they need?
- Are their tools instruments of communication and creative change?

Too often, the answer to each of these questions is no, or not enough, or not yet. This lack of response can mean that the full potential of productivity in the product development environment is not understood or used.

When a new tool is introduced in the product development environment, managers and employees must continually monitor its performance. You must not only get to know the present capabilities of a tool, but how you want that tool to improve your product development process. It's a mistake to evaluate the performance of a new tool in the old process. For example, in a typical process, at the end of placement, routing, and artwork, a check plot is generated for the engineer to review. However, new tools allow engineers to do that checking on-line, saving the time it takes to generate the plot and deliver it to the engineer. On-line checking can save approximately two hours per check point. But to use the new time-saving tools, the process must change—in this example, the drafting work order would state the deliverable as completed work, not a generated plot.

And how do you introduce a new tool without causing problems? A company needs a consistent (but not rigid) approach to managing the dynamics of change. For example, introducing new tools can cause changes in job processes, scheduling, cost models, and communications. Depending on how a company manages these changes, managers and employees alike welcome it or reject it.

So a more basic question quickly arises: How do you successfully introduce and manage change? W. Edwards Deming, in his book *Out of the Crisis*, proposes 14 things that companies, large and small, can do to ensure that change is an ongoing and positive experience:

1. Create constancy of purpose for improvement of product and service.
2. Adopt the new philosophy of a new economic age.
3. Cease dependence on inspection to achieve quality.
4. End the practice of awarding business on the basis of price tag alone. Instead, minimize total cost by working with a single supplier.
5. Improve constantly and forever every process for planning, production, and service.
6. Institute training on the job.
7. Adopt and institute leadership.
8. Drive out fear.
9. Break down barriers between staff areas.
10. Eliminate slogans, exhortations, and targets for the work force.
11. Eliminate numerical quotas for the work force and numerical goals for management.
12. Remove barriers that rob people of pride of workmanship. Eliminate the annual rating or merit system.
13. Institute a vigorous program of education and self-improvement for everyone.
14. Put everybody in the company to work to accomplish the transformation.

Change should not be an earthquake on anyone's scale. But if change is successfully introduced and managed, the product development environment will not split apart into those all-too-common islands of automation. Each employee will feel involved in the group process that is commonly known as teamwork.

INCREASINGLY COMPLEX TASKS

As tool technology evolves from manual to automated, it's worthwhile to use tools to get rid of some of the mundane tasks. That means lots of power in the hands of individual engineers.

That concentration of power and ensuing information can be a problem if there are no communication paths that allow ideas and data to flow freely and creatively through the product development environment. It's also a problem if complex tasks are not well managed and integrated into the overall product development process so that design errors are caught early and their effects minimized. Otherwise, automation simply may help you get costly, error-riddled designs faster. In other words, don't automate a bad process.

"Civilization advances by extending the number of important operations [tasks] we can perform without thinking of them."

–Alfred North Whitehead, philosopher

AUTOMATING TASKS: A PROTOTYPICAL EXAMPLE

The associated costs in detecting software, hardware, and mechanical errors rises over 1000 times from the time the product is specified to the time the product is released to the field. A study by the Rome Air Development Center indicates that a software defect costs $450 at the requirements stage, $1150 at the coding stage, and $2300 at the software debugging and testing stage. These figures illustrate that one of the most effective ways to prevent costly design errors is to create a product development process that considers the downstream effects of a design as early in the design cycle as possible. Don't overlook the fact that the cost of design errors is measured in both dollars and resources.

In the past, building prototypes may have been the answer, but that approach will not quickly resolve the diverse issues that companies are facing with today's complex technologies. Prototypes are costly and require several turns—and still don't work correctly. For example, there is an average of three prototype turns on ASICs, and fewer than 50% of the functional ASICs work in the PCB. Electronic Engineering Times recently published an article titled "An End to Over the Wall Engineering—Engineers Take On the Board Layout Decisions." This article indicates that, due to complexities, there is an average of five prototype turns for each new PCB design.

At $20,000 to $60,000 per turn, it is no wonder that companies are looking for ways to shorten the cycle time by achieving first-pass success.

The costs of making changes are measured in both dollars and resources

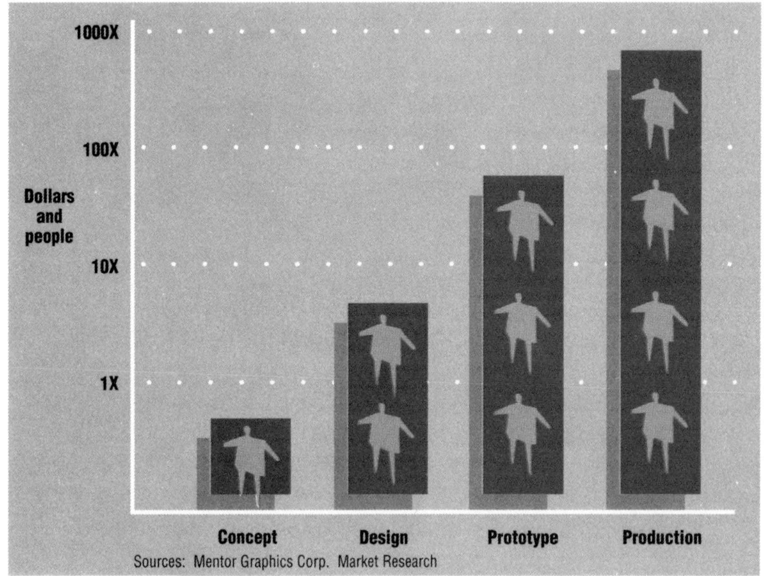

Many companies continue to spend millions of dollars in needless prototype turns of ASICs and PCBs to test their conformance to such specifications as:

- Timing and functionality of the ASIC or ASICs on the PCB
- Testability of the ASIC (individually and on the PCB)
- Pin-out trade-offs for optimization of multilayer PCBs
- Power requirements
- Thermal tolerances (each IC and the PCB)
- Reliability
- Packaging requirements
- Software and hardware integration

Multiple prototype turns are wasteful and time-consuming because these various considerations and specifications can be included early in the design process and tested without

Two unsettling and connected issues for managers can be:

- A greater number and variety of communication paths exist for taking action and exerting influence.
- Empowerment and responsibilities are shifting from the vertical to the horizontal, from chain of command to peer networks and teams.

Both of these situations blur the distinction between managers and those being managed, at least on the surface. Managers play fewer authoritative roles in setting schedules or work expectations without consulting their immediate employees and other managers.

Managers today are losing the simple carrots and sticks based on salary and promotions. In fact, most social research shows that sticks don't engender the loyalty, commitment, and dedication in an employee that result in greater productivity. So what managers need are varied and more effective ways to encourage high productivity and build commitment. They must confront changes in their own base of power and recognize the need for new ways to motivate people.

But managers are not of one cloth. The roles and problems of top managers can differ sharply from those of middle managers.

Top Managers

In 1988, the United Research Company asked CEOs what they believed was the key to managing a company to gain a competitive edge. Change was never mentioned. But in 1990, almost 45 percent said the number one way to win in business is to have an organization that can respond quicker and make change a way of life.

A survey in *Chief Executive* magazine showed that 70 percent of CEOs believe they can slice 10 to 20 percent off total cycle time in the next two years. But only 40 percent believe their companies are good at making change happen.

In the 1980s, top managers began learning that they must manage change. In the 1990s, they must learn to manage surprise. With the pace of events getting faster and faster and opportunities opening up, companies need to be able to respond rapidly, flexibly, and imaginatively.

One problem for top managers in the 1990s is identifying management tools—strategies and processes—that increase productivity, decrease time to market, and generate the pride of product ownership in all employees throughout the product development environment.

In the 1990s, top managers need strategies and processes that facilitate continuous improvement and change. The acceptance of change in the product development environment comes from the company's vision and its commitment to managing and promoting change effectively. And it is the role of top managers to define the initial vision, keep it in mind, and push for change.

Middle Managers

Middle managers also need new strategies and processes so that once and for all they can get out of the bog of giving orders. Too often, managers act as poor role models for the employees they manage, demonstrating by their inability to share decisions that responsibility is a burden. The job of middle managers in the 1990s is to be facilitators of change, and that job is not easy.

Middle managers must have a general understanding of relevant technical issues so they can communicate the company's vision in a way that everyone buys into it. Also, the social organization in a manager's work group must reflect the egalitarian tools that are revolutionizing the product development environment. Middle managers, while keeping their team focused, must lead from within the team and not from outside it, sensitively taking on and balancing the roles of coach, captain, and teammate. If they can't, people who don't believe in the company's goals become responsible solely to themselves and push their own personal goals.

Not least, managers at all levels must remain doggedly determined to keep examining their assumptions and be ready to change them if the facts don't fit. Decisions based on myths are poor decisions.

SLAYING THE DRAGONS OF THE PAST

Myths that should have died long ago still stalk managers' offices. And only those managers who lay those myths to rest and step with an open mind into the 1990s will become heroes and heroines.

Here are a few of the many myths that lie in wait to cloud a manager's vision and undercut his or her decisions:

Myth 1: Labor costs are killing the company. In the United States, companies have traditionally assumed that labor costs are all that matter, even though labor is actually less than 15 percent of the cost of most products. In the high technology markets, labor costs are less than 10 percent, according to the chief financial officer of a major EDA company.

The typical product's development cycle will be vastly more complex in the 1990s with far more data to manage and many more process steps to coordinate than in the 1980s. Even the scope of this cycle will need to be broadened into areas previously considered separate and distinct. An example of this need can be seen by the early miscalculations made by the implementors of just-in-time manufacturing.

Just-in-time manufacturing caused companies to focus almost exclusively on one phase of the product development cycle—manufacturing. However, up to 90 percent of the critical competitive cycle times lie outside of manufacturing, according to the Thomas Group Inc., a Texas-based consulting firm. Reducing the total cycle time for product development can improve profit as a percentage of sales up to an astounding 26 percent.

Product development cycle times that are not competitive result in greater losses of profits than either development or manufacturing cost overruns.

Lost profits when a product is not competitive

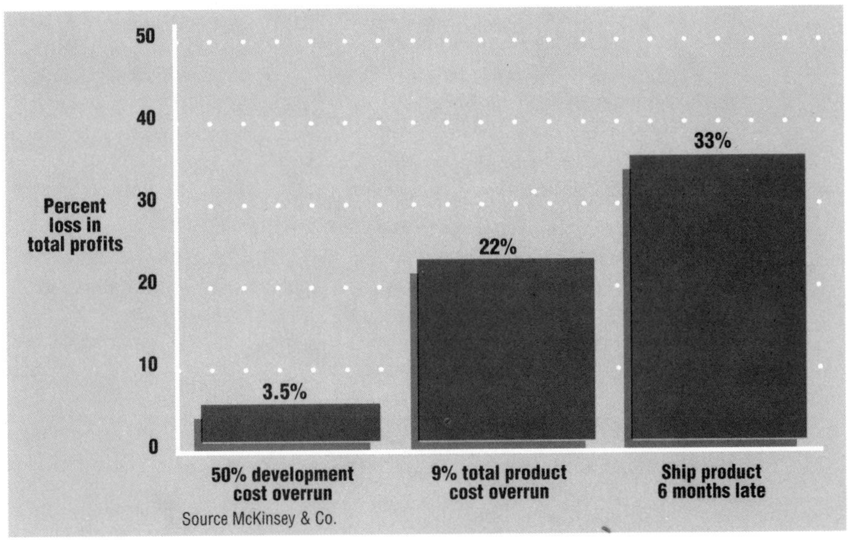

Source McKinsey & Co.

Significantly reducing total cycle time by 50 percent and greater can benefit companies in many ways. Companies can be more responsive to customer needs as well as improve time to market. Reducing total cycle time can accelerate improvements in cost, quality, yields, productivity, and effectiveness.

Companies can improve the effectiveness of resources; for example, how plant space, tools, inventories, and talent are utilized.

Competitiveness is more important now than ever before. Products and services reach the market with increasing frequency and variety, as any aisle in a large electronics store demonstrates. Product development cycles are shorter, which means that companies must structure their product development environment to respond quickly.

The following figure illustrates how a company can measure the impact of potential delays in bringing a product to market. Every market has a growth phase and a decline phase. The goal is to introduce a product as early as possible in the market growth phase.

Revenue lost from delayed market entry

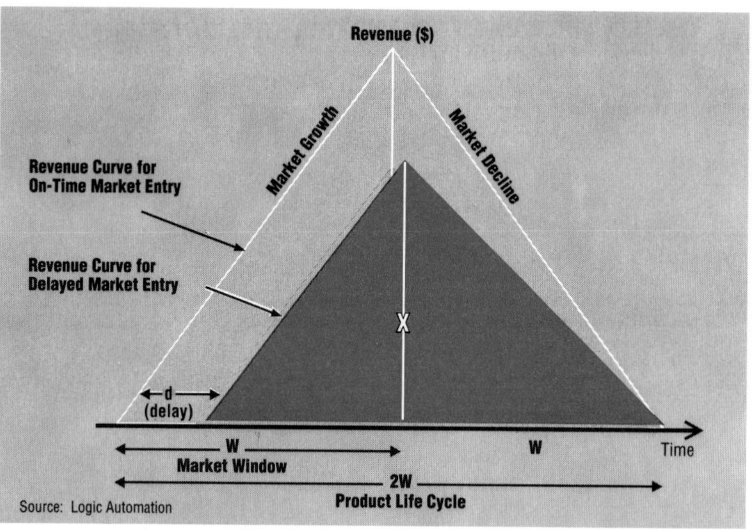

By delaying a product's entry into the market, significant revenues can be lost for each month the product is late. Companies can use the following formula to calculate the percent revenue lost due to market delays. The data shown with the formula shows the percent revenue lost by the delayed market entry of a product with a 12-month market window. The losses are significant, indeed.

Formula for revenue loss

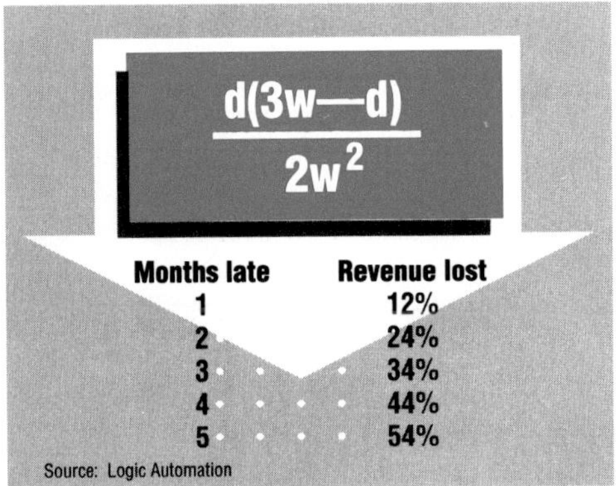

d(3w—d)
2w 2
Months late
Revenue lost
1 12%
2 24%
3 34%
4 44%
5 54%
Source: Logic Automation

Improve quality
Decrease costs because of less rework, fewer mistakes, fewer delays, snags; better use of machine-time and materials

Capture the market with better quality and lower price
Stay in business
Provide jobs and more jobs
Source: W. Edwards Deming

CUSTOMERS WANT IT NOW!

Today's customers want it now and pay a premium price to get exactly what they want as soon as possible. So today's market demands short cycle times. Many companies have responded to that market and made such items as fax machines, copy machines, cellular telephones, scanners, and laser printers readily available.

Customers also demand quality. When companies produce the high quality their customers demand, they are sometimes surprised to discover that quality is an investment that more than pays for itself. Companies realize unexpected savings by eliminating the hidden costs of imperfect products. For example, fewer employees are needed to deal with imperfect products, and intermediate inventories of parts can be greatly reduced. More can be done in less space, which leads to a decline in capital requirements.

Giving customers exactly what they want as fast as possible has many benefits. It cements customer loyalty, leads to premium competitive prices, and reduces costs for both the company and the customer. But this can only happen in a fine-tuned product development environment that understands that building in quality does not mean sacrificing time-to-market.

THE CONTINUING CHALLENGES

It's clear that what ties automation to technology, tools, tasks, and talent is the thread of time. And it is inevitable that the clock in the product development environment will continue to speed up as complex tasks and processes become more interactively automated. This must happen because in tomorrow's product development environment, savings will be measured not in years or months, but in weeks or days.

Time is a company's enemy only when the company can't respond quickly to change and provide what the market needs and wants.

Yet how does a company collapse its traditional and sequential schedule for product design, production, and marketing into a process that is not just parallel, but fully integrated? In short, how does a company take actions that create and sustain a successful product development environment for the 1990s?

So far, you only have the outline of a vision based mostly on what's not working and what needs to change. Now you're ready to take the next step and find out about the solutions to the problems described in this chapter. In the rest of this book, you can start the process of defining your company's future and vision in the positive light of concrete solutions. The next chapter introduces you to concurrent engineering—a strategy and process for the product development environment that promotes corporate renewal and success.

TWO

CONCURRENT ENGINEERING—RENEWAL AND SUCCESS.

TO STAY A WINNER, YOUR COMPANY MUST LEARN THE ART AND SCIENCE OF CONCURRENT ENGINEERING—BALANCING ITS FOUR KEY DIMENSIONS OF ORGANIZATION, COMMUNICATION INFRASTRUCTURE, REQUIREMENTS, AND PRODUCT DEVELOPMENT.

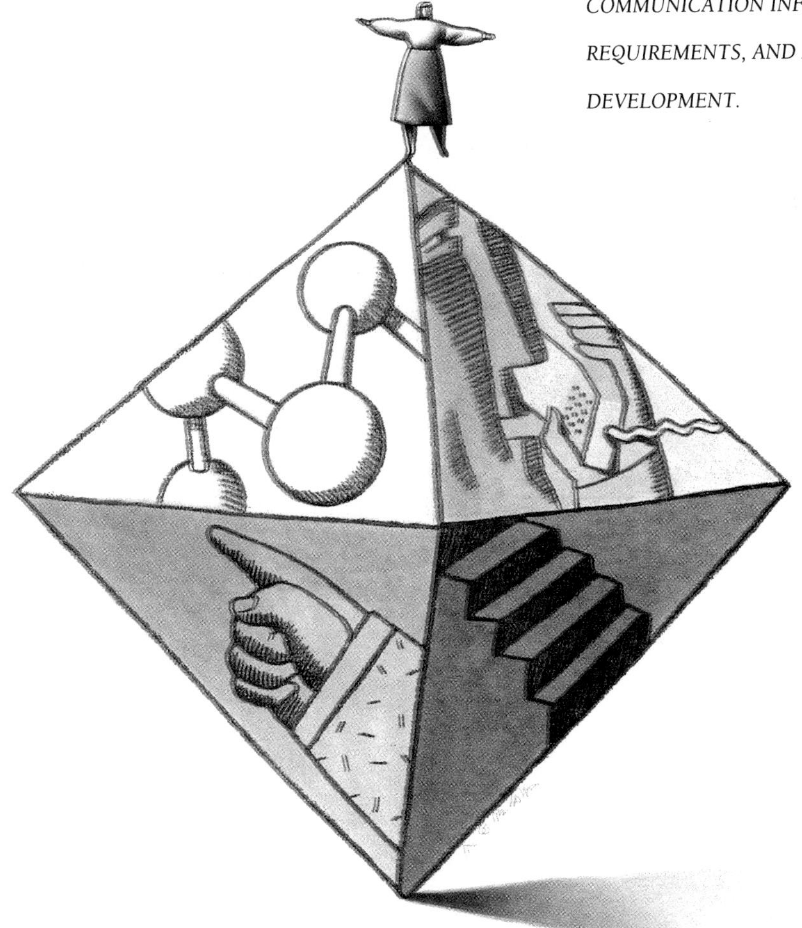

BALANCING THE FOUR DIMENSIONS

Concurrent Engineering—Renewal and Success

Successful companies in the 1990s will learn to manage the changes needed to ensure continued productivity in the global marketplace—getting the highest-quality, lowest-cost product to market in the least time. To manage the forces of change, your company (or division in a corporation) must have a product development environment that uses concurrent engineering to produce its basic product—whether it is as complex as a space shuttle or as simple as a pressure gauge. Simply stated, the often sequential and fragmented product development environment of the 1980s must transform itself into a concurrent engineering environment for the 1990s.

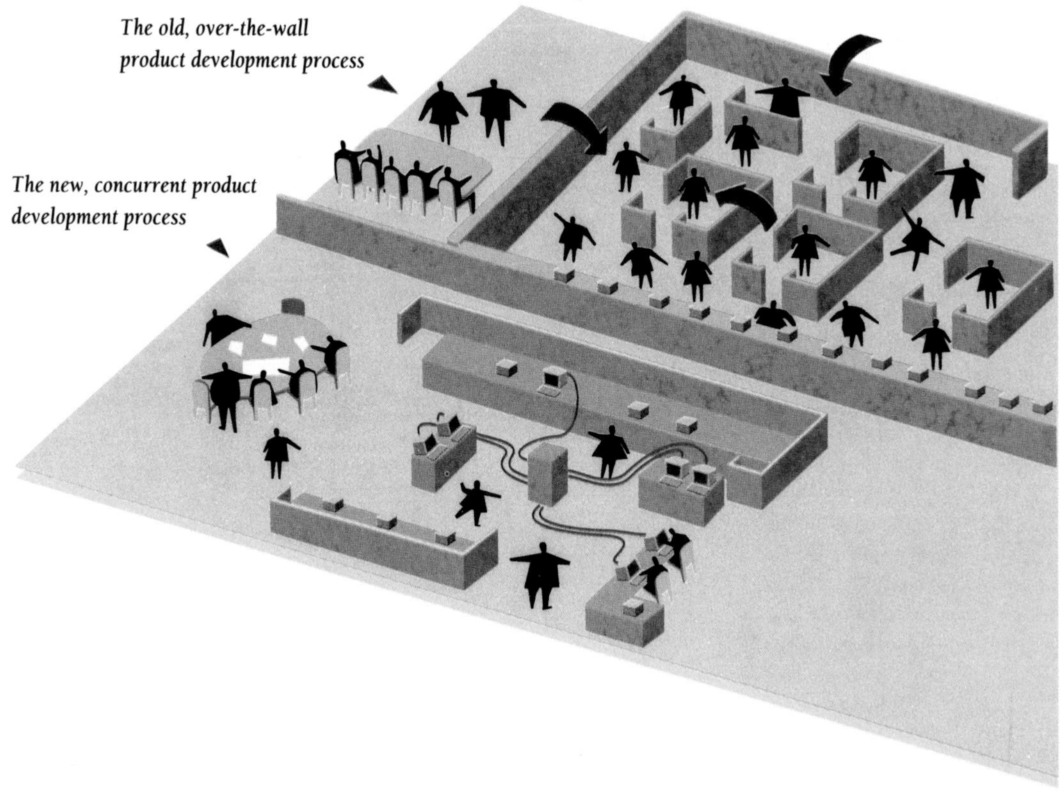

When your company decides to initiate the transition to a concurrent engineering environment for development of its product, it makes a commitment to harness and control the five forces of change that keep sweeping through the product development environment: technology, tools, tasks, talent, and time.

The way to nurture and keep control of these forces—reshaping them into resources for change—is to create a dynamic environment whose foundation is not cast in concrete, rather in four interconnected dimensions: the organization of managers and employees, their means of communicating, their unwavering focus on what the customer wants, and the development process by which the product evolves, adapts, and continues to sell.

THE FOUR DIMENSIONS OF CONCURRENT ENGINEERING

It's chancy to be dogmatic in an ever-changing global economy, but here goes: the concurrent engineering environment always has at least four key dimensions. The shape of these dimensions and their relative balance continually shift, depending on the specific product and the current market forces. Here's a capsulated view of each dimension.

Organization. Two managerial entities inhabit and shape this dimension—managers and the product development teams. Managers must create, empower, and support product development teams whose number, members, and included disciplines are based on the complexity of a product. The development teams must assume the authority and responsibility for their design decisions, and individual members must commit themselves to what the team, as a whole, decides.

Communication infrastructure. Good communication is always important, and a sound infrastructure makes communication possible—linking people, ideas, specifications, processes, and feedback. Relevant information from the other three dimensions should permeate this dimension and be available as team members need it.

Requirements. This dimension has a given shape at a particular moment in time: the total set of customer, company, and industry requirements for a product. The focus of this dimension is customer requirements, and most requirements should be viewed, to some extent, in terms of factors that affect customer satisfaction. A company must determine what a customer wants, ensure that a customer is getting it, make sure the product meets internal company standards and external industry standards. Two important internal requirements are to use appropriate planning methodologies and planning perspectives. All these requirements have a driving, energetic effect on the other dimensions, and the dynamo that powers this dimension is a good design.

Product development. For each company and its product, this dimension has a fairly stable outline because of its integrated vision of the total product development process—from design conception to manufacturing and support. This approach develops libraries of components, considers downstream processes early in the design, and strives to continually improve the product development process.

A balanced concurrent engineering environment, where each dimension is in relative harmony with the other three, is not that uncommon. But where you find this environment is usually in a company of one—an individual who is in business with no other employees and who is developing a product that is fairly simple.

This one person is both the manager and product development team. There is one communication path for all information. Also, this person alone is responsible for meeting customer requirements and keeping in mind the total product development process. In this ideal environment, this manager and team of one person has the same vocabulary, purpose, and priorities; the technology for a communication infrastructure may be an answering machine, a computer, and a few tools; the end product is likely to satisfy the customer requirements because only one person needs to understand the requirements and keep track of their implementation; and all development processes, from design to manufacturing to marketing, are in the hands and mind of a single individual and are almost simultaneously applied to all aspects of the product's development.

But as mentioned, this ideal concurrent engineering environment, where each dimension is almost automatically brought into balance with the others, rarely exists beyond a single-employee company.

Typically, larger companies must continuously examine the dimensions of concurrent engineering and adjust each one to bring it into balance with the others. Each dimension has its own internal factors that can be strengthened and can affect the entire environment. So the trap to beware of is the assumption that solving a problem in one dimension can solve a problem in another. For example, changing the customer requirements does not solve problems in the communication infrastructure. And solving product development issues does not empower product development teams.

Because the concurrent engineering environment is four separate but interacting dimensions, you can focus on fine-tuning that environment for success. Understanding these four dimensions makes the company's shift to a concurrent engineering environment both possible and manageable. You are able to assess to what degree these dimensions are already in place and working effectively.

Before you take a closer look at each of these four dimensions of a concurrent engineering environment, it's important to point out that the dimensions of organization and communication infrastructure have a "philosophical aspect." Their creation is based on some person(s)—usually top management—deciding what constitutes effective teams, the boundaries of authority and responsibility, and the most effective means of communication. These two dimensions reflect someone's belief about what will work for a particular company producing a specific set of products of a certain complexity.

The dimensions of requirements and product development have a "methodical aspect." You must follow specific procedures to capture and specify customer requirements and to integrate a product with development processes.

In a sense, the concurrent engineering environment is where dimensions of philosophy (organization and communication) and methodology (requirements and development processes) converge.

THE ORGANIZATION DIMENSION

ORGANIZATION

The existing culture and organizational policies in a company are often opposed to concurrent engineering, where it is necessary to match authority to responsibility in a meaningful context. Only in this kind of organizational arrangement will the employees within a company and its culture be supportive of the concurrent engineering environment and committed to its success.

As within any company, managers should play a key role in preparing the culture of the company for changes, including those involved in creating a concurrent engineering environment. Managers must create product development teams and then empower those teams with the authority and responsibility to make decisions. Managers must continually assess the professional and technical needs of the team and provide the necessary training and education, tools, and rewards.

Everyone must understand the positions that both managers and the product development teams occupy in the organization dimension. Every employee must feel, as an individual and team member, that he or she has a key role in increasing the productivity and effectiveness of a company. Then everyone can consciously and proudly take ownership of the product.

The interactive concurrent engineering environment requires that authority and decision-making belong to the team and that the influence of team members shifts as the development proceeds.

THE MANAGER'S ROLE

Vision comes from the top.

The decision to implement concurrent engineering is a strategic decision that falls on managers' shoulders. In the 1990s, using concurrent engineering is essential if your company intends to be the technological leader in a product or industry.

If you are a manager, you have four responsibilities in providing an efficient organization for a concurrent engineering environment.

Responsibility 1: You must get the vision of concurrent engineering–understand its implications and believe in its value.

Everyone must make sure that "the design has a customer focus and the design is closely related with the rest of the organization."

–Richard J. Schonberger

Richard J. Schonberger states in his book *World Class Manufacturing* that "R&D people are often the butt of some version of the heave-it-over-the-transom joke. It's a bum rap. The R&D people are not to blame. The blame belongs to their [managers] for not making sure that (1) the design has a customer focus and (2) the design is closely related with the rest of the organization. When (1) and (2) are true, problems disappear like dirt in a laundry detergent ad."

Schonberger has identified the source and the keeper of a company's vision—the managers—who must understand the value of a concurrent engineering environment. He also spells out the two main tenets of concurrent engineering as a design that has a customer focus and is closely related with the rest of the organization. When company strategies are guided by these tenets, he suggests that the results are: "The designers have enormous power to prevent—or cause—later [more costly] problems." However, when all the dimensions of concurrent engineering are in balance, design engineers will not cause problems later, but will, in fact, detect and correct all types of problems early in the product development process.

Responsibility 2: You must prepare your employees for the culture shock of changing to a concurrent engineering environment.

To quote Hayes, Wheelwright, and Clark in their book *Dynamic Manufacturing*, "there are fundamental, wrenching, far-reaching transformations required throughout the enterprise." And it is these types of changes that the shift to a concurrent engineering environment often requires.

People are used to doing things the way they've always done them in the past. If you change how employees do their jobs, this causes some amount of culture shock for most of them—even for yourself and the other managers who are implementing the changes. This culture shock is a natural form of resistance to change.

In their book *Changing Ways*, Murray M. Dalziel and Stephen C. Schoonover provide practical suggestions for implementing change: get ready for change, get the right people, and implement change with elegance. The authors identify and suggest solutions to three critical problems that you, as a manager of change, must overcome: motivating people to change, obtaining the right resources, and avoiding the common pitfalls during implementation.

"People resist change when it is not understood, is imposed, is perceived as threatening, has risks greater than its potential benefits or interferes with other priorities."

–Andy van de Ven,
Professor of Management
University of Minnesota

Dalziel and Schoonover also explore the context for change by asking questions that can be phrased and expanded in the context of making the change to a concurrent engineering environment. For example, can you define precisely what you are changing? In which dimension of concurrent engineering are you making changes, and why? Does everyone understand the reasons for the change?

Because it is both the managers and employees who together make change work, the key to successful change in a company is for you and other managers to personalize the changes so that every employee has a stake in their success.

Responsibility 3: You must not only show commitment but must stay involved.

To implement concurrent engineering successfully requires hands-on management. You must make sure your company's organization and culture will allow the dimensions of concurrent engineering to prosper in a way that ensures they remain in balance. It is also your responsibility to make sure the development process is continuously improved.

One of the keys to the successful implementation of concurrent engineering is the support of hands-on managers.

Here are seven guidelines for best meeting the needs of your particular company and products:

1. Understand your current goals.
2. Understand the process for attaining your goals and determine metrics for measuring success.
3. Understand how your design goals depend on the goals of other disciplines.
4. Understand who depends on your result and why.
5. Recognize design conflicts and resolve tradeoffs quickly.
6. Gauge the quality of your solution.
7. Get feedback for continuous improvement.

To monitor and evaluate improvement, you must develop a communication infrastructure that includes systems for continuously measuring the quality of the design solution with regard to cost, schedule, and conformance to customer requirements. For example, Dr. Genichi Taguchi did some pioneering work on methods of quality engineering for low cost. You might want to investigate what methods exist for managing quality and have your systems conform to the methods you want to use. One part of monitoring any aspect of product development is to maintain a complete record of the decision process. A history of design decisions (lessons learned) will help with future designs and design changes. For example, computer-aided problem reporting systems are useful for categorizing and storing design decisions.

Responsibility 4: You must be willing to create and empower product development teams.

Depending on the scope of the tasks involved in producing a product, you must create product development teams that represent all the disciplines involved in the total product development process.

For example, if your product is a redesign of an existing product, it's possible that the development team would be as small as four people: an engineer, a component engineer, a representative from manufacturing, and a representative from purchasing. This team might meet only at the beginning, middle, and end of the development process. But if your product is as complex as a jumbo jet, if many changes are specified for components and their manufacture, if the market is competitive and world-wide, and if many complex processes are needed to support product development, managers will need to create single-discipline and mixed-discipline teams to ensure that various development processes can proceed concurrently. Managers may even need their own teams to coordinate resources.

After you and other managers share your vision of a concurrent engineering environment and organize development teams to represent the various disciplines in that environment, you should empower those teams to solve problems and make decisions. Both you and the teams must understand the role of the team in the concurrent engineering environment and how that role is supported by managers (from the outside) and a group process (from the inside).

One way managers can help their teams' chances of success is to take some training in learning how to build a team. According to Bill Vitaliano, manager of the hardware design process at Harris Corporation, managers can use team-building skills to help team members value each other's potential for contribution, develop a team purpose statement that is aligned with the organization's vision for the future, and establish norms for the team to guide future teamwork.

Another way to help the team succeed is to physically move team members to the same location. Co-location means desk-next-to-desk, not different floors of the same building. According to Jack Abramowitz, technical advisor at Grumman Aerospace, co-located teams have more opportunity for interaction and collaboration than dispersed teams. In the case of large teams, it may only be possible to co-locate the key team members and then hold weekly team meetings for the entire team.

And the team must understand that you as a manager have the responsibility and authority to oversee team actions so that they stay in line with the company's vision.

THE DEVELOPMENT TEAM'S ROLE

In *Break Through Thinking*, Gerald Nadler and Shozo Hibino describe "The People Design Principle," which, in effect, describes what a product development team is and why the company benefits from the resulting group interaction.

- Members of the development teams should be from every discipline affected by problems and their solutions. This makes sure that all aspects of a problem and solution are covered.
- On a team, each member should understand another member's intricate techniques and complex situations as they relate to a common problem and solution.
- Team meetings, in which all members participate, are more productive than conventional review meetings where one member explains his or her progress and problems with the design.
- Members of teams relish accepting responsibility for and working together on a product (or portion of a product) rather than working in isolation.
- Individual members are the source for most ideas, and their interaction on a team can increase the number of creative and productive ideas.

With the other dimensions in place, the development teams formed in the concurrent engineering environment allow a freer exchange of information between traditionally separate disciplines. A team approach also permits a clear statement of goals to which everyone contributes and subscribes. But how does this happen? How does the team communicate, define the overall purpose of the team, and set priorities?

Consensus—achieving relevant decisions

An important way to motivate team members to reach decisions that resolve differences—in effect, to focus their actions toward a common purpose—is to arrive at decisions through consensus. According to William Ouchi in his book *Theory Z*, a team reaches consensus when "it finally agrees upon a single alternative and each member of the group can honestly say to each other member three things:

1. I believe that you understand my point of view.
2. I believe that I understand your point of view.
3. Whether or not I prefer this decision, I will support it, because it was arrived at in an open and fair manner."

Members of a development team must understand the importance of consensus and feel a loyalty to the team and the company so that, even in disagreement, they never try to undermine team decisions. As Mentor Graphics CEO Tom Bruggere says, "Once consensus is reached on a decision, everyone must support that consensus regardless of one's personal belief. Disagreements should focus on ideas and what is best for the customer, not on people or individuals." But exactly what does a team need to do to reach a consensus?

Collaborating to reach a consensus

The typical result of enlarged communication paths between different levels in a management chain is a greatly increased area of misunderstanding.

A sign of our corporate times is the ability of a group of people to meet for hours, talk excitedly about what they are doing, and communicate nothing of value to others in the meeting. In *Groupthink*, Irving Janis explains that most groups think they're communicating when they're not. "They think they're exploring the interesting aspects of a question when they're not. They think they're taking a collective innovative approach to the challenges that confront them—and they're not." This self-deception explains why people think meetings are a waste of time. This type of communicating can be extremely frustrating.

What's missing in most meetings and in most communication is collaboration. Michael Schrage, in his book *Shared Minds: The New Technologies of Collaboration*, says that "the practical reality of collaboration is that it requires a higher order of involvement as well as a different approach to sharing and creating information." Schrage says communication is the exchanging of information, brainstorming, making a list of ideas and definitions, whereas collaboration is the creating of a shared understanding. Collaboration is "a different quality of interaction; a collective playground of shared ideas and information."

A concurrent engineering environment encourages the creation and empowerment of development teams, but their effectiveness depends on the members' abilities to collaborate. In a meeting with a collaborative atmosphere, team members spend more time understanding what one another is saying and doing. There are three stages of collaboration that lead a team to a consensus about its role, about a problem, or about a solution.

"Communication is the exchanging of information, brainstorming, making a list of ideas and definitions, whereas collaboration is the creating of a shared understanding."

–Michael Schrage

Stage 1: Define a common vocabulary.

For team members to communicate with one another and for what they say to be understood and therefore useful, they must first develop a common vocabulary. This is particularly necessary for mixed-discipline teams.

Sometimes mixed-discipline development teams bring to the table many language barriers. For example, design engineers might not fully understand the jargon of CAD experts. Other times, mixed-discipline team members may be using the same words for which they have different understandings. Words and phrases like system and quality are tossed back and forth without an agreement on their definition and connotations. Buzz words like design for manufacturing include a built-in barrier to productive discussion because "to be in the know," you're already supposed to understand and be using them.

After everyone is using a precise, common vocabulary, true communication begins, and the team can start the next stage of collaboration.

Stage 2: Agree on a common purpose.

The team's decisions and actions must always relate to the company's vision and the customer's requirements. This common purpose ensures that resources are shared and allocated as needed. The focus by team members on such a purpose places the emphasis on cooperation, not competition. When there is agreement on a common purpose, then individual priorities are successfully addressed.

For example, if your purpose is to manage one project in a program and if someone else's purpose is to manage separately another project in that program, both of you will be competing for resources, visibility, rewards, and so on, to the detriment of both projects. However, if you both believe that your purpose is to support the same program, you can allocate resources according to the needs of the program, and visibility will be focused on the program, not projects within it.

Stage 3: Agree on individual priorities.

If everyone has the same purpose, then individual priorities tend to fall into place—but not always. Priorities still must be stated and agreed on because team members may agree on the overall purpose but have different priorities. Your priority may be to get out a perfect design, and someone else's priority may be to get the design out on time. Once these differences are openly defined in the team setting, then the team can decide which trade-offs to make to achieve the key factors of the customer's requirements.

The basis for the difference in how people set priorities is often in their personalities, so along with the team, the manager must monitor that agreed-on priorities are being followed in order to keep the team on track. These personality traits, such as being a perfectionist or being obsessed with schedules, must be respected, valued, and used as resources.

When a team is collaborating rather than just communicating, it is easier for a team to reach a consensus about a problem or its solution. The constant process of defining a common vocabulary, stating the team purpose, and setting priorities enhances the productivity of the team and the company.

A reminder: The specific organization of managers and teams throughout the concurrent engineering environment cannot be prescribed. It depends on your company and your belief in what will work best. Managers can, however, avoid the three most common mistakes made when putting a team together: making the team too big, making the team too small, and putting the wrong people on a team.

An oversized team creates too many lines of communication, causes too much overhead, and is too expensive. An undersized team is like not having a team at all, because all the required disciplines are not represented. Not least, the wrong people can make the wrong decisions, resulting in a released product that doesn't meet the customer's needs.

In general, creating development teams should result in pyramidal hierarchies becoming flattened and authority flowing to those who have the corresponding responsibility.

THE COMMUNICATION INFRASTRUCTURE DIMENSION

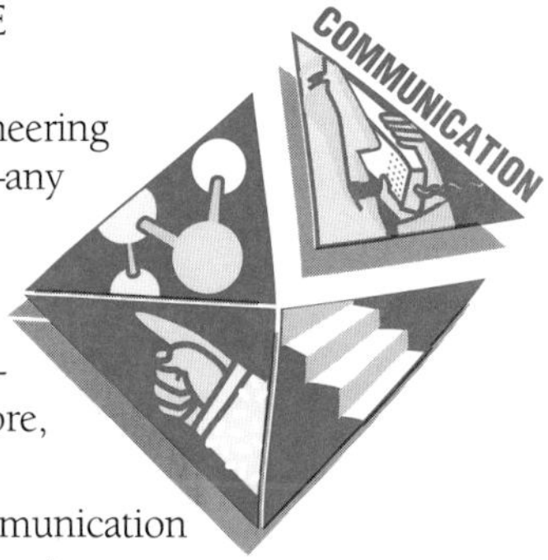

The second key dimension of a concurrent engineering environment is the communication infrastructure—any system, equipment, and software that facilitates the meaningful transfer of information relating to the product. Concurrent engineering requires that one or more teams work and share information in an integrated product development environment; therefore, effective communication is critical to success.

However simple or complex the product is, communication issues arise that can thwart team activities. Even when teams are clear about the purpose of their work and their priorities and have plenty of employees, enough time, abundant materials, and adequate technology, the overall purpose of the team effort—task, project, program, or enterprise—doesn't always succeed. As product complexity increases, the development of the product can fail before reaching its technological limitations if a communication infrastructure doesn't support the necessary kinds and volume of information. The infrastructure must also expedite important information to the right people.

The concurrent engineering environment does not focus on numbers of people in determining the shape and contents of the communication infrastructure dimension, though clearly it's a factor. The more people involved in a project, the greater the chances of poor communication. On a 1,000 person project, even if you eliminate 99% of the communication paths, that still leaves nearly 5,000 paths! But thousands of paths of communication between thousands of people can be accomplished rather simply through electronic mail. Because it's basic for these person-to-person communication paths to be in place, the focus of this dimension quickly shifts to collaboration, and the infrastructure determines the degree to which data from different disciplines can be meaningfully organized and accessed by development team members in order to create a shared understanding of the product and the processes involved in developing it.

Potential communication paths in a project

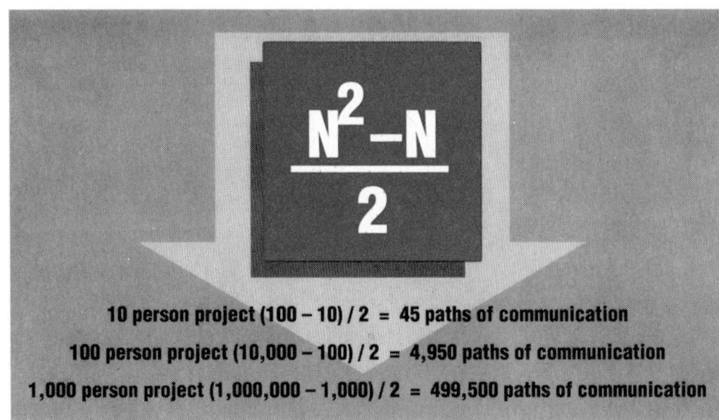

N2–N
2
10 person project (100 – 10) / 2 = 45 paths of communication
100 person project (10,000 – 100) / 2 = 4,950 paths of communication
1,000 person project (1,000,000 – 1,000) / 2 = 499,500 paths of communication

To a great extent, product complexity determines the number of disciplines involved, and both of these determine the type of infrastructure needed to share information. The more components and disciplines, the more varied and unintegrated the component data is—which requires a more complex infrastructure that can integrate the data and keep everyone informed about activity in the concurrent engineering environment and each person's respective role.

When in balance with the other dimensions, the communication infrastructure supports and nourishes the other dimensions. However, when the communication infrastructure is not in balance, the process of collaboration breaks down, and the development teams lose or distort the original, desired behavior of the product. This misdirection can result in a loss of product functionality, problems in testability, delays in manufacturing, and a loss of customers. That's why companies cannot ignore the technological requirements of this dimension.

TECHNOLOGIES FOR COMMUNICATING AND COLLABORATING

A communication infrastructure provides the technologies to facilitate the communication and collaboration necessary for product development. Specifically, these technologies facilitate the discovering and defining of what should be built, followed by carefully tracking how to build it and verifying that the end product meets the original design goals. When considered in this way, these communication technologies are potentially as critical to the product's success as the technologies used in the actual development of the product.

Changes needed in the communication infrastructure

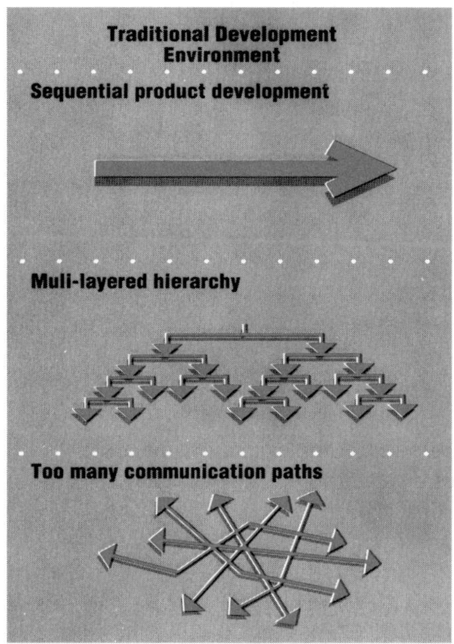

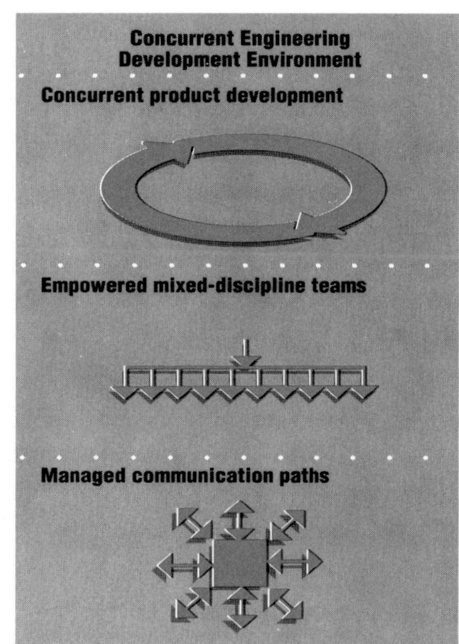

Databases that handle customer requirements, electronic mail systems, and other product data (such as warranty information on field defects), monitoring and evaluation systems, and closed-loop corrective action systems (such as problem-reporting systems) are examples of the technologies that must be in place to support discovery and definition, enhance communication of published discoveries, and glean requirements and definitions from ongoing development activities.

The level of technological support should correspond to the level of effort and complexity in the concurrent engineering environment. The levels of support are additive—meaning that the concurrent engineering environment for a complicated product includes all the more basic communication technologies required for simpler products as well as those required for the more complex infrastructure.

Supporting a design database

You can use communication technologies to support discovery and definition throughout product development in several ways.

With few disciplines involved on the development team—implying that the team is small and that the product, current customer requirements, and development process are fairly simple—you might only need an electronic mail system as a means of linking information about the design to ongoing tasks. In this instance, individuals may hold pertinent information in their heads or in their file cabinets or computers, and to find out what you want to know, you just ask the right person.

With more disciplines involved, you might want to use a design database that has query and reporting capability, accessible by both team members and design tools, to compile information about the design into various usable forms, such as a history of design problems and lists of possible substitute parts.

At a greater level of product complexity, you might need interactive browsing capability, such as provided in the Powerframe recently available from Digital Equipment Corporation or in the Falcon Framework recently available from Mentor Graphics Corporation. An interactive browser should be accessible by both team members and design tools, to facilitate rapid interactive access to a design database that may actually be composed of the design-related data contained in several databases of several disciplines. In fact, a single database for design data might not exist. For example, a design engineer might easily check all the information about a specific design feature—including what was problematical in manufacturing and in customer acceptance—by browsing through all the databases in the concurrent engineering environment.

From database to knowledgebase

When your company needs to manage an enterprise composed of programs that include projects with many defined tasks, you need to automate as much of the process of discovery and definition as possible. You can use a design decision database to organize project design requirements, design decisions, and discipline-specific design data. This type of database would serve as the design knowledgebase and could include, among the other database capabilities previously mentioned, automatic and interactive decision support for the ongoing product development process.

INTERACTIVE MONITORING AND REPORTING SYSTEMS

To use the design knowledgebase, you need systems that organize, evaluate, and retrieve the information in usable ways. You must also have managing and reporting systems that expand the knowledgebase. Managing and reporting systems should:

- Track the decision process.
- Monitor and evaluate the progress and quality of your decisions.
- Track the problems associated with product development activities.
- Maintain links to outside sources of information.

To deal with a very complex product, managing and reporting systems need to be interactive with all phases of the development process. For example, as the engineer is designing, the reporting system should tell the engineer if a component over-spends the projected budget or requires unusual manufacturing procedures.

Capturing and utilizing the decision path

The design knowledgebase should be interactive with a managing and reporting system that can capture the decision path—the thought process about a product's design and development. (Some problem reporting systems can do this today in a limited way.) While team members communicate the discovery and changing definitions of what is going to be built, the knowledgebase should keep a record of evolving design requirements and decisions so that later anyone can trace the decision path—what requirements and decisions led to a design change.

The managing and reporting system should be active at the beginning of the design process. It should capture and trace the conceptual requirements that lead to the behavior of the design, and along the way, it should capture and trace the detailed design decisions. The record of this decision path ideally includes all the interactions among team members, customers, and industry standards committees that lead to design decisions. The managing and reporting system that tracks and documents the decision path and stores the related data in the knowledgebase must be thorough and discriminating so that the reasons behind decisions are clear.

As a product matures and new features are added, a monitoring and evaluation system can use the knowledgebase to assist team members in making decisions that result in the clean maturation of the product's design and implementation. This approach increases product reliability and extends product life.

New projects can also benefit from the experiences captured in the design decision path associated with prior projects. A design knowledgebase can help bring new people on a project up to speed quickly by understanding why decisions were made. In addition to design data, the knowledgebase reflects the organization of a project, including what tools were required and what processes were used. For example, an enormous number of design decisions are made with each product enhancement. A majority of these decisions get lost or forgotten, often because key people involved in those decisions are no longer available. If those decisions were stored as part of a design knowledgebase, think of the benefits to the engineers working on the next release, helping them understand the decision path to previous decisions.

Reporting problems now to avoid them later

Just as problem reporting systems help in the support phase of a project, the concepts can be extended to a similar system that supports the entire product development process. The design knowledgebase would contain information about problems associated with the design and the development process. As designs become more complex and more design dependencies are created, the managing and reporting system could help solve current problems and avoid problems by generating new action items, by reminding people of pending action items, and by reporting on the status of existing action items.

As with other managing and reporting systems, you should be able to trace the information path and understand a problem's history and solutions. At the least, you could query the knowledgebase for all of a particular product's problem reports—from design to delivery—and find a single solution to what seems like separate problems. And of course, whatever you discover becomes immediately available to everyone else in the concurrent engineering environment.

3. Define how components interact.

When the team starts thinking about real-world components, the specific team disciplines come into play, and team members have to define how the various components interact. For example, if the team is defining a graphics subsystem, the team might get to the point where it defines a component that is a graphics accelerator card. Then the team needs to define how the other components of the system will interface to it. In defining these interfaces, the team members are just defining more behaviors—how to translate a sequence of inputs into a sequence of outputs—and are generating more detailed requirements, such as a standard or proprietary interface or a specified range of performance.

4. Define product integration and testing procedures.

The team must constantly take into consideration how the components of the product will be integrated and tested. The team must determine not only if the product is supposed to work (feasibility) but also if it actually does work (testability). Because if the components can't be integrated and tested, the product can't be built. And if it can't be built, it is useless. This bottom-up look is an ongoing necessity in the overall top-down design process.

If the components can't be integrated and tested, the product can't be built.

For example, with a complicated product the development team must figure out the best way to integrate components into subsystems and then integrate subsystems into a larger and larger part of the whole. No matter how simple or complex the product, the team must develop strategies that will be used to verify that the parts are actually working. Since the product to be built was initially described in terms of how it would behave under various conditions, the team has a head start on a comprehensive test suite. The team can use as test cases the same scenarios that were earlier constructed to define conceptual behaviors. This permits early feedback to the design process and promotes "design for testability."

Another benefit of specifying early how the components of the product fit together and interact with each other is that the development team, by representing and considering all disciplines, also promotes "design for manufacturability." With this early look at your product's integration and testing needs, the team gets a jump on alpha and beta site planning.

There's no point having a requirement that can't be verified or tested as correct.

With all the requirements defined, it's a good idea to remember that validating and redefining those requirements are processes that should have been going on throughout the initial definition phases of the product and should continue to go on throughout the entire development process.

EVALUATING AND VALIDATING WHAT YOU DO

Traditionally, designers stick with their first concept of the design and make additions or deletions to that original idea. However, a complex product is in a constant state of flux: design oversights are uncovered, new requirements are added, new constraints are imposed, and new competitors rise from the murky depths. The design should accommodate this desirable state of flux in a concurrent engineering environment, where one or more development teams are encouraged to develop, evaluate, and validate the design.

In a concurrent engineering environment, the product must be continually evaluated and validated—from the smallest component and its requirements to the integrated product and its requirements. For a complex product, the design tool an engineer uses should be able to check interactively with the design knowledgebase that requirements for the component being designed are being met. Then while the product is designed, it can be validated in terms of cost, performance, reliability, and customer perception. And by keeping track of the decision process, the design knowledgebase can reaffirm why a certain alternative was selected. But however careful a design decision, changes to requirements always need to be made and must be part of the ongoing product development process.

Teams find the best way to design and build a complex product by going through trade-off analysis—a process of analyzing the design choices through what-if scenarios. Trade-off analysis occurs, either intuitively or formally, when the development team makes any important decision by one of the following:

- Identifying the constraints that cause the team members to make a choice between features.
- Evaluating the features based on some criteria.
- Trading off some features to keep or gain others.

Trade-off analysis is the heart of design: the process of selecting the best choice after a detailed evaluation of all the possible choices. By using trade-off analysis to challenge and refine the focus of the product design, teams can make more pivotal and lasting design decisions.

This design rationale—the decision path created through trade-off analysis—must be captured and passed on to the subsequent developers. Without a documented decision path, a new engineer who is reusing an existing design could change the design and then spend months chasing subtle problems and modifying the design to handle them. But if a new engineer can refer to the original rationale for design decisions, he or she can move quickly to add already specified features to the original design or have reasons to challenge the previous design decision. With a thoroughly interactive design knowledgebase, a challenge can be done quickly in a what-if query before actual design changes are tried, and if a change in a customer requirement is made, everyone on the development team should know about it and agree with it.

Each individual team member must be able to trace the path from the collaborative design decision to the functionality and behavior under their responsibility.

It's during the trade-off analysis on large projects that you see team members earnestly collaborating. After the team reaches a decision and implements it, then traceability to product behavior becomes important. Each individual team member must be able to trace the path from the collaborative design decision to the functionality and behavior under their responsibility. As mentioned earlier, the communication infrastructure must adequately support traceability in all directions—top-down, bottom-up, and across disciplines.

The focus of the concurrent engineering environment on requirements as one of its four dimensions provides a greater chance of actually meeting customer needs—and meeting them quickly. The product that the customer wants initially is usually not the same product that the customer wants delivered. Customer requirements change throughout the development process. The concurrent engineering environment is always ready to adapt to a customer's changing needs. As customer requirements and available technology change throughout the development process, products can be redesigned fast.

So it's basic to know how requirements direct the current decision process and future decisions. This understanding promotes a product development environment that is "of one mind"—another way of characterizing the concurrent engineering environment. The team members of different disciplines grow to understand each other's point of view as they share their opinions and ideas, and the design converges to reflect the product that the customer wants.

THE PRODUCT DEVELOPMENT DIMENSION

DEVELOPMENT

Many companies are struggling to simplify their design process and to use design automation effectively. They are beginning to realize that organizational changes or the latest, souped-up tools aren't enough to be competitive in the 1990s. What they are lacking is a process for total product development—an integrated vision of how the product moves from design conception to manufacturing and beyond. The product development dimension includes all those processes that link the activities for designing and building what the requirements specify. Even the process of defining the requirements and using trade-off analysis is really part of this dimension. But it also includes all those other processes related to such areas as marketing and customer support that are necessary for continued product success over the years.

As you might expect in a concurrent engineering environment, all these activities are ongoing and happening at the same time. Companies must concurrently enhance the product while assessing its status. Development processes must integrate all disciplines. Then the knowledge gained during this process of concurrent product development must be captured and recycled to provide for decision support and timely product and process enhancements—creating an environment of continuous change and improvement.

Some of these needed changes have already been discussed from the vantage point of each of the other three key dimensions involving the organization, communication infrastructure, and requirements. To understand the product development dimension, you can focus on its three key factors: the design process, the development and use of component (or parts) libraries, and the continuing optimization of the development process.

THE DESIGN PROCESS

As in the other dimensions, what is appropriate for your company's product development process depends on the complexity of your product—its parts and the processes needed to develop it. But while the requirements dimension focuses on the what of the product, this dimension focuses on the how and the specific methods and processes needed to make the what (the product) happen.

Design in the "-abilities" -don't add them on.

In the requirements dimension, you saw how defining and redefining product specifications affects the design process and other phases of the product development process. From the very start, product development teams must include information from downstream processes in their design. These processes involve testability, manufacturability, reliability, serviceability, and accountability. In the best case, the design process is part of a feedback loop where downstream processes help to shape the design and then downstream engineers keep assessing the impact of early design decisions on their processes. This flow of information can, for example, cause the number of engineering change notices to drop dramatically. By moving downstream processes upstream, companies can focus on process improvement rather than fixing poorly conceived designs.

So it's the attention that a company gives to how a product is developed that ensures a good design and a timely product that can compete successfully. A quality product is one that satisfies the customer's needs over the life of that product. An example of how the product development processes work in a concurrent engineering environment can be found in that continual search for a good design process or methodology that results in continuously improving products.

Capturing the good design

It makes sense that at the heart of product development and the design process is a good design. Without a good design, the best organization and the best communication technologies won't do you any good at all.

The fundamentals of product development

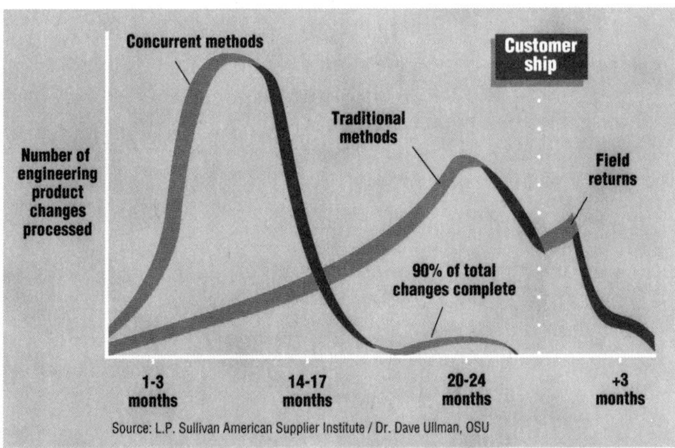

On the surface, a good design is one that meets the customer's requirements and also meets the company's requirements—that is, a design developed on time and within budget. In addition, a good design must be based on engineering requirements and targets, follow a functional model of the product, incur a decreasing number of design changes throughout the design process, and incorporate mature technology.

Studies by Dr. David G. Ullman in the Department of Mechanical Engineering at Oregon State University have identified the five shoulds of a good design:

1. *A good design should clearly represent the customer's needs and wants for the product.*

   This requirement is often accomplished in great detail for military procurements but not often for commercial products. Part of this effort is to identify exactly who the customer is and to find cost-effective methods of recording what the customer wants.

2. *A good design should be based on engineering requirements and targets.*

   Based on the customer requirements, a set of engineering requirements must be developed. These requirements are reflective of the customer's requirements but are clearly measurable in a laboratory situation and have specific targets based on benchmarks. For any newly developed product, it is important to know and understand the competition from both the existing products produced in-house and those produced by outside vendors.

3. *A good design should follow a functional model of the product.*

   In VLSI (Very Large Scale Integration) circuitry design, an early step is to design the logic that determines the chip's function. In the design of mechanical devices, there are no techniques for directly modeling the function of a product. In fact, as the structure of a mechanical device evolves, more functions are added. It is important to monitor the functional development of any electrical or mechanical device.

4. *A good design should incur a decreasing number of design changes throughout the design process.*

   Early in the process, many alternatives and changes should be considered. As the product evolves toward the final design, the number of changes should reduce to zero. Late design changes are expensive and are usually caused by design decisions that altered the original functions.

5. *A good design should use technology that is mature.*

   In a competitive market, companies face high incentives to include new technologies in their products. However, if the technology is not ready, resulting problems may be attributed to the design, rather than the technology.

"A design that meets specifications is the engineer's view of a good design. However, a design that solves the problem is the customer's view of a good design."

–Dr. Geoff Bunza, Mentor Graphics

In the concurrent engineering environment, the development team has a method for finding and producing a good design, and it's called collaborating on knowledge. A good design comes from the total development process—how well the development team has a shared understanding of the problem to be solved. And perhaps the major problem to be solved is to meet the customer's expectations.

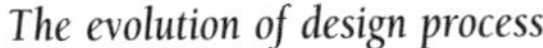

The evolution of design process

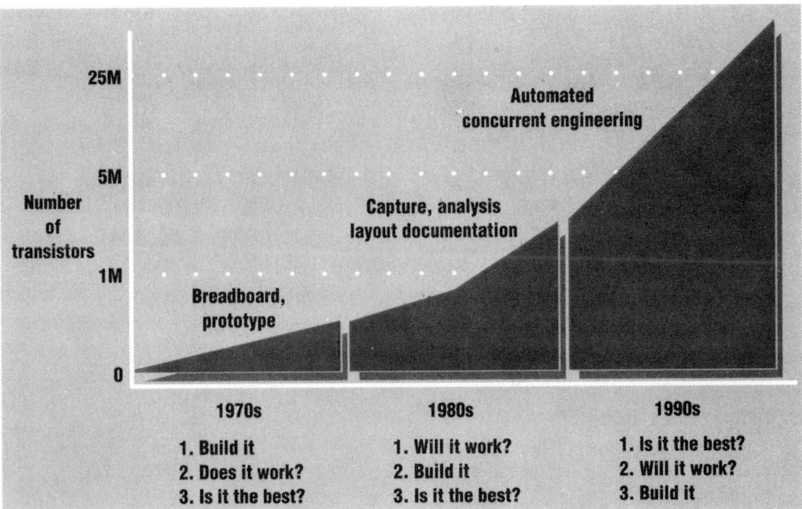

Those expectations must be legitimate, clearly expressed in the customer's mind, and precisely understood by the team. For example, to get this understanding, the team might decide it needs to mix the academic knowledge of new engineers with the experience of veteran engineers who have previously solved similar problems. The team might send its members to talk directly to a customer and look at products previously built to solve similar problems. Or if the new product is to be a tool that a customer will use to develop another product, team members might actually try to do the things that the customer is currently doing and is expecting the newly designed product to do better, such as build complex integrated circuits or develop software.

In a concurrent engineering environment, the engineers don't go away to design and build what's agreed on. This is especially true with brand-new products that might take eighteen months to develop. In eighteen months, the whole market could be completely different. A company could build the wrong product for all the right reasons. Instead, the engineers, as members of the product development teams, stay in contact with the customer and closely monitor customer expectations as they change over time to ensure the product's competitiveness.

QFD–House of Quality

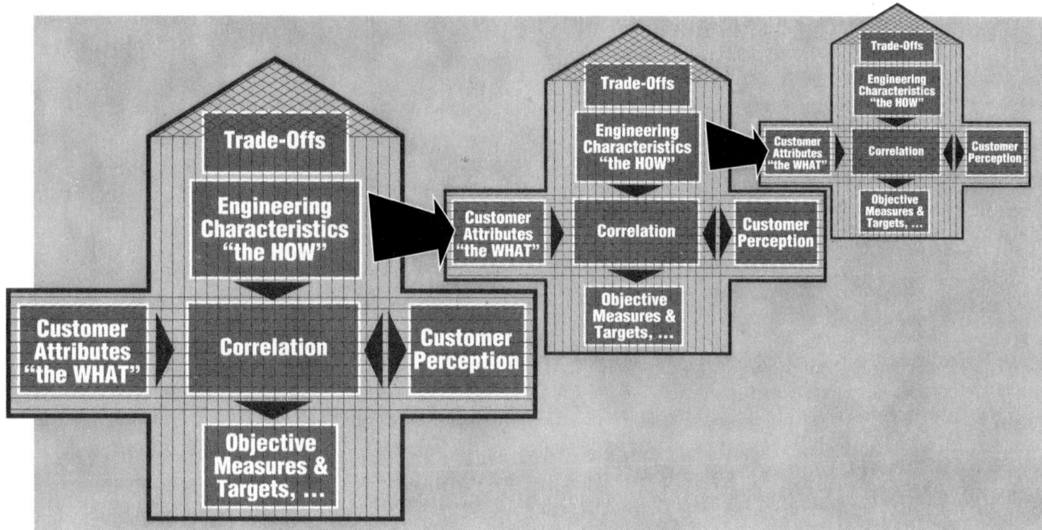

Designing quality into the product

Quality function deployment (QFD) is one management method for designing products that meet customer requirements. QFD methods involve constructing and evaluating a matrix-style chart called the house of quality. The chart forms a conceptual map of the characteristics that the customer wants most in a product (the whats) and the engineering decisions necessary to build it (the hows).

Eventually, the hows from one house of quality become the whats of another house as the details for the product design are fleshed out. For example, engineering characteristics (hows) like horsepower needed for driving a golf cart up an incline with a full load of players and clubs, can become the customer attributes (whats) for another house of quality that is built around the ability of the motor and gears to perform the hill-climbing feat many times without a problem. Then, those parts characteristics, like the materials that are used to construct the motor and gears so that they have a long mean time before failure, become the engineering characteristics (hows) for that new house of quality.

QFD methods in the conceptual stage of design are valuable in a number of ways. QFD focuses on quality from the customer's point of view and offers reasonable alternatives to engineering decisions. Quality is designed into a product—not added on. And as the effort to develop a product becomes more complicated, QFD promotes more interaction between product development teams that include a mix of disciplines.

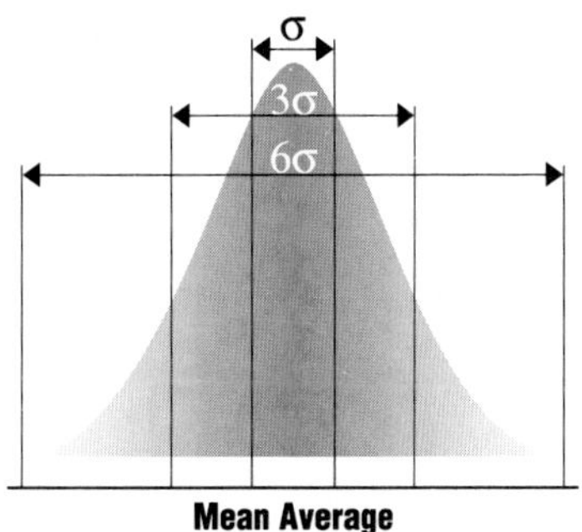

Another management goal for designing quality into a product is Six Sigma. As a statistical way of measuring quality control, achieving Six Sigma means catching defects 99.9997 percent of the time. Companies must shed the old notion that they have to expect a certain amount of defects and errors in their products. "Do you know what 99.0 percent quality means?" asks Phil Kelly, vice president for Motorola's customer response center. "It means the US Postal Service would lose 17,000 pieces of mail every hour." Kelly stresses that "*all* errors are preventable."

Ultimately, how well the product meets the ever-changing customer expectations determines whether the company is delivering a product of high quality. And it's good to remember that if the product is to meet those expectations, the customer must know how to use the product—which means documentation or customer training may need to be another concurrent process in product development.

It is important to remember that there is no one path to product quality or the highest degree of excellence. So it is important for a company to be aware of the different approaches to quality that have been tried with success and to evaluate and use whatever works for a particular product.

COMPONENT LIBRARIES

A key factor to sustaining a successful design process is the creation and use of component libraries. These libraries contain the building blocks of the actual design and, for a product composed of many subsystems and components, will contain many alternatives from which to choose. The completeness and accuracy of the component libraries are critical to ensuring an efficient development team and a defect-free design. The component library must contain all the specifications and operational characteristics of all the building blocks to be used in the design; and all members of the design team must simultaneously receive the component information or they cannot design concurrently.

Component libraries, among other things, keep track of what parts are in stock, which were used in previous products, and what the specifications for the individual parts are. These libraries usually mean that you never have to design an entire product from scratch. Using previously designed and tested components speeds the overall design and manufacturing processes and ensures greater product reliability.

Component libraries come in many different forms, such as symbols, physical packaging footprints, in-circuit test descriptions, signal integrity models, and simulation models. Simulation models are the most complex form of component libraries. A simulation model of a component is a representation of how that component behaves. Simple components may be represented by a gate-level description. More complex components are often described in software behavioral models or hardware models.

The rapid growth of VLSI circuit complexity is changing the way these simulation models are generated. Rather than using component data sheets, the semiconductor supplier who builds the component must be involved in ensuring the completeness, accuracy, and timeliness of the simulation model. One provider of some 10,000 behavioral simulation devices is Logic Automation, Inc. of Beaverton, Oregon. Logic Automation does involve the semiconductor supplier to generate libraries with the semiconductor supplier's proprietary information.

In a concurrent engineering environment for a complex product, the component libraries are part of the design knowledgebase that must be available throughout the development process. The component library information in the design knowledgebase documents when a specific component was used and why. In an environment with interactive reporting systems, information from the library may be automatically chosen and used, based on customer requirements or specific trade-offs.

OPTIMIZING PRODUCT DEVELOPMENT

After component libraries, the next key factor in a successful development process is the continual evaluation and change of the product and the processes that produced it. The company can begin by using the information that flows through the concurrent engineering environment to pinpoint how to improve a product and its development process the next time the design process starts. For example, a company needs to look closely at product defects and determine where the design process allowed the defect to occur and pass undetected. All the links between different parts of a design and the recorded behaviors and decisions form a block of design knowledge that should be in a database and serve as the basis for design reuse.

One concept for promoting design reuse is CARE, Computer-Aided Reusable Engineering, developed by Logic Automation, Inc. CARE promotes reusing engineering designs developed from schematic capture and board-level simulation tools. These designs include simulation models that allow engineers to simulate and reverify their new design that is based on the existing design. This makes possible a method of reusing engineering ideas throughout the concurrent engineering environment. Texas Instruments used CARE concepts to develop the TI Simuboard. A complete board-level design, using new graphics processors, was captured in an EDA database. Engineers who accessed this design could understand how the design worked and then borrow design elements for their own designs. TI's customers were able to reuse design information from the Simuboard in their own products.

Another way to optimize product development is to evaluate customer requirements continuously so that product development teams, when possible, can design a basic product to which features can be added. For example, no one stereo can service everyone because there are many varied needs. Instead, a company can build a stereo that services a particular class of customer needs and then adapt the product for specific customer needs with expansion and follow-on products. By continually gathering and analyzing information about customer requirements and market directions, the development teams can keep redefining the basic product and the individual customer add-ons.

Yet another way to optimize product development is to use tools that continually assess whether customer requirements are being met. For complex products, the software modeling and simulation tools that were previously discussed might allow a product to be tested carefully so that fewer prototypes need to be built. But many components have become so complex that developing a full and accurate software representation of every component is not practical. Hardware models have evolved as a rapid and cost-effective way to fill this need. Hardware models can be constructed in a few days or a few weeks. Logic Modeling Systems, of Milpitas, California, a company who designs and manufactures a hardware modeler, is the leading provider of hardware models and systems.

Hardware models can also be used to optimize the concurrency of design tasks. All hardware models provide the full behavior of a component, including how that component will process executable code in the case of microprocessors. This allows designers to run code, such as diagnostics, against the design. The design becomes a virtual prototype or virtual breadboard, and valuable information can be provided to the software designer or diagnostics engineer, as well as to the hardware designer. For example, the design can debug the diagnostics and the diagnostics can debug the design. This allows concurrent development and feedback on hardware and software design, especially for embedded or target-specific software. An important benefit is that the designer can use the actual software to build confidence in the quality of the design.

Keep in mind that it's desirable and inevitable for this optimization process to spread through and affect all the dimensions of concurrent engineering. This causes the dimensions to change and shift so that the concurrent engineering environment adapts successfully to the ever-changing marketplace.

With these descriptions of the four key concurrent engineering dimensions in mind, it's time to mention once again that you can transform the forces of change into resources. The concurrent engineering environment nurtures technologies, tools, tasks, talents, and time and employs them wisely throughout the product development process as development methodologies change, new hardware becomes available, new standards are incorporated, and trade-offs are made. The concurrent engineering environment and its dimensions welcome and support change because change is a way to ensure the desired product behaviors continue throughout the product development process. Change is a necessity for product success and survival.

The last figure in this chapter illustrates the benefits of concurrent engineering. In general, the positive impacts of concurrent engineering are felt most in three important areas: time to market, quality improvements, and lower costs due to productivity gains. It's ambitious to seek improvement in all three areas at the same time, but that's what concurrent engineering with its integrated approach can allow a company to do.

Concurrent engineering benefits

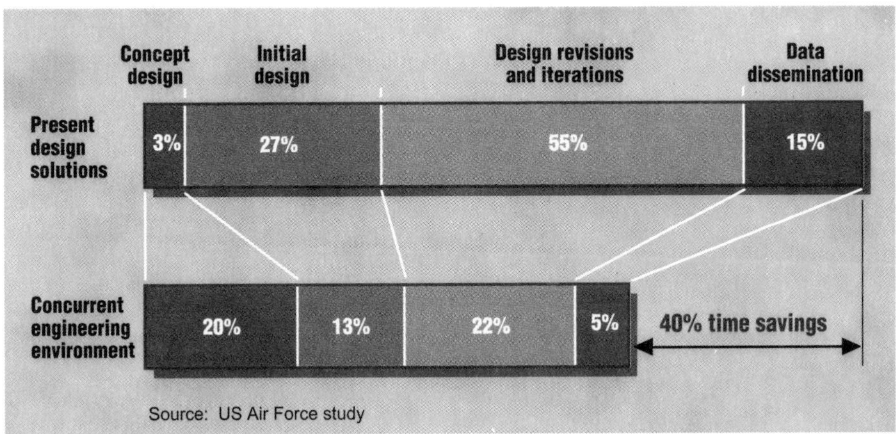

But you may already be convinced that your product could benefit from concurrent engineering, and you don't know where to start to make it happen. If so, the best place to start is to read the next chapter, which will help you assess where your company is and how much it needs to do in order to implement and balance the four dimensions of concurrent engineering.

THREE

APPLY A CONCURRENT ENGINEERING APPROACH.

IT'S TIME TO TAKE ACTION.

START BY ASSESSING WHERE

YOUR COMPANY IS AND

WHERE IT SHOULD BE.

TAKE THE RIGHT APPROACH.

CREATE A ROADMAP FOR SUCCESS.

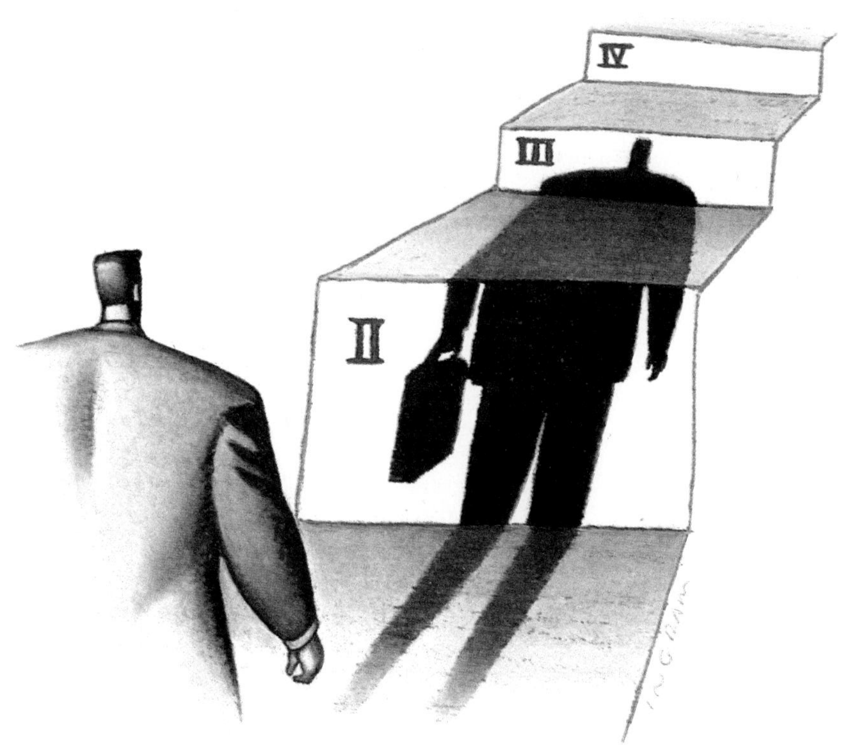

WHERE ARE YOU? WHERE SHOULD YOU BE?

Apply a Concurrent Engineering Approach

The concurrent engineering environment is an environment of necessity for companies who want to compete successfully in the 1990s. The factors that influence a customer's purchase decisions—is it faster, cheaper, and better?—demand changes in the four dimensions: organization, communication infrastructure, requirements, and product development. So the first question is not whether your company needs concurrent engineering, but this: Which concurrent engineering approach does your company need?

Generally speaking, it's your product—its parts and the processes needed to develop it—that determines the scope of your concurrent engineering environment. Simpler products usually allow a simpler approach. If your product is similar to a power supply, your concurrent engineering approach may be simple, as well as the kind and number of methods to implement it, because the overall purpose and the tasks of individuals are basically the same—to produce the power supply.

But if your product is complex, like a jumbo jet with many parts, add-on features, or a complicated development process, individual tasks only contribute to the development process. The gap between your company's overall purpose and the individual tasks must be bridged. The product makes it necessary to have a more extensive concurrent engineering environment. In this case, the most successful concurrent engineering approach would probably be the one that populates the four dimensions with many appropriate technologies, tools, tasks, and talents—the resources for change that are necessary to develop the product in a timely fashion. This environment would employ whatever methods needed to make productive use of these resources.

Whatever type of product you have, you must apply these resources for change by using methods that bring into balance the four dimensions of concurrent engineering. In general, the methods can be grouped into four concurrent engineering approaches. Each approach corresponds to a specific type of team effort—task, project, program, enterprise—that the company must make to have a concurrent engineering environment that works.

Here is an overview of each approach. When reading these descriptions, keep in mind that they are meant to be general enough to apply to most products and specifically are crafted to serve the purpose of the concurrent engineering assessment tool you'll soon use in this chapter.

Task. If your product has only one major unit and requires only a few individuals to develop it, then it requires a task effort.

Project. If your product has more units and requires a group of individuals who are in the same engineering discipline, this single-discipline team constitutes a project effort *(which includes task efforts)*.

Program. If your product requires separate engineering disciplines for its different units, each unit may need its own team *(project team)*. Then representatives from these project teams can form a mixed-discipline program team to manage the overall development process and promote communication across disciplines. In effect, your product uses a program effort *(which includes task and project efforts)*.

Enterprise. If your product is so complicated that it requires many mixed-discipline teams *(program teams)* that may include third-party vendors, you need a level of communication that requires an enterprise team. This signals that your company-wide team effort is an enterprise effort *(which includes task, project, and program efforts)*.

From these four descriptions, you should have a sense of which overall concurrent engineering approach your company needs to use, but the real value is in knowing which methods can implement each approach. It's important to note that the approaches are additive—for example, to implement the program approach, you must first implement the task approach and then the project approach. Also, keep in mind that your company may already have some of the resources for the changes that a concurrent engineering environment requires. If so, you'll soon learn more about the methods of using them effectively to keep the four dimensions in balance. Bringing these dimensions into balance creates a highly efficient and productive development process that is strategic to winning and keeping markets and customers.

So now, the next question is this: What are the different methods that implement the approach your company needs, in a way that brings the four dimensions of concurrent engineering into balance? To learn the answer, you must go through a process—assessing where your company is and where it should be. Out of this assessment comes an overall vision of a concurrent engineering environment—a vision that you can use to further explore the changes that you need to continue implementing to stay successful.

ASSESS YOUR PRODUCT DEVELOPMENT ENVIRONMENT

The assessment tool in this chapter is a concurrent engineering assessment. It combines elements from other assessment tools, including the Carnegie Mellon University Software Engineering Institute *(SEI)* Assessment Questionnaire, the Department of Defense CALS/CE Task Group for Electronic Systems Self Assessment, and the Mentor Graphics Corporation Process Maturity Assessment Questionnaire.

This tool will help you look at your company's current product development environment, will suggest a vision for what kind of concurrent engineering environment would help your product flourish, will illustrate what your company needs to do to bring the dimensions of concurrent engineering into balance, and will help you plan a roadmap to transform your company's product development environment into a concurrent engineering environment.

The tool presented here is made up of four parts:

The company assessment questionnaire helps you determine the current state of your company's product development environment in relation to the four dimensions of concurrent engineering and to key areas within each dimension.

The methods matrix helps you determine, dimension by dimension and approach by approach, the general concurrent engineering methods that your company needs in order to develop a given product successfully. It's the concurrent engineering vision your company should have.

The dimensions map helps you see the variances between where your company is and where it should be in each concurrent engineering dimension. It illustrates what you need to do to implement the vision so that the dimensions are in balance.

The priority roadmap helps you determine priorities for starting to bring the dimensions into balance—the priorities for implementing the concurrent engineering vision for your company.

The assessment tool in this chapter is only a starting place—a vision for the near future. Though you cannot use this tool as a scientific measure to prescribe exactly what you need to do, you can use it to give yourself a general idea of what kind of change is necessary in your company to create a concurrent engineering environment. You can use it to find out where you should be focusing your attention and possibly adding resources. For more comprehensive assessments that deal with individual practices or processes, you'll need to use such tools as a Best Practices assessment. Additional assessment tools are listed in the Appendix.

FIND OUT WHERE YOU ARE NOW

The company assessment questionnaire characterizes the present development environment in which your company develops its product. If your company is large enough to have very distinct products, focus on the development environment for only one product that you market. For this assessment to be useful, you must answer the questions as they relate to your company's current product development environment, not according to plans you may have to change it. *(Another copy of the questionnaire is in the Appendix.)*

The questions are grouped according to the four dimensions and further grouped into key areas in each dimension. Answer each question yes **Y** or no **N** with the best information you have. Answer yes only if your company is consistently and adequately implementing the action implied by a question. Answer every question unless you don't know the answer or unless what is asked is not relevant to your product. Completing this questionnaire should take less than 30 minutes.

ORGANIZATION

This part of the company assessment questionnaire explores where your company presently stands in terms of the key factors that characterize the organization dimension in a concurrent engineering environment. To successfully apply a concurrent engineering approach, a company's organization of its employees focuses on individuals and often on teams who understand the product development process and their role in it. It is the responsibility of managers to empower these individuals and teams with the authority they need in order to complete their tasks. Managers also need to ensure other kinds of support, such as training, education, and tools that allow the company to adapt and meet each new challenge of the marketplace.

Team Integration

Individual employees and teams understand their roles and tasks in the context of the overall product development process.

Y N **1.** Are the specifications and priorities for the assigned tasks understood by the individuals?

Y N **2.** Is the product development process understood by each single-discipline team?

Y N **3.** Is there a common vocabulary, priority and purpose established for the mixed-discipline product development team?

Y N **4.** Are the requirements, specifications, interdependencies, and priorities of the product understood by the enterprise team *(which includes the customer and third-parties)*?

Empowerment

The levels of authority and responsibility that coexist within your company play a significant role in its productivity, and both individuals and teams are rewarded.

Y N **5.** Are design decisions made by the supervisors and managers?

Y N **6.** Are design decisions made by the single-discipline team?

Y N **7.** Are design and tradeoff decisions made by the mixed-discipline team?

Y N **8.** Do representatives from the enterprise team *(which includes the customer and third-party vendors)* participate in your decisions?

Y N **9.** Are individuals responsible for scheduling and then completing their tasks on time and responsible for the outcome of their tasks?

Y N **10.** Is a single-discipline team responsible for the development of engineering specifications and their correlation to interdependent specifications?

Y N **11.** Is a mixed-discipline team responsible for program-wide specifications, scheduling, and correlation to requirements?

Y N **12.** Is an enterprise team *(which includes the customer and third-party vendors)* responsible for the system design specifications?

Y N **13.** Do you reward individuals for their contributions?

Y N **14.** Do you reward teams for their contributions?

Training and Education

Managers provide appropriate training and education for an individual or team. Effectiveness training includes how to solve problems, set goals, think creatively, use standards, utilize experts, and work with other disciplines.

Y N **15.** Is adequate training provided for each individual on the procedures, tools, and standards he or she should use?

Y N **16.** Does the single-discipline team have adequate cross-discipline awareness regarding procedures, tools, and standards?

Y N **17.** Is adequate team effectiveness training provided for the mixed-discipline team members?

Y N **18.** Is adequate team effectiveness training provided for the enterprise team members *(including the customer and third-party vendors)*?

Automation Support

Managers ensure that the necessary tools are available. These tools are integrated and provide access to product data.

Y N **19.** Are the tools for each discipline provided as stand-alone tools?

Y N **20.** Are centralized tools provided for the single-discipline team?

Y N **21.** Are the tools for each individual integrated within the mixed-discipline team?

Y N **22.** Are the tools for each individual integrated within the enterprise team *(including any vendor-supplied parts or assistance being available on-line)*?

COMMUNICATION INFRASTRUCTURE

This part of the questionnaire explores where your company stands in terms of the key factors that characterize the communication infrastructure dimension in a concurrent engineering environment. Concurrent engineering involves the co-design of the product by all disciplines. Therefore, using effective communication paths and tools to manage product information, employees, tasks, and changes to the product becomes critical for success. Working product data, lessons learned, decision rationales, and decision sequences need to be tracked so that individuals and teams understand the product development process at any time. Communication between individuals and between all workstation tools is crucial and determines how data is acquired and shared within the task, project, program, and enterprise.

Product Management

Effective communication paths are crucial to product management so that individuals and teams can understand their assigned goals and roles, help to plan the development process, monitor the fulfillment of their goals and roles, and improve the process as needed.

Y N **23.** Are electronic mail capabilities available to each individual?

Y N **24.** Are query and online reporting capabilities available to each individual?

Y N **25.** Are interactive product data browsers available to each individual?

Y N **26.** Is decision support available to each individual?

Y N **27.** Are technical reviews and inspections conducted at the appropriate milestones?

Y N **28** Is disciplined and consistent product management used for a project effort?

Y N **29.** Is there a communication path between all aspects of project management and system requirements?

Y N **30.** Are managers and interdependent project teams automatically and concurrently informed of problems and their status?

Product Data

Product data is complete and accurate at all times, and individuals and teams can access, manipulate, and change that data as appropriate.

Y N **31.** Is product development data controlled by the individual?

Y N **32.** Do individuals on the single-discipline team have access to all the product development data related to their discipline?

Y N **33.** Do individuals have electronic access to the product development data related to the different disciplines involved in product development?

Y N **34.** Do individuals and teams have electronic access to company-wide product development data that includes data from customers and third-party vendors?

Y N **35.** During the development process, are the product development specifications and designs utilized and documented in an established manner?

Y N **36.** Is the product development data stored, controlled, changed, and versioned in a similar or common computer database?

Y N **37.** Is the data in the product development database interoperable among the various design automation tools?

Y N **38.** Are evolving product requirements, specifications, and development data under automatic change and versioning controls?

Feedback

Feedback keeps the product development process on track and permits individuals and teams to handle deviations from customer expectations, product specifications, industry standards, and other requirements. Feedback from reviews and inspections generates action items as well as suggestions for enhancements to the product.

Y N **39.** Are problems analyzed as to their root cause and then corrected?

Y N **40.** Are problem reports logged, prioritized, scheduled for correction *(or rejection)*, and tracked until the problems are corrected?

Y N **41.** Are action items, problem reports, and enhancement requests stored in a decision database and then used as indicators for customer satisfaction?

Y N **42.** Are the trends of action items, problem reports, enhancement requests, and all other decisions analyzed to continuously improve the product development process?

REQUIREMENTS

This part of the questionnaire explores how your company handles the key factors that characterize the requirements dimension in a concurrent engineering environment. Concurrent engineering broadens the interpretation of requirements to include all product attributes that affect customer satisfaction. Adequately capturing and expressing the total set of these specifications is crucial to concurrent engineering. In addition, the organization imposes other requirements, such as planning, scheduling, and documentation, on individuals and teams. These internal requirements, as well as the validation of the total set of customer requirements, must work in concert to ensure successful concurrent engineering.

Requirements Definition

Your company converts customer needs upfront to the definitions, specifications, and designs of the product. At every stage in the development process, individuals, teams, and managers can check that requirements, specifications, and designs are meeting customer needs.

Y N **43.** Are customer expectations determined and converted to established, documented customer or marketing requirements?

Y N **44.** Are the customer or marketing requirements partitioned into established, documented functional specifications?

Y N **45.** Is there traceability from the individual functional specifications back to the customer or marketing requirements?

Y N **46.** Can the enterprise team access the customer or marketing requirements as part of decision support?

Y N **47.** Are internally imposed expectations determined and converted to established, documented product life cycle *(PLC)* requirements?

Y N **48.** Are the internal requirements partitioned into established, documented PLC specifications?

Y N **49.** Is there traceability from the individual functional specifications back to the PLC requirements?

Y N **50.** Can the enterprise team access the PLC requirements as part of decision support?

Planning Methodology

Product planning, evaluation, and design methods can happen from both the bottom-up and top-down. These methods may include trade-off analysis and integrating the tasks and processes that develop the product.

Y N **51.** Is there a bottom-up design process in which all individuals contribute to the planning, evaluation, or creation of the product or functional specifications?

Y N **52.** Is there a top-down design process in which the customer, product, or system design requirements lead to documented specifications for the functional subsystem design?

Y N **53.** Is it required that the mixed-discipline team consider tradeoffs that may change the product technology, design architecture, or development-to-manufacturing process?

Y N **54.** Do the product requirements and system design requirements lead to interrelated tasks and processes?

Planning Perspective

When determining the development process required for a given product, your company includes planning perspectives as part of that process.

Y N **55.** Do individuals document short-term planning prior to the start of a task?

Y N **56.** Does your company require documented long-term planning for your product?

Y N **57.** Does your company use multiphased, multi-year planning methods for each product family?

Y N **58.** Does your company measure best-value product designs for cost, functionality, fitness for use, reliability, performance, and supportability?

Validation

The requirements for the development process are validated to determine whether the specifications meet the customers requirements and if all specified processes accomplish the intended result.

Y N **59.** Are the individual functional subsystem specifications validated according to the customer requirements?

Y N **60.** Are the discipline-specific requirements validated according to the customer requirements?

Y N **61.** Are the mixed-discipline and process requirements validated to the customer requirements?

Y N **62.** Are interactive methods used to monitor and warn the enterprise team when a requirement mismatch occurs?

Standards

Your company documents and communicates to individuals and teams the conventions, guidelines, and procedures used for design standards. The standards cover customer needs, testing, manufacturing, and customer support.

Y N **63.** Does your company have a mechanism to monitor compliance with applicable design standards?

Y N **64.** Does your company use design standards to ensure product reliability?

Y N **65.** Does your company use design standards to ensure product testability, manufacturability, supportability, and usability?

Y N **66.** Does your company regularly review and improve its design standards?

PRODUCT DEVELOPMENT

This final part of the company assessment questionnaire explores how your company handles the key factors that characterize the product development dimension. The process of concurrently enhancing the product and assessing its status is very much a part of a concurrent engineering environment. In particular, verification, optimization, and development processes are continually redefined. This ongoing effort affects the role of data libraries, reviews, and product architectures.

Component Engineering

When a team is part of the development process, all the design data and the data on components, both simple parts and units, are available to all individuals.

Y N **67.** Are individuals responsible for the development of their own components and component libraries?

Y N **68.** Are company-wide standards used to represent the component data?

Y N **69.** Is a single library system used to manage the component data of all the different disciplines involved?

Y N **70.** Is the library system database linked to a decision support tool to assist each designer in making component or unit selections?

Design Process

The methodologies and validations for the design process are documented and measured.

Y N **71.** Are design process specifications methodically documented so that function-specific designs *(system, software, hardware, or mechanical)* are both repeatable and consistent?

Y N **72.** Is deterministic analysis used to measure how well the product functions—for example, logic simulation for gauging functionality, fault simulation for determining the detectability of a failure, analog simulation for verifying parameters, finite element analysis for measuring mechanical tolerances?

Y N **73.** Is there adequate evaluation of the reuse and shared use of product technology and product design units?

Y N **74.** Are adequate methods used to integrate the product and processes?

Y N **75.** Is information extracted from the physical design *(back-annotated)* to perform more detailed analyses of the product features and performance?

Y N **76.** Are analysis methods used to account for downstream processes, such as cost, testability, reliability, manufacturability, and supportability at the conceptual or detailed design stage?

Y N **77.** Are the computing environment and product development tools interoperable for all disciplines?

Y N **78.** Are decision support and process management systems in use?

Optimization

Managers must respond to the continuing evolution of technology.

Y N **79.** Are there goals for product and process improvements?

Y N **80.** Are major project decisions and the factors leading to them documented, distributed, and analyzed for guidance on other projects?

Y N **81.** Are process modeling and simulation tools used in planning and improving the design process?

Y N **82.** Are product designs, development processes, requirements, and tools concurrently analyzed and continuously improved as part of a company-wide optimization strategy?

Y N **83.** Is a supplier qualification program used to select third-party vendors for products or tools?

Later, in the third part of this assessment, you'll use the answers you gave to the questions in this questionnaire. For now you're ready to continue with the second part of this concurrent engineering assessment—the methods matrix.

DETERMINE WHERE YOU SHOULD BE

The methods matrix helps you determine what methods your company can use in its product development environment to reap the full benefits of concurrent engineering. Before you look closely at the matrix, first choose a product—a current or future product. You will be assessing which concurrent engineering methods would enhance your company's success in developing that product. *(Another copy of the matrix is in the Appendix.)*

Using the matrix is straightforward: Read the descriptions across from each key factor, and circle each description whose methods would be necessary for successful development of your chosen product. You may circle one description, more than one, all four, or none—however many you think are necessary for implementing that key factor and the overall process it suggests. One thing that can help guide your choices is noting that the more complicated your product is, the more likely you'll circle more descriptions for a particular key factor. The matrix should take less than fifteen minutes to complete.

ORGANIZATION

Key Factors	Task Approach	Project Approach	Program Approach	Enterprise Approach
Team Integration	Individuals have specific task and discipline perspectives, with little interaction between engineers or between disciplines. Data is controlled by individuals.	A single-discipline team has a project perspective. Data is not easily accessible by other disciplines.	A mixed-discipline team has a program perspective. Team members receive training to better understand other disciplines. Data is easily accessible by other disciplines.	Mixed-discipline teams have members from the entire enterprise, including management, suppliers, manufacturing. purchasing, customers, service, and all the "-abilities."
Empowerment	Management provides the only leadership. Individuals have responsibility. Rewards are given to individuals.	Management selects a team leader from within the single-discipline team. Decisions are a team responsibility. Rewards are given to the single-discipline team.	A mixed-discipline team selects its own leader. The team has the authority to make decisions; single-discipline teams have the responsibility to carry them out. Rewards are given to the mixed-discipline team.	Mixed-discipline teams select a leader. The teams have authority to make decisions and to carry them out. Rewards are given to mixed-discipline teams.
Training and Education	Individuals receive training in specific specialities.	Individuals receive training in cross discipline procedures, tools, and standards.	A mixed-discipline team receives training in team effectiveness. Team members think holistically and use tools, such as QFD. Training is on-demand and situation specific.	Mixed-discipline teams throughout the enterprise receive training in team effectiveness. Interactive simulation tools may be used to teach methods of data generation and force examination of issues from different perspectives.
Automation Support	Stand-alone tools are interfaced vertically within disciplines. Data is gathered and stored for later use. Discipline-specific hardware and software are available on a single platform. Documentation is created on desktop systems.	Centralized single-discipline tools can access data within a project. Data is gathered and is available for use. A single-discipline team can share hardware and software data.	Mixed-discipline tools are integrated for each individual throughout the program. Data is gathered, processed, and updated immediately. A mixed-discipline team can share hardware and software data. Documentation is integrated within the product development environment.	Mixed-discipline tools are integrated for each individual throughout the enterprise. Data is utilized to initiate action prior to a problem or issue arising. Mixed-discipline teams can share hardware and software data throughout the enterprise. Documentation is integrated within the enterprise-wide product development environment.

When you know which concurrent engineering approach your product needs, it's important to examine the inconsistencies in the matrix and understand why all the methods for each key factor work best as part of a single consistent approach. Inconsistencies occur where a description for a simpler approach is not circled or a description for a more complicated approach is circled. The example shows an instance of each type of inconsistency.

If you didn't circle the description in a simpler approach below the general approach your product needs, you likely should reconsider the methods for that key factor. Not implementing the methods of the simpler approach first may cause problems to ripple throughout the development process, because the methods that add up to the approach your product needs are so interrelated. Circling a description for a more complicated method than your product needs will skew the effective use of resources. Both types of inconsistencies in approach, if allowed to remain, can throw the dimensions off balance. It's also these inconsistencies that point to which factors in a dimension warrant your further attention and study.

Because you've determined the concurrent engineering approach for the product you chose to assess, the matrix gives a good picture of what processes and methods define and balance the dimensions for successful development of that product. In short, you have a concurrent engineering vision for that product. Next, you'll take a step on the road to understanding what your company would need to do to make that vision a reality.

CREATE A ROADMAP TO SUCCESS

To create a customized roadmap for preparing a successful concurrent engineering environment, you will compile your assessment data from both the company assessment questionnaire and the methods matrix and then analyze the results. From these results, you can begin to define the actions your company would need to take in order to realize a concurrent engineering environment that matches the vision you got from the methods matrix.

PLOT YOUR ASSESSMENT RESULTS

Use the dimensions map, which is the third part of this concurrent engineering assessment tool, to map your assessment data for a graphic view of where you are now and where you should be. *(Another copy of the map is in the Appendix.)*

The Dimensions Map

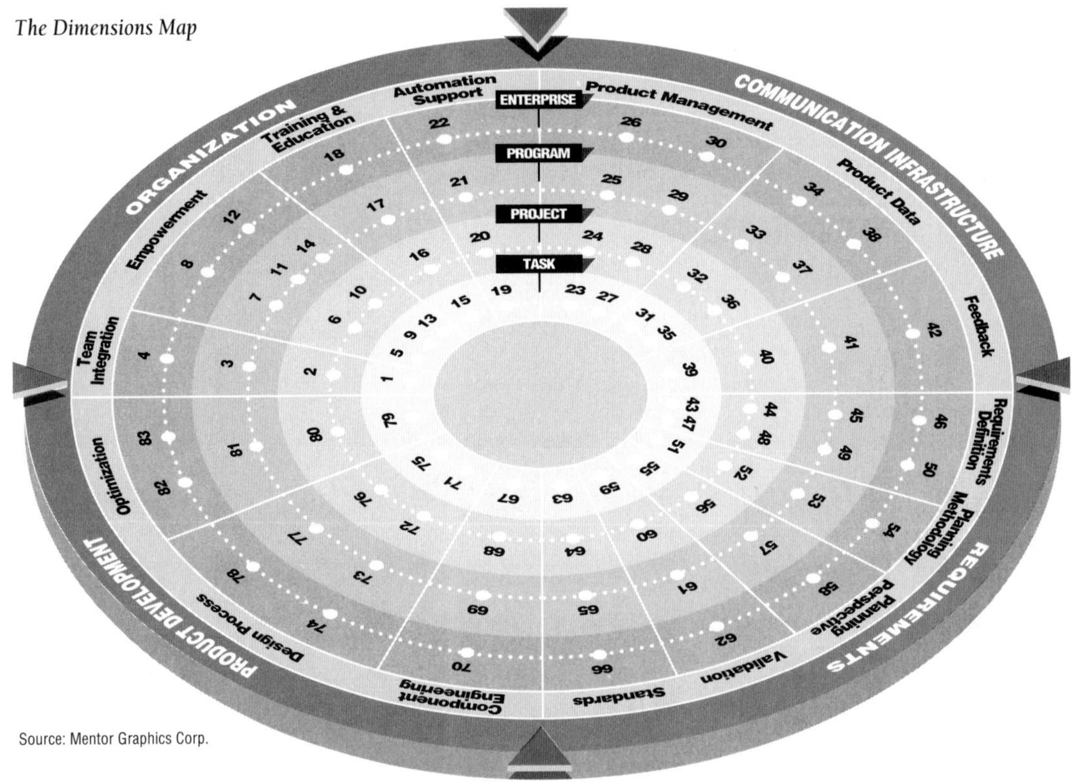

Source: Mentor Graphics Corp.

Note that the dimensions map has four quadrants representing the four dimensions of concurrent engineering, which are divided according to the key factors for each dimension. Four concentric rings represent the four different concurrent engineering approaches—task, project, program, and enterprise. The numbers in the rings refer to the questions in the company assessment questionnaire, and they are distributed according to the key factors and approaches to which they correspond.

First, transfer your yes **Y** answers from the company assessment questionnaire to the dimensions map by blackening the white dot beneath the corresponding question number. *(The no answers aren't plotted.)*

Next, connect the outermost blackened dots, as in the following example.

Your company's assessment questionnaire data

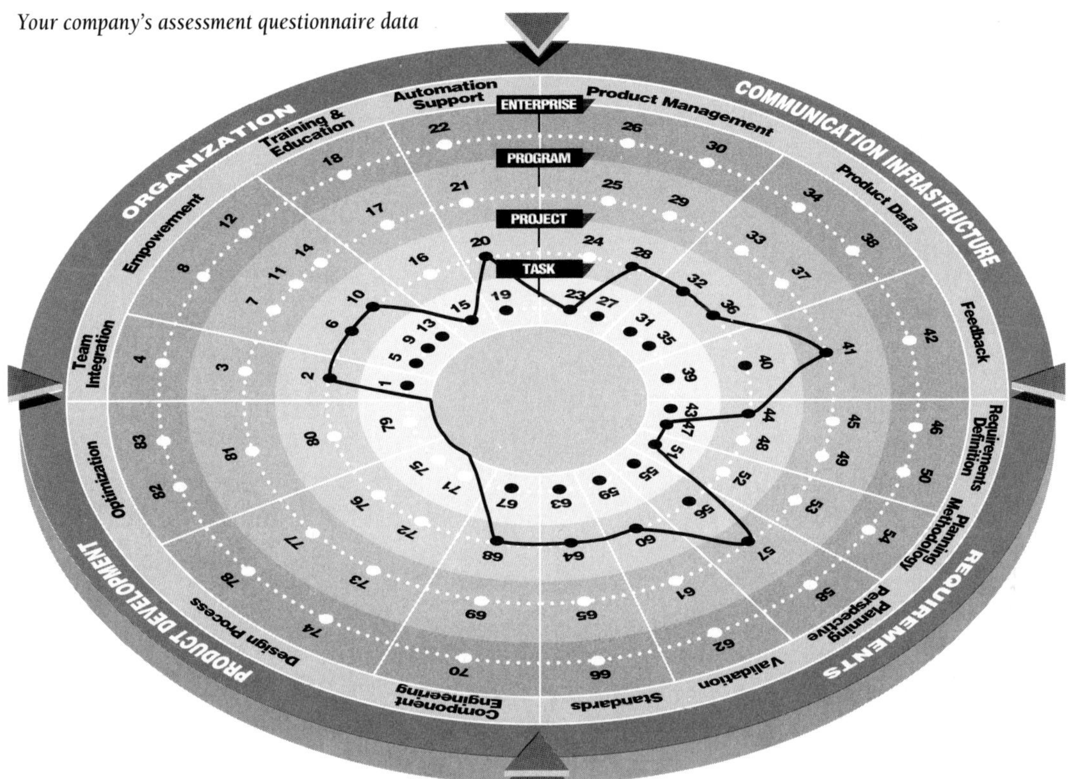

From the methods matrix, you determined the concurrent engineering approach necessary to develop your chosen product. That information relates to one of the concentric rings in the dimensions map. So draw a thick line along the top of the ring that corresponds to the approach your product needs, as in the following example.

Now you're ready to analyze and use these results.

Your product's methods matrix data

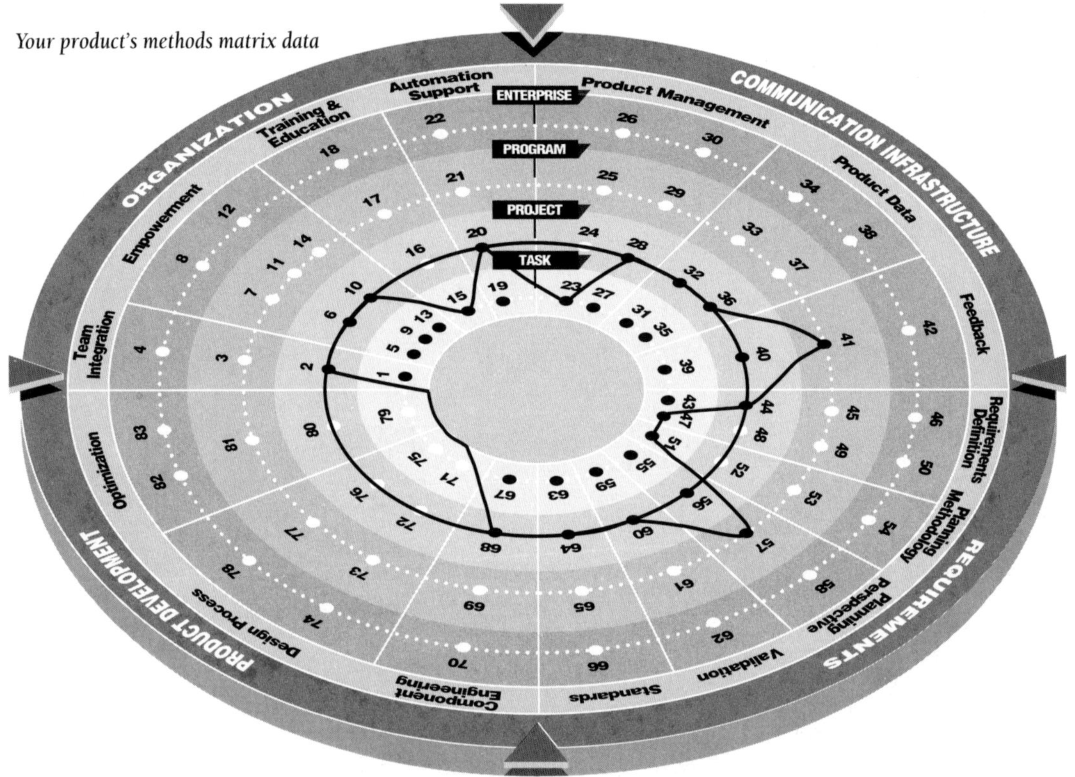

ANALYZE THE RESULTS

By comparing your company assessment questionnaire data with what seems to be the appropriate concurrent engineering approach your chosen product needs, you can see the differences between where you are in your current product development environment and where you should be in a fully implemented concurrent engineering environment. The line you drew by connecting the outermost dots shows what concurrent engineering methods your company has as part of its present-day product development environment. The darkened concentric ring illustrates what type of concurrent engineering approach your company needs in order to develop your chosen product. And the variances in the two boundaries illustrate where your company may need to take action.

In the example, the methods needed to implement a concurrent engineering environment are in a project approach *(which first assumes implementing the task approach)*. Where the line

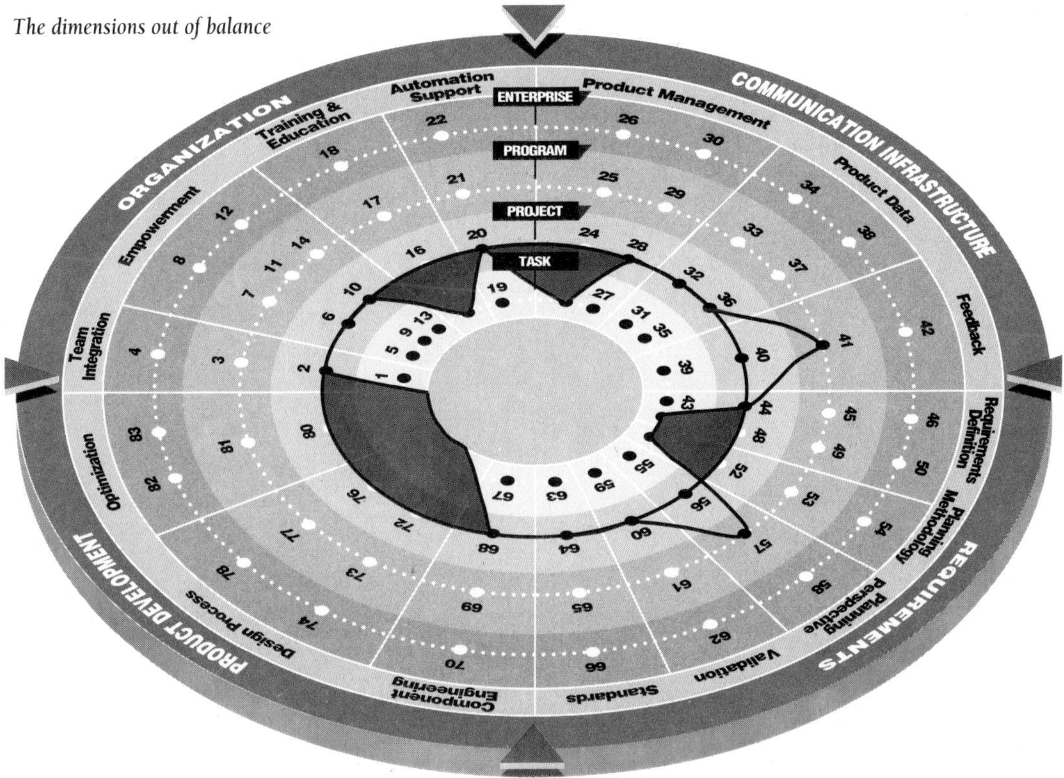

The dimensions out of balance

of connected dots is in the concentric ring just below the project approach, the key factors have the necessary resources and processes for that dimension. But as the jagged line that connects the dots makes clear, the current product development environment falls short of resources and processes for some key factors in each dimension *(and in a few instances exceeds what is needed)*.

What you have is a snapshot that illustrates how balanced *(or imbalanced)* your current product development environment is in relation to the concurrent engineering environment you would need to develop your chosen product.

Focus your attention on the dimensions that are out of balance because of a deficiency of resources and applied methods. As in this example, highlight those areas on your own concurrent engineering dimensions map to get a clearer overview of your goals. You'll soon use this knowledge to create a more specific plan for balancing the dimensions.

But first, notice on your dimensions map *(as in the example)* if a dimension is out of balance because of an excess of resources to implement a key factor. If that has happened, don't assume that you've got that key factor "more than covered" and that you can forget about it. In such a case, you may want to reallocate some of those excess resources to deficient areas or keep them in place and ready for a future product that you know will require a more complicated concurrent engineering approach. However you handle areas where methods and resources exceed what is needed, keep an eye on how this imbalance affects your efforts to create a concurrent engineering environment.

Finally, as part of understanding these results, organize information about what your company needs to do to create this desired concurrent engineering environment. Make note of the unblackened dots that are at the level of or below the approach your product would need. *(You would have answered the corresponding questions yes if your current product development environment had the necessary resources and processes to implement the concurrent engineering environment your chosen product needed.)* Return to the company assessment questionnaire and reread these questions to reinforce where your company needs to take action.

Then use these same questions with the fourth part of this concurrent engineering assessment tool—the priority roadmap—to organize and prioritize a list of action items. First, list by each dimension and key factor the questions that you ideally should have answered yes. Use the content of the question and information from the methods matrix *(which corresponds to where the question is located on the dimensions map)* to create an action item. Then assign what you think should be the priority for that item and the team member responsible for it.

You have just defined the steps you think your company needs to take to implement your vision of a concurrent engineering environment. But if you stop here, it won't happen. You must create a company-wide vision that all employees share.

COMMUNICATE AND REFINE YOUR CONCURRENT ENGINEERING VISION

Your priority roadmap is not yet the finished path your company should take. You must communicate its message to others in your company so that a common vision evolves.

Priority Roadmap example

Key Factor	Question #/Action Item	Priority	Completed
■ Organization Dimension			
Training & Education	16. Provide cross-discipline training for procedures, tools, and standards.	2	☐
■ Communication Infrastructure Dimension			
Product Management	24. Provide querry and online reporting capabilities to disciplines.	2	☐
■ Customer Requirements Dimension			
Planning Methodology	46. Document customer design requirements for the functional subsystem design.	2	☐
■ Product Development Dimension			
Design Process	68 Determine measures for function-specific tasks.	3	☐
	71. Extract information from the electronic physical design.	1	☐

You might want to start by using the assessment tool in this chapter as a communications tool—to get others thinking about concurrent engineering approaches and methods. Ask both managers and development teams to complete the four-part assessment. Their views will undoubtedly be different than yours and form a basis for further discussion in creating a shared company vision. Then managers and teams can begin the process of collaborating to reach a consensus on common purposes and priorities. They can determine the best way to apply concurrent engineering methods to transform the current product development environment into a concurrent engineering environment.

One important result should be a priority roadmap that all employees support with their best efforts.

VALIDATE WITH A PILOT

With roadmap in hand, one way you can introduce and, more importantly, gauge the effectiveness of your concurrent engineering approach is by implementing it with a pilot.

The pilot can serve several purposes. For example, it can demonstrate the expected improvements and verify the concurrent engineering approach you're putting in place. The members of the pilot team learn the actual operation of the new procedures and organization from the pilot and then serve as experts for propagating the new methods and practices to the rest of the company. Also, the pilot flushes out unexpected problems with new approaches before they can affect ongoing projects, programs, or products.

But in order to properly evaluate a pilot and the approach used to develop the pilot product, you must evaluate beforehand how the costs, implications, and changes of using a pilot will affect the overall operations of your company. Usually it's wise to start with a small pilot that does not seriously disrupt your current product development environment, so you need to choose your pilot product carefully.

Here are some suggestions: The pilot product should be a real product, one that represents the levels of product development and difficulty normally expected at the company. The product should also have some schedule flexibility—not so much in terms of delivery date but in the scheduling of individual milestones. This flexibility allows the new concurrent engineering approach a measure of experimentation and adjustment as the pilot ensues. For example, you might want to use, as a pilot product, one unit that is currently part of a major product—or one product version that is in a family of products. Or in some cases, you might want to run your pilot with a new product.

These comments about validating with a pilot are sketchy at best and only meant to point you toward one reasonable strategy in the process of implementing a concurrent engineering environment. Outside consultants are helpful when setting up the various complexities of a pilot and in helping you gauge its proper scope, so that you succeed and get meaningful results that apply to the company as a whole.

IMPROVE CONTINUOUSLY

As market forces change the requirements for your company's product, you can repeat the assessment in this chapter from several points of view—using different managers and teams—and at different times. Then you can adjust the four dimensions as necessary. Constant assessment and evaluation provides direction for continuous improvement in the product and the processes that produce it.

One more thing is clear: this continuous improvement is always going to be made necessary by those underlying and permeating forces of change that flow through the concurrent engineering environment—in particular, the combination of evolving technologies and tools. And as products continue to evolve, become more complicated, and require program and enterprise approaches to development, companies must understand the value and use of automation technologies in revitalizing and implementing their concurrent engineering environments.

Either now or at some time in your company's future, automated concurrent engineering is going to be the key to long-term success.

FOUR

AUTOMATING THE CONCURRENT ENGINEERING ENVIRONMENT.

LOOKING FOR A STRATEGY FOR THE FUTURE? IT'S AUTOMATION! REMOVE THE BARRIERS TO SUCCESS BY SYSTEMATICALLY AUTOMATING YOUR CONCURRENT ENGINEERING ENVIRONMENT IN FIVE PHASES.

MORE THAN JUST TOOLS & ENVIRONMENT

Automating the Concurrent Engineering Environment

Sometimes when you want to plan for the future, it seems as if you're staring at a door trying to guess what's on the other side. Or you're peeking through the keyhole and see a daunting vision of an endlessly long assembly line of products blurred by the speed as they roll through manufacturing. Everything is getting more complicated and moving much faster.

Sooner, rather than later, the future is now for companies that need a program or enterprise approach to their products. And the key to the door of their increasingly complex future is automation.

In a concurrent engineering environment that is trying to absorb and keep track of billions of bits of information, the technologies of automation are the enablers of productive change. It is these technologies that reshape and further integrate the resources of tools, tasks, talent, and time throughout the four dimensions—stabilizing the concurrent engineering environment and sharpening the possibilities for success. If your company's effort to develop and produce a product entails the complexity of an enterprise (or sometimes a large program), your company needs to start automating its concurrent engineering environment.

If your product and development processes are less complicated and need only a task or project approach, you need to start planning for the automation that will inevitably be needed as your company grows. It's likely that one day you'll find yourself agreeing with Mitsuo Shimizu, General Manager of the IC-CAD Development Division, Software Business Operations for Canon, Inc., when he describes how the need for automated concurrent engineering in Japan has arisen: "When product development is done on a small scale, the Japanese work together as a team extremely well regardless of whether they know concurrent engineering or not. There is good communication not only among the development team but also with the manufacturing and marketing people. This 'natural concurrent engineering' is no longer adequate in today's product development environment, and we need to develop a more systematic approach, what you call an automated concurrent engineering environment."

The increasing use of automation in the concurrent engineering environment is inevitable when your company has a philosophy of continuous improvement that searches for mastery of the product development process and realizes the desire to remain close to the voice of the customer.

In Chapter 3, the methods matrix points to the results of automation strategies applied as part of an enterprise approach—interactive and interoperable tools, integrated data and interrelated tasks, and mixed-discipline teams that use concurrent approaches to design, problem solving, and decision support. It's the job of this chapter to tell you how to get those results and how to create an automated concurrent engineering environment step by step.

You'll find that some of the automation technologies you need are available now while others soon will be. But first, you need to understand five specific roadblocks that tend to impede the flow of work and ideas and unbalance the concurrent engineering environment. Then you will learn how to remove those roadblocks with the appropriate automation technology, which must be implemented methodically in five phases.

UNDERSTANDING THE ROADBLOCKS TO AUTOMATION

Empowered to be part of an enterprise approach to product development, mixed-discipline teams will discover quite a few barriers to implementing a successful concurrent engineering environment. The initial barriers are a lack of common vocabularies, priorities, and purposes. These problems act like speed bumps: they slow things down for a while, but then the teams smooth them out through collaboration and consensus and are soon past them. However, some barriers are more serious: there are five roadblocks that are sure to stop your company on the road to an automated concurrent engineering environment.

Roadblock 1: Existing tools that can no longer perform the new requirements of design tasks.

Although the individuals on the teams tend to apply state-of-the-art technology to their respective designs, they rapidly discover where new "islands of automation" exist. The current technology and tools for integrating data, processes, and decisions are not adequate for the tasks.

For example, creating speedier computer processors as the hardware brains for tools, as happened in the 1980s, was not a panacea for reducing time to market. In the same decade, designs grew more complex, and the amount of time required to prepare the design data for each step in the design process increased. So while computer processing time decreased, a significant percentage of the overall throughput of data had been to input and output the data. This is in accordance with Amdahl's Law.

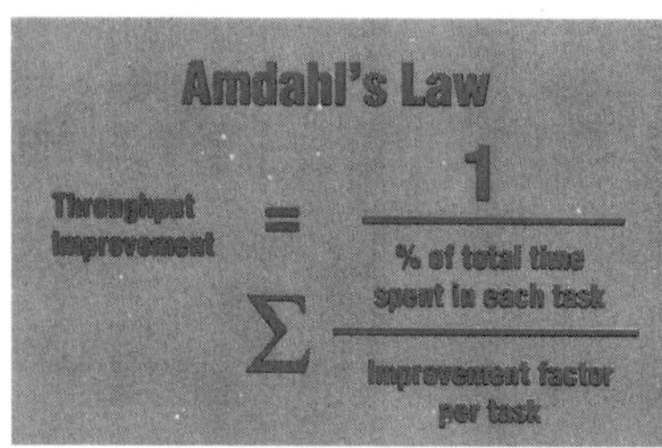

Dr. Amdahl observed that computer processing power was increasing at a rate several times greater than the time required to input and output the data. He predicted that it wouldn't be long before a significant percentage of the overall throughput would be consumed by the requirement to manage input and output. Dr. Amdahl developed a formula, called Amdahl's Law, to determine overall throughput: the time it takes to gather, analyze, and output data. That formula is still useful today to determine how long it will take to get something done from beginning to end.

For example, suppose you had a one-million gate design and you wanted to transfer that design from schematic capture to simulation. Translating that million-gate design from the symbol format to the simulation table format may take 50 instances per second. That means putting the data into the simulator would take 20,000 seconds or 333 minutes. With a reasonably fast simulator, it should take 40 to 60 minutes to simulate the entire one-million gate design. So, in this example, it could take up to eight times longer to get the data ready to simulate than it would to do the simulation.

Shared data should be created once and used many times.

This example points out a major issue of the product development environment of the 1980s that must be solved in the concurrent engineering environment of the 1990s. The tools of the 1990s will need to:

- Share the same data management facilities
- Directly interact at the process level
- Be alerted to incremental changes in the database
- Have the same user interface
- Provide common on-line help, query facility, browsers, reference data, and documentation

In other words, the time to gather and output data to those who need it must be shortened by new communication technologies.

Roadblock 2: The proliferation of different kinds of computers, networks, user interfaces, and operating systems throughout a company.

It's great that an engineer from one discipline can communicate information to an engineer in another discipline who has a different computer and operating system. The use of translation devices to link tools and information is becoming more common and is a necessary step in allowing different computers and tools to work together. But it's only a first step.

Imagine how much more effective the work of a mixed-discipline team would be if each individual could walk over to another engineer's workstation and be able to work with that engineer's computer. Better yet, imagine an automated concurrent engineering environment where two or more engineers could sit at their own workstations anywhere in the world and simultaneously work on the same design and see it change.

Bill Gates, chairman and co-founder of Microsoft Corporation, gives this example of what the future can offer as part of an integrated computing environment: "Right now the user has to learn how to use all the different applications required to produce various types of data, locate all the files that contain the necessary information, and figure out how to link them all together. The user also has to keep all the applications up-to-date when data in one or more of the files changes. Software should be able to do all this by hooking the information together and tracking the connections. For instance, if you insert a drawing into the text, you can alter the drawing in the word processor without going out to the drawing application and then coming back to the word processor."

The way tools communicate with each other and with the people using them can change how the teams work and how fast they get their work done, and the lack of integrated standards for tools is what will hold companies back.

Roadblock 3: The lack of appropriate data management.

If a company removes the first two roadblocks, one result is a fresh wave of data that must be properly sorted and stored, and sometimes discarded. The data must be made meaningful to each discipline on the team.

For example, what commonly happens in the development of a design is that each discipline on the product development team has its own point of reference for the design. The designer has the schematic as a reference, the purchasing manager has the bill of materials, the PC board layout engineer has the PC board layout drawing, and so forth. But whose reference is the primary reference? Which disciplines are dependent on another discipline's reference? And at what stages in the development process does the point of reference change?

Only with the fast and ongoing analysis of the appropriate data can an enterprise approach succeed. This is made possible through an automated product data management facility.

Roadblock 4: Downstream processes that get stuck downstream and never make it upstream.

It's one thing to make data available to all members of a product development team and another thing to make sure it is used at the right time in the development process. The organization of teams can help to reinforce the need for members to tag changes that will affect processes downstream and upstream. But without a consistent and automatic process of informing team members and requiring them to take notice, design problems will fall through the cracks—only to surface when making the needed change will be very costly in money, resources, and time.

This roadblock goes away when a company automates the "-abilities," such as testability, manufacturability, reliability, serviceability, and accountability.

Roadblock 5: The correct decisions not made soon enough.

To enable a flexible and adaptable product development process, teams must make decisions when the timing of those decisions is critical to the success of the product's quality, cost, or schedule. To do this, team members must know the history of a design and the design decisions, up to the present moment. Because of the sheer number of decisions, an automated decision support facility is necessary to keep track of them and can actually make many mundane decisions for the team. Only with this automated support is it possible for the team to do instantaneous trade-off analyses and try out what-if scenarios.

As mixed-discipline teams encounter these roadblocks in a concurrent engineering environment, the teams keep returning to an important fact: technology, tools, tasks, and time must be made to yield a value that is consistent with the customer and product requirements and the team goals. To repeatedly get this result is an overwhelming effort—one that only automation technologies can begin to manage. And to choose the right technology, a company must understand what's involved in automating a concurrent engineering environment.

REMOVING THE ROADBLOCKS

You can think of this figure as a roadmap. It can show you several things about the relation of automation to your company's concurrent engineering environment. As teams and their tools need to use data in differing ways, that data must be linked into more meaningful forms of information. And the way to do this when using an enterprise approach is through automation.

Roadmap for an Automated Concurrent Engineering Environment

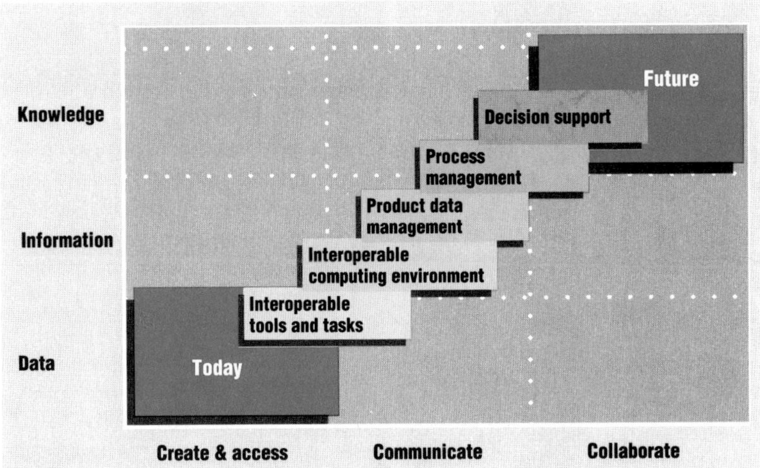

In a sense, this roadmap is a more specific explanation of how many of the methods suggested in Chapter 3 for an enterprise approach can be accomplished systematically. It illustrates the direction a company needs to go in order to get rid of the five roadblocks. Notice that there are five enabling phases of automated concurrent engineering that your company must systematically pass through in order to resolve the issues the five roadblocks raise. These phases are:

- Interoperable tools and tasks
- Interoperable computing environment
- Data management
- Process management
- Decision support

To do this, your company must start at the bottom-left corner of the roadmap. Many companies have already begun this journey. Team members usually create, archive, and access data that is then available to other teams, tools, or databases. This is the raw data of team members' experiences in the development process.

But when a company is implementing an enterprise approach, only with the automation of these five phases can teams and tools communicate these enormous amounts of data so that the data informs both upstream and downstream processes. In this way, the data effortlessly circulates as useful information. For example, a previously agreed-on and tested subsection of an existing design could be reused in a new design.

One foreseeable goal of an automated concurrent engineering environment is to have team and tool collaboration. This could occur on the level of instantaneous trade-off analysis of selected or monitored events. In such an environment, information is shaped and presented through an interactive filter of product goals and constraints (requirements). Decisions in a previous design process will not only be available as information, but they will automatically be used to shape current design decisions. In such an environment, the information becomes part of a general awareness of process and constitutes the knowledge of past and present as well as plans for the future. The raw data has finally been transformed to bring the lessons learned throughout development into an ongoing understanding of product and processes.

There is an obvious question about automating a company's concurrent engineering environment: Is there a technology and tool that can do it automatically? Is there a resource for making the changes needed?

THE FRAMEWORK STRATEGY

One strategy that is increasingly favored as the way to automate a concurrent engineering environment is called a framework. Ideally, a framework provides the software perspective needed to let your company move through the five phases of automating its concurrent engineering environment.

Andy Graham, president of the Computer Aided Design Framework Initiative (CFI), describes a framework as a collection of software program facilities, or a set of extensible services, that are the foundation for an integrated electronic design automation system. The framework should comprise the following:

- A common design data management facility
- A standard representation for data
- A product data management facility
- A process management facility
- A common user interface facility
- An open architecture that allows any tool to be used within the framework

The primary goal of a framework is to increase a company's productivity by supporting the interaction of mixed-discipline teams and enabling the early prediction of downstream impacts on design decisions. So a framework is an electronic design automation environment that empowers teams and tools to collaborate through the concurrent sharing of product and process knowledge.

Even when implementing a framework strategy, a company must still pass through five phases that will enable it to remove the five roadblocks and fully automate its concurrent engineering environment. By implementing automation in phases, a company using an enterprise approach continues the ongoing coordination needed among team activities, priorities, goals, and processes.

THE FIVE PHASES OF AUTOMATION

To implement automation so that your company's development teams can successfully collaborate on the basis of knowledge, the concurrent engineering environment must have the capabilities of five enabling phases. A few companies are already implementing strategies that will allow them to collaborate on knowledge. But as mentioned, many companies are only able to create, archive, and access data and are just now starting to evaluate the methods required to communicate design and process information across mixed disciplines.

For all of these companies, using the five phases can be a valuable approach for implementing an automated concurrent engineering environment. Each phase lays the foundation for the next phase, so it's important to proceed methodically through each phase.

In the following descriptions of these phases, note that phases one and two concentrate on getting the necessary interoperability in place, phases three and four deal with issues a bit more complicated, requiring more changes in your organization and product development process, and ultimately, the fifth phase promotes a decision support system. To demonstrate how a strategy such as a framework can enable your company to make these phases a reality, the discussion for each phase will mention the value of using a framework strategy to implement that phase.

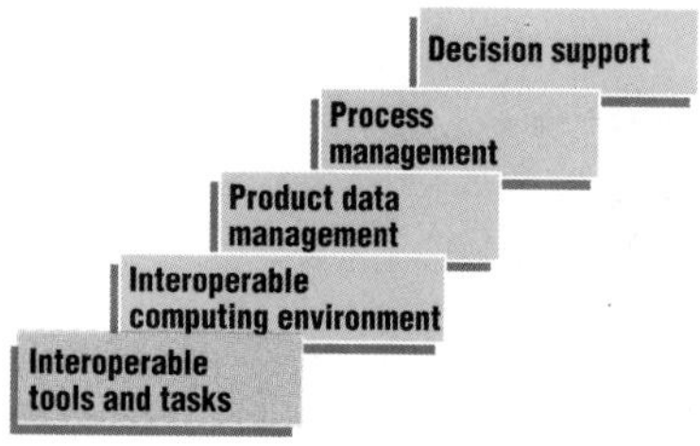

PHASE 1: MAKE TOOLS AND TASKS INTEROPERABLE

The first phase of implementing an automated concurrent engineering environment involves making tools and their associated tasks interoperable. As the number of tools continues to increase, so will the need for direct communication among these tools.

In the January 10, 1991 issue of *Electronic Design* in an article titled, "Concurrent Engineering Meets Design Automation," Jose DeCastro and Peter Hoogerhuis give us a peek at what will be possible with tools in the mid-1990s. "The evolving design automation environment that supports concurrent engineering has seen the power and scope of its tools expand steadily. One interesting area is the relationship between advanced simulation tools and concurrent engineering. As simulation technology grows more comprehensive, designers are approaching the capability to produce 'virtual prototypes' that embody all aspects of the product. It will eventually become possible to model the user interface of a product so that customers can interact directly with the virtual prototypes. Their feedback can then be incorporated into quality function deployment (QFD) maps, which help redirect the design to accommodate their suggestions."

Only with the adoption of existing standards and the evolution of new ones can a company bring about this opaque quality of tool and task integration. The adoption of standards as part of a strategy for integrating current tools and purchasing new ones is a necessary first step for an efficient and productive development process in an automated concurrent engineering environment.

Interoperable Tools and Tasks

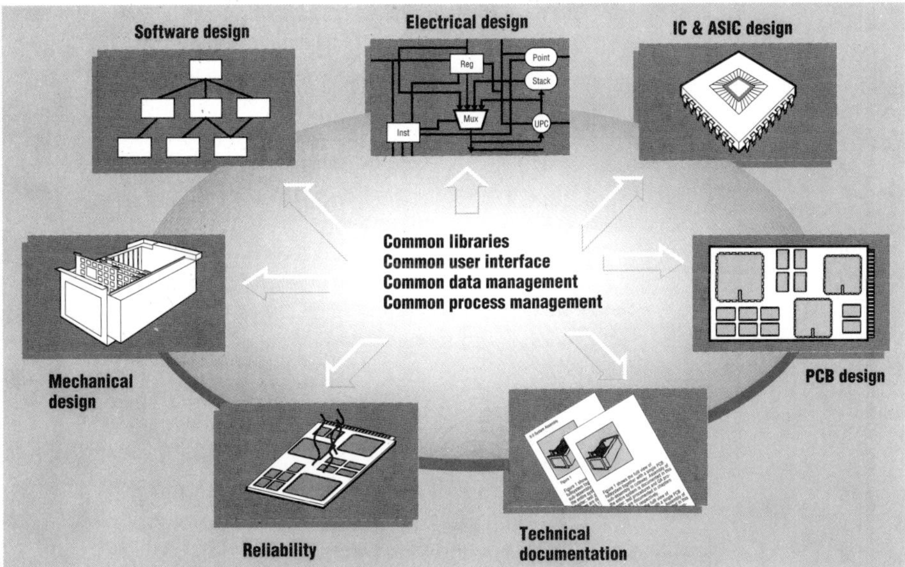

Standardizing the Standards

In the 1980s, standards evolved out of the need for electronic design, engineering, and manufacturing tools, each with its own interface, to communicate data. This necessity propelled the creation of a standard format for interchanging electronic data among CAD/CAE tools and systems—the Electronic Design Interchange Format (EDIF). Specifically, EDIF gives users the ability to move graphics or data between different tools and includes a way for updating, improving, and maintaining the format.

In that same era, another standard came into use: the Initial Graphics Exchange Specification (IGES), which is a project of the Air Force Integrated Computer-Aided Manufacturing (ICAM) program. IGES is for the exchange and archiving of data between CAD/CAM systems. This standard has a user-extensible interface for geometric, drafting, and structural entities and can graphically represent most of the information in a CAD/CAM system.

These initial standards for integrating tools and tasks were an important advance, but they didn't necessarily save any time in the design process because designs were still created many times and used many times. Data could be passed from one tool to the next, but there was no data management system for integrating all the data that each tool contained.

The tools of the 1990s require new standards that will allow them to interact with each other and a data management system. This process has begun. The CAD Framework Initiative (CFI) is a forum where users of CAD/CAE systems can voice their needs and vendors can listen to them.

In place for over two years, the CFI has begun to define industry requirements for the database consistency and inter-tool communication needed to track and control design data in the complex, heterogeneous tool environments of the future. CFI's procedural interface (PI) enables design tools from multiple vendors to communicate with each other in one environment. Through the interface, design tools from the different vendors can pass information or data directly and in real time.

In addition, another standard is needed to make it possible for tools to electronically represent a product in an accurate and unambiguous language. An emerging standard that promotes the exchange and integration of physical and functional product information over the life cycle of a product is PDES—the Product Definition Exchange using STEP (the international Standard for the Exchange of Product Model Data). PDES is a cornerstone of the more comprehensive CALS/CE standard—the Department of Defense's Computer-Aided Acquisition and Logistic Support/Concurrent Engineering standard.

In 1990, Robert M. White, undersecretary of technology in the Commerce Department, said that "the successful implementation of STEP [which PDES uses] means hundreds of billions of dollars worth of sales at home and abroad. Successful national implementation of STEP is not a matter of choice; it is a matter of survival." Colin McMillan, assistant secretary of defense for production and logistics, added: "When PDES becomes commercially available, it will be a requirement in [Department of Defense] contracts."

PDES is so important because it provides a complete and unambiguous computer definition of the physical and functional characteristics of a product. PDES has four implementation levels:

- Level 1: a passive file exchange
- Level 2: an active file exchange
- Level 3: a shared database
- Level 4: an integrated product knowledgebase

The guidelines and standards of CFI and PDES, when PDES is ready, will provide the capability to exchange product models that can be interpreted directly by advanced CAD/CAE tools—

the kind of automated environment that Jose DeCastro and Peter Hoogerhuis envisioned earlier. This is a major advance over the common practice in the 1980s of using ASCII netlist files as program interfaces.

Of course, all of these current and emerging standards must be seamlessly integrated into the concurrent engineering environment of today and tomorrow. Their complexity, driven by the increasing number of complex tools and tasks, requires an automation strategy that has an open architecture and accepts evolving standards.

Integrating Tools and Tasks—A Strategy

One of the most difficult problems with the integration of tools and tasks is knowing where a company should start. The following list has some suggestions for building bridges of communication between two tools at a time in order to accomplish a group of related tasks more efficiently.

By starting simply so that the concurrent engineering environment is not thrown into turmoil, many companies have been very successful with these basic approaches to tool and task integration on their journey to an automated concurrent engineering environment. Perhaps this list can serve as a basis for creating a simple level of integration for your company's existing tools and tasks.

Existing tools	**Tasks**
Software Development and Simulation	To develop, analyze and debug software while considering the trade-offs with simulated hardware.
ASIC Design and Synthesis	To create an optimum ASIC for speed, die area, power dissipation, package type, cost, and so forth.
PLA Design and Synthesis	To automatically select a PLA according to propagation delay, package type, temperature range, and cost.
Schematic Capture and Library Management	To ensure that all schematic components have required parameters, conform to industry standards, and are reliable components, and to assist the designer in the selection of a component given a desired set of parameters.
Schematics and Design Rule Checking	To provide for loading analysis, technology mismatches, connectivity errors, drafting standards, initial reliability estimates, cost estimates, and other user-defined rule checks.

Existing tools	Tasks
(continued)	
Schematic and Layout	To attach the engineer's expertise to the schematic for the benefit of the layout system, relative to critical component placement and routes.
Documentation Design and Synthesis	To ensure that all references to text, tables, and graphics in documentation are on-line to revisions, conform to industry standards, and are on-line to the users in a hypertext/hypertag format that allows for rapid browsing and queries.
Timing Analysis and Layout	To determine the critical timing paths that affect the proximity of components during placement before layout routing begins.
Testability and Layout	To determine, by means of a statistical fault grader, the location of observable test points, JTAG elements, and partial SCAN elements before layout routing begins.
Simulation and Layout	To simulate the physical parameters and component variance before layout is complete.
Reliability and Layout	To determine the reliability stresses that affect the proximity of components during placement before layout routing begins.
Simulation and Test	To correlate the automatic test equipment (ATE) specifications with the design specifications, and to create the required ATE inputs for a given design before a prototype is built.
Layout and Manufacturing	To correlate the manufacturing process requirements with the layout and design specification before a prototype is built.

Building a bridge between two existing tools to accomplish related tasks is a short-term tactic that should not replace a long-term strategy. The next useful advance is to build bridges of communication and understanding among all the tools in the concurrent engineering environment. To do this, a company must focus on a standard that insists on an "open" data architecture. This architecture should incorporate advanced technologies that integrate and promote interoperability between tools, teams, and development processes.

In a recent article in *Electronic Engineering Times*, Stephen Evanczuk proposes that the needed architecture be a framework, which will simplify the task of incorporating standards and integrating tools and tasks. "A framework provides common services and utilities for orchestrating a collection of individual applications programs toward a common objective—such as the design of an integrated circuit or printed circuit board or a complete system. A framework builds on and augments the utilities of an operating system with specific services necessary for the application environment. Those services include a common user-interface management capability, [to] provide a consistent metaphor for accessing the tools and design environment; data management services, to support reliable shared access to design data; and tool-management services, to coordinate the operation of individual tools and tool sequences."

The dominant factors in this open framework architecture will be to provide perceptive views and consistent and flexible tools for all disciplines. The architecture should be perceptive about the diverse mixed-discipline views of each tool. The data model underlying the architecture should have consistent semantics, and the tools need to be flexible enough to promote the principles associated with balancing the dimensions in a concurrent engineering environment.

PHASE 2: MAKE YOUR COMPUTING ENVIRONMENT INTEROPERABLE

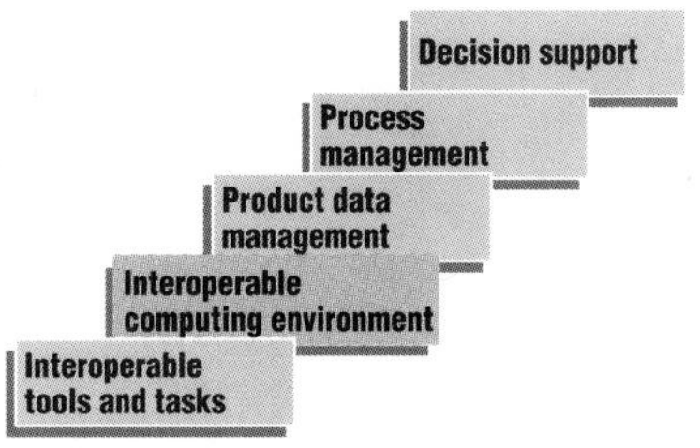

A logical outgrowth of the first phase of implementing an automated concurrent engineering environment is the second phase, during which a company must provide interoperability between the various computers, databases, and user interfaces. A computing environment can successfully provide this interoperability if:

- Tools and databases communicate as part of a common network and the processing power of computers can be shared
- The same data is available to all
- The ways of communicating and manipulating information are consistent for all team members

This type of environment-wide communication and information network allows companies to plug and play the best-in-class tools and maintain them with little effort.

Creating a Common Computing Network

Several network standards are emerging that are worth watching, and the most promising seems to be the Open System Foundation's Distributed Computing Environment (OSF DCE), whose application developer's kit has been available since January 1991. It has been licensed to over 70 developers and has received many worldwide endorsements. These endorsements are from leading universities, such as Carnegie Mellon and Stanford; from leading software developers, such as Oracle, Informix, Interactive, Mentor Graphics, Microsoft, and Sybase; and from almost every leading computer manufacturer, including Groupe Bull, Siemens-Nixdorf, Digital Equipment, Hewlett-Packard, Hitachi, IBM, Silicon Graphics, and Stratus Computer. Significant endorsements have also come from the user community, such as from Nippon Telephone and Telegraph; and the European Commission plans to use DCE on a network of more than 10,000 personal computers.

At the CeBIT '91 computer show in Hanover, Germany, a demonstration provided proof that computer workstations with different hardware architectures and operating system software can be combined on a network to function as a single, stand-alone computer and share the task of processing application programs. The participants were the Open Software Foundation and five of the world's leading computer vendors: Groupe Bull, Siemens-Nixdorf, Digital Equipment, Hewlett-Packard, and IBM. An Ethernet local area network of computer workstations, each running DCE, was connected to a common data information system. The DCE software consolidated the processing power of all the computers on the network and enabled each workstation to act automatically as either a client or server in order to retrieve and process information and, using OSF Motif, to display it simultaneously in real time on each workstation's screen.

In essence, DCE works as a layer of software, sometimes called "middleware," that resides between the computer's operating system and the application program running on the computer. It is designed to distribute one or more application programs to many computers on a network to take advantage of the combined processing power and unique capabilities of each computer. Instead of having one computer fully occupied by one large, complex application, DCE subdivides applications into smaller sections and then assigns those sections to the first available computer on the network that is best suited for processing the application segment.

With a computing environment like DCE, team members will find that their work is processed easier and more efficiently than ever before, while they are completely insulated from the complexity of the different computers and their connections to the network. DCE does this by integrating a series of components, such as:

- The remote procedure call (RPC) that makes the complexities of DCE opaque to programmers and users
- A naming or directory service that makes information accessible to team members regardless of their location or type of computer
- Threads for controlling the flow of information within a program
- A time service that synchronizes the clocks of all the computers on the network
- A distributed file system that gives team members access to data stored on computers other than their own
- Personal computer integration that lets MS-DOS computers access files and print services from UNIX computers
- Distributed management that provides centralized management and control of all computers in a distributed environment

DCE may very well become the de facto standard for solving many of the problems in a complex computing environment.

Understanding Other Computing Environment Issues

DCE is not the total answer to functional interoperability of the computing environment. Other issues include how the following aspects of interoperability are going to be implemented:

A graphics support system. A successful computing environment needs a graphics support system that ensures that any two-dimensional or three-dimensional graphics created in an application on one computer can function on any other computer.

A common user interface. A common user interface that allows team members to manage and interact with data—for example, OSF Motif, Microsoft Windows 3.0, or Sun Microsystems OpenWindows—is necessary for all tools used in the product development process. This user interface should allow multiple tools to be available at the same time and have a set of general commands that are common and intuitive.

A database file management system. An interoperable computing environment needs a system that manages the files in and between databases. Relational data systems, such as a structured query language (SQL), allow many types of databases to be used. It's also worth noting that Object Oriented, a rapidly emerging database architecture, is being selected by many companies to fulfill this aspect of interoperability.

The licensing of software. Network-licensed software sometimes works by allowing a team member to check out an application program in the same way that a person might rent a video movie. When the application is in, the team member gets to use it; however, when it's out, the team member has to wait until the current user returns it. Although this system of licensing is not ideal, it does work. A better way is needed for team members to use application programs as they need them.

Systems for security access, electronic mail, and backing up and archiving of data. The computing technology that a company chooses in order to implement an automated concurrent engineering environment should support a security access system, a network backup/archive system, and electronic mail system.

Standards that are adopted today must consider these aspects of interoperability. As the figure shows, the Open Software Foundation is leading the way.

Interoperable Computing Standards

	AT&T (UNIX)	IEEE (POSIX)	X/OPEN	OSF (AES Level 0)
Graphics				Adopted
User interface			Adopted	Adopted
Windowing			Adopted	Adopted
Data Management			Adopted	Adopted
Languages C++	Adopted	In Progress	Adopted	Adopted
NLS		In Progress	Adopted	In Progress
Security		In Progress	In Progress	In Progress
Real-time		In Progress	In Progress	In Progress
Networking	Adopted	In Progress	In Progress	Adopted
Commands	Adopted	Adopted	Adopted	Adopted
Kernal	Adopted	Adopted	Adopted	Adopted

Adopted (interoperable) · In Progress

Source: Hewlett-Packard Technical Computer Group

All of these issues involved in setting up a flexible and automated computing environment are likely to be addressed most successfully by an open framework strategy. For example, the issue of licensing may be simplified if a company adopts an open framework that already supports many of the workstation and application vendors and offers a comprehensive network licensing package.

Suppose an engineer is trying to decide which tool to use next when he or she is new to a design automation system. A process management facility can sequence and support each design process. For example, one method could prevent schematics from going to layout without undergoing logic or timing simulation; or another method could prevent a design from going to test before it has first passed a statistical fault grading and then, in sequence, passed a simulation within the parameters that are already set up in the automatic test equipment. Because of the mixed disciplines, various tools, and process steps in an enterprise effort, the process management facility is the engineering equivalent of a traffic-control system that is universally used and understood.

A process management facility should also manage the flow of work and processes among mixed-discipline teams and their members. It should assist teams in setting targets for improving time to market, lowering costs, and getting higher quality products. It should help managers and teams in identifying, understanding, and measuring existing processes so that it's clear which processes have the most influence on the success of the product development process. Then it should allow the analysis of those processes into smaller tasks so that the number of different inputs required by the tasks as well as the outputs from those tasks can be measured. In short, the development process must be understood and tracked with quantitative as well as qualitative measures so that the development process can be evaluated and then easily changed to keep a company more competitive.

Lastly, an automated process management facility must interactively assist each team member throughout the product development process. It should establish a process flow that is a simple set of concurrent tasks which balance the talent and tools available to complete the task. It should allow for the mixed skills of team members and require appropriate input from all team members when one member proposes a change in the process.

Working Within a Framework

The kind of automated process management facility just described is only partially available today. If a company is committed to an open framework strategy, this facility, as it is developed, can be integrated into the concurrent engineering environment. Already, frameworks are beginning to support managing the design process at the four different levels of product and process complexity: task, project, program, and

"A framework is more than just a common user interface and a database. It has to support the design process ..."

–Gerry Langeler, president of Mentor Graphics Systems Group

enterprise. Team members are increasingly able to create and manage their own data and process flows as part of an overall strategy in managing the development process.

In the future, the automated concurrent engineering environment will produce intelligent process flows that control the design throughout the product development process and provide detailed feedback on the status of the design and the individual processes. All of this will yield a smooth development process that ensures the consistency and completeness of a design and simplifies the task of redesign.

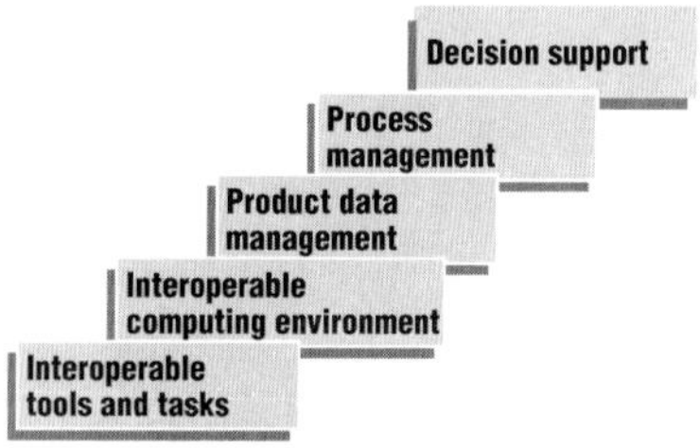

Decision support
Process management
Product data management
Interoperable computing environment
Interoperable tools and tasks

PHASE 5: AUTOMATE DECISION SUPPORT

In the fifth and final phase of implementing an automated concurrent engineering environment, a company must provide a decision support facility to help team members make decisions. Because these decisions can affect the success of the product's quality, cost, or schedule, not only do team members have to consider downstream processes, but they must also know how all the decisions were reached at every step in the development process.

When fully implemented in the future as part of a framework strategy, here's what an automated decision support facility will do:

- Keep track of the number of changes that occur throughout a product's development and help evaluate their impact on the process
- When used with process management, precisely indicate what requirements have or haven't been met and make sure that the design fully meets each requirement before routing it on to the next team member, tool, or process step
- Assist teams in deciding between design alternatives and in making design tradeoffs
- Help individual customers design products that are unique to their own needs by providing a rapid prototyping environment that allows customers and development teams to quickly model a product's required development process
- Support the creation of prediction tools for team members so they can consider downstream finished-product characteristics, such as manufacturability and cost
- Integrate corporate data and design data outside of the product data model

When development teams are able to use this kind of decision support facility, they will be able to analyze design choices and rapidly develop and prototype new tools. This automated decision support system will be an active partner in the product development team and represent a collaboration of effort and knowledge that transcends individual contributions.

REWARDS ARE WORTH THE RISKS

The ultimate perspective of concurrent engineering and the key perspective for the 1990s is automated concurrent engineering. By automating concurrent engineering in the electronic design automation environment of a framework, a company provides teams and tools with computer-assisted interactions throughout the entire enterprise effort. As mentioned, a framework can perform many manual tasks, making them invisible, and provide guidance and feedback so that engineers can concentrate on developing creative solutions to development problems. A framework cradles all the design automation tools and gives them a way to talk to each other, manage and share enterprise-wide information, prescribe successful product development processes, and assist in making design decisions. A framework helps to clear the road for continued growth and success.

Even though creating an automated concurrent engineering environment is an appropriate and measurable response to the competitive pressures of the 1990s, there is associated risk with any change. Perhaps the greatest risk is in trying to advance too quickly through the five phases of implementing an automated concurrent engineering environment. Companies that try to skip phases are not as successful as companies that proceed methodically, one phase at a time, until they reach the final phase of automating decision support.

Also, if a company's culture is not ready, implementing automation technologies in a concurrent engineering environment can slow down the development process. There are numerous examples of when automation was invasive and people worked to get around the system because they felt the need to "get the job done." It is important to make automation occur as a natural part of ongoing daily work and emphasize that it minimizes the tedium of repetitive tasks, such as data re-entry. Managers must be actively involved in selling this environment to teams and other employees and make them both committed to their roles and comfortable with using new tools and processes.

The road to automated concurrent engineering is a journey, not an event.

Frankly, the alternative to creating an automated concurrent engineering environment for an enterprise effort is the future loss of market share and profitability. The rewards of automation are indeed worth the risks; the main rewards are your company's robust survival and success.

Appendix A. Other Assessment Tools

The assessment tool described in Chapter 3 is only a starting place, providing a general view of your product development process and concurrent engineering environment. Several other comprehensive assessment tools that you can use to evaluate specific practices or processes are listed below.

For software process:

- The Carnegie Mellon University, *Software Engineering Institute (SEI) assessment questionnaire*. SEI documents are available from the National Technical Information Service, United States Department of Commerce, Springfield, VA 22161. Department of Defense and other US Government agency personnel and contractors should write to the Defense Technical Information Center, Attn: FDRA, Cameron Station, Alexandria, VA 22304-6145.

For electrical process:

- The United States Department of the Navy, *Best Practices: How to Avoid Surprises in the World's Most Complicated Technical Process,* NAVSO P-6071, March 1986. For sale by the Superintendent of Documents, United States Government Printing Office, Washington, D.C. 20402.
- The CALS/CE Electronic Task Group, *First Principles of Concurrent Engineering: A Competitive Strategy for Electronic System Development,* available after June, 1991. For copies, contact CALS ISG, Suite 300, 1025 Connecticut Avenue, NW Washington, D.C. 20036 (202) 775-1440.
- Mentor Graphics Corporation Consulting Services, *Electronic Design Process Product Maturity Assessment Questionnaire.* For information, contact 8005 SW Boeckman Road, Wilsonville, OR 97070-7777 (503) 685-7000.

For mechanical process:

- The CALS/CE Industry Steering Group Technical Report 002, *Application of Concurrent Engineering to Mechanical Systems Design: Final report of the Reliability and Maintainability (R&M) Mechanical Design Study,* June 16, 1989. For copies, contact CALS/CE ISG, Suite 300, 1025 Connecticut Avenue, NW Washington, D.C. 20036 (202) 775-1440.

For manufacturing process:

- The Oliver Wight Companies, *ABCD Checklist.* For information contact 5 Oliver Wight Drive, Essex Junction, VT 05452 (800) 343-0625.

For process quality:

- The Malcolm Baldridge National Quality Award program. For information, contact the United States Department of Commerce, National Institute of Standards and Technology, Gaithersburg, MD 20899.

Appendix B. Copy of the Assessment Tool

This appendix contains a copy of the assessment tool in Chapter 3, which includes the company assessment questionnaire, the methods matrix, and the dimensions map.

FIND OUT WHERE ARE YOU NOW

The company assessment questionnaire characterizes the present development environment in which your company develops its product. If your company is large enough to have very distinct products, focus on the development environment for only one product that you market. For this assessment to be useful, you must answer the questions as they relate to your company's current product development environment, not according to plans you may have to change it.

The questions are grouped according to the four dimensions and further grouped into key areas in each dimension. Answer each question yes **Y** or no **N** with the best information you have. Answer yes only if your company is consistently and adequately implementing the action implied by a question. Answer every question unless you don't know the answer or unless what is asked is not relevant to your product. Completing this questionnaire should take less than 30 minutes.

ORGANIZATION

This part of the company assessment questionnaire explores where your company presently stands in terms of the key factors that characterize the organization dimension in a concurrent engineering environment. To successfully apply a concurrent engineering approach, a company's organization of its employees focuses on individuals and often on teams who understand the product development process and their role in it. It is the responsibility of managers to empower these individuals and teams with the authority they need in order to complete their tasks. Managers also need to ensure other kinds of support, such as training, education, and tools that allow the company to adapt and meet each new challenge of the marketplace.

Team Integration

Individual employees and teams understand their roles and tasks in the context of the overall product development process.

Y N **1.** Are the specifications and priorities for the assigned tasks understood by the individuals?

Y N **2.** Is the product development process understood by each single-discipline team?

Y N **3.** Is there a common vocabulary, priority and purpose established for the mixed-discipline product development team?

Y N **4.** Are the requirements, specifications, interdependencies, and priorities of the product understood by the enterprise team *(which includes the customer and third-parties)*?

Empowerment

The levels of authority and responsibility that coexist within your company play a significant role in its productivity, and both individuals and teams are rewarded.

Y N **5.** Are design decisions made by the supervisors and managers?

Y N **6.** Are design decisions made by the single-discipline team?

Y N **7.** Are design and tradeoff decisions made by the mixed-discipline team?

Y N **8.** Do representatives from the enterprise team *(which includes the customer and third-party vendors)* participate in your decisions?

Y N **9.** Are individuals responsible for scheduling and then completing their tasks on time and responsible for the outcome of their tasks?

Y N **10.** Is a single-discipline team responsible for the development of engineering specifications and their correlation to interdependent specifications?

Y N **11.** Is a mixed-discipline team responsible for program-wide specifications, scheduling, and correlation to requirements?

Y N **12.** Is an enterprise team *(which includes the customer and third-party vendors)* responsible for the system design specifications?

Y N **13.** Do you reward individuals for their contributions?

Y N **14.** Do you reward teams for their contributions?

Training and Education

Managers provide appropriate training and education for an individual or team. Effectiveness training includes how to solve problems, set goals, think creatively, use standards, utilize experts, and work with other disciplines.

Y N **15.** Is adequate training provided for each individual on the procedures, tools, and standards he or she should use?

Y N **16.** Does the single-discipline team have adequate cross-discipline awareness regarding procedures, tools, and standards?

Y N **17.** Is adequate team effectiveness training provided for the mixed-discipline team members?

Y N **18.** Is adequate team effectiveness training provided for the enterprise team members *(including the customer and third-party vendors)*?

Automation Support

Managers ensure that the necessary tools are available. These tools are integrated and provide access to product data.

Y N **19.** Are the tools for each discipline provided as stand-alone tools?

Y N **20.** Are centralized tools provided for the single-discipline team?

Y N **21.** Are the tools for each individual integrated within the mixed-discipline team?

Y N **22.** Are the tools for each individual integrated within the enterprise team *(including any vendor-supplied parts or assistance being available on-line)*?

COMMUNICATION INFRASTRUCTURE

This part of the questionnaire explores where your company stands in terms of the key factors that characterize the communication infrastructure dimension in a concurrent engineering environment. Concurrent engineering involves the co-design of the product by all disciplines. Therefore, using effective communication paths and tools to manage product information, employees, tasks, and changes to the product becomes critical for success. Working product data, lessons learned, decision rationales, and decision sequences need to be tracked so that individuals and teams understand the product development process at any time. Communication between individuals and between all workstation tools is crucial and determines how data is acquired and shared within the task, project, program, and enterprise.

Product Management

Effective communication paths are crucial to product management so that individuals and teams can understand their assigned goals and roles, help to plan the development process, monitor the fulfillment of their goals and roles, and improve the process as needed.

Y N **23.** Are electronic mail capabilities available to each individual?

Y N **24.** Are query and online reporting capabilities available to each individual?

Y N **25.** Are interactive product data browsers available to each individual?

Y N **26.** Is decision support available to each individual?

Y N **27.** Are technical reviews and inspections conducted at the appropriate milestones?

Y N **28** Is disciplined and consistent product management used for a project effort?

Y N **29.** Is there a communication path between all aspects of project management and system requirements?

Y N **30.** Are managers and interdependent project teams automatically and concurrently informed of problems and their status?

Product Data

Product data is complete and accurate at all times, and individuals and teams can access, manipulate, and change that data as appropriate.

Y N **31.** Is product development data controlled by the individual?

Y N **32.** Do individuals on the single-discipline team have access to all the product development data related to their discipline?

Y N **33.** Do individuals have electronic access to the product development data related to the different disciplines involved in product development?

Y N **34.** Do individuals and teams have electronic access to company-wide product development data that includes data from customers and third-party vendors?

Y N **35.** During the development process, are the product development specifications and designs utilized and documented in an established manner?

Y N **36.** Is the product development data stored, controlled, changed, and versioned in a similar or common computer database?

Y N **37.** Is the data in the product development database interoperable among the various design automation tools?

Y N **38.** Are evolving product requirements, specifications, and development data under automatic change and versioning controls?

Feedback

Feedback keeps the product development process on track and permits individuals and teams to handle deviations from customer expectations, product specifications, industry standards, and other requirements. Feedback from reviews and inspections generates action items as well as suggestions for enhancements to the product.

Y N **39.** Are problems analyzed as to their root cause and then corrected?

Y N **40.** Are problem reports logged, prioritized, scheduled for correction *(or rejection)*, and tracked until the problems are corrected?

Y N **41.** Are action items, problem reports, and enhancement requests stored in a decision database and then used as indicators for customer satisfaction?

Y N **42.** Are the trends of action items, problem reports, enhancement requests, and all other decisions analyzed to continuously improve the product development process?

REQUIREMENTS

This part of the questionnaire explores how your company handles the key factors that characterize the requirements dimension in a concurrent engineering environment. Concurrent engineering broadens the interpretation of requirements to include all product attributes that affect customer satisfaction. Adequately capturing and expressing the total set of these specifications is crucial to concurrent engineering. In addition, the organization imposes other requirements, such as planning, scheduling, and documentation, on individuals and teams. These internal requirements, as well as the validation of the total set of customer requirements, must work in concert to ensure successful concurrent engineering.

Requirements Definition

Your company converts customer needs upfront to the definitions, specifications, and designs of the product. At every stage in the development process, individuals, teams, and managers can check that requirements, specifications, and designs are meeting customer needs.

Y N **43.** Are customer expectations determined and converted to established, documented customer or marketing requirements?

Y N **44.** Are the customer or marketing requirements partitioned into established, documented functional specifications?

Y N **45.** Is there traceability from the individual functional specifications back to the customer or marketing requirements?

Y N **46.** Can the enterprise team access the customer or marketing requirements as part of decision support?

Y N **47.** Are internally imposed expectations determined and converted to established, documented product life cycle *(PLC)* requirements?

Y N **48.** Are the internal requirements partitioned into established, documented PLC specifications?

Y N **49.** Is there traceability from the individual functional specifications back to the PLC requirements?

Y N **50.** Can the enterprise team access the PLC requirements as part of decision support?

Planning Methodology

Product planning, evaluation, and design methods can happen from both the bottom-up and top-down. These methods may include trade-off analysis and integrating the tasks and processes that develop the product.

Y N **51.** Is there a bottom-up design process in which all individuals contribute to the planning, evaluation, or creation of the product or functional specifications?

Y N **52.** Is there a top-down design process in which the customer, product, or system design requirements lead to documented specifications for the functional subsystem design?

Y N **53.** Is it required that the mixed-discipline team consider tradeoffs that may change the product technology, design architecture, or development-to-manufacturing process?

Y N **54.** Do the product requirements and system design requirements lead to interrelated tasks and processes?

Planning Perspective

When determining the development process required for a given product, your company includes planning perspectives as part of that process.

Y N **55.** Do individuals document short-term planning prior to the start of a task?

Y N **56.** Does your company require documented long-term planning for your product?

Y N **57.** Does your company use multiphased, multi-year planning methods for each product family?

Y N **58.** Does your company measure best-value product designs for cost, functionality, fitness for use, reliability, performance, and supportability?

Validation

The requirements for the development process are validated to determine whether the specifications meet the customers requirements and if all specified processes accomplish the intended result.

Y N **59.** Are the individual functional subsystem specifications validated according to the customer requirements?

Y N **60.** Are the discipline-specific requirements validated according to the customer requirements?

Y N **61.** Are the mixed-discipline and process requirements validated to the customer requirements?

Y N **62.** Are interactive methods used to monitor and warn the enterprise team when a requirement mismatch occurs?

Standards

Your company documents and communicates to individuals and teams the conventions, guidelines, and procedures used for design standards. The standards cover customer needs, testing, manufacturing, and customer support.

Y N **63.** Does your company have a mechanism to monitor compliance with applicable design standards?

Y N **64.** Does your company use design standards to ensure product reliability?

Y N **65.** Does your company use design standards to ensure product testability, manufacturability, supportability, and usability?

Y N **66.** Does your company regularly review and improve its design standards?

PRODUCT DEVELOPMENT

This final part of the company assessment questionnaire explores how your company handles the key factors that characterize the product development dimension. The process of concurrently enhancing the product and assessing its status is very much a part of a concurrent engineering environment. In particular, verification, optimization, and development processes are continually redefined. This ongoing effort affects the role of data libraries, reviews, and product architectures.

Component Engineering

When a team is part of the development process, all the design data and the data on components, both simple parts and units, are available to all individuals.

Y N **67.** Are individuals responsible for the development of their own components and component libraries?

Y N **68.** Are company-wide standards used to represent the component data?

Y N **69.** Is a single library system used to manage the component data of all the different disciplines involved?

Y N **70.** Is the library system database linked to a decision support tool to assist each designer in making component or unit selections?

Design Process

The methodologies and validations for the design process are documented and measured.

Y N **71.** Are design process specifications methodically documented so that function-specific designs *(system, software, hardware, or mechanical)* are both repeatable and consistent?

Y N **72.** Is deterministic analysis used to measure how well the product functions—for example, logic simulation for gauging functionality, fault simulation for determining the detectability of a failure, analog simulation for verifying parameters, finite element analysis for measuring mechanical tolerances?

Y N **73.** Is there adequate evaluation of the reuse and shared use of product technology and product design units?

Y N **74.** Are adequate methods used to integrate the product and processes?

Y N **75.** Is information extracted from the physical design *(back-annotated)* to perform more detailed analyses of the product features and performance?

Y N **76.** Are analysis methods used to account for downstream processes, such as cost, testability, reliability, manufacturability, and supportability at the conceptual or detailed design stage?

Y N **77.** Are the computing environment and product development tools interoperable for all disciplines?

Y N **78.** Are decision support and process management systems in use?

Optimization

Managers must respond to the continuing evolution of technology.

Y N **79.** Are there goals for product and process improvements?

Y N **80.** Are major project decisions and the factors leading to them documented, distributed, and analyzed for guidance on other projects?

Y N **81.** Are process modeling and simulation tools used in planning and improving the design process?

Y N **82.** Are product designs, development processes, requirements, and tools concurrently analyzed and continuously improved as part of a company-wide optimization strategy?

Y N **83.** Is a supplier qualification program used to select third-party vendors for products or tools?

Later, in the third part of this assessment, you'll use the answers you gave to the questions in this questionnaire. For now you're ready to continue with the second part of this concurrent engineering assessment—the methods matrix.

DETERMINE WHERE SHOULD YOU BE

The methods matrix helps you determine what methods your company can use in its product development environment to reap the full benefits of concurrent engineering. Before you look closely at the matrix, first choose a product—a current or future product. You will be assessing which concurrent engineering methods would enhance your company's success in developing that product.

Using the matrix is straightforward: Read the descriptions across from each key factor, and circle each description whose methods would be necessary for successful development of your chosen product. You may circle one description, more than one, all four, or none—however many you think are necessary for implementing that key factor and the overall process it suggests. One thing that can help guide your choices is noting that the more complicated your product is, the more likely you'll circle more descriptions for a particular key factor. The matrix should take less than fifteen minutes to complete.

ORGANIZATION

Key Factors	Task Approach	Project Approach	Program Approach	Enterprise Approach
Team Integration	Individuals have specific task and discipline perspectives, with little interaction between engineers or between disciplines. Data is controlled by individuals.	A single-discipline team has a project perspective. Data is not easily accessible by other disciplines.	A mixed-discipline team has a program perspective. Team members receive training to better understand other disciplines. Data is easily accessible by other disciplines.	Mixed-discipline teams have members from the entire enterprise, including management, suppliers, manufacturing. purchasing, customers, service, and all the "-abilities."
Empowerment	Management provides the only leadership. Individuals have responsibility. Rewards are given to individuals.	Management selects a team leader from within the single-discipline team. Decisions are a team responsibility. Rewards are given to the single-discipline team.	A mixed-discipline team selects its own leader. The team has the authority to make decisions; single-discipline teams have the responsibility to carry them out. Rewards are given to the mixed-discipline team.	Mixed-discipline teams select a leader. The teams have authority to make decisions and to carry them out. Rewards are given to mixed-discipline teams.
Training and Education	Individuals receive training in specific specialities.	Individuals receive training in cross discipline procedures, tools, and standards.	A mixed-discipline team receives training in team effectiveness. Team members think holistically and use tools, such as QFD. Training is on-demand and situation specific.	Mixed-discipline teams throughout the enterprise receive training in team effectiveness. Interactive simulation tools may be used to teach methods of data generation and force examination of issues from different perspectives.
Automation Support	Stand-alone tools are interfaced vertically within disciplines. Data is gathered and stored for later use. Discipline-specific hardware and software are available on a single platform. Documentation is created on desktop systems.	Centralized single-discipline tools can access data within a project. Data is gathered and is available for use. A single-discipline team can share hardware and software data.	Mixed-discipline tools are integrated for each individual throughout the program. Data is gathered, processed, and updated immediately. A mixed-discipline team can share hardware and software data. Documentation is integrated within the product development environment.	Mixed-discipline tools are integrated for each individual throughout the enterprise. Data is utilized to initiate action prior to a problem or issue arising. Mixed-discipline teams can share hardware and software data throughout the enterprise. Documentation is integrated within the enterprise-wide product development environment.

COMMUNICATION INFRASTRUCTURE

Key Factors	Task Approach	Project Approach	Program Approach	Enterprise Approach
Product Management	Electronic mail capabilities are available to each individual. Technical reviews and inspections are conducted at the appropriate milestones.	On-line reporting and query capabilities are available to each individual. Disciplined and consistent product management is used.	Interactive product data browsers are available to each individual. Product design and system design are interconnected.	Decision support is available to each individual. Problems and their status are automatically and concurrently reported.
Product Data	Product specifications and designs are used and documented during the development process by individuals.	Product development data is stored, controlled, changed, and versioned in a similar or common computer database.	Mixed-discipline data in the product development database is interoperable among design automation tools.	Real-time data is available throughout the enterprise. Requirements, specifications, and product data are under change and version controls.
Feedback	Problems are analyzed as to their root cause and then corrected.	Problem reports are logged, prioritized, scheduled for completion, and tracked until the problems are corrected.	Action items, problem reports, and enhancement requests are stored in a decision database and then used as indicators for customer satisfaction.	The trends of action items, problem reports, enhancement requests, and all other decisions are analyzed to continuously improve the product development process of the enterprise.

REQUIREMENTS

Key Factors	Task Approach	Project Approach	Program Approach	Enterprise Approach
Requirements Definition	Customer expectations and internally imposed expectations are determined and converted to established and documented requirements.	Customer or marketing requirements and internal requirements are partitioned into established, documented functional specifications and product life cycle specifications.	Mixed-discipline requirements are traceable from the individual functional specifications back to the customer or marketing requirements and product life cycle specifications.	Enterprise-wide mixed-discipline teams have on-line access to the customer or marketing requirements and product life cycle requirements as part of decision support.
Planning Methodology	The design process is bottom-up. All individuals contribute to the planning, evaluation, or creation of the product or functional specifications.	The design process is top-down. The customer, product, or system design requirements lead to documented specifications for the functional subsystem design.	Mixed-discipline teams consider trade-offs that may change the product technology, design architecture, or development-to-manufacturing process.	Product requirements and system design requirements lead to interrelated tasks and processes.
Planning Perspective	Individuals document short-term planning prior to the start of a task.	A company requirement is to document long-term planning for each product.	A company requirement is to use multi-phased, multi-year planning methods for each product family.	A company requirement is to measure best-value product designs for cost, functionality, fitness for use, reliability, performance, and supportability.
Validation	Individual subsystem specifications are validated according to the customer requirements.	Discipline specific requirements are validated according to the customer requirements.	Mixed-discipline and process requirements are validated according to the customer requirements.	Enterprise-wide mixed-discipline teams are automatically and concurrently warned when a requirement mis-match occurs.
Standards	Compliance with applicable design standards is monitored.	Design standards are used to ensure product reliability.	Design standards are used to ensure product testability, manufacturability, supportability, and usability.	Design standards are regularly reviewed and continuously improved.

PRODUCT DEVELOPMENT

Key Factors	Task Approach	Project Approach	Program Approach	Enterprise Approach
Component Engineering	Individuals are responsible for development, control, and maintenance of their own component libraries. These libraries are discipline-specific.	Company-wide standards are used to represent components.	A single library system is used to develop, control, and maintain the component data from all the different disciplines involved.	The library system database–developed, controlled, and maintained across the enterprise–is linked to a decision support tool.
Design Process	Standard methods and practices are documented and used for managing design activities so that designs are both repeatable and consistent. Information extracted from the physical design (back-annotated) is used to analyze product features and performance.	Deterministic analysis is used to measure how well the product functions. Analysis methods are used to account for downstream processes (the "-abilities") at the conceptual or detailed design stage.	Reuse and sharing of product technology and design units are adequately evaluated. The computing environment and product development tools are interoperable for all disciplines.	Downstream processes are accounted for at the concept or detailed design phase. Decision support and process management systems are in use throughout the enterprise.
Optimization	Product and process improvement goals are in place.	Major product decisions and the factors leading to them are documented, distributed, and analyzed for guidance on other projects.	Process modeling and simulation tools are used in planning and improving the design process.	Product designs, development processes, requirements, and tools are concurrently analyzed and continuously improved as part of an enterprise-wide optimization strategy. A supplier qualification program is used to select third-party vendors for products or tools.

The Dimensions Map

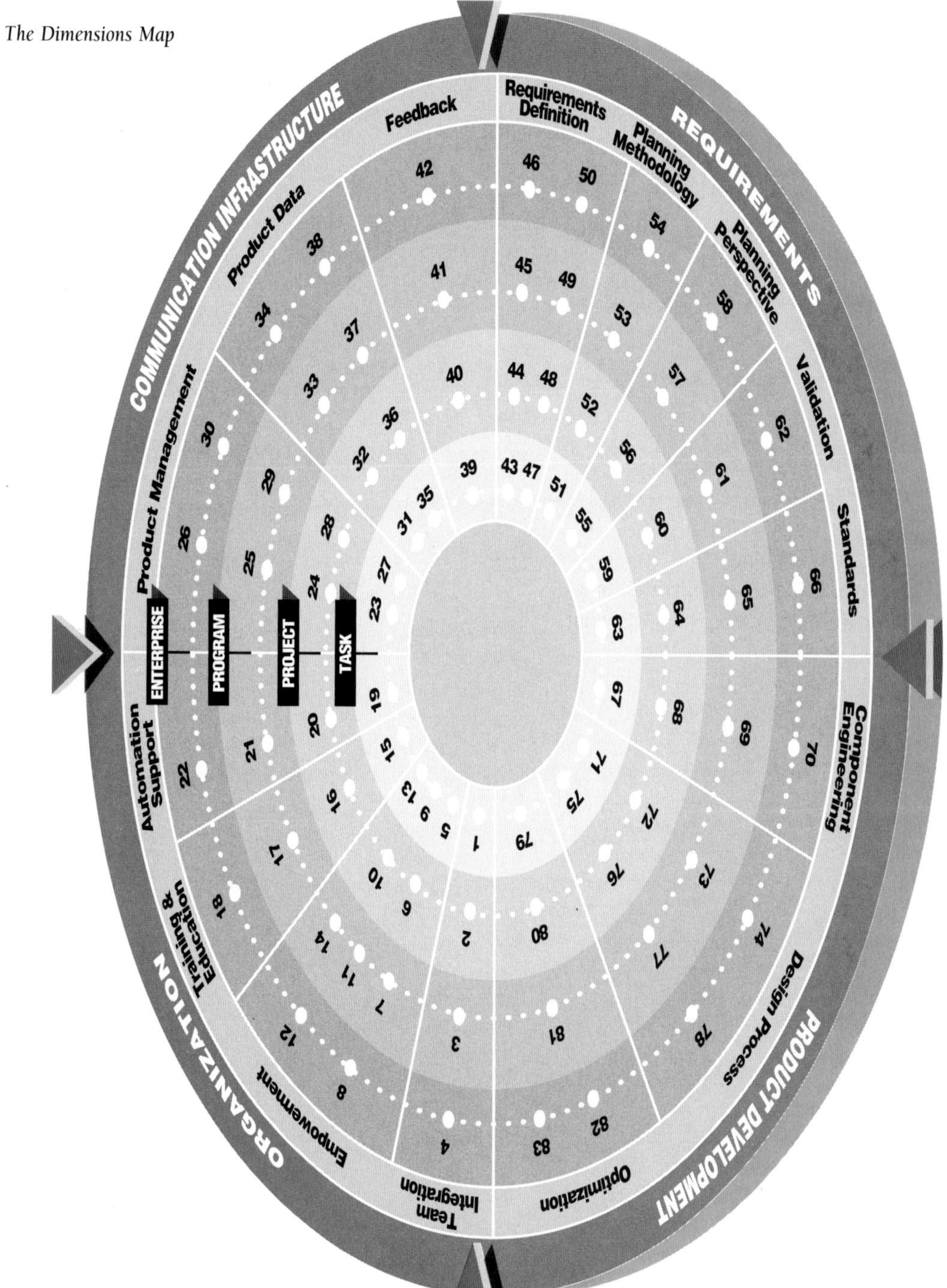

Source: Mentor Graphics Corp.

Abbreviations

ASIC Application Specific Integrated Circuit
CAD Computer-Aided Design
CAE Computer-Aided Engineering
CAM Computer-Aided Manufacturing
CASE Computer-Aided Software Engineering
CALS/CE Computer-Aided Acquisition and Logistics Support/ Concurrent Engineering
CFI CAD Framework Initiative
CIM Computer-Integrated Manufacturing
CERC Concurrent Engineering Research Center
CM Configuration Management
CIP Continuous Improvement Process
DARPA Defense Advanced Research Projects Agency
DFT Design For Testability
DCE Distributed Computing Environment
EDIF Electronic Design Interchange Format
IC Integrated Circuit
IDA Institute for Defense Analyses
IGES Initial Graphics Exchange Specification
JIT Just In Time
MRP Materials Requirements Planning
MTBF Mean Time Between Failure
NIH Not Invented Here
OSF Open Software Foundation
OSA Open System Architecture
PCB Printed Circuit Board
PDES Product Data Exchange using STEP
QA Quality Assurance
QFD Quality Function Deployment
STEP Standard for the Exchange of Product model data
TQC Total Quality Control
VLSI Very Large Scale Integration

Glossary

Amdahl's law A formula, developed by Dr. Amdahl, to determine overall throughput: the time it takes to gather, analyze, and output data.

assessment A view of the present state of concurrent engineering within a product development environment. An assessment tool is included in chapter three and is made up of four parts: the company assessment questionnaire, the methods matrix, the dimensions map, and the priority roadmap.

automated concurrent engineering The result when design automation and framework technology is applied to the process by which products and their related manufacturing and support processes are developed.

best value-based design A design or decision methodology where the overall "value" of a product is considered. Value can be a combination of several factors, including cost, performance, reliability, and features. All of these factors are considered when making tradeoff decisions during the product development process.

bottom-up design A structured approach to organizing design data where the lowest level primitive elements are defined first, then the higher level functions are built using these elements. As the hierarchical definition process concludes, the overall design structure is expressed in terms of high level functional blocks and their interconnections. See also *top-down design.*

breadboard design A time-consuming method used to evaluate and verify the functional correctness of the proposed design using physical components electrically interconnected with either wire-wrap or some form of hand-wired connections. Simulation tools eliminate the need for breadboard design.

browser See *product data browser.*

Computer-Aided Design (CAD) The use of computer-based tools to assist in the physical layout of electronic designs, including preparation of manufacturing tooling. CAD also refers to automated mechanical design.

Computer-Aided Engineering (CAE) The use of computer-based tools to assist in one or more aspects of electronic design, from initial detailed design specification through physical layout and test.

Computer-Aided Manufacturing (CAM) The use of computer-based tools to program, direct, and control production equipment in the fabrication of manufactured items.

Computer-Aided Software Engineering (CASE) The use of computer-based tools to aid in the software engineering process. CASE tools are used in software design, requirements tracing, code production, testing, document generation, and other software engineering activities.

Computer-Aided Acquisition and Logistics Support/Concurrent Engineering (CALS/CE) A Department of Defense and Industry initiative designed to improve the accuracy, timeliness, and use of technical information. Started in 1985, CALS/CE objectives were to accelerate the integration of R&M design tools into CAD/CAE systems, automate processes for generating logistic technical information, and to increase the capability to receive, distribute and use technical information in digital form. In 1988 the Secretary of Defense required the implementation of CALS/CE by contractors. Industry steering groups formed sub-task groups to aid this implementation. These task groups include the Frameworks, Electronic Systems, Mechanical Systems, Reliability and Maintainability, CE Bibliography, Tech/Admin Interface and Manufacturing sub-groups.

CAD Framework Initiative (CFI) A forum where users of CAD/CAE systems can voice their needs and vendors can listen to them. CFI has begun to define industry requirements of the database consistency and inter-tool communication needed to track and control complex design data. CFI's procedural interface (PI) enables design tools from multiple vendors to communicate with each other in one environment. Through the interface, design tools from the different vendors can pass information or data directly and in real time. For more information, write to:

CAD Framework Initiative
7490 Clubhouse Road, #102
Boulder, CO 80301

change control See *configuration control.*

Computer-Integrated Manufacturing (CIM) An approach to production in which a hierarchy of networked computers control and monitor the manufacturing process by determining what parts, materials, and subassemblies will move to which stations on what schedules, by selecting tools and operations to be performed, by controlling operations, and by testing to ensure that pre-specified tolerances are being met.

collaboration To work together in a joint intellectual effort to create a shared understanding. There are three stages of collaboration that lead a team to consensus: first define a common vocabulary, agree on a common purpose, and then agree on individual priorities.

component One of the hardware or software parts that make up a system. A component may be subdivided into other components. The terms "component" and "unit" are often used interchangeably.

component data All the information that describes the electronic or mechanical component or device. This data should contain the information required by all design disciplines.

concurrent The occurrence of two or more activities within the same period of time, achieved either by interleaving the activities or by simultaneously executing the activities.

concurrent engineering Defined by IDA Report R-338 titled, The Role of Concurrent Engineering in Weapons System Acquisition, as "a systematic approach to the integrated, concurrent design of products and their related processes, including manufacture and support. This approach is intended to cause the developers, from the outset, to consider all elements of the product life cycle from conception through disposal, including quality, cost, schedule, and user requirements."

concurrent engineering environment The collection of services and the culture necessary to support concurrent engineering. A concurrent engineering environment has four key dimensions: organization, communication infrastructure, requirements, and product development.

Concurrent Engineering Research Center (CERC) Promotes the transfer of concurrent product development technology to US industry to improve its competitiveness. Through pilot studies, CERC is gaining valuable understanding and experience in implementing concurrent engineering. These pilots yield information such as documented case studies, scenarios, and metrics; system requirement documents; and software technology validation and integration experience. CERC is located at West Virginia University, Morgantown, West Virginia.

configuration The grouping of a computer system or component as defined by the number, nature, and interconnections of its constituent parts.

configuration control Part of configuration management, where configuration items are evaluated, coordinated, approved or disapproved, and implemented after formally establishing their configuration identification.

Configuration Management (CM) An engineering discipline that provides direction and monitoring of configuration items. CM responsibilities include: to identify, document, and control changes to the functional and physical characteristics, to document change processing and implementation status, and verify compliance with specified requirements. See also *configuration control.*

Continuous Improvement Process (CIP) An approach to steadily improving quality of a specific product or service through identifying and correcting root sources of defects. These may, in some cases, be subtle factors with small but cumulative effects.

correct-by-construction Design data and design rules are monitored throughout the construction process to ensure that the finished product accurately conforms to the input data.

customer requirements The performance, features, and general characteristics of a product as defined by a customer. Customer requirements are an important consideration in the design specification for a product.

Defense Advanced Research Projects Agency (DARPA) A Department of Defense agency that began a study in 1982 to look for ways to improve concurrency in the design process. When DARPA released their results five years later, the study proved to be an important foundation upon which future groups would base further study of concurrent engineering.

database A collection of data that is interrelated and is stored together in one or more computer files. A concurrent engineering environment supports a common database for all tools.

decision support Design decisions made with the aid of online data. For example, a decision support tool could determine component selection based on factors such as cost, availability, and power consumption.

design The process of defining the architecture, components, interfaces, and other characteristics of a system or component. Also, the result of this process.

design capture The process of formally stating a design, as when a person uses a computer-aided tool to draw a schematic or other drawing.

design cycle The sequence of phases through which a design evolves. For example, the typical electronic design cycle consists of concept, design, simulation, layout, and test.

design elements Explicitly identifiable portions of a design that can be described and modeled as entities. Design elements may be primitives, interconnections of primitives, or interconnections of larger elements.

Design For Testability (DFT) A design process whereby deliberate effort is expended to assure that a product may be thoroughly tested with minimum effort, and that high confidence may be ascribed to test results.

design methodologies Approaches or techniques that are used in solving certain aspects of design problems.

design process The set of activities, tools, methods, and procedures used to produce a product or component design. Specific design processes include electronic design, mechanical design, and software design.

design productivity Measures of the rate at which designs can be produced, usually expressed in terms of gate equivalents per day of design effort, or design cost per gate.

development process See *product development process.*

Distributed Computing Environment A layer of software that resides between the computer's operating system and the application program running on the computer. The Open Software Foundation (OSF) supports this environment. DCE is designed to combine computers with different hardware architectures and operating system software on a network to function as a single, standalone computer that shares the task of processing application programs.

downstream processes Processes that are at the back end of the design cycle, including testability, manufacturability, reliability, serviceability, repairability, maintainability, and usability. These processes are also known as the "-abilities."

Electronic Design Interchange Format (EDIF) The EIA-548 Standard for interchanging electronic data among CAD/CAE tools and systems. EDIF gives users the ability to move graphics or data between different tools and includes a way for updating, improving, and maintaining the format.

electronic mail A program, commercial, or public domain, that facilitates the electronic distribution of messages and data to addressed subscribers on a network.

enterprise approach The effort required to develop a very complicated product that has more than one program and requires many mixed-discipline teams, that may include third-party vendors, to develop it.

feedback The ability to return all analyses and reviews of team members.

framework A collection of software program facilities, or a set of extensible services, that are the foundation for an integrated electronic design automation system. The key facilities provided by a framework include common design data management, product data management, process management, and a common user interface.

global optimization The result when product designs, processes, multi-requirements, and tools are concurrently analyzed and continuously improved.

Institute for Defense Analyses (IDA) Responsible for publishing the report (IDA Report R-338) that first coined the term "concurrent engineering."

Initial Graphics Exchange Specification (IGES) An ASME/ANSI Y14.26M-1989 standard for interchanging electronic data among CAD/CAM tools and systems and for archiving that data. This standard has a user-extensible interface for geometric, drafting, and structural entities and can graphically represent most of the information in CAD/CAM systems.

inter-discipline team See *mixed-discipline team.*

interoperability The ability of two or more systems or components to exchange information and to use the information that has been exchanged. For example, interoperable tools have access to and use the original data, not translated data nor copies of the data. Making a change to data in one tool automatically changes the data used by all other tools.

integrate To coordinate, or blend two or more systems or components into a functioning or unified whole. For example, integrated tools are a collection of computer tools that share a common user interface and a common database. When moving from one design phase to the next, the design data is translated for each tool so that all tools have the same "look-and-feel."

integrated circuit A tiny electronic component which contains hundreds or thousands of permanently connected transistors and other devices. Also known as "chips" or "microchips."

intra-discipline team See *single-discipline team.*

just in time (JIT) manufacturing A production system where materials or parts used in manufacturing are brought to the work site just as they are needed for assembly, not maintained in inventories. The benefits include reduced work-in-progress, lower inventory costs, and reduced rework costs when errors in design or manufacture are detected.

layout That portion of the electronic design cycle during which the logical or electrical definition of the design is transformed into a physical equivalent that can be manufactured. Layout can be gate array, standard cell, custom integrated circuit, or printed circuit board.

Materials Requirements Planning (MRP) An approach to inventory management that usually draws on suppliers' information to frequently update forecasts of materials needs so that production plans can be made.

Mean Time Between Failure (MTBF) A measure of the reliability of a product.

metric A quantitative measurement of a system, component, or process to determine the degree to which it possesses a given attribute. Metrics are often used to measure quality.

mixed-discipline team A team whose members represent all the various expertise necessary to satisfactorily perform the job.

network A system used to connect multiple computers together so that they can communicate and exchange information.

Not Invented Here (NIH) An attitude that all major components in a product should be designed and manufactured in-house.

Open Software Foundation (OSF) An industry group promoting a standard interoperable computing environment. OSF supports the distributed computing environment (DCE).

Open System Architecture (OSA) An architecture for a system which allows for the incorporation of new product technologies and new tool technologies.

on-line A system or mode of operation in which input data enter the computer directly from the point of origin or

Resources

This is a complete list of all the sources and works consulted by the authors, including both quoted sources and sources that influenced the authors' thinking. It indicates the volume and range of reading upon which the authors formed their ideas.

This comprehensive list is provided for those who wish to pursue the subject of concurrent engineering in greater detail than is presented in the text of this book.

The sources are organized alphabetically by title in each of the following categories:

- The five forces of change: technology, tools, tasks, talent, and time
- The four key dimensions of concurrent engineering: organization, communication infrastructure, requirements, and product development
- The books and manuscripts that comprise a popular reading list

TECHNOLOGY

Fox, Geoffrey C. and Paul C. Messina, "Advanced Computer Architectures," *Scientific American*, (October, 1987), pp. 67-74.

Meindl, James D., "Chips for Advanced Computing," *Scientific American*, (October, 1987), pp. 78-88.

Hagel, John III, "Conquering complexity: How winners leverage simpler design," *Electronic Business*, (February 6, 1990), pp. 62-64.

Badawy, Michael K., "The Enemies Are Within," *Industry Week*, (March 20, 1989), pp. 39-43.

Rohan, Thomas M., "Keeping In Touch With Technology," *Industry Week*, (October 3, 1988), pp. 39-42.

Dahl, Aubrey, "The Last of the First," *Datamation*, (June, 1978), pp. 145-149.

"Living With The Chip," *The Royal Bank of Canada Newsletter*, (1988).

DeYoung, H. Garrett, "Managing technology at warp speed," *Electronic Business*, (January 21, 1991), pp. 53-57.

Gilder, George, "The New American Challenge," *Electronic Business*, (August 7, 1989), pp. 36-40.

Peled, Abraham, "The Next Computer Revolution," *Scientific American*, (October, 1987), Volume 257, Volume 4, pp. 57-64.

Gelerneter, David, "Programming for Advanced Computing," *Scientific American*, (October, 1987), pp. 91-98.

Reich, Robert B., "The Quiet Path to Technological Preeminence," *Scientific American*, (October, 1989), Volume 261, Number 4, pp. 44-47.

"The 30TH Anniversary of the Integrated Circuit," *Electronic Engineering Times*, (September, 1988).

Aerospace Industries Association of America, Inc., "Ultra-Reliable Electronic Systems," *Aerospace Industries Association of America, Inc.*, (April, 1990).

TOOLS

Carter, Donald E., "Better Software for Analog Simulation," *Computer-Aided Engineering*, (January, 1987), pp. 56-57.

Burrows, Peter, "Coming Soon: Design automation with interchangeable tools," *Electronic Business*, (June 11, 1990), pp. 72-75.

Carter, Donald E., "Designing Reliability and Maintainability Into Today's Complex Products," *Mentor Graphics Corporation white paper*, (August, 1989).

DeBella, Neil A., "Full Custom IC Layout," *Mentor Graphics Corporation white paper.*

McLeod, Jonah, "A Giant Leap For Simulation," *Electronics*, (February, 1989), pp. 73-80.

Palesko, Chet, "IC Tools Target the Big Chips," *Computer-Aided Engineering*, (September, 1989), pp. 80-84.

Freuler, Tom and Michael McSherry, "Interactive Compaction Controls The Squeeze," *High Performance Systems*, (October, 1989), pp. 69-74.

Carter, Donald E., *An Introduction To Digital Logic Simulation.* (Portland, Oregon: Mentor Graphics Corporation, December 1986)

Teresko, John, "New Tools From Technology," *Industry Week*, (April 18, 1988), p. 59.

Goering, Richard, "Rapid Prototyping How To Stay The Course," *High Performance Systems*, (October, 1989), pp. 21-25.

Gifford, Paul, "Sequent's Symmetry Series," *VLSI Systems Design*, (June, 1988), pp.1-6.

Vasko, David A., and Dan Weyer, "Simulation Sorts Out System Schemes By Surveying Trade-Offs," *Electronic Design*, (September 27, 1990).

Siemiatkowski, Richard T., "Standards And The Electronic Engineer," *American Institute Of Aeronautics and Astronautics AIAA Aerospace Engineering Conference.*

Huber, John P., "System Simulation at the Board-Level with Electronic Design Automation Tools," *Mentor Graphics Corporation white paper*, (March 27, 1988).

Evanczuk, Stephen, "Tool integration poses challenge for designers," *Electronic Engineering Times*, (March 18, 1991), pp. 41-44.

"USAF R&M 2000 Process," *Headquarters, United States Air Force Office of the Special Assistant for R&M report*, (October, 1987).

Nurie, Ghulam M. and Paul J. Menchini, VHDL Model Portability, *High Performance Systems*, (July, 1989), pp. 76-85.

Goering, Richard, "VHDL synthesis, simulation good, but not good enough," *Electronic Engineering Times*, (January 21, 1991), pp. 71-74.

Smith, David, "What is Logic Synthesis?", *VLSI Systems Design*, (October, 1988), pp. 18-26.

Hines, John, "Where VHDL Fits Within The CAD Environment," *Printed Circuit Design*, (December, 1987), pp. 8-12.

TASKS

Evanczuk, Stephen, "Back-End Engineering Moves To The Front," *High Performance Systems*, (November, 1989), pp. 18-25.

Department of the Navy, "Best Practices - How to Avoid Surprises in the World's Most Complicated Technical Process," *United States Navy report.*

Research Newsletter, "CAD/CAM/CAE Preliminary Market Review: A Repeat Of 1988 As Vendor Consolidation Abounds, 1989," *Dataquest Incorporated*, (January, 1990).

Hales, H. Lee, "CimPlan The Systematic Approach to Factory Automation," *Cahners Publishing Company.*

Palesko, Chet, "Computer Aided Engineering - Composite design paves way to ULSI," *Electronics Times*, (May 9, 1989).

Causey, Rob, "The confidence to ditch prototypes," *Electronics Weekly*, (February 24, 1990), p. 19.

Garda, Robert A., "Developing, Disseminating, and Utilizing Marketing Knowledge," *Journal of Marketing*, (October, 1988), pp. 20-29.

Thryft, Ann R., "Getting concurrent no simple task," *Computer Design*, (March 18, 1991), pp. 1, 30.

Rinholm, Brenda L., "New products often die from internal disease," *Marketing News*, (October 29, 1990), p. 7.

"That Old-Time Accounting Isn't Good Enough Anymore," *Business Week Special Report*, (June 6, 1988), p. 107.

"The Productivity Paradox," *Business Week Special Report*, (June 6, 1988), pp. 100-102.

Whiting, Rick, "What are the secrets of success for product transition?", *Electronic Business*, (February 19, 1990), pp. 34-40.

TALENT

Soderberg, Leif, "America's Engineering Gap," *The Wall Street Journal*, (January 30, 1989), p. 11.

Berkman, Barbara N., "The best and brightest speak out," *Electronic Business*, (June 12, 1989), pp. 29-37.

Crapo, Ray, "Dealing with EEs who know more than you do," *Electronic Engineering Times*, (April 22, 1991), pp. 81, 84.

Altany, David R., "Decision-Making Trickles Down To The Troops," *Industry Week*, (April 18, 1988), p. 34.

Rohan, Thomas M., "Designer/Builder Teamwork Pays Off," *Industry Week*, (August 7, 1989), pp. 45-46.

Bellinger, Robert, "Engineers: don't blame me for delays," *Electronic Engineering Times*, (January 21, 1991), p. 101.

Ryan, Margaret, "An EE career isn't what it used to be," *Electronic Engineering Times*, (February 18, 1991), pp. 73-74.

Bellinger, Robert, "The EE degree: Is four years enough?," *Electronic Engineering Times*, (February 11, 1991), pp. 97-99.

Teresko, John, "Engineering: Where Competitive Success Begins," *Industry Week*, (November 19, 1990), pp. 30-34.

Woolnough, Roger, "Europe's Engineer Shortage," *Electronic Engineering Times*, (August 28, 1989), p. 20.

Cox, Allan, "The Homework Behind Teamwork," *Industry Week*, (January 7, 1991), pp. 21-23.

Shea, Kevin, "Improving engineering productivity by using solutions-based strategies," *Electronic Engineering Times*, (January 21, 1991), p. 34.

Kelleher, Joanne, "The Labor Crisis Builds," *Computer World*, (August 13, 1990), pp. 23-24.

Sheridan, John H., "Lessons From The Gurus," *Industry Week*, (August 6, 1990), pp. 35-41.

Crapo, Raymond F., "Managing the project engineer," *Electronic Engineering Times*, (April 23, 1990), p. 85.

Gabarro, John J. and John P. Kotter, "Managing your boss," *Harvard Business Review.*

Soderberg, Leif, "Merging engineering skills that give you the edge," *Electronic Business*, (September 4, 1989), p. 55.

Ryan, Margaret, "The Out Of Work Engineer: Part 1 - Finding engineering's 'lost grads'," *Electronic Engineering Times*, (September 25, 1989), pp. 99, 110.

"People Needs: Work Trends and Shortages," *Aviation Week & Space Technology*, (November 20, 1989), pp. S5-S13.

Pascarella, Perry, Vince DiBianca and Linda Gioja "The Power of Being Responsible," *Industry Week*, (December 5, 1988) pp. 41-54.

Verespej, Michael A., " 'Shelves' Emptying In Skills Markets," *Industry Week*, (November 20, 1989), p. 54.

Buffington, Perry W., "Star Quality," *Sky*, (September, 1990), pp. 101-104.

Ryan, Margaret, "Transatlantic EE teams," *Electronic Engineering Times*, (November 12, 1990), p. 128.

Welter, Therese R., "Wanted: Technical Skills," *Industry Week*, (July 3, 1989), pp. 36-37.

Lawler, Edward, "When You Put The Team In Charge," *Industry Week*, (December 3, 1990), pp. 30-32.

Rohan, Thomas M., "White collar Wisdom," *Industry Week*, (September 3, 1990), pp. 33-34.

TIME

Thomas, Philip R., "Executive weaponry: Short cycle times slay competitors," *Electronic Business*, (March 6, 1989), pp. 116-121.

Chu, Al, "Fast Decisions Made Easy," *Bell Lab News*, (December 18, 1990), Employee Newspaper.

McClenahen, John S., "Is Myopia A Myth?", *Industry Week*, (May 7, 1990), p. 64.

Boston Consulting Group, "Perspectives Time-based Competition Series," *Boston Consulting Group white paper.*

Meyer, Christopher, "Reducing Cycle Time for Sustained Competitive Advantage," *Strategic Alignment Group*, (1990), pp. 1-13.

Peters, Tom, "Speed Becomes a 'Leading Edge'," *Industry Week*, (June 19, 1989), p. 12.

Teresko, John, "Speeding The Product Development Cycle," *Industry Week*, (July 18, 1988), pp. 40-41.

Welter, Therese R., "10 Weeks' Design Collapses To One," *Industry Week*, (July 16, 1990), pp. 58-59.

ORGANIZATION DIMENSION

Sheridan, John H., "Aligning Structure with Strategy," *Industry Week*, May 15, 1989, pp. 15-23.

Ohmae, Kenichi, "Companyism and Do More Better," *Harvard Business Review,* January-February 1989, pp. 70-77.

Peters, Tom, "Creating The Fleet-Footed Organization," *Industry Week,* April 18, 1989, pp. 35-39.

Baker, Darrel, "EDA success calls for some reorganization," *Electronic Engineering Times,* November 26, 1990, pp. 64-66.

McKenna, Joesph F., "A few Good Heros," *Industry Week,* October 15, 1990, pp.16-19.

McClenahen, John S., "Flexible Structures to Absorb the Shocks," *Industry Week*, April 18, 1988, pp. 41-44.

Ohmae, Kenichi, "The Global Logic Of Strategic Alliances," *Harvard Business Review*, March-April 1989, pp. 64-75.

Cox, Allan, "The Homework Behind Teamwork," *Industry Week*, January 7,1991, pp. 21-23.

Goldstein, Mark L., "Just Managing Won't Be Enough," *Industry Week*, April 18, 1988, p. 21.

Haavind, Robert, "Lean and Limber will Describe the Company of the Future," *Electronic Business*, April 30, 1990, pp. 58-60.

Kanter, Rosabeth Moss, "The New Managerial Work," *Harvard Business Review*, November-December 1989, pp. 85-92.

Peet, W. James and Karen J. Hladik, "Organizing for global product development," *Electronic Business*, March 6, 1989, pp. 62-64.

Modic, Stanley J., "Strategic Alliances," *Industry Week*, October 3, 1988, pp. 46-52.

Hamel, Gary and C.K. Prahalad, "Strategic Intent," *Harvard Business Review*, May-June 1989.

Tregoe, Benjamine B. and Peter M. Tobia, "Strategy and The New American Organization," *Industry Week*, August 6, 1990, pp. 28-34.

Kotter, John P., "What Leaders Really Do," *Harvard Business Review*, May-June 1990, pp. 103-111.

Shapiro, Benson P., "What the Hell is 'Market Oriented'?", *Harvard Business Review*, November-December 1988, pp. 119-125.

Hayes, Robert H., "Why Strategic Planning Goes Awry," *The New York Times*, Sunday, April 20, 1986.

Verespej, Michael A., "Yea, Teams? Not Always," *Industry Week*, June 18, 1990, pp. 104-105.

COMMUNICATION INFRASTRUCTURE DIMENSION

Vanfossen, Roe, "Automation: A Must For Industrial Survival," *Automation*, December 1990, p. 41.

Beasley, William G., "Aerospace & Defense: Bridging Islands of Automation," *Aviation Week & Space Technology*, March 5, 1990, pp. S3-S26.

Rauch-Hindin, Wendy, "Communication Standards," *System & Software,* March 1984, pp. 104-131.

Bucher, Robert, "Cim-can we integrate the process plant," *Automation,* February 1991, pp. 24-25.

Crawford, John D., "EDIF: A Mechanism for the Exchange of Design Data," *IEEE Design & Test,* February 1985, pp. 63-69.

Eurich, John P. and Gene Roth, "EDIF grows up", *IEEE Spectrum,* September 1990, pp. 68-72.

Smith, David, "An Engineering Information System," *VLSI System Design,"* November 1988, pp. 60-68.

Sheridan, John H., "The Fortress Walls Come Tumbling Down," *Industry Week,* April 18, 1988, p. 50.

Sanders, Al, "How to get the best design tools working as one," *CAD Framework Initiative,* June 1990, pp. 1-4.

Gates, Bill, "Information at Your Fingertips™," *Fall Comdex,* November 12, 1990, pp. 1-9.

Gillin, Paul, "Information Age, Japan Style," *Computerworld,* August 13, 1990, pp. 4-6.

Iversen, Wes, "Information Systems: Tying it all Together," *Industry Week,* August 20, 1990, pp. 20-30.

Krouse, John, et al., "Linking Computers for Team Engineering," *CAD/CAM Planning: 1990 Supplement,* July 26, 1990, pp. CC38-CC48.

Welter, Therese R., "Network Interference," *Industry Week,* May 2, 1988, pp. 43-45.

Goldstein Mark L., "The Networked Organization," *Industry Week,* April 18, 1988, pp. 46-47.

Davenport, Thomas H., and James E. Short, " The New Industrial Engineering: Information Technology and Business Process Redesign," *Sloan Management Review,* Summer 1990, pp. 11-27.

McCaskey, John, "Object-oriented database keeps the house in order," *Electronic Design,* March 19, 1987, pp. 129-134.

Schulman Marc G.,"Open System," *Salomon Brothers Inc.,* July 25, 1988, pp. 1-13.

Sheridan, John H. and John Teresko, "Open Systems," *Industry Week,* April 15, 1991, pp. 25- 56.

House, Charles H., and Raymond L. Price, "The Return Map: Tracking Product Teams," *Harvard Business Review,* January-February 1991, pp. 92-100.

Sorgie, Charlie, "Systems Engineering and Communications in a Large Project," *Mentor Graphics Corporation white paper,* March 8, 1990, pp. 1-15.

Till, Johna, "Standard protocols bridge LAN islands as networks go global," *Electronic Design,* May 26, 1988, pp. 80-90.

Schuldt, Ronald L. "Universal Data Classification, The Key to Enhanced Communications in a TQM Environment," *Martin Marietta Corporation*, pp. 1-10.

Evanczuk, Stephen, "U.S. 'Steps' toward product data standard", *Electronic Engineering Times,* December 10, 1990.

Karsh, Arlene, "We the people: standards give government more bang for our bucks," *Electronic Publishing & Printing,* June/July 1989, pp. 36-48.

Teresko, John, "What MIS Should Be Telling You About CASE," *Industry Week,* April 2, 1990, pp. 82-85.

Grout, Steve, "White Paper- an Phased Approach to PDES Electrical," *Martin Marietta Corporation MCC CAD Program,* July 12, 1989, pp. 1-12.

REQUIREMENTS DIMENSION

Lanning, Michael J. and Edward G. Michaels, "A Business is a Value Delivery System," *McKensie Staff Paper,* June 1988 No. 41.

Conrades, G.H., "Today's IBM: Closing In On Customer Satisfaction," *Management Digest.*

Reinertsen, Donald, "Good products start with good specifications," *Electronic Business,* June 15, 1986, pp. 118-120.

Hauser, John R. and Don Clausing, "The House of Quality," *Harvard Business Review,* May-June 1988, pp. 63-73.

Phillips, Stephen, "King Customer," *Business Week* , March 12, 1990, pp. 88-94.

King, Peggy, "Listening to the Voice of the Customer," *HP Professional,* May 1989, pp. 12-13.

Gragert, P.J., "Managers Must Shape Mere Data Into Information," *Management Information Systems Week,* September 10, 1980.

Finkelman, Dan, “McKensey's Secrets of Satisfying Customers,”*Boardroom Reports,* July 1, 1990, pp. 56-57.

Weimer, George, etal, “Quality: The Driving Force In Manufacturing,” pp. IM1-IM16.

Sullivan, Lawrence P., “Policy Management Through Quality Function Deployment,” *Quality Progress,* June 1988, pp. 18-20.

Carlzon, Jan, “Putting the customer first: the key to service strategy,” *The McKensey Quarterly,* Summer 1987, pp. 38-51.

“Reconciling conflicting design-automation standards,” *IEEE Spectrum, March 1990.*

Ross, Phillip J., “The Role of Taguchi Methods and Design of Experiments in QFD,” *Quality Progress,* June 1988, pp. 41-47.

Ballard, Carl, “Requirements Driven Developer,” *Ascent Logic Corporation white paper,* December 1989, pp. 3-60.

Cook, Brian M., “In Search of Six Sigma: 99.9997% Defect-Free,” *Industry Week,* October 1, 1990, pp. 60-65.

Gormley, Joseph and Donald A. Mac Isaac, “The System Design Approach,” *Ford Motor Company white paper,* pp. 1-12.

Kauffman, Draper L., “System 1: An Introduction to Systems Thinking,” *Future Systems Inc.,* 1980, pp. 1-41.

M'Pherson, P.K. “Systems engineering: a proposed definition,” *IEEE Proceedings, vol 133, Pt. A, No. 6,* September 1986, pp. 348-SR-47 to 348-SR-48.

Chambers, George J., “What is a System Engineer,” *IEEE Proceedings, vol 133, Pt. A, No. 6,* September 1986, pp. 348-SR-3 to 348-SR-7.

PRODUCT DEVELOPMENT DIMENSION

Murphy, Robert J., and Joseph N. Shea, “Analysis Promotes Continuous Product/Process Improvement,” Evaluation Engineering, December 1990, pp. 38-46.

Baker, Darrel, “Better procedures can boost EDA success,” *Electronic Engineering Times,* November 19, 1990, pp. 50-64.

McEachnie, William,”Bridging the Gap: Product Design Groups vs. Computer-Aided Design,” *Printed Circuit Design,* March 1988, pp. 23-35.

Rosenthal, Charles W., "Computer Aids for the System Design Process," *Elseviar Science Publishers B.V.*, 1990, pp. 51-57.

McKinnis, Craig, "Convair Goes Concurrent," *Computer-Aided Engineering,* February 1991, pp. 18-27.

Boudette, Neal E., "Creating the Computer-Integrated Enterprise," *Industry Week* , June 18, 1990, pp. 43-50.

Krubasik, Edward G., "Customize Your Product Development," *Harvard Business Review,* November-December 1988, pp. 3-7.

Evanczuk, Stephen, "Designers are checking out library management," *Electronic Engineering Times,* December 17, 1990, pp. 39-41.

Walsh, Thomas J., "Designing for Post-manufacturing Safeguards," *Journal of Engineering Computing and Applications, Vol. 2 Number 4,* Summer 1988, pp. 15-21.

Needham, Paul, "Documentation tools provide design cycle management," *Computer Design,* October 15, 1986.

"Evaluating design process problems," *Electronic Engineering Times,* July 16, 1990, pp. 34-38.

Evanczuk, Stephen, "Frameworks build toward design process management," *Electronic Engineering Times,* July 23 1990, pp. 45-46, 54.

Haavind, Robert, "Groupware: Addressing a need for improving productivity," *Electronic Business,* September 17, 1990, pp. 69-72.

"Guidelines for Creating and Managing an Integrated Product Development Process," *Air Force Support Command white paper,* June 16, 1990, pp. 1-25.

Richardson, D. Kenneth, "Implementing Concurrent Engineering," *University of Southern California - Concurrent Engineering Conference, Los Angeles,* January 14, 1991, pp. 1-14.

Shea, Kevin, "Improving engineering productivity by using solutions-based strategies," *Electronic Engineering Times,* January 21, 1991, p. 34.

Henry, William I., "Integration of R&M into CAE for Product Excellence," *Boeing Aerospace white paper,* Summer 1988, pp. 1-6.

Sanders, Lester, "Manufacturing-Based Designs," *High Performance Design*, July 1989, pp. 65-72.

Whitney, Daniel E., "Manufacturing by Design," *Harvard Business Review*, July-August 1988, pp. 83-91.

Mayer, John H., "Manufacturing joins design at product starting line," *Computer Design/News Edition*, February 11, 1991, pp. 19-22.

Ullman, David G., *The Mechanical Design Process*. (New York: McGraw-Hill Publishing Company, August 1991)

Binnendyk, Frank, "Move test up in the design cycle," *Electronic Engineering Times*, August 28, 1989, p. 33.

Yeh, Chao-Pin, etal, "A Multidisciplinary Approach to PWB Design," *The American Society of Mechanical Engineers*, Winter Annual Meeting, November 25-30, 1990.

Collett, Ron, "The New Battlefield of the 1990's EDA Market: Top-Down Design," *Dataquest Inc. white paper*, April 1990.

Brown, David H., etal, "Product Information Management," *D.H. Brown Associates, Inc. white paper*, July 1989.

Kitzmiller, Charles T., "RAMCAD: Design Process Description," *Wright Research and Development Center white paper*, May 31, 1989, pp. 1-233.

Hall, Donald D., "Roadmaps for CAE Evolution," *Defense Systems and Program Office white paper.*

Hill, Bert, "Supporting Tradeoff Analysis," *Mentor Graphics Corporation white paper*, December 22, 1989, pp. 1-22.

Welter, Therese R., "Ten Ways to Mismanage Technology," *Industry Week*, November 30, 1987, pp. 37-42.

Stein, Richard J., "Twelve rules for building bad products," *Electronic Business*, September 1, 1987, pp. 124-126.

BOOKS AND MANUSCRIPTS

CALS Industry Steering Group. *Application of Concurrent Engineering to Mechanical Systems*. (Washington D.C.: CALS Industry Steering Group, June 16, 1988)

CALS Industry Steering Group, CE Frameworks Task Group. *Information Architecture Considerations for Concurrent Engineering*. (Washington D.C.: CALS/ISG/CE Frameworks Task Group, 1991)

Nadler, Gerald, and Hibino, Shozo. *Breakthrough Thinking.* (Rochlin, Ca.: Prima Publishing & Communication, 1990)

Editors of CAD/CIM Alert. *CALS: An Industry/User Report.* (Boston Mass.: CAD/CIM Management Roundtable, Inc., 1990)

Dalziel, Murray M, Schoonover, Stephen C. *Changing Ways.* (New York: American Management Association, 1988)

Stalk Jr., George, Hout, Thomas M. *Competing Against Time.* (New York: Free Press a Division of Macmillian, Inc., 1990)

Thomas, Philip R. *Competitiveness Through Total Cycle Time.* (New York: McGraw-Hill Publishing Company, 1990)

Hickman, Craig R., Silva, Michael A. *Creating Excellence: Managing Corporate Culture, Strategy, and Change in the New Age.* (New York: New American Library Books, 1984)

Hays, Robert H., Wheelwright, Steven C., and Clark, Kim B. *Dynamic Manufacturing.* (New York: Free Press a Division of Macmillian, Inc., 1988)

Burstein. Daniel, *Euro-quake.* (New York: Simon & Schuster, 1991)

CALS/Concurrent Engineering Task Group. *First Principals of Concurrent Engineering: A Competitive Strategy for Electronic System Development.* Review Draft, (Wash. D.C.: CALS Industry Steering Group, February 1991)

IEEE Standard Glossary of Software Engineering Terminology, Std 610.12-1990. (New York: the Institute of Electrical and Electronics Engineers, Inc., December 10, 1990)

Goldzimer, Linda Silverman. *"I'm First".* (New York: Rawson Associates, 1989)

Juran, J.M. *Juran on Planning for Quality.* (New York: Free Press a Division of Macmillian, Inc., 1988)

Bennis, Warren, and Nanus, Burt. *Leaders.* (New York: Harper & Row, 1985)

Dertouzos, Michael L., Lester, Richard K., Solow, Robert M., and the MIT Commission on Industrial Productivity. *Made in America: Regaining the Productive Edge.* (Cambridge, Mass: MIT Press, 1989)

Curtis Donald A. *Management Rediscovered: How Companies Can Escape the Numbers Trap.* (Homewood, Illinois: Dow-Jones Irwin, 1990)

Pingry, Julie. *Manufacturing Cost Management: Beyond Financial Justification.* (Arlington Mass.: Cutter Information Corp., 1989)

Davidow, William H. *Marketing High Technology.* (New York: Free Press a Division of Macmillian, Inc., 1986)

Levitt, Theodore. *Marketing Imagination.* (New York: Free Press a Division of Macmillian, Inc., 1986)

Gilder, George. *Microcosm: The Quantum Revolution in Economics and Technology.* (New York: Simon & Schuster, 1989)

Lareau, William. *Millennium Management: Last Chance for American Business.* (Piscataway, New Jersey: New Century Publishers, Inc.)

Deming, W. Edwards. *Out of the Crisis.* (Cambridge, Mass: Massachusetts Institute of Technology, Center for Advanced Engineering Study, 1986)

Seidman, William L., Skancke, Steven L. *Productivity, The American Advantage: How 50 U.S. Companies are Regaining the Competitive Edge.* (New York: Simon & Schuster, 1990)

Pittiglio Rabin Todd & Roth. *Reducing Time-to-Market.* (Portland, Oregon: Regis McKenna Inc., 1991)

Winner, Robert I., etal *The Role of Concurrent Engineering In Weapons System Acquisition.* (Alexandria, VA.: Institute for Defense Analyses, 1988)

Schrage, Michael. *Shared Minds: The New Technologies of Collaboration.* (New York: Random House, 1990)

Schonberger, Richard J. *World Class Manufacturing.* (New York: Free Press, a Division of Macmillian, Inc., 1986)

Index

Biographies

Don Carter is Technical Director for the Corporate Marketing group within Mentor Graphics Corporation. With over 17 years experience in Automatic Test Equipment, Simulation, and Design Automation, he is recognized as one of the leading industry experts in these fields. He is an active member of the Department of Defense CALS/CE Task Group, Electronic Systems. He has written several papers on the subjects of Simulation, Design-to-Test, and Concurrent Engineering. His first book, "Introduction to Digital Logic Simulation," in its second release, is used by universities worldwide today. His educational background is in Biomedical Engineering. He lives in Lake Oswego, Oregon.

Barbara Stilwell Baker is a freelance writer with over eleven years experience writing for the computer and electronics industries. She is a member of the Society for Technical Communication and has won numerous awards from that society, including an International Award of Merit, two Awards of Distinction, and an Award of Achievement. She holds a Bachelor's degree in English from Pacific Lutheran University in Tacoma, Washington. She lives in Lake Oswego, Oregon.

Colophon

This book was designed from the outset to be both readable and visually interesting. The typefaces used in this book were chosen with that in mind. ITC Berkeley Oldstyle was chosen for the text and subheads, Avant Garde for major heads, and Helvetica Condensed is used for running heads and folios. The paper stocks are 100# Remarque Cover and 70# Evergreen Matte. Both were chosen for their good overall brightness, finish and opacity qualities among the recycled stocks now available. The entire book was formatted on a Macintosh® IIci using Aldus® PageMaker®. Since the authors' files were created and edited on Macintosh systems, simple styles were designed for their system early in the process, facilitating a smooth transition into the final layout system. The illustrations, with the exception of the cover and divider illustrations, were drawn in color using Adobe Illustrator® and then placed into final page formats. All pages were proofed from laser-printed pages, then separated and output to film using a Linotype® L300 imagesetter.

This book is printed entirely on recycled paper.

Printed in the USA